The
Prophets

P9-APO-861

BS
1505.2
.P76
1996

The Biblical Seminar
42

edited by
Philip R. Davies

Sheffield
Academic Press

GOSHEN COLLEGE LIBRARY
GOSHEN, INDIANA

Copyright © 1996 Sheffield Academic Press

Published by Sheffield Academic Press Ltd
Mansion House
19 Kingfield Road
Sheffield S11 9AS
England

Printed on acid-free paper in Great Britain
by The Cromwell Press
Melksham, Wiltshire

British Library Cataloguing in Publication Data

A catalogue record for this book is available
from the British Library

ISBN 1-85075-788-7

CONTENTS

READING PROPHECY

ABBREVIATIONS

AB	Anchor Bible
AbrN	*Abr-Nahrain*
AJSL	*American Journal of Semitic Languages and Literatures*
AnBib	Analecta biblica
ANET	J.B. Pritchard (ed.), *Ancient Near Eastern Texts*
AOAT	Alter Orient und Altes Testament
ARM	Archives royales de Mari
ATANT	Abhandlungen zur Theologie des Alten und Neuen Testaments
ATD	Das Alte Testament Deutsch
BA	*Biblical Archaeologist*
BARev	*Biblical Archaeology Review*
BETL	Bibliotheca ephemeridum theologicarum lovaniensium
BEvT	Beiträge zur evangelischen Theologie
BHS	*Biblia hebraica stuttgartensia*
Bib	*Biblica*
BJS	Brown Judaic Studies
BKAT	Biblischer Kommentar: Altes Testament
BZ	*Biblische Zeitschrift*
BZAW	Beihefte zur ZAW
CBQ	*Catholic Biblical Quarterly*
CBQMS	*Catholic Biblical Quarterly*, Monograph Series
EBib	Etudes bibliques
EvT	*Evangelische Theologie*
ExpTim	*Expository Times*
FRLANT	Forschungen zur Religion und Literatur des Alten und Neuen Testaments
HAT	Handbuch zum Alten Testament
HeyJ	*Heythrop Journal*
HKAT	Handkommentar zum Alten Testament
HSM	Harvard Semitic Monographs
HSS	Harvard Semitic Studies
HTR	*Harvard Theological Review*
HUCA	*Hebrew Union College Annual*
IBS	*Irish Biblical Studies*
ICC	International Critical Commentary
Int	*Interpretation*
JAAR	*Journal of the American Academy of Religion*
JAOS	*Journal of the American Oriental Society*
JBL	*Journal of Biblical Literature*

JCS	*Journal of Cuneiform Studies*
JJS	*Journal of Jewish Studies*
JNES	*Journal of Near Eastern Studies*
JPOS	*Journal of the Palestine Oriental Society*
JQR	*Jewish Quarterly Review*
JR	*Journal of Religion*
JSOT	*Journal for the Study of the Old Testament*
JSOTSup	*Journal for the Study of the Old Testament*, Supplement Series
JTS	*Journal of Theological Studies*
KAT	Kommentar zum Alten Testament
NCB	New Century Bible
NICOT	New International Commentary on the Old Testament
OBO	Orbis biblicus et orientalis
OTG	Old Testament Guides
OTL	Old Testament Library
OTP	*Old Testament Pseudepigrapha*
OTS	*Oudtestamentische Studiën*
OTWSA	*Die Ou Testamentiese Werkgemeinskap in Suid-Afrika*
RB	*Revue biblique*
RHR	*Revue de l'histoire des religions*
SBLDS	SBL Dissertation Series
SBLMS	SBL Monograph Series
SBLSBS	SBL Sources for Biblical Study
SBLSP	SBL Seminar Papers
SBS	Stuttgarter Bibelstudien
SEÅ	*Svensk exegetisk årsbok*
SJT	*Scottish Journal of Theology*
SPB	Studia postbiblica
TBT	*The Bible Today*
Tbü	Theologische Bücherei
ThWAT	G.J. Botterweck and H. Ringgren (eds.), *Theologisches Wörterbuch zum Alten Testament*
TynBul	*Tyndale Bulletin*
TZ	*Theologische Zeitschrift*
USQR	*Union Seminary Quarterly Review*
VD	*Verbum domini*
VT	*Vetus Testamentum*
VTSup	*Vetus Testamentum*, Supplements
WBC	Word Biblical Commentary
WMANT	Wissenschaftliche Monographien zum Alten und Neuen Testament
WUNT	Wissenschaftliche Untersuchungen zum Neuen Testament
ZAW	*Zeitschrift für die alttestamentliche Wissenschaft*
ZTK	*Zeitschrift für Theologie und Kirche*

LIST OF CONTRIBUTORS

A. Graeme Auld, Edinburgh, UK

Hans M. Barstad, Oslo, Norway

J. Blenkinsopp, Notre Dame, IN, USA

Athalya Brenner, Haifa, Israel

David Carr, Columbus, OH, USA

Robert P. Carroll, Glasgow, UK

R.E. Clements, Cambridge, UK

A.R. Pete Diamond, Carpinteria, CA, USA

Fokkelien van Dijk-Hemmes†

John C. Holbert, Dallas, TX, USA

Thomas W. Overholt, Stevens Point, WI, USA

Robert B. Robinson, Philadelphia, PA, USA

John F.A. Sawyer, Lancaster, UK

Bebb Wheeler Stone, Pittsburgh, PA, USA

Louis Stulman, Findlay, OH, USA

Anthony J. Tomasino, Chicago, IL, USA

H.G.M. Williamson, Oxford, UK

INTRODUCTION

Some thirty years ago, students enduring a course on 'The Prophets' might expect to be dealing pre-eminently with theological and form-critical questions: what were the forms of speech used by prophets (and their redactors) and what were the prophetic messages they brought?

In this volume, intended to serve today's students of the prophetic literature of the Hebrew Bible/Old Testament, what issues ought to be highlighted? Certainly, form-criticism and theological issues remain of general interest. But these are well catered for in most commentaries and dictionary and encyclopaedia articles. What is distinctive about recent writing on the prophets? For this is the question I have set myself to address in this *Reader*.

It is often helpful to consider such questions in the light of the three links of the hermeneutical chain: author, text, reader. It seems to me that in each area important developments have taken place. For 'author' we should perhaps read 'prophet', those figures whom an even earlier generation than mine treasured as the *real* recipients of the divine revelation, whose *ipsissima verba* represented the purest contact between divine and human. But awareness of the role of redaction in the shaping and reshaping of the 'prophetic message' has left the prophet's imprint blurred or even illegible. What is the link between a prophet and his book? The emergence of social-historical alongside literary analysis has very much altered the posing of this question. The phenomenon of 'intermediation', which Robert Wilson's *Prophecy and Society in Ancient Israel* did much to highlight, has sharpened our focus on the type of persons traditionally deemed to be the 'authors' of prophetic books, but can such analysis reclaim prophetic authors of scrolls like Jeremiah or Isaiah? In the end, we are forced to make our decision about the texts we have, and how they came into being.

The atomizing tendency of form-criticism, implicitly or explicitly assigning to the prophets short and dramatic outbursts, has been countered in recent years by a concern for the finished product, the 'final form of the text', the 'canonical' dimension. In such a process the prophet can easily tend to become not only the mere originator of a tradition but even less: the memory, witness of subsequent 'communities of faith'. However problematic such entities are historically, this approach at least legitimately addresses the question of how we have the kinds of prophetic books that we have and what purposes they served. The historical prophet becomes simultaneously a moment and an idea, as the 'message' of the book transcends whatever historical context its parts may have reflected. As Scripture, prophecy must be, after all timeless, whereas the chief value of prophets is their address to their own specific situation. And no less is true of their supposed 'redactors' who also 'adapted' the prophetic 'message' for their own specific times. But were these redactors, who contributed little or much to the prophetic books, themselves 'prophets'?

Is *biblical* prophecy, then, a social phenomenon or a literary one? If both, what is the connection between ancient Israelite/Judaean intermediaries and the biblical prophetic literature? This is a basic, fundamental and urgent question and yet one hardly addressed with any directness until a certain configuration of scholarly interests—anthropological, canonical—forced it to become explicit. The first part of this reader contains a discussion which first erupted in *JSOT* in 1983, then resurfaced in 1990 and was still echoing in 1993. I make no apology for devoting a good deal of space to this debate, which ranges across a range of historical and literary issues. In the first set of articles, Graeme Auld proposes that the term *nabiʾ* and the concept of 'prophecy' is substantially a creation of a literary tradition, while Jeremiah and Amos, for instance, appear to eschew the title and indeed, Jeremiah even criticizes prophets. The initial discussion (in which Robert Carroll supported and Hugh Williamson opposed Auld's position) was resumed several years later by Thomas Overholt, who protested that the biblical 'prophets' were indeed genuine prophets and acknowledged as such by those who produced an 'anthology' such as the book of Jeremiah: there is a match between the literature and the social reality which cross-cultural studies of intermediation confirm. This time Auld and Carroll take the opposite view and Overholt has a last word.

Overholt's title, 'It is Difficult to Read', is a fitting caption to the entire controversy, though the final say in this volume goes to Hans Barstad, who applauds the methodology of Auld and Carroll, but contrasts his 'positive scepticism' with Auld's and Carroll's 'negative scepticism' when it comes to the historical profiles of the biblical prophets. For regardless of how the producers of the biblical books regarded their eponymous prophets, the *content* of these books must, in the light of the considerable comparative evidence now available, be categorized as 'prophecy'. Such parallels, limited though they are, also suggest the writing down and keeping of prophetic sayings, a process that makes it plausible to consider the biblical books of prophecy as repositories of real prophetic sayings in an earlier time.

An important issue in recent years has been the composition of the prophetic books. The unity of the Book of the Twelve has been reasserted, and the book of Jeremiah has been assigned at one extreme to the prophet and his secretary, and at the other extreme to a long process of elaboration or accretion. But the book of Isaiah has occupied the front of the stage. The long-established consensus over its tripartite structure, with First, Second and Third Isaiahs often effectively treated as three different authors and books, has been gradually undermined in a new search for the unity of the 66 chapters. Three articles chart that revaluation. The article by Ronald Clements, who deserves as much credit as anyone for instigating the new direction in Isaiah research, points out the many parallels of phraseology and topic between 1–39 and 40–55 and, of course, the role of chs. 36–39, which has become pivotal in the debate. Anthony J. Tomasino argues that the final chapters (66–68) of the book have been patterned on the opening passage (1.1–2.4). Although these are redactional, Tomasino raises, as other scholars have recently, the question of whether there ever was a 'Proto-Isaiah' to which 40–65 were later attached or 1–39 came into existence over a longer period of time, extending beyond the actual composition of 40–55 and even 56–66.

David M. Carr's article surveys the various proposals being developed concerning the 'reunification' of the book of Isaiah and doubts whether a desire for 'unity' is well grounded, or the criteria by which proponents convince themselves of such a unity so apparent as they claim. Perhaps, he suggests, the structure and composition are ultimately unamenable to 'closure', and coherence unattainable. If this implies a return, even if only part way, to previously articulated views on the haphazardness, untidiness, even arbitrariness of the contents and arrangement of prophetic books, that view can only lead once again to the question of what function such ill-organized corpora ever exercised. Perhaps scholarship will always be tempted to find coherence; perhaps its absence is threatening. In any case, lack of coherence can never be ultimately proved, and can always be interpreted as a challenge to better comprehension. Is coherence, in the end, more important for readers than for authors or editors?

The term 'ideology' as opposed to 'theology' is not uncontroversial, because 'ideology' is both variably used and for many retains a negative (Marxian) connotation. However, 'theology' is equally inappropriate: prophets are not 'theologians' and the prophetic books do not have a 'theology' in the modern sense of the word. Perhaps the decisive advantage of the term 'ideology' is that it provokes the reader to some kind of relativity, some critical distance. 'Ideology' is what any person, group or class may have, and used in a neutral sense (as social scientists and most ideology critics do) it relativizes all value systems. Thus, while we once affirmed that Amos's 'theology' was that God required the rich to practise social justice for fear of ultimate punishment (a view which, as 'theology'—even biblical theology—implied a divinely endorsed perspective, Amos's 'ideology' is now to be explained as a result of his own intellectual formation, his class roots, his formation, his interest (or, at least, those of the authors of the book named after him). Ideology, put another way, is a human perspective in a more obvious way than theology.

Hence examination of prophetic ideology leaves the way open for a shift in the way the contents and worldview of the prophetic books is addressed. The articles in the third part of this collection deal with Isaiah 40–55, Jeremiah and Ezekiel. Joseph Blenkinsopp reads these chapters from a social and political perspective, though he finds, in his own words, not 'actual proposals and strategies' but 'attitudes, even dreams and fantasies, entertained in one segment of post-exilic Judaism'—which he nevertheless evaluates positively. Daniel Smith's analysis of Jeremiah 29 endorses the prophet's letter as a call to 'nonviolent resistance', again politicizing the prophet's stance, which, he says, 'gives us insights on the continued social psychology of a group under stress' but which also initiates a Jewish ethic, evident later (as he sees it) in Daniel and in Pharisaic-rabbinic Judaism.

Other essays in this section deal with issues of gender. Feminism has exploited the prophetic literature in many ways, which range from redemption to denunciation of the values in these texts. Typically (though not inevitably), feminist critique is drawn away from the political to the personal, from agenda to rhetoric, where prophetic ideology is no less clearly to be identified. Bebb Wheeler Stone's article offers the boldest thesis in suggesting that features of Isaiah 40–55 show the author to have been a woman (or a community of women), who experienced both the political victimization of exile and the sexual victimization of patriarchy. Here, as in John F.A. Sawyer's article, the figure of the 'Servant of Yahweh' comes into play, though for Sawyer the 'masculinity' of the Servant contrasts with the femininity of the 'daughter of Zion', another very important image in this corpus.

But if the 'gendering' of prophetic texts is one feminist issue, another, more controversial, is pornography. It can hardly be denied that the metaphor of Israel as unfaithful wife and its god as injured husband raises questions about the privileging of maleness and the politics of sexuality, but the accusation of pornography, notably in the case of Hosea and Ezekiel, is a much more dramatic and troubling issue. To some modern readers, the very linking of 'pornography' and 'Bible' is offensive. Athalya Brenner's article, which is very recent, is included because it tries both to explain and press the charge that some prophetic texts are pornographic. It also introduces the term 'pornoprophetics', which may well enter the currency of biblical scholarship! A number of ethical as well as historical issues are obviously ignited here. In an ancient patriarchal society, what counts as pornography? How far can we impose modern categories on ancient texts? On the other hand, how can women readers of the Bible embrace such explicit joy and venom as Ezekiel appears to entertain in his detailed descriptions and denunciations of female sexual behaviour? Might one not even be tempted to revise such a metaphor with the emphasis on male marital brutality, a rather more common occurrence of modern Western life? The wider problem here, of course, is the appropriation of ancient patriarchal metaphors in a modern egalitarian culture, if that is where we are yet. Finding female voices, metaphors and even authors in the Bible is one recourse, but it may not always be sufficient.

'It is Difficult to Read'—and as with biblical prophecy itself, the hearing is all. Brenner's article is as much about the individual reader as about the ideology of patriarchal texts. The articles in the final section of this *Reader* are concerned with writing and reading strategies; in other words, with the confrontation not of prophet and hearers but of prophetic literature and reader. Since *JSOT* has been something of a forum for

newer literary criticism, it is not surprising that a number of articles of
this kind can be found. The first, by van Dijk-Hemmes picks up where
the previous section left off by comparing Hosea 2 with the Song of
Songs. It belongs, however, in this final section as an example of an
intertextual reading consciously chosen by the reader, although this
particular female reader/author suggests that the textual features she
reads also convey social meaning. There are ideological issues here too:
in a patriarchal context a call for 'justice' means the reassertion of male
authority. Van Dijk-Hemmes concludes by suggesting a reading strategy
which displaces the woman's quoted words in Hosea into the context of
the love songs of the woman in the Song of Songs. This not only
constitutes an interesting reading strategy but also suggests an interesting development within 'canon(ical) criticism'; displacing texts and
reading them against each other. Numerous possibilities suggest themselves.

Two articles on Jeremiah explore literary patterns and aspects but
both also extend their analysis to the social contexts that generated
them. In this regard they represent not the 'pure' literary criticism of the
1970s which abandoned the historical world and addressed texts as
enclosed systems. Rather, they reflect the historical agenda that has
begun to return in the 1990s, a concern to extrapolate from the social
world accessible by means of literary analysis a real social context, or at
least a historical world-view. Thus the end of the Judaean monarchy and
its aftermath are posited as the context in which features of the book
which emerge from *literary* analysis may be explained. This new historical programme differs from earlier ones in that it does not presuppose
historical events nor read the text as a historical document, but rather
accepts that literary structures are not idealistically separable from real
contexts. Yet the methodology remains a literary one, and not literary-
historical, as with source- form- and tradition-criticism.

Louis Stulman's article addresses the literary code of 'insider-outsider',
which plays a role, of course, in much of the biblical literature. Stulman
argues that the invocation of foreign oppression serves not to undermine
internal cohesion but to buttress it by punishing transgression against the
structures established by prophetic authority. Put in simpler terms, external oppressors are Yahweh's agents in punishing lawbreakers within
Israel. However, the experience of national disaster which Jeremiah experienced leads to an overthrow of this ordered universe, so that even
Yahweh becomes an 'untamed participant' who cannot be controlled and

who seems to contribute to chaos. This inversion leads to a conflict of codes within the book of Jeremiah.

A.R. Pete Diamond's article deals with the 'narrative management' of oracles in Jeremiah by those responsible for the shape of the book, and it focuses on the oracles to Zedekiah in chs. 37–38. Here Diamond finds evidence both of a theodicy of the exile and of postexilic party conflicts. But the obvious inconsistency in the portrayal of Jeremiah's message is explained not by redactional layers but by the adoption of a deliberate strategy of opposing two Deuteronomistic models of prophecy: announcement of disaster and intercession. He suggests that by means of this ambiguity the stance of the ancient reader (and the reader's community) are invited to play some role in the validation of the disaster and its outcome. Here Diamond is closer to the older method of reconstructing editorial intentions, positing indeed two discreet redactors with differing intentions. But in analysing a narrative 'Jeremiah' as a character constructed and manipulated according to the requirements of editors, this article also defines 'prophecy' as a literary phenomenon.

The final articles deal exclusively with literary analysis, and also with 'minor' prophets. Although a good deal has been written before and since on satire in Jonah, Holbert's article (from 1981) neatly and elegantly presents a reading in which Jonah emerged very clearly as the target of the book's satire. His final question, Who does Jonah stand for?, may be left for the modern reader to expand upon. On the broader front, this persuasive reading of Jonah raises the canonical-theological question of why in the middle of the Book of the Twelve is a story lampooning not only a prophet but the typical language of biblical prophecy? Is it not carnivalesque, to say the least?

Robert B. Robinson's article, though discussing that least-regarded of prophetic books, Obadiah, is essentially about reading poetry. Using recent literary theory, he introduces the notion of 'naturalization' as the process by which the reader aligns a text with the external world. The features of poetry oblige the competent reader to abandon a mimetic (literal, 'realistic') level of naturalization and move to a 'higher' one. This movement is then illustrated with reference to Obadiah, and especially to the references to 'Edom' which, though understood partly as a simple historical reference to Judah's neighbour, also requires 'naturalization' as Esau (and thus in terms of ancestral, *Urzeit*), and also naturalization at the level of eschatology. Finally, the eschatological and historical 'time' confront each other. It is a confrontation which can, indeed, be perceived throughout the prophetic literature of the Hebrew Bible/Old Testament, and perhaps offers us a clue as to the existence of these curious books. For curious they are; without parallel in the literature of the ancient world, often hard to read and to understand. 'Why are there books of prophecy in the Bible' may be ultimately unanswerable; it is hoped that this *Reader* illuminates the quest, if it does not deliver any answer.

WHAT ARE PROPHETS?

JSOT 27 (1983), pp. 3-23

PROPHETS THROUGH THE LOOKING GLASS:
BETWEEN WRITINGS AND MOSES

A. Graeme Auld

1. *Orientation*
The Room this Side of the Glass

This paper seeks to extend a study on 'Prophets and Prophecy in Jeremiah and Kings',[1] and to explore some of its implications. To try to spread the blame, I should like to mention first some recent publications which appear to me to furnish the room through whose mirror I want to take you.

1.1 In his discussion of 'Poetry and Prose in the Book of Jeremiah' at the Vienna Congress, W. McKane has commented on the very different approaches—and indeed presuppositions—of Thiel and Weippert to the prose tradition in Jeremiah.[2] He follows this with an examination of closely related poetry and prose in Jer. 3.1-13 and 12.7-17. McKane concludes that

> the kind of activity uncovered in 3.6-11 and 12.14-17...is a type of enlargement and elaboration which operates within narrow contextual limits and does not have the comprehensive systematic theological objectives which it is customary to ascribe to prose redactions of the book of Jeremiah.

Further:

> Those who claim a systematic theological activity for a Deuteronomistic editor and identify compositions in which this is realised are perhaps

---

1. *ZAW* 96 (1984), pp. 66-82.
2. W. McKane, 'Poetry and Prose in the Book of Jeremiah', *Congress Volume, Vienna 1980* (VTSup, 32; Leiden: Brill, 1981), pp. 220-37.

professing to know more of the inner workings of his mind than can be gathered from the text.

I suggest that these comments may have a wider relevance—to the production of Joshua to Kings.

1.2 In his massive Genesis commentary, C. Westermann has strongly advanced the argument—in itself not at all novel—that much of the present text of Genesis was generated from material already within earlier forms of the book.[3] He presents a cogent case for understanding Genesis 20 as a development from Gen. 12.10-20 for largely exegetical reasons. Having read the fuller subsequent account of Abraham's dealings with a foreign king over his wife, the reader becomes disposed to a 'proper' approach to the briefer and possibly misleading prior text. However the generation of narrative in Genesis from narrative already in the text does not always serve local exegetical needs. The use of the same material again in Genesis 26 may have been simply to help build up an 'independent' series of traditions about the middle patriarch Isaac.

1.3 E. Tov has usefully summarized his own and others' researches into the interesting textual history of the book of Jeremiah in his contribution to the Louvain Colloquium on Jeremiah: 'Some Aspects of the Textual and Literary History of the Book of Jeremiah'.[4] One welcomes his linkage of textual and literary matters. Tov and Bogaert are persuaded that the shorter Greek text of Jeremiah represents a first edition of that book, while our traditional Hebrew text is an expanded second edition. In somewhat similar vein to McKane's comments noted above Tov writes:

> Editor II was not consistent, so that the inconsistency of his rewriting cannot be taken as an argument against our working hypothesis. In fact, very few revisions are consistent—in the biblical realm only 'inconsistent' revisers are known, such as the deuteronomistic reviser of Josh.-2 Kgs and Jer., the 'Elohist' in the Psalms, the Lucianic reviser of the LXX, and, on a different level, the Samaritan Pentateuch.

1.4 H.G.M. Williamson's note on the 'The Death of Josiah and the Continuing Development of the Deuteronomic History' seeks to account for the differences between Kings and Chronicles in their reporting of

3.   C. Westermann, *Genesis*, I (ET; Minneapolis: Fortress Press, 1984–86 [1966–]).

4.   E. Tov, 'Some Aspects of the Textual and Literary History of the Book of Jeremiah', in P.-M. Bogaert (ed.), *Le Livre de Jérémie* (BETL, 54; Leuven: Peeters, 1981).

the death by positing 'a revised and expanded form of Kings, which the
Chronicler can at most have worked over only lightly' as 'the best way
of accounting for the literary development of this passage'.[5]

1.5 These four studies do not all tend in exactly the same direction.
But it may be helpful to underline some elements in them before proceeding further: *a*. Poetic nucleus and prose development. *b*. Narrative
generated from difficult material within a corpus, then added to that
corpus. *c*. Greek Jeremiah as translation of an earlier version of the book
than the familiar Hebrew. *d*. Biblical revisers as inconsistent. *e*. Development of the text of the book of Kings.

2. *Prophets and Prophecy in Jeremiah and Kings*
Through the Glass

My own study mentioned above focuses on the usage of the noun *nābî*'
('prophet') and its related verbal themes in the books of Jeremiah and
Kings.

2.1 In writings associated with the Latter Prophets, the attitude to
'prophets' appears to change radically during or soon after the exile.
The eighth- and seventh-century figures are mostly hostile, and at best
neutral, about 'prophetic' contemporaries. (Hosea is the most neutral.)
By contrast, post-exilic figures are readily titled 'prophet' and this title is
extended in the writings associated with them to earlier individuals like
Elijah and Isaiah. The large books of Jeremiah and Ezekiel stand at the
crossroads.[6] There is still critique of contemporary prophets in plenty
within these collections. However each book as it now stands is concerned to present its hero as a 'prophet'. And in addition to the plentiful
criticism of prophets there is a new theme of a tradition of faithful
'servants the prophets'. Exploration of these two larger books helps to
locate where and how the change of attitude occurred. It may be significant that Ezekiel is not directly accorded the title 'prophet', although a
hope is expressed concerning him twice (2.5; 33.33) that his people 'will
know that a prophet has been among them'. If frequency of usage is
significant, it may be more important to note that Ezekiel's words are
introduced some thirty times by a reported command to 'prophesy'.
Perhaps during the period when attitudes were changing the verb was

5.   H.G.M. Williamson, 'The Death of Josiah and the Continuing Development
of the Deuteronomic History', *VT* 32 (1932), pp. 242-48.
6.   Full documentation is available in my *ZAW* article, cited in note 1 above.

more acceptable than the noun 'prophet' as a designation of acceptable 'prophetic' activity.

2.2 These rather broad generalizations about the book of Ezekiel as a point where certain trends intersect within the Latter Prophets as a whole can fortunately be tested with a degree of objectivity in the book of Jeremiah, with its different editions, and its blend of poetry and prose. Of course argument is legitimate over the classification of this or that element of the text as poetry or prose, over the historical conclusions that are proper from such a decision, and even over the very relevance to the biblical material of the 'western' distinction between poetry and prose.[7] I still hold that such a decision is helpful—and hope that the following discussion may be held to offer it some support. However, two versions of Jeremiah are objectively to hand; and the longer stresses a number of concerns which are either peripheral or much less formed in the shorter version. If the widely accepted distinction between earlier poetic nuclei and later prose development is combined with the evidence of less and more developed versions of Jeremianic prose, then three stages in the development of our inherited Hebrew text of Jeremiah are available for comparison: the poetry; the shorter prose development translated into Greek; and the familiar fuller prose development. The book of Jeremiah is doubly suited to our requirements: in the stratification of its traditions just described; and in the fact that *nābî*ʾ ('prophet') and its related verbs are used as often in this book alone as in all the rest of the Latter Prophets.

Analysis of this rich stock of 'prophetic' terminology in the three sections of Jeremiah produces the following results:

2.2.1 'Prophets' are mentioned in Jeremiah's poetry mostly to be criticized. There are a couple of exceptions in which they appear in a more neutral light.

2.2.2 In the prose common to Hebrew and Greek, such criticism still bulks very large; however some new features appear. The verb 'prophesy' comes to be used in passages critical not just of 'the prophets', but also of certain named individuals who are never so described. Even more novel, it is used positively of the activity of Jeremiah himself, and also of Uriah and Micah. Four times at this stage in the book's development Jeremiah is accorded the title 'prophet'; and (perhaps more importantly) he is strategically designated 'prophet to the nations' at the

---

7. So J.L. Kugel, *The Idea of Biblical Poetry: Parallelism and its History* (New Haven, CT: Yale University Press, 1981).

beginning of the book (1.5). And finally we meet five positive references to an otherwise obscure group termed Yahweh's 'servants the prophets'.

2.2.3 In the extra material of the received Hebrew text we find a further small expansion of censure of 'prophets'—the theme that dominates the other sections of the book. But most noteworthy is the multiple insistence (24 extra references) that Jeremiah is a 'prophet'—not to speak of the further six times in chapter 26 in which Hananiah too is accorded this title.

2.2.4 It appears that the scattered instances of 'prophetic' terminology in other (Latter) Prophetic books can be successfully correlated with the more abundant—relatively datable—evidence in the book of Jeremiah. It was only after the exile that such figures became termed 'prophet'. And until this development was successfully completed, it may have been easier to use the verb 'prophesy' of them (whatever that means!) than to term them 'prophet'.

2.3 Kings is the other biblical book replete with talk of 'prophets'. Much of this is concentrated in the middle third of the book: the Elijah/Elisha narratives in 1 Kings 17–2 Kings 10. We find there all five instances of the verb; 33 of the 38 occurrences of the plural noun; but only 12 of the 41 appearances of the noun in the singular. Half the usage of the singular noun is in the form of the title 'prophet' with a proper name; and this title features only in the first and last thirds of Kings— once certainly in 1 Kings 18.36 (MT) but not LXX. The only other singular prophet in these parts of Kings is the unnamed one from Bethel in 1 Kings 13 and 2 Kings 23.

The textual leverage on this material is provided not by the LXX version of Kings, although it does offer two significant scraps of evidence, but by the alternative account of the monarchy in the book of Chronicles. Chronicles is also interested in the phenomenon of 'prophecy'; but what it has to report about 'prophets' and 'prophesying' diverges much more from the material in Kings than the broad similarities between the two books would lead us to expect. And variation over the title *hannābî'* is as interesting here as between MT and LXX in Jeremiah. For example, while Kings uses the title 'prophet' 20 times (and never in the special Elijah/Elisha material that is without parallel in Chronicles), and while part of Chronicles that mirrors the traditions in Kings uses this title 13 times, there is only one perfect overlap in usage: the mention of 'Huldah the prophetess' in 2 Kgs 23.22 and 2 Chron. 35.18. The Chronicler's mention of 'Isaiah the prophet' in 2 Chron. 32.20 is clearly related to 2 Kgs 19.1-2. But apart from these two cases, the title is used quite differently. This is all the more striking since the story linking the king of Israel, Jehoshaphat of Judah, and Micaiah son of Imlah, with its frequent use of 'prophet(s)' and 'prophesy', appears almost identically in 1 Kgs 22.1-35 and 2 Chronicles 18.

The most economical account of the 'prophetic' materials in Kings and Chronicles—and one that accords well with our account of 'prophetic' terminology within the Latter Prophets—is that each of the familiar books was developed from a common original that used the title 'prophet' rarely, and knew the Micaiah story.

The account of true and false prophecy in this story of Micaiah may well emanate from circles close to those who told similar stories about Jeremiah and his opponents. I argue that the distinctive expression in that story, 'a prophet of the Lord' (*nābî' l'yhwh*), in 1 Kgs 22.7, and 2 Chron. 18.6, is in fact the source of the remaining limited biblical usage of the phrase: it appears elsewhere only in the neighbouring 1 Kgs 18.22 of Elijah (where it is a later supplement), and 2 Kgs 3.11 of Elisha (within a narrative largely dependent on the Micaiah story); at the end of the introduction to Samuel in 1 Sam. 3.20 (of which more anon) and then of Oded in 2 Chron. 28.9—'a prophet of the Lord' in Samaria.

Three further appearances of the word 'prophet' in the singular occur in the Naaman story in 2 Kings 5. Elisha urges his king to invite the Syrian 'that he may know there is a prophet in Israel' (v. 8) Naaman's Israelite maid has already wished (v. 3) that her lord might be 'with the prophet who is in Samaria'. These expressions are most reminiscent of the hope that Ezekiel's people 'will know that a prophet has been among them' (Ezek. 2.5; 33.33).

If many instances of the title 'prophet' in Kings may have been added after the Kings text was used by the Chronicler, and if the rare phrase 'a prophet of Yahweh' was coined in the Micaiah story with its links with the theme of true and false prophecy in Jeremiah, and if references to Elisha in the Naaman story remind us of the presentation of Ezekiel, then we have a plausible post-exilic context for almost all singular uses of 'prophet' in Kings. The main group remaining are the eight references in 1 Kings 13 (and the one back reference in 2 Kings 23) to the unnamed prophet from Bethel who encountered the 'man of God' from Judah: another story, like the Micaiah one, that handles questions about the true and false prophet, and may plausibly be related to those

discussions of the proper norms for 'prophecy' which also shaped some
of the Jeremiah prose traditions.

Most occurrences of 'prophets' in the plural are in a few localized
groups: 'prophets of Yahweh', 5 times in 1 Kings 18 and 19; 'prophets
of Baal (and Asherah)', 8 times and mostly in 1 Kings 18; 'prophets of
the king of Israel', 7 times and only in the Micaiah story and the
dependent story of Jehoshaphat and Elisha in 2 Kings 3; 'the sons of the
prophets', 4 times in 2 Kings 2 and 6 times more in chs. 4–9. No one
within these prophetic groups is ever named but they all have a clear
(even if only chorus-like) role to play in the stories that feature them.

The other 'prophets' in Kings are Yahweh's 'servants the prophets'
who make five appearances: in 2 Kgs 9.7; 17.13, 23; 21.10; 24.2. In the
last two of these passages the relevant phrase is absent from the related
passage in Chronicles. And I have suggested grounds for considering
Yahweh's 'prophetic servants' an addition to the first three texts that
mention them as well. These prophets have no narrative role—they are
simply acknowledged agents of the divine 'word'. And it may well be
the case that this acknowledgment was a theological afterthought.

3. *The Wider Prophetic Family*
Still in the Room on the Other Side

If it be granted, at least for the sake of argument, that the classical
'prophets' of the Bible began to be *called* so only some time after the
exile, is it possible to strip away from the Biblical traditions this *nābîʾ*
overlay and recover the prophets' own estimate of themselves? It may
be helpful to review from our new vantage point the usage of some
other related biblical expressions.

3.1 'Man of God' is used to introduce or address 'prophetic' figures
several times in the Bible, but the usage is far from widespread. It occurs
but once in the Latter Prophets: in Jeremiah 35.4, which gives no clue
why Igdaliah is so designated. The term is used most often of Elijah (5
times) and Elisha (27 times) in Kings.[8] That book uses *ʾîš hāʾelōhîm* also
of Shemaiah in 1 Kgs 12.22 (= 2 Chron. 11.2), who bears the word of
God to Rehoboam that he should not attack the north after Jeroboam's
defection; and a dozen times immediately afterwards in 1 Kings 13 of
the 'man of God' from Judah who spoke against Bethel. Other unnamed

---

8.   Of Elijah, in 1 Kgs 17.18; and 2 Kgs 1.9, 11, 12, 13. Of Elisha, 10 times in
2 Kgs 4; 4 times in 2 Kgs 5; 6; 7; 8; and then in 2 Kgs 13.19.

men of God appear in Judg. 13.6, 8 and 1 Sam. 2.27. Samuel himself is so introduced in 1 Sam. 9.7, 8, 10. The date of these passages may be variously assessed; however the remaining nine instances of 'man of God' are in certainly late texts, six referring to Moses and three to David.[9]

3.2 Haggai bears the title 'messenger of Yahweh' in Hag. 1.13. Then it is often supposed that *mal'akî* ('my messenger') is a title not a name- at least in Mal. 3.1. And the set for our next problem is complete when we note that in the intervening book of Zechariah 'a messenger' appears some 20 times—but this time as a visionary (*rō'eh*) intermediary.[10] Outside these three late books, Yahweh's 'messenger' figures in the Latter Prophets only in Hos. 12.5, of the opponent over whom Jacob prevailed, and in Isa. 37.36 (= 2 Kgs 19.35; cf. 2 Chron. 32.21) of the divine agent that disposed of large numbers of Assyrians in Judah. He reappears as a similar agent of death in 2 Samuel 24—and even more often in the parallel 1 Chronicles 21—in the punishment that follows David's census.[11] Then (apart from Ps. 34.8 and 35.5, 6) the remaining scattered appearances of the 'messenger' are in earlier episodes of the biblical story: from Abraham to Elijah.[12] It is often unclear whether the *mal'āk* was human. In the promise of Samson's birth (cf. Judg. 13) 'messenger' and 'man of God' are used side by side. Earlier in the same book, it seems likely that 6.7-10 was drafted to underscore that Yahweh's envoy in the following verses was in fact a human prophet. Maimonides understood Exodus 23.20 to refer to Moses. And we are left to speculate on what sort of being supplied food to Elijah (1 Kings 19.5, 7) or dispatched him to King Ahaziah (2 Kgs 1.3, 15).

3.3 The regular Hebrew word for 'seeing' (*r'h*) is used not infre- quently in the Bible of special, enhanced, second 'sight'. Quite exacting exegesis may often be necessary before deciding that such a sense is appropriate in any given occurrence of the *qal* theme. Of course

9. Of Moses, in Deut. 33.1; Josh. 14.6; Ps. 90.1; Ezra 3.2; 1 Chron. 23.14; and 2 Chron. 30.16. And of David in Neh. 12.24, 36; and 2 Chron. 8.14.

10. In fact, 20 times in Zechariah 1–6, and then once in 12.8.

11. I shall have more to say below on divergences between 2 Samuel 24 and 1 Chronicles 21. W.E. Lemke's 'The Synoptic Problem in the Chronicler's History', *HTR* 58 (1965), pp. 349-63, has helpfully pinpointed the complex relationship between our inherited texts of Samuel—Kings and Chronicles.

12. See for example Gen. 16 (×4); 21.17; 22.11, 15; 24.7, 40; 28.12; 31.11; 32.2; Exod. 3.2; 14.19; 23.20, 23; 32.34; 33.2; Num. 20.16; 22.22-35 (×10); Judg. 2.1, 4; 5.23; 6.11, 12, 20, 21, 22; 13.3-21 (×12); 1 Kgs 13.18; 19.5, 7; 2 Kgs 1.3, 15.

interpretation is eased when we meet other themes of the verb with a
divine subject—whether the *hiphᶜil* in the sense of 'show' or 'let see',
or the *niphᶜal* in the sense of 'is seen' or 'shows himself'. God may
make things seen, and may let himself be seen. The related noun *marʾeh*,
often rendered 'vision', is used of phenomena as substantial or insubstantial as are denoted by the English 'appearance'.

Given all this, it is noteworthy that neither Amos nor Jeremiah is ever
described as a 'seer' (*rōʾeh*), although each is 'let see' things by Yahweh
and asked what they 'see'.[13] In fact the title *rōʾeh* is used very rarely in
the Bible: (a) of Samuel, first in 1 Samuel 9, from halfway through the
story in which he was first styled 'man of God', then in 1 Chron. 9.22;
26.28; 29.29; (b) of Hanani in 2 Chron. 16.7, 10; (c) in the plural and
paired with *ḥōzîm* of 'seers' generally in Isa. 30.10.

3.4 The other 'seeing' verb, *ḥzh* is used much less frequently, and
occurs only in the qal theme although there are several related noun
forms—*ḥāzôn*, *ḥāzût*, *ḥezyōn*, *maḥzeh*. Some would suggest that the
word is not Hebrew at all, but a loan word from Aramaic. Many of its
appearances are in technical prophetic contexts, often in close association
with *nābîʾ*. Accordingly, to achieve some 'purchase' on these, it may be
helpful to review first those biblical passages in which this is *not* the
case.

3.4.1 In one psalm (63.3), *ḥzh* and *rʾh* are used in close proximity—of
gazing on God in the sanctuary. The four other psalms in which *ḥzh*
appears use it alone: in 11.4 and 17.2, of what God sees; in 11.7 and
17.15, of people seeing God; in 46.9, of seeing God's actions; while 58.9,
11 talk of the premature child never seeing the sun and the joy of the
righteous at seeing vengeance. In Proverbs the verb is used of
observation and discernment, twice alone and one paired with *rʾh*. Then
in Job *ḥzh* is used of insight in 15.17 and 34.32, and of seeing God in
19.26, 27 and 23.9. In Job the noun is always paired with 'dream',
whether as a means of revelation (4.13 and 33.15), or as something
ephemeral (20.8; cf. Isa. 29.7), or a divine visitation in a nightmare
(7.14). Proverbs 29.18 pairs *ḥāzôn* with *tôrâ*.[14] And Ps. 89.20 recounts
how God 'spoke in a vision' of his promise to the Davidic house.

The technical sense of both verb and noun which is almost standard

13. Amos 7.1-8; 8.1-2; 9.1; Jer. 1.11-13 (cf. 4.23-26; 23.18).
14. McKane has noted (*Proverbs* [OTL; London: SCM Press, 1970], pp. 640-
41) that LXX took *ḥāzôn* as referring to a person—a 'guide'; but retains this 'solitary
reference...to prophetic vision...in the book of Proverbs'.

elsewhere in the Bible is already encountered in some of these poetic texts. Indeed the only other non-technical usage is in Exod. 24.11, of the elders 'seeing' God on his mountain—and even there the reading is less than certain.[15] We meet the term in only two other Pentateuchal contexts: in connection with (Aramaean?) Balaam in Numbers, and in Gen. 15.1 of how the 'word of Yahweh' came to Abram.

3.4.2 In Chronicles, as we shall see shortly, *ḥōzeh* ('seer') alternates with *nābîʾ* (and indeed *rōʾeh*) in a quite stylized way. The situation is quite different in Samuel–Kings. 'Seer' and 'vision' make only four appearances in these books—and 'prophet' is part of each context, though perhaps not always an original part. In 2 Sam. 24.11 and 2 Kgs 17.13 they are paired. 1 Samuel 3 opens with a comment on the state of *ḥāzôn* in Samuel's youth and closes with him designated *nābîʾ leyhwh*. And 2 Samuel 7, which introduces Nathan as 'the prophet' in v. 2 and talks of Yahweh's word coming to him by night in v. 4, describes the whole event in v. 17 as 'this vision'. Perhaps we should note that, of all the patriarchs, it is Abraham with whom Yahweh had communicated 'in a vision' and by his 'word' (Gen. 15.1), who bears the title 'prophet' in Gen. 20.7. Within the *text* of the Latter Prophets, the 'seer' enjoys the same rating as the 'prophet'. Amos (7.12) sidesteps the title with a denial that he is a 'prophet'. Micah (3.7) has 'seers' disgraced along with 'diviners'. Jeremiah mentions 'visions' only twice, and both times within critique of the 'prophets': in 14.14 blaming their 'lying visions', and in 23.16, 17 complaining of 'visions of their own hearts' which promise peace. These two themes recur in Ezekiel 13 (vv. 7 and 16); while problems of false or unrealized 'vision' are handled in 12.21-28. And in 7.26 'vision' is simply what is expected of a 'prophet' (just as Jer. 18.18 expects of him 'word'). We might note that Lamentations in much the same period mentions the 'prophet' four times: twice to link him with the 'priest' (2.20; 4.13); once to complain that they 'obtain no vision from the Lord' (2.9); and once to blame them for their 'false and deceptive visions' (2.14). Then in Zech. 10.2 'diviners see lies', while according to 13.4 'every prophet will be ashamed of his vision'. In fact in the main text of the Latter Prophets it is only in Hab. 2.2, 3 and the manifestly late Joel 3.1 that 'vision' is a clearly positive term—and in Joel that goes also for prophecy, dreaming and possession by the spirit.

3.4.3 In a final group of passages, *ḥzh* and its related nouns are used

---

15. MT's *wyḥzw* is certainly the *lectio difficilior*: LXX offers the passive 'were seen'; while some Samaritan MSS attest *wyʾḥzw*, 'caught'.

in what is certainly a technical, broadly 'prophetic' context, but not in close association with the terin *nābî*. It is used in the title verse of many books: Isaiah, Amos, Obadiah, Micah, Nahum, and Habakkuk. Indeed in Isaiah its use is even more widespread: it heads individual sections of the book in 2.1 and 13.1; and figures also in 21.2; 22.1, 5; and 29.11—some at least of which may be post-Isaianic.

3.5 To return briefly to the *nābî*, the burden of the first part of our argument was to show that the great majority of occurrences of this term belonged to the late biblical period. Although contemporary *nᵉbîʾîm* are often castigated in the Latter Prophets, some references to them are neutral, and even favourable.

3.5.1 We noted earlier that in Ezekiel and also in the earlier prose tradition in Jeremiah, the verb 'prophesy' was used very much more often than the noun 'prophet' in connection with these two figures. It may be appropriate to correlate this fact with two elements in the book of Amos. In the short narrative of his encounter with Amaziah, Amos refuses the appellation 'prophet' but accepts the divine command to 'go, prophesy' (7.14, 15). Then following the series of questions in 3.36, the conclusion is drawn that 'prophesying' after hearing Yahweh speak is as much anyone's business as is being afraid after hearing a lion roar. May it be that the use of the verb in connection with these now classical figures preceded and facilitated the later application to them of the title *nābî*? If so, what did the verb mean?

The verb is attested in only two themes—*niphʿal* and *hithpaʿel*—both of which themes are occasionally used in Hebrew to create verbs from nouns.[16] The use of this verb in connection with Amos, Jeremiah and Ezekiel, but not the noun—or at least the noun only very sparingly and perhaps only afterwards—may suggest an absence of appropriate terminology for these figures, filled by the application of a denominative verb meaning 'to act like a *nābî*', 'to play the part of a prophet'.

3.5.2 Many of the non-redactional occurrences of *nābî* have already been noted in other contexts. The remainder of our reduced stock of evidence for plotting the earlier biblical sense(s) of our term should now be mentioned. Amos complains equally of stopping 'prophets' and making 'Nazirites' break their vows. The Elisha stories portray their hero in some sort of association with the 'sons of the prophets'. Elijah is in despair over Jezebel's treatment of Yahweh's 'prophets' and is in

---

16. GKC cites for the *niphal* (§51g) *nzkr* from *zkr*, *nlbb* from *lb* and *nbnh* from *bn*; and for the *hithpael* (§54i) *htyhd* from *yhwd(h)*, and *hṣṭyd* from *ṣydh*.

conflict with Baal's. Saul has sought enlightenment from *ʾûrîm*, dreams and prophets before resorting to the medium at En-Dor.[17]

The remaining passages use verb as well as noun, and are notoriously hard to interpret. In the two stories of Saul falling in with bands of 'prophets', the related verb apparently denotes remarkable behaviour. Yet the interpretation of 1 Samuel 10 and 19 is immediately complicated by their offering different explanations of the same saying: 'Is Saul too among the prophets?' We can be sure that 'prophesy' in the intervening MT 'plus' in 1 Sam. 18.10 is pejorative: the second is caused by an 'evil spirit'. And this is equally true of the only use of this verb in Kings, outside the Micah story, in 1 Kgs 18.29, of what Baal's prophets do to arouse him. The only occurence of the verb in the Pentateuch (Num. 11.25, 26, 27) describes behaviour that pillars of the community want to see stopped forthwith. We are left to ponder whether Saul's association with the prophets is evaluated in the text, or simply remarked on.

3.6 Remarkably little contemporary evidence for an estimate of pre-exilic 'prophecy' has survived this review. 'Man of God' and 'Yahweh's envoy' appear in scattered passages that may be early. On the other hand it is unlikely that *rōʾeh* was used as a title until a later writer used the occasion of Saul's visit to Samuel 'the man of God' to equate this designation with the subsequent 'seer' and 'prophet'. The use of *ḥāzâ* and *ḥāzôn* in the titles of several prophetic books is similar to the positive development of 'prophet' and 'prophesy': *within* the text of several of the Latter Prophets its associations are pejorative. However non-prophetic parts of the Bible do use *ḥzh* positively, of insight and discernment; and they may have contributed to the development.

It seems unlikely that earlier designations of these figures were suppressed by later tradition. The evidence reviewed suggests refinement by supplementation, rather than alteration or suppression of terminology already in our texts. The earlier biblical tradition may have been less interested in designation—and so too perhaps in 'office'.[18] It

---

17. Amos 2.11-12; 2 Kgs 4.1; 6.1; 9.1; 1 Kgs 18–19; 1 Sam. 28.6, 15.

18. Two differences between the related 2 Sam. 24.11 and 1 Chron. 21.9 seem relevant here, cf. note 12 above. The texts are as follows:

Sam.	wdbr-yhwh hyh	ʾl-gd hnbyʾ	ḥzoh dwyd lʾmr...
Chron.	wydbr yhwh	ʾlgd	ḥzoh dwyd lʾmr...

It is arguable that Chronicles preserves the earlier reading; and what we have read in Samuel has made plain that the divine communication came through the proper channels.

remembered some of the names: of those who had 'stepped out of line'? of those whose words had a special quality? And, if this is so, then sound method requires us to start our quest from these words, and not from any institution or office.

4. *Deuteronomist and Chronicler*
Sortie Down the Corridor

This section is only partly relevant to our main theme. But perhaps you will indulge this sortie—since we are in the room through the glass any-way—down a corridor which I can never properly see from our regular side of the mirror.

It is remarkable how little communication there is between students of Chronicles and students of Joshua to Kings. In treatment of the latter, there are often few if any references to the largely parallel biblical narrative of the Chronicler;[19] while those who focus on his work assume that what we know as the Deuteronomistic History was available to him in substantially the shape we know.[20] The actual text the Chronicler used may differ frequently from our MT of Samuel–Kings;[21] but the basic materials were all there. However some of our observations about the distribution of 'prophetic' vocabulary in the two corpora invite some reconsideration.

4.1 We have already noted that there is very little overlap between

---

19. W. Dietrich's argument for three main Deuteronomistic strata in Kings (*Prophetie und Geschichte* [Göttingen: Vandenhoeck & Ruprecht, 1972]) cites Chronicles not at all. Then neither R.D. Nelson, who advances Cross's arguments in *The Double Redaction of the Deuteronomistic History* (JSOTSup, 18; Sheffield: JSOT Press, 1981), nor H.-D. Hoffmann, who argues for a single author of the History in *Reform und Reformen* (Zurich: Theologischer Verlag, 1980), cites Chronicles more than a few times.

20. T. Willi insists (*Die Chronik als Auslegung* [Göttingen: Vandenhoeck & Ruprecht, 1972], pp. 54-56) that the Deuteronomistic History in its present form was the Chronicler's main source—he paid close attention even to those sections of his source he did not repeat. P. Welten, in his conclusion to *Geschichte und Geschichtsdarstellung in den Chronikbüchern* (Neukirchen–Vluyn: Neukirchener Verlag, 1973), is clear that the Chronicler wrote some 300 years after the Deuteronomist.

21. Cf. above, nn. 12, 19. Willi, *Die Chronik* and Williamson, *1 and 2 Chronicles* (London: Marshall Morgan & Scott; Grand Rapids: Eerdmans, 1982) are fully aware of the textual problems.

Kings and Chronicles in the way they use the title 'prophet'. And, with the notable exception of the Micaiah story, this is equally true of the way they use noun and verb as a whole. Chronicles uses 'seer' language very much more frequently than Samuel–Kings; and it may help if we plot this richer usage before we proceed. Chronicles agrees with its assumed *Vorlage only* over titling Gad 'seer' and Nathan, Isaiah and Huldah 'prophet(esse)s'.[22] Half the remaining titles (24) appear in the cross-references at the end of the report of a reign to the further available information in Samuel–Kings.[23] And only the remaining 12 occur in the 'main text' of Chronicles. There Samuel and Hanani are styled *rōʾeh*; Jehu ben-Hanani is styled *ḥōzeh*—along with the heads of the three musical families whose business is to 'prophesy'; and Elijah, Nathan, Samuel and Jeremiah are termed 'prophet'.[24]

4.2 Two quite different, but equally substantial attempts have recently been made (by Hoffmann[25] and Polzin[26]) to defend Noth's view that the Deuteronomist was a single writer, his history representing a unified conception.[27] Hoffmann even enhances the Deuteronomist's achievement by ascribing to him even more of the material in the relevant books than Noth had done. However most scholars are persuaded by either of two main accounts that reckon with a substantial revision of the history by a second Deuteronomist. These accounts differ in several ways, including whether Noth was right to deem the (first) Deuteronomist

22. Cf. 1 Chron. 21.9 and 2 Sam. 24.11; 2 Chron. 17.1 and 2 Sam. 7.2; 2 Chron. 32.20 and 2 Kgs 19.2; and 2 Chron. 34.22 and 2 Kgs 22.14.

23. In 1 Chron. 29.29 and 2 Chron. 9.29; 12.15; 13.22; 26.22; 32.32; 33.18. Contrast 2 Chron. 20.34 which cites Jehu ben-Hanani without a title.

24. In fact in the inherited MT the remaining dozen instances form a neat pattern: each of the three titles appears four times:

> *rōʾeh* in I, 9.22; 26.28; II, 16.7, 10
> *ḥōzeh* in I, 25.5; II, 19.2; 29.30; 35.15
> *nābîʾ* in II, 21.12; 29.25; 35.18; 36.12

However some indications from both LXX and Syr suggest that later adjustments have been made to some of these verses.

25. Cf. above, n. 20.

26. R.M. Polzin, *Moses and the Deuteronomist: A Literary Study of the Deuteronomistic History*, I (San Francisco: Harper & Row, 1980).

27. M. Noth, *The Deuteronomistic History* (JSOTSup, 15), 1981.

exilic (so Smend,[28] Dietrich,[29] Veijola[30]), or whether the earlier draft closed with its hero Josiah (so Cross,[31] Nelson[32]). However both accounts ascribe 'prophetic' material to their second hand. If our earlier observations have force, then the rewriting of the 'Deuteronomistic' traditions in 'prophetic' terms continued long after the exile. And the absence of Judg. 6.7-10 (the major reference in that book to the 'prophetic' role) from the relevant Quern fragment of Judges[33] only serves to confirm this conclusion.

4.3 In studies of the book of Joshua I have noted links between Chronicles and some elements of an *early* revision of the basic (Deuteronomistic?) draft of that book.[34] How much of Joshua–Kings was *not* available to the Chronicler? And if we have reasonable ground for suspicion that the Deuteronomistic History was far from complete before the Chronicler's work was being composed then several new questions will have to be asked. The more it is recognized that biblical revisers were inconsistent and that narrative could be generated piecemeal for exegetical purposes, the harder it may be to answer many of them.

4.4 Only one simple 'manipulation' of Noth's magisterial account of the Deuteronomistic History is required if we want to remove much of the evidence for the Chronicler having radically altered by subtraction what he inherited from the Deuteronomist (plus a few supplements). The story of David in his court (2 Samuel 9–20 + 1 Kings 1–2) and the Elijah/Elisha narratives (much of 1 Kings 17–2 Kings 10) are readily identifiable and separable entities. Why not deem them *supplements* to the Deuteronomist's work, not *sources* for it? The Chronicler is deafeningly silent over each corpus. But *is* he the innovator?

4.5 Von Rad's argument is often quoted: that repeated examples of

28. R. Smend, *Die Entstehung des Alten Testaments*, 1978.

29. Dietrich, *Prophetie und Geschichte*.

30. T. Veijola, *Die Ewige Dynastie: David und die Entstehung seiner Dynastie nach der dtr Darstellung* (STAT, 193; 1975).

31. F.M. Cross, *Canaanite Myth and Hebrew Epic: Essays in the History of the Religion of Israel* (Cambridge, MA: Harvard University Press, 1973).

32. Nelson, *Double Redaction*.

33. Reported in R.G. Boling, *Judges* (AB; Garden City, NY: Doubleday, 1975), p. 40, on the basis of a communication from F.M. Cross.

34. A.G. Auld, 'Judges I and History: A Reconsideration', *VT* 25 (1975), pp. 261-85 (especially pp. 280-82); and *Joshua, Moses and the Land*, 1980 (esp. pp. 101, 108-109).

prophecy and fulfilment form one of the structural elements of the Deuteronomistic History.[35] To the extent that the main point is true, we should now say more cautiously that (before all the prophetic titles were added) it was a narrative about the fulfilment of what Yahweh had said. Yet this is another important feature of Joshua–Kings which looks different when viewed from Chronicles. Von Rad does not make explicit that only the first two of his eleven examples of Deuteronomistic notes of fulfilment write of Yahweh 'establishing the word he had spoken' (*hēqîm ʾet-dᵉbārô ᵃšer dibber*). It is only these same two examples (1 Kgs 8.20 = 2 Chron. 6.10; and 12.15 = 10.15) that reappear in Chronicles. Selection from Deuteronomistic tradition—or common source? Williamson writes that Chronicles suppressed the story of Ahab's fate from the end of the Micaiah story in part because the fulfilment of a prophecy was involved which it had not reported.[36] But *was* it in his source? Is there between the 'Matthew' of Samuel–Kings and the 'Luke' of Chronicles a lost 'Mark' that told the whole story of the Jerusalem monarchy? What relation does this 'chronicle of the kings of Judah' bear to Deuteronomistic thought and style?

5. *Between Writings and Moses*
Back to the Room through the Glass

The discussion in the earlier part of this paper encourages the view that both parts of the 'prophetic' canon of the Hebrew Bible received much of their distinctive and positively intended 'prophetic' vocabulary over a briefer and in a later period of the biblical tradition than is regularly supposed. The process which has been sketched appears to imply recognition that these 'prophetic' writings were different from the other 'writings': it was on to these books and not others that 'prophetic' and 'visionary' terminology was grafted.

5.1 John Barton has recently discussed canonical development relating to the 'prophets', and in particular Josephus' talk of the prophets after Moses writing the history of their times in thirteen books.[37] He suggests this points to a bipartite canon of Law and Prophets—with 'prophets'

35. G. von Rad, *Studies in Deuteronomy* (London: SCM Press, 1953), esp. pp. 78-81.

36. H.G.M. Williamson, *1 and 2 Chronicles*, p. 286.

37. J. Barton, '"The Law and the Prophets": Who Are the Prophets?', *OTS* 23 (1984), pp. 1-18.

implying a certain level of inspiration or authority. It was a further stage
that what we have inherited as Former and Latter Prophets were selected from Josephus' Prophets, with the remainder assigned to Writings.

Our own discussion belongs to a rather earlier period, and appears to
point in a different direction. We have noted the emergence of two
standard terms, 'prophets' and 'seer' in Isaiah, Jeremiah, Ezekiel and
the Twelve; and an analogous proliferation of 'prophetic' vocabulary in
Kings, which extended into Samuel and even, in time, Judges. This
process itself appears to recognize a 'prophetic' *je ne sais quoi*.

5.2 To an extent our account of the 'prophetizing' of Chronicles too
would appear to undercut this conclusion. But the situation in that book
is rather more complex. I incline to the view that the references in both
Kings and Chronicles at the end of almost every king's reign to the
availability of further information elsewhere are in fact cross-references
between these two narratives that have diverged from their common
source. This is widely recognized in the case of the Chronicler's references. But I wonder whether the references to 'chronicles of the kings
of Judah' within Kings are not an invitation to scrutinize the other
biblical book, and not extant state archives. Be that as it may, the form
of many of the acknowledgments in the present text of Chronicles of
material in Samuel–Kings recognizes those traditions as 'prophetic' or
'visionary',[38] or it notes that the familiar texts of Kings is a
development, or exposition (*midrāš*) of an earlier 'book of kings',[39] or it
points to 'prophetic' supplementation of a shorter account of the
monarch.[40] The invitations in 1 Kgs 29.29 and 2 Kgs 9.29 to consult
dibrê nātān hannābî for further information on David or Solomon will
more likely be a reference to the 'court history' which is not reflected in
Chronicles, than to Nathan's dynastic oracle which is. Parts of the main
text of Chronicles have received 'prophetic' supplementation—and of
course this may be the contribution of the Chronicler himself. However
the marginal references in Chronicles as we have received the work (the
references to Samuel–Kings) tend to emphasize the prophetic character
of that other parallel work. Perhaps those who drafted them would not
have been averse to deeming Samuel and Kings part of restricted
'prophetic' canon that excluded Chronicles.

38. Cf. note 24 above.
39. On Joash, in 2 Chron. 24.27.
40. Cf. 2 Chron. 26.22, and also 13.22.

5.3 While late passages mainly in Jeremiah and Kings,[41] but also in some other hooks,[42] talk in a stereotyped way of Yahweh's 'servants the prophets', the last chapter of Chronicles handles the same theme by making an explicit and unique link between 'his prophets' and 'his messengers'.[43] I have already noted that I find this implied in Judges 6.7-10; the first prophetic passage in Joshua–Kings.[44] These verses attribute Israel's suffering under the Midianites to her spurning Yahweh's voice and revering Amorite gods. This developed understanding of a prophet's message prefaces the rather more practical approach taken to Gideon by Yahweh's messenger (6.11ff.) in response to Israel's lament over Midian. This preface deftly claims prophetic influences in other episodes of the Judges even where the actual accounts use different terminology—so helping to make explicit the prophetic character of yet another part of this whole narrative corpus.

5.4 This late addition to Judges rather takes away some of the force of 1 Samuel 3. There we encounter the heaviest concentration of words and phrases relating to the whole phenomenon of prophecy and its importance of any score of verses in the Bible. However ancient the origins of this story of Samuel's night-time audition, it seems clear that it has been redrafted to highlight the institution of biblical prophecy.[45] Noth may have been right to detect behind the present book of Judges and the opening chapters of Samuel an earlier 'Deuteronomistic' conception of a period of the Judges that extended to and concluded with Samuel's transfer of power to a king. Samuel had been the last judge (cf. 1 Sam. 7.15). This conception is largely neutralized by the present division of 'books'; with the birth narrative and this audition underscoring a prophetic portrayal of this early leader, a view again shared with Chronicles when we read of 'the days of Samuel the prophet' in preference to Kings' 'days of the judges'.[46]

5.5 H.-C. Schmitt has recently drawn our attention again to certain parts of the Pentateuch—or more strictly Genesis to Numbers—which

41. Jer. 7.25; 25.4; 26.5; 29.19 (not LXX); 35.15; 44.4. 2 Kgs 9.7; 17.13, 23; 21.10; 24.2.

42. Amos 3.7; Zech. 1.6; Dan. 9.6, 10; Ezra 9.11.

43. 2 Chron. 36.15-16.

44. Cf. §4.2 above.

45. There is further discussion of this chapter in my paper in *ZAW*; cf. n. 2 above.

46. Contrast 2 Chron. 35.18 with 2 Kgs 23.22.

have clear relations with prophetic concerns.[47] Elements of Exodus 3–4 are very like narratives of prophetic call. Chapter 4, and also the report of the act of exodus itself in chapter 14, both culminate in reports of the people's belief in Moses and his God. The terminology is that of Isaiah 7.9 and 2 Chron. 20.20. Almost identical expressions constitute important moments in other blocks of Pentateuchal tradition: Exod. 19.9 at Sinai; Num. 14.11; 20.12 in the desert; and Gen. 15.6 in the time of the patriarchs—and we have already noted other prophetic links in that chapter. Schmitt argues that these passages are part of a 'redaction of the Pentateuch in the spirit of prophecy'; and that they post-date the 'priestly' strata of the Mosaic tradition. Torah before Prophets!

5.6 It is commonplace to recognize Deuteronomy too, and its figure of Moses, as influenced by prophetic conceptions. He himself proclaimed 'the word of Yahweh', and promised the raising up of a *nābî* like himself (18.15, 18). This passage is part of the same discussion of true and false prophecy as we have seen already in Jeremiah and Ezekiel. Polzin has recently attributed it to the Deuteronomist, who here claims authority equal to that of Moses for *his own* exposition of the divine will.[48] Mayes equally views 18.15ff as a late addition to the Deuteronomistic law; and states that here Moses is not so much viewed as the archetypal prophet as the standard by which to judge the validity of the prophetic word.[49] Mayes's alternative I find puzzling: Moses is surely regarded as a 'prophet', the sort of 'prophet' which Jeremiah and Ezekiel, and also Elijah and Samuel, become. He is also the standard by which they are validated and their opponents condemned. Yet this is not the Pentateuch's last word on prophecy.

5.7 There are too many uncertainties about Num. 12.6-8 for us to know whether Moses is there a privileged prophet, or of a different category. God speaks to him 'mouth to mouth' or 'face to face', and not in vision, dream or 'riddles'. The clue to his categorization may lie in the words: *bᵉkol-bêtî neᵉᵉmān hûᵃ*—'in all my house it is he who is established/faithful/trustworthy'. Now it is possible that these words have a similar force to Ahimelech's attempt (1 Sam. 22.14) to reassure Saul over David's intentions towards him: 'who among all your servants is

---

47. H.-C. Schmitt, 'Redaktion des Pentateuch im Geiste der Prophetie', *VT* 32 (1982), pp. 170-89.

48. Polzin, *Moses and the Deuteronomist*.

49. A.D.H. Mayes, *Deuteronomy* (NCB; London: Marshall Morgan & Scott; Grand Rapids: Eerdmans, 1979).

faithful as David?' It could be that Moses is portrayed as *the* trusty servant. But Ahimelech's words have a deeper sense. Reinforced shortly afterwards by Abigail's 'Yahweh will make of (or for) my lord a sure (or established) house' (1 Sam. 25.28), they echo through Psalm 89, Samuel–Kings and Chronicles[50] as a promise of the institution of the Davidic line. Indeed we find this promise first, and rather obliquely, at the end of 1 Samuel 2, concluding Eli's message from the man of God. It is surely to contrast Samuel with Eli, and to compare the institution of prophecy with that of monarchy, that the immediately following story of Samuel's call concludes with him *established* as a prophet of Yahweh.[51] Is it fanciful to see that claim outdone in Moses' favour in Numbers 12.7? Be that as it may, the concluding verses of the Pentateuch effectively neutralize the earlier promise in Deuteronomy 18. At whatever date they were penned they simply note that (despite all appearances to the contrary?) the expected prophet like Moses still has not arisen. Moses—and that means the whole Torah associated with his name—is incomparable.

5.8 They are surely right who see these verses as the end of the Pentateuch, and not just of its last book, and who hear them say something about Torah and Prophets and Canon, and not just something about Moses and historical successors.[52] Certainly, if our arguments have force, they confirm this reading. It is common to view the preaching of the prophets as one of the influences which helped form the teaching of Deuteronomy. I have attempted to show that the *nābîʾ*, the 'prophet' who Moses is or with whom he is compared is no historical 'prophet'—but the reconstructed, post-exilic 'prophet' of the Prophetic Canon. The last word of the Torah knows the Prophets substantially as we know them—even the earlier Deuteronomy 13 and 18 would seem to know Jeremiah 1 and 23.

5.9 Prophets then precede—but have no precedence over—Moses. Prophets are also 'Writings', 'writings' that have been redefined as 'prophetic' at a quite advanced stage in the development of the earlier of them. We must leave it to another study to clarify what about these writings let them become prophetic; but conclude with an Alice-like

---

50. Ps. 80.29, 38; 1 Kgs 8.26 (= 1 Chron. 6.17); 11.38; 1 Chron. 17.23 (n.b.: not equivalent to 2 Sam. 7.25); 2 Chron. 1.9

51. Cf. 1 Sam. 2.35; 3.20.

52. J. Blenkinsopp, *Prophecy and Canon* (Notre Dame, IN: University of Notre Dame Press, 1977), pp. 85-95.

view of the Bible—with Prophets between Writings and Moses. Torah, having been nurtured at several stages by the prophetic traditions, sought to control them, and does so in the Hebrew Bible. Yet the argument between Sadducee (Jewish or Samaritan) and Pharisee was not whether to add Prophets as new scripture beside Torah, but whether to retain Prophets once it had been ensured that Moses had said enough.

JSOT 27 (1983), pp. 25-31

POETS NOT PROPHETS
A RESPONSE TO 'PROPHETS THROUGH THE LOOKING GLASS'

Robert P. Carroll

I am in basic agreement with the thesis of Dr Auld's paper.[1] I do not propose to make any comments on the Chronicles section, but will confine my remarks to its essential thesis about the prophets. For some time I have held the view, theoretically I grant but based on a posteriori grounds, that the individuals traditionally known as prophets should not be regarded as prophets (i.e. *nᵉbîʾîm*) but require a different description.[2] They were certainly poets, probably intellectuals, and possibly ideologues. Dr Auld's careful analysis of biblical texts has now provided a sound basis for developing such a view.

The competent reader, to use Northrop Frye's phrase, of the Bible will have noticed a serious problem in evaluating prophecy. There appear to be two very different attitudes towards prophets in the biblical traditions. There is a very positive view, most likely emanating from prophetic circles, which approves of the prophets as revealers of the divine will, speakers of the word of Yahweh to Israel (cf. Amos 3.7 and the stereotypical phrase 'thus says Yahweh...). These speakers are simply categorized in the later literature as 'his servants the prophets'

1. I am grateful to Dr Auld for my having had access to his earlier study 'Prophets and Prophecy in Jeremiah and Kings' (to be published in *ZAW* 96 [1984]). Dr Auld's SOTS paper is dedicated to Professor G.W. Anderson, and I would certainly wish to be associated in this response with that dedication as a mark of my respect and esteem for an outstanding British Old Testament scholar and in memory of the years (1963–67) when I was a research student of Professor Anderson's.

2. Expressions of this view may be found in R.P. Carroll, *From Chaos to Covenant: Uses of Prophecy in the Book of Jeremiah* (London: SPCK, 1981) especially pp. 11-13. See also A.G. Auld, 'Poetry, Prophecy, Hermeneutic: Recent Studies in Isaiah', *SJT* 33 (1980), pp. 567-81.

(e.g. 2 Kgs 9.7; 17.3, 23; 21.10; 24.2; Amos 3.7; Jer. 7.25-26; 25.4; 26.5; 29.19; 35.15; 44.4; Zech. 1.6; Dan. 9.6, 10; Ezra 9.11), a phrase which clearly indicates redactional approval. Such a positive attitude is epitomized by the story of Eldad and Medad in Num. 11.24-30. There Moses is represented as so approving of the spirit of prophecy that he can say 'Would that all Yahweh's people were prophets, that Yahweh would put his spirit upon them!' (v. 29).[3] It would be difficult to find a more positive evaluation of prophecy than such a statement attributed to the greatest prophet who had ever lived in Israelite memory (Deut. 34.10-12; cf. 18.15, 18). However, there is an equally negative perception of the prophets in the Bible. The prophets are dismissed as false, as misleaders of the community (e.g. Isa. 9.14-16; Mic. 3.5-7; Jer. 23.9-32). They are denigrated as madmen (cf. 2 Kgs 9.4, 11; Hos. 9.7; Jer. 29.26), condemned as the source of godlessness in society (Jer. 23.15), and blamed for the fall of Jerusalem (Lam. 2.14). These negative views are epitomized in Zech. 13.2-5 where the claim of any youth to be a prophet will be dealt with most severely by parents and all future claims to function as a prophet will be a source of shame.[4] Here there is no sense of the prophet as the servant of the living God. These two different attitudes towards prophets in the Bible produce a very odd evaluation of the prophetic role in late Israelite society. The destruction of the community was caused by its failure to pay attention to its prophets (positive evaluation of prophets) on the one hand, but on the other hand the community was destroyed because it followed its prophets who misled it (negative perception of prophets). This formal contradiction is usually resolved by invoking notions of 'true' and 'false' with reference to various prophets, but this resolution is both too facile and too problematic to be maintained.[5] Dr Auld's thesis points to a way of resolving this problem.

3.   It should be recognized that Num. 12.1-8 corrects this overvaluation of prophets in favour of the authority of Moses based on his special, i.e. superior to a prophet, relationship with Yahweh. Cf. M. Noth, Numbers: *A Commentary* (OTL; London: SCM Press, 1968), p. 96.

4.   See D.L. Petersen, *Late Israelite Prophecy: Studies in Deutero-Prophetic Literature and in Chronicles* (SBLMS, 23; Missoula, MT: Scholars Press, 1977), pp. 33-38.

5.   See J.L. Crenshaw, *Prophetic Conflict: Its Effect upon Israelite Religion* (*BZAW*, 124; Berlin: de Gruyter, 1971); Carroll, *From Chaos to Covenant*, pp. 158-97 and the literature cited there on pp. 319-24. There are some useful observations on this vexed question in S.J. De Vries, *Prophet against Prophet: The Role of the*

Describing the figures usually called 'prophets' as poets is a relatively problem-free description in that there can be no disagreement that individuals such as Amos, Hosea, Isaiah, Jeremiah or Ezekiel were poets. The speakers of the oracles in the anthologies we call 'prophetic' literature were clearly poets. That is indisputable. All other descriptions are highly disputable. Calling them intellectuals may involve using a term which is controversial still in our own cultural history, but it is, I believe, a useful category for considering these poets.[6] It .would also help to account for the connections various scholars have made between their work and the wisdom traditions.[7] A common feature of these poetic collections is the open and, quite often, extreme hostility shown towards social institutions in ancient Israel. The fierce denunciation of every aspect of social and religious life, king and temple, sacrifice and prayer, worship and values, indicate that these poets were social critics operating with a high level of theory.[8] They may even have been social reformers putting forward radical critiques of society and arguing for serious changes in the life of the people. These critiques may well have had an ideological basis, hence the tendency for them to be viewed as ideologues.[9] By ideology here I would understand not only a system of ideas, but also those distorting elements characteristic of ideology in the Marxian sense which breed 'false consciousness'.[10] Such distortion can

Micaiah Narrative (1 Kings 22) in the Development of Early Prophetic Tradition (Grand Rapids: Eerdmans, 1978).

6. On intellectuals in modern culture see E. Shils, 'Intellectuals', in David L. Sills (ed.), *International Encyclopedia of the Social Sciences*, VII (New York: Macmillan, 1968), pp. 399-415.

7. On this issue see, most recently, R.N. Whybray, 'Prophecy and Wisdom', in *Israel's Prophetic Tradition: Essays in Honour of Peter R. Ackroyd* (Cambridge: Cambridge University Press, 1982), pp. 181-99.

8. There are many problems here, some of which relate to the presence of critical elements in the framework sections of prophetic texts (e.g. the polemic against sacrifice appears in Isa. 1.10-15; Amos 5.25; Jer. 7.21-26). Some theoretical account needs to be provided for these collections and for connections between the original sayings of the poets and the subsequent redactional holdings. For a recent attempt to provide a theoretical treatment of these poets see K. Koch, *The Prophets: The Assyrian Period* (London: SCM Press, 1982); Koch certainly differentiates between the 'prophets' and the *nᵉbîʾîm*.

9. Cf. L.S. Feuer, *Ideology and the Ideologists* (Oxford, 1975), pp. 197-202; M.A. Cohen, 'The Prophets as Revolutionaries: A Sociopolitical Analysis', *BARev* 5.3 (1979), pp. 12-19.

10. On this see K. Marx and F. Engels, *The German Ideology* (London, 1963).

GOSHEN COLLEGE LIBRARY
GOSHEN, INDIANA

be seen in the sweeping judgments of the community which condemn everybody (especially Jer. 5.1-5; 8.4-7; 9.2-6), the denunciation of opponents without argument (especially Jer. 23.9-32), and the stereotyped analyses of disparate situations (e.g. Jer. 7.16-20; 44.15-23). The ideological slant is a keen characteristic of intellectual attitudes and activities. I think Max Weber was on the right lines when he described the prophets as 'demagogues and pamphleteers': 'The preexilic prophets from Amos to Jeremiah and Ezekiel, viewed through the eyes of the contemporary outsider, appeared to be, above all, political demagogues and, on occasion, pamphleteers.'[11] It is probably the case that the redactors of the anthologies shared some, if not all, of the ideological traits of the original poets and this may account for the development of these poets in the direction of a more structured account which eventually produced the correlation of poet and prophet in post-exilic times.

If the demand to rethink the category of prophet for these poets is correct then a number of consequences will follow from this analysis. We will have to rewrite the history and structure of prophecy. The role of the redactors' ideology (theology may be a preferred word but only if it includes a connotation of ideological holdings) will be seen as having a much more creative and constructive part to play in the emergence of the traditions than has often been allowed in the past. Recent work done by American scholars on anthropological, ethnographical and sociological investigations of prophecy will need to be modified to apply to the redactional frameworks of the traditions more than to the original poems.[12] The book of Jeremiah provides perhaps the best paradigm of how redactional transformation of a poet's work eventually produced the fullest account of the life and times of a 'prophet'. Although the debate about the book of Jeremiah is a matter of controversy, the

---

For a very fine treatment of the history of ideology and its changing meaning see H. Barth, *Truth and Ideology* (Berkeley: University of California Press, 1976).

11. M. Weber, *Ancient Judaism* (New York: Free Press, 1952), p. 267.

12. I have in mind here the valuable work done by scholars such as T.W. Overholt, D.L. Petersen and R.R. Wilson. E.g. R.R. Wilson, *Prophecy and Society in Ancient Israel* (Philadelphia: Fortress Press, 1980); D.L. Petersen, *The Roles of Israel's Prophets* (JSOTSup, 17; Sheffield: JSOT Press, 1981); T.W. Overholt, 'Commanding the Prophets: Amos and the Problem of Prophetic Authority', *CBQ* 41 (1979), pp. 517-32. See also R.C. Culley and T.W. Overholt (eds.), *Anthropological Perspectives on Old Testament Prophecy* (Semeia, 21; Chico, CA: Scholars Press, 1982).

tradition itself constitutes one of the primary areas for this discussion.[13] This is partly because of the poetry–prose differentiations in the book. Here are focused many of the problems of orality and textuality so beloved of structuralists and deconstructionists, but also of importance for conventional biblical scholars who, however much they may dislike contemporary theorizing, face nevertheless many similar problems in interpretation. Dr Auld's analysis of the use of *nābîʾ* in Jeremiah, and especially the contrasts between its use in the MT and in the LXX, indicates quite clearly the centrality of the book of Jeremiah to this debate.

The canonical understanding of scripture which has become an important aspect of biblical interpretation in recent years, partly due to Brevard Childs's advocacy of it, will insist on treating these poets as prophets because the final form of the text presents them as such.[14] We therefore cannot avoid treating them as prophets at some stage of our interpretation of the text, but 'final form' interpretation should not be allowed to so dominate our thinking that we are misled into giving it an importance it should not have. The canonical reading of a text is very much a process of narrowing down meaning until it is limited to the redactors' intention and ideology. The original poets were free spirits, poets of the imagination, denouncing the social structures of their own time, but through redactional transformation have become conventional 'prophets', a fixed form of institutional activity, and thereby made to serve purposes which they themselves might very well have despised (even denounced on occasions)! Such a process deprives them of much of their force because it serves ends other than their own. Unfortunately

13. See Carroll, *From Chaos to Covenant*; W. McKane, 'Relations between Poetry and Prose in the Book of Jeremiah with Special Reference to Jeremiah III 6-11 and XII 14-17', *Congress Volume, Vienna 1980* (VTSup, 32; Leiden: Brill, 1981): 220-37. A rather fine study of the way the redaction of Jeremiah has transformed the private individual into a public figure is to be found in W.E. March, 'Jeremiah 1: Commission and Assurance', *Austin Seminary Bulletin: Faculty Edition* 86 (1970), pp. 5-38. For similar developments in the Isaiah tradition see now O. Kaiser, *Isaiah 1–12* (OTL; London: SCM Press, 2nd edn, 1982), especially pp. 114-218 on Isa. 6.1–9.6 (this is the section of the commentary which Kaiser (p. viii) would prefer to be read first of all).

14. See B.S. Childs, *Introduction the Old Testament as Scripture* (London: SCM Press, 1979). For reactions to his approach see *JSOT* 16 (1980), pp. 2-60; R.P. Carroll, 'Childs and Canon', *IBS* 2 (1980), pp. 211-36; R.N. Whybray, 'Reflections on Canonical Criticism', *Theology* 84 (1981), pp. 29-34

canonical criticism or the interpretation of the final form of the text is an approach which elevates one particular 'freezing' of the traditions into an authoritative reading of the text, often to the exclusion of consider-ations of other readings or the various stages of construction through which the text has gone. In place of a very rich reading of the text it substitutes a rather etiolated and most undialectical reading which approx-imates to a supposed ancient 'orthodoxy'. This is a most unsatisfactory approach to understanding the Bible and therefore I welcome Dr Auld's thesis as a way towards restoring a richer reading of the text.

No biblical scholar is required or bound to take a canonical approach to the interpretation of the text. Yet in tracing the stages of the growth of the biblical traditions some analysis is needed of those forces which gave rise to the *need* to turn the highly individual poetic traditions of Amos, Isaiah or Jeremiah into conventional works of prophecy. Did some crises in the community (the inevitable candidate for such a crisis is invariably the exile) or some breakdown in authority demand such a development? Did some developing or emerging ideology of the word or some pressure group of theologians utilize such a transformation to put forward a programme of social construction or control? The inevitable candidate for such a group would be the Deuteronomists; although some scholars may feel that too much has been made of the Deuteronomistic redaction of the prophets.[15] I have always found it problematic that there should have been two levels of canonicity in the Bible: Torah *and* Prophecy. One would have been sufficient. If Torah had been the binding force in the community, what possible grounds could there have been for adding a supplement to it? It simply does not make sense (and did not for various Jewish communities of the second temple period). Between Torah and Prophecy there are substantive tensions (e.g. the word given once for all in the past and the word given regularly in the immediate present: Moses versus the prophet) and these tensions point in a different direction from the conventional account

15. See W. Thiel, *Die deuteronomistische Redaktion von Jeremia 1–25* (WMANT, 41; Neukirchen–Vluyn: Neukirchener Verlag, 1973); *idem*, *Die deutero-nomistische Redaktion von Jeremia 26–45* (WMANT, 52; Neukirchen–Vluyn: Neukirchener Verlag, 1981); J. Vermeylen, *Du Prophète Isaïe à l'apocalyptique: Isaïe I–XXXV, miroir d'un demi-millénaire d'expérience religieuse en Israël* (vol. 2; Paris: Gabalda, 1978), pp. 693-709; W.H. Schmidt, 'Die deuteronomistische Redaktion des Amosbuches: Zu den theologischen Unterschieden zwischen dem Prophetenwort und seinem Sammler', *ZAW* 77 (1965), pp. 168-93.

given of the rise of canonical writings.[16] Could Prophecy have been 'canonical' in some circles before Torah achieved that status or did it appeal to circles which felt quite unrepresented by Torah? Was the model of canonical utterance derived from the 'prophetic' collection in the first place (cf. Isa. 8.16-20) and then taken over by Torah circles? Was then the radical shift which transformed the poets and intellectuals of the past into 'prophetic' mediators of the divine word in the present a movement necessitated by questions of authority in the post-exilic period? It is, I suspect, along these lines that the debate about canon might fruitfully pursue its investigations and it is certainly here that Dr Auld's main arguments have much to contribute.

Although I am in agreement with Dr Auld's thesis I am aware of many questions which it raises, some of which I have already voiced. Were there 'prophets' in ancient Israel? Were these individuals or groups? What relationship or similarity, if any, did the intellectual poets (the so-called literary prophets) have to these *nᵉbîʾîm* What were the processes whereby individual poets were transformed into prophets? Why? What movements or ideologies (when and where?) turned such individuals into figures from conventional patterns of behaviour? At-tempts to answer such questions must inevitably be speculative because there is so little information, if any at all, in the Bible. The biblical data for answering such questions are invariably the output of ideological circles and it is now very difficult (if not impossible) to get behind such material in order to trace the stages in the transformation. But the approach of Dr Auld offers one way of raising the questions and answering them. That makes it an exciting thesis. If it is accepted it will alter radically the way we think about the poets and prophets of the Bible. Such a radical alteration means that his thesis will be resisted vigorously by many in contemporary biblical scholarship, but I warmly welcome it for its promise of a complete rethinking of a very old subject.

---

16. The best book on these tensions within the canon that I know of is Joseph Blenkinsopp's *Prophecy and Canon* (Notre Dame, IN: University of Notre Dame Press, 1977).

JSOT 27 (1983), pp. 33-39

A RESPONSE TO A. GRAEME AULD

H.G.M Williamson

Graeme Auld has presented us with suggestions of great interest is evident, and if they could he substantiated they would entail a considerable revision of the general consensus about the development of the historical books. Note at once that I do not include here the subject with which he ended, the development of the Jewish canon. This point seemed to me somewhat separate from the rest of the discussion and could probably stand without it purely as an exegesis of the closing verses of Deuteronomy; nor is it, in any case, the most novel part of the paper. I shall therefore concentrate my remarks rather on some of his earlier and more controversial points.

First, much of this paper is based on a presentation of statistics, relevant in particular to *nābî'* and related verbal stems and, to a lesser extent, to other words referring to prophetic figures. The argument is that only quite late did *nābî'* come to be used of those whom we now generally regard as prophets. Broadly speaking, if we set the testimony of the latter prophets against the former prophets, then, judged by this criterion, the historical books have, at the very least, been subjected to a late 'prophetic' redaction.

Now, since the dangers of handling statistics are well known, one may hesitate to rush in here. Nevertheless, by the same token there are some obvious points which the uninitiated are likely to raise and against which Dr Auld will wish to protect himself.

1. Since the pre-exilic biblical prophets seem, generally speaking, to have been 'loners', it does not occasion much surprise to find that there are not many positive references to *nābî'* in their oracles, for they would have had only themselves to refer to. Where one might expect such references would be in (prose) editorial references to them by their

support groups. There is not a great deal of this for the earliest prophets; it comes to the fore particularly, of course, with Jeremiah, and here, as Dr Auld has observed, we find them. Must we assume, however, that Jeremiah himself would have rejected the designation?

2. By the same token, it is not surprising that when the pre-exilic prophets refer to other prophets they are critical of them, as has been shown. However, account should be taken here of the point that evidently better was expected of them. It is not that they are rejected because they are *nᵉbîʾîm* but because they are bad ones.

3. Again, it is not particularly surprising that 'the prophets' as a group gain positive appraisal only in the post-exilic period. Obviously, they could not be positively appraised until there was in fact such a group to be appraised! It could scarcely have happened, therefore, at the start of the tradition of written prophecy. It is generally recognized, however, that it was only with the vindication of their message of judgment in the exile itself that many came to realize that the prophets had been right all along. To put the point in other words, Zech. 1.3-6 fits its historical context and could hardly have been written sooner.

4. I should like also to have seen some account taken of the results of recent sociological approaches to the study of the prophets. Now, in many people's opinion sociology is often as slippery as statistics, but it is at least of interest that the studies of Petersen[1] and Wilson,[2] though they approach the texts from quite different points of view, both independently agree that specifically in this area of terminology regional variation may have played a larger role than we are accustomed to acknowledge. If so, the richer usage of the exilic and post-exilic writers may be due in part to the merging of this earlier diversity.

5. Finally, we should not underplay such hints at a positive evaluation of prophecy as do exist in the early sources. Amos 2.11 and 13 come particularly to mind, for there the prophets are raised up by God only to be silenced by antagonistic Israelites.

The other main area which the paper discussed and which, not surprisingly, I should like to probe, is the relationship between the Deuteronomic History and Chronicles. In my own note on the subject ('The Death of Josiah and the Continuing Development of the Deuteronomistic History',

---

1. D.L. Petersen, *The Roles of Israel's Prophets* (JSOTSup, 17; Sheffield: JSOT Press, 1981).

2. R.R. Wilson, *Prophecy and Society in Ancient Israel* (Philadelphia: Fortress Press, 1980).

VT 32 [1982], pp. 242-48), to which a kind reference was made, I suggested that there was evidence to suppose that the Chronicler's account of the death of Josiah did not come from some alternative source, but was actually a part of the version of the Deuteronomic History which the Chronicler was following. I hinted that alongside our canonical Kings, which took final shape in Babylon, the development of the history continued a little elsewhere—presumably in Palestine. Recent studies of the growth of Jeremiah have advanced similar suggestions, and it may also help account for the purely textual differences between the Massoretic Text of Samuel, 4QSam^a and the form of text to which it seems the Chronicler had access.

Now, I think it possible that there may be another odd paragraph or two of this nature in Chronicles; for instance, I have wondered about part of the account of Hezekiah's reform at the start of 2 Chronicles 31. But of course the proposal of Dr Auld's paper would undercut my position entirely, first by arguing that both present texts are independently based on some other common source and, secondly, by postulating a much longer and far more substantial degree of later activity on the Deuteronomic History than my modest proposal envisaged. Let us, therefore, examine the principal arguments advanced in this section of the paper.

1.   First, it seems rather a large conclusion to draw from a fairly narrow base. This becomes particularly acute when it is remembered that the Chronicler certainly—and the Deuteronomist probably—had his own distinctive point to make about the nature of prophecy.[3] His ascription of prophetic terminology to the Levitical singers, coupled with his characteristic use of Levitical sermons in which the canonical prophets are quoted as 'texts', are sufficient to suggest that his concern is with the reapplication of written prophecy in his own day. If, as Seeligmann has argued in detail, this represents a development from the position in Kings, with the prose of Jeremiah holding the middle ground, then the terminology should be studied initially to see how it relates to that conceptual development, rather than in complete isolation.

---

3.   As the evidence has been frequently rehearsed, it is not necessary to go into detail here; see, for instance, D.L. Petersen, *Late Israelite Prophecy: Studies in Deutero-Prophetic Literature and in Chronicles*, SBLMS, 23, 1977; I.L. Seeligmann, 'Die Auffassung von der Prophetie in der deuteronomistischen und chronistischen Geschichtsschreibung (mit einem Exkurs über das Buch Jeremia)', VTSup, 29 (1978), pp. 254-84; T. Willi, *Die Chronik als Auslegung* (FRLANT, 106; Göttingen: Vandenhoeck & Ruprecht, 1972), pp. 216-29.

2. The hypothesis that Kings and Chronicles both drew on an independent source was widely held by conservative scholars in the last century,[4] although of course on grounds rather different from those advanced here; only so could they harmonize a number of the discrepancies between the two texts. That belief eventually died out, first because there was no evidence whatsoever for the existence of this 'phantom' source,[5] and, secondly, because so much of Chronicles explicitly presupposes knowledge of the earlier account in substantially its present form.

Auld's treatment of the source citation formulae rules out any attempt to counter in terms of the first point, but he also suggests explicitly that the Chronicler could have worked with a text of the Deuteronomic History which included neither the court history of David nor the Elijah/Elisha narratives. Does this not, therefore, fall foul of the second point referred to above, namely that Chronicles can only be explained on the basis of the present text of Samuel–Kings? Let me illustrate with regard to the court history.

(a) At 1 Chron. 20.1-3 we have a brief account of Joab's and David's Ammonite campaign. In 2 Sam. 11–12 this is intertwined with the story of Bathsheba and Uriah. This is why it is there said at first that 'David tarried in Jerusalem' (11.1). This note, however, is retained by the Chronicler, at the expense, in fact, of strict consistency, because two verses later (1 Chron. 20.3) he also includes the statement that 'David and all the people returned to Jerusalem' (Cf. 2 Sam. 12.31). This is

---

4. See, for instance, the summary of Keil's discussion of the Chronicler's sources in the introduction to his commentary:

> But our canonical books of Samuel and Kings are by no means to be reckoned among the sources possibly used besides the writings which are quoted... The single plausible ground which is usually brought forward to prove the use of these writings, is the circumstance that the Chronicle contains many narratives corresponding to those found in Samuel and Kings, and often verbally identical with them. But that is fully accounted for by the fact that the Chronicler used the same more detailed writings as the authors of the books of Samuel and Kings...

C.F. Keil, *The Books of the Chronicles* (Edinburgh: T. & T. Clark, 1872), p. 38 (trans. from *Biblischer Commentar über die nachexilischen Geschichtsbücher: Chronik, Esra, Nehemia und Esther* [Leipzig, 1870]).

5. This point was stressed particularly by C.C. Torrey, 'The Chronicler as Editor and as Independent Narrator', *AJSL* 25 (1908–1909), pp. 157-73 and 188-217, reprinted in *Ezra Studies* (Chicago: University of Chicago Press, 1910), pp. 208-51.

probably a case, then, where extracting from the fuller account has led
to a slight redundancy and inconsistency rather than a case in which the
latter have been made the peg on which to hang the longer account. It
need hardly be said that good reasons have been advanced to explain
why the Chronicler should have wished to omit the longer story but to
include this and other accounts of David's wars and victories.

(b) Another allusion to the court history is probably to be found in
1 Chron. 29.24, where the statement that 'and all the sons likewise of
King David submitted themselves unto Solomon the king' seems rather
pointless unless it alludes to the account of Adonijah's rebellion
(1 Kings 1).

(c) There is a possibility—I put it no higher than that, although others
are more convinced[6]—that it was reflection on the opening of 1 Kings 2
which triggered the whole of the Chronicler's presentation of the
patterning of the accession of Solomon on that of Joshua, a patterning
which is now generally recognized.[7]

(d) Finally, without the hypothesis that the Chronicler knew 2 Samuel
in substantially its present shape, we are left with an odd method of
composition by whomever was responsible for this part of the Deuteronomic History. For instance, 2 Samuel 21–24 is generally agreed to
have been added to a text of Samuel which already included the court
history. It interrupts the latter in order to present miscellaneous material
about David at the end of the account of his reign. Since the Chronicler
drew on these chapters at several points in his narrative, the view under
discussion has to follow the less plausible hypothesis that they stood in
an earlier version of the continuous history and that the court history
was wrapped around them by a subsequent editor.

3. I can now deal more briefly with the Elijah/Elisha stories (1 Kings
17–2 Kings 10).

(a) Nearly all these chapters relate to the northern kingdom of Israel
alone. They thus fall into the category of material which, for reasons of
his own, the Chronicler has consistently omitted. So their absence from
his account is in no way remarkable.

(b) The exceptions to this, namely incidents in which kings of the
southern kingdom of Judah are involved, neatly prove the rule. First,

6. Cf. R.L. Braun, *JBL* 95 (1976), p. 587 n. 17 and VTSup, 30 (1979), pp. 61-
62 n. 32.

7. Cf. Williamson, 'The Accession of Solomon in the Books of Chronicles',
VT 26 (1976), pp. 351-61.

1 Kings 22 is cited extensively, prophets and all, in 2 Chronicles 18. Secondly, 2 Kings 3 is replaced by an alternative account in 2 Chronicles 20 because it served better the Chronicler's total presentation of the reign of Jehoshaphat.[8] Thirdly, 2 Chron. 22.7-9 (the death of Ahaziah) seems to be based on 2 Kgs 9.1-28 with 10.12-14 and to presuppose knowledge of it. The differences, I have argued,[9] can all be explained on the basis of the Chronicler's well-attested principles of interpretation, familiar from other passages. Here we should note in particular, however, the passing reference to 'Jehu the son of Nimshi, whom the Lord had anointed to cut off the house of Ahab' (2 Chron. 22.7). This undoubtedly betrays knowledge of part, at least, of the Elisha cycle.

4. Finally, I am not sure how much should be made of the lack in Chronicles of the fulfilment formulae in Kings to which von Rad drew our attention. While Auld clearly regards it as significant, it should be remembered that, with one important exception to which we shall return, they too all relate to the northern kingdom. Meanwhile, it may be noted in passing that instances of a looser connection between prophecy and fulfilment as noted by von Rad are included in Chronicles from Kings.

It is thus no use my trying to hide the fact that I find myself unable to accept a number of the conclusions of Dr Auld's paper as they relate to areas of particular interest to me. Of course, this does not rule out the possibility of a prophetic redaction of the Deuteronomic History after the exile but before Chronicles[10] (unless we follow the growing fashion for dating Chronicles as early as 520–515 BCE[11]); nevertheless, to adopt the analogy which was suggested with the New Testament synoptic problem, I still favour a two document hypothesis rather than a hunt for an elusive Q.

Let me end, however, on a positive note, for, among much else of interest, Dr Auld's paper has thrown up one possibility that could be well worth pursuing. Attention was drawn to references to prophets in the books of Kings which are omitted by Chronicles. These are not

8. See my commentary, *1 and 2 Chronicles* (NCB; Grand Rapids: Eerdmans, 1982), pp. 277-80 and p. 291ff

9. Williamson, *1 and 2 Chronicles*, pp. 311-12.

10. For a survey of opinions on this, cf. R.D. Nelson, *The Double Redaction of the Deuteronomistic History* (JSOTSup, 18; Sheffield: JSOT Press, 1981).

11. I have set out my reasons for rejecting this date in *TynBul* 28 (1977), pp. 123-26, and in *1 and 2 Chronicles*, pp. 15–16.

numerous, and for some (e.g. 1 Chron. 21.9) I favour more mechanical explanations. It is of interest to note, however, that two relate to Manasseh and his doleful effects on the history of Judah—and that in just the way that 1 Esdras 1 differs most from 2 Chron. 35–36. Those who argue for a 'double redaction' view of Kings generally attribute the theme of blaming Manasseh for the exile to the latest phase. Meanwhile, as is well known, the Chronicler handles this theme quite differently because of his characteristic understanding of retribution. While this latter point adequately explains the omissions in Chronicles, the different approach adopted by 1 Esdras 1 may be sufficient to reopen the question of the status of that enigmatic document.[12] Perhaps we may ask whether in these instances we should not be talking so much of purely textual assimilation at a late, even translation, stage, but of an earlier contribution to the development of the definitive history and interpretation of the closing years of the Judean monarchy.

12. For some preliminary orientation, cf. my *Israel in the Books of Chronicles*, (Cambridge: Cambridge University Press, 1977), pp. 12-36.

JSOT 27 (1983), pp. 41-44

PROPHETS THROUGH THE LOOKING GLASS:
A RESPONSE TO ROBERT CARROLL AND HUGH WILLIAMSON

A. Graeme Auld

I give a very warm welcome to the two foregoing reactions to my journey through the looking glass. Each in its quite different way helps to clarify some of the issues raised in my paper. Robert Carroll demonstrates none of the famed antipathy between Glasgow and Edinburgh. His comments are reassuringly supportive: indeed he sketches very accurately the wider context which my paper sought to address.

I draw attention to only two of the points he has made, where I should like to place the emphasis rather differently, or perhaps just say a little more. The first concerns 're-think[ing] the category of prophet for these poets'. My first aim is a negative one: to discount the inherited suggestion that these poets were 'prophets' in their own eyes or in the eyes of their contemporaries. That is a simple issue of archival accuracy. However when we talk about re-thinking a category we are most often talking about our own categories. While I agree with Carroll that 'the canonical reading of a text is very much a process of narrowing down meaning until it is limited to the redactors' intention and ideology', I think it would be wrong to claim that the category 'prophet' simply narrows our understanding of figures like Isaiah, Amos, Jeremiah and the like. When they—and Elijah with them—are re-presented as 'prophets' in the later biblical tradition, then the meaning of 'prophet' is also shifted, expanded, enriched. Our category *is* closer to the developed biblical category then to the ancient Israelite category. Yet the canonical term which is partly shaped by the great individuals it now encompasses is more worthy of these poets than the earlier historical term against which they so strongly reacted.

Secondly and more briefly I am increasingly one of those who 'feel that too much has been made of the Deuteronomistic redaction of the prophets'. Certainly many of the later materials in the prophetic books share the language and concerns of parts of the Books of Kings. However, as I tried to suggest in my paper, my unease over 'Deuteronomistic redaction' is two-fold. On the one hand 'redaction' may have altogether too systematic overtones. On the other hand—and even if the first point is too strongly stated—much of the 'prophetic' material in both Kings and Jeremiah is late and, if anything, post-Deuteronomistic.

Hugh Williamson's patient and detailed observations deserve a full article for proper discussion. Here I can only point to a few cases in which his textual data seem to favour my hypothesis even better than his.

2 Chron. 22.7-9 on the death of Ahaziah is clearly related to the material in 2 Kings 9–10. But how? These last two chapters of the material in 1 Kings 17 to 2 Kings 10 are hardly the conclusion of an early source on Elijah and Elisha. Several editorial concerns overlap. But our starting point must be in the material which precedes these portions in both Kings and Chronicles. 2 Chron. 21.5 to 22.6 (with the exception of 21.11-19) is a repetition of 2 Kgs 8.17-29. It is precisely 2 Chronicles 22.7-9 which continues this material in style. The much more expansive treatment in 2 Kings 9–10 not only added much more detail but in fact suppressed the original brief record. Williamson draws our attention to a rather similar situation in 1 Chron. 20.1-3 and 2 Sam. 11–12, both on David and the Ammonite war. The short record in Chronicles must be defended against the charge of inconsistency: brief it is—but to the point! Joab led out the army with David at home. Joab was successful and David took over active command at the point of success. It reads like a very formal Minute. But is the related material in 2 Samuel 11–12 the story which the Minute records or a story created from the Minute? Williamson is clear that the account of the Ammonite campaign 'is intertwined with the story of Bathsheba and Uriah'. I argue that the insertion of the Bathsheba story into something like the short Chronicler's record has led to some redundancy in 2 Sam. 11.1 and 12.26. However the note that David remained in Jerusalem is the opportunity for the insertion and not a relic of it. Three footnotes may underscore this conclusion.

1.   The participle *yšb* has the (later?) *plene* spelling only in 2 Samuel 11.1.

2. 2 Sam. 12.26 like 1 Chron. 20.1 talks of Joab in the singular. 2 Sam. 11.1 has corresponding plural expressions.

3. There is some Greek testimony for a further element in the Chronicler's record. If this text identical to part of 2 Samuel 12 is accepted then the Chronicler's original Minute would have been less cryptic and the familiar MT text would be the result of homoioteleuton.

The brief list of David's officials with which 2 Samuel 8 ends is repeated *with some significant redrafting* as the closing verses of 2 Samuel 20. These verses resume the original text after the major insertion of most of 2 Samuel 9–20. 1 Chron. 18.15-17 is almost indistinguishable in text from the end of 2 Samuel 8 and, like 2 Samuel 8, it is positioned before the first mention of David and the Ammonites. I still find it preferable to suppose that the elements of the David story common to Samuel and Chronicles were a text that actually existed—a text which was considerably and variously supplemented to produce the two canonical versions.

Williamson raises a key point when he commends setting my statistics in a wider context and seeks to persuade me that 'the terminology should be studied initially to see how it relates to conceptual development rather than in complete isolation'. He quotes with approval Seeligmann's argument that Kings, the prose text of Jeremiah, and Chronicles represent a linear development in attitude to the prophets. The argument in question is a very important one. My own present guess is that the many secondary and late elements in all the texts Seeligmann is studying and to which he draws very clear attention should no longer be seen as exceptions to the old account, but become rather the basis for a new one. An account of conceptual development may only be hazarded when one is certain of documentary history. If supplementation (= 'redaction'?) was often piecemeal, if the 'Chronicler' did not abbreviate from his source as much as is often supposed, if MT pluses in Jeremiah are no evidence for Deuteronomistic thought, then our intellectual history of the post-exilic period requires too much alteration for it to offer any moderation of statistical speculation.

I plead for a radical rescrutiny of many biblical texts free from any recourse to inherited historical reconstructions whether ancient or modern. There are still remarkably few externally documentable facts in the area of biblical history. If 2 Samuel 9–20 was not part of the text of Samuel available to the Chronicler then that deduction of literary history should carry more weight in the final assessment of David than the common observation that these chapters portray character well and could be true. The present Books of Samuel and Kings may be a much later text than commonly supposed—independent of rather than prior to the Books of Chronicles. The fact that Kings ends with the fate of Judah's last king tells us no more about the date of composition (generally believed exilic) than the fact that the Pentateuch ends with the death of Moses.

JSOT 48 (1990), pp. 3-29

PROPHECY IN HISTORY:
THE SOCIAL REALITY OF INTERMEDIATION

Thomas W. Overholt

There *were* prophets in ancient Israel and Judah, and persons like Amos and Jeremiah were recognized by their contemporaries as being among them. This proposition may seem to many a banality—a piece of common knowledge and hardly something to be argued—but in recent years it has come under explicit attack by two British scholars, A. Graeme Auld and Robert P. Carroll. My proposition, then, provides an occasion to appraise their arguments and to make a modest proposal about how cross-cultural studies can contribute to our appreciation of the historical reality of biblical prophecy.

Poets Not Prophets

The position that Auld seeks to defend is that 'it [is] at least plausible that [the terms] "prophet" and "prophesy" only came to be attached to those whom we regard as the towering prophets of the Bible in a period no earlier than when Jeremiah and Ezekiel became similarly re-presented' (1984: 82). Stated in a slightly stronger way, he informs us that his 'first aim is a negative one: to discount the inherited suggestion that these poets were "prophets" in their own eyes or in the eyes of their contemporaries' (1983b: 41). Recent studies by Carroll have tended toward a similar conclusion. These two scholars have studied different material, and their arguments are not identical. Still, they are in basic agreement that figures like Amos, Hosea and Isaiah were poets and were not thought of as prophets until exilic times. Between them, Auld and Carroll marshal four arguments in support of this 'poets not prophets' hypothesis.

The first argument is linguistic. Auld in particular has been preoccupied with what he calls the 'history of terminology' (1984: 82).
Several of his studies center on the noun and verb forms of *nb'* and
conclude that there are three identifiable stages in the use of these terms
in the prophetic and historical books of the Hebrew Bible. First, at an
early stage the terms were applied to groups that were the objects of
criticism. During this period, the canonical prophets—Isaiah, Micah,
Zephaniah and Jeremiah (in the poetic sections of the books)—were not
referred to as 'prophets'. 'The usage is rather more nuanced' in Amos
and Hosea, but 'there is no suggestion that Hosea was himself a
"prophet"; and that label is specifically rejected by Amos in 7.14'
(1984: 68). The books of Jeremiah and Ezekiel represent a second,
transitional stage. In addition to criticism of the prophets as a group,
these books contain positive references to past prophets and apply the
title 'prophet' to Jeremiah and Ezekiel themselves. The latter book
regularly uses the verb to describe Ezekiel's functioning. Auld concludes,
however, that neither Jeremiah nor Ezekiel used the noun to describe
himself or the verb to refer to his own activity (1984: 73). Finally, there
is a late stage in which the view of prophets is essentially favorable, and
individuals—Haggai, Zechariah and Habakkuk—are given the title
'prophet'. The favorable attitude toward prophets in Kings is the result
of late editorial additions.

In this view, Jeremiah and Ezekiel 'stand at the crossroads' of a
development from eighth- and seventh-century hostility (or at best
neutrality) toward 'prophetic contemporaries' to the post-exilic period
when persons were 'readily titled "prophet"' (Auld 1983a: 5). The
validity of this scheme can be tested with 'a degree of objectivity' in the
book of Jeremiah, 'with its different editions, and its blend of poetry and
prose' (1983a: 5-6). References to 'prophets' in the Jeremiah poetry are
mostly critical. In the earliest stratum of prose (the material common to
LXX and MT) there are many critical references to prophets, but
Jeremiah, Uriah and Micah are referred to positively as prophets. The
latest prose ('extra' material in MT) has a few critical references, but
gives the title 'prophet' to Jeremiah (24×) and Hananiah (6×). Carroll
also notes the development that has taken place between the two
editions of the book of Jeremiah: while the first (represented by LXX)
gives Jeremiah the title 'the prophet' only four times (all refer to the
period after the fall of Jerusalem), the second (represented by MT) does
so 26 times, making him 'the prophet par excellence' (1989a: 23).

Auld observes that the verb 'prophesy' seems to have been used positively earlier than the noun 'prophet'. For example, Amos 3.3-8 (Auld eliminates v. 7 as a later prose addition) groups prophesying with other matters of general human experience. Thus '*prophesying*...[is] an activity that is not confined to official *prophets*, but open to *anyone* who has heard Lord Yahweh speak' (1986: 32). This line of argumentation involves the supposition 'that for the author of the narrative one did not have to be a "prophet" in order to receive the divine imperative to "prophesy"; and indeed that such a command did not turn one into a "prophet"' (p. 30). Amos 7.10-17, a late addition included to explore 'the nature of Amos's authority' (1986: 28), has the same tendency: 'the designation "prophet" is rejected but the activity of "prophesying" [is] acceptable' (1984: 68). Thus, neither 7.10-17 nor 3.3-8 provides 'evidence for Amos's own attitude to the business of prophecy' (1986: 35).

In another study Auld examines the use of the phrase 'the Word of God' in order to call into question 'the widespread confidence that in the classical Hebrew prophets we meet the quintessential bearers of the divine word' (1988: 245). He points out that the phrase rarely occurs in books associated with the eighth-century prophets. In Hosea, for example, the only two occurrences (1.1; 4.1) are in secondary editorial insertions (1988: 246). This phrase and others (like 'says the Lord' in passages which on other grounds can be considered secondary) may be 'used to claim authority for a later insertion to the message of the eighth-century figure', and it is doubtful that prophets like Isaiah, Hosea or Jeremiah 'ever actually said "Hear the Word of the Lord" or "The Word of the Lord came to me"' (1988: 246-47).

A second argument in support of the 'poets not prophets' theory follows from the observation that there is no unanimity in the Hebrew Bible on 'what a prophet is or should be' or on the evaluation of prophets. Carroll points out that 'the Bible offers no definition of what a prophet is (1 Sam. 9.9 is a most curious statement!) nor does the biblical word *nabi'* have any definite meaning in Hebrew that we can discern'. It is impossible to derive from the biblical texts a clear understanding of the relationship between prophets and diviners or the cult, and attempts to delineate 'the various roles specified by different terms in the Hebrew Bible' must negotiate the twin hazards of scanty data in the texts and inexact matches between ancient roles and modern activities. Furthermore, the Hebrew Bible displays 'a strange tension between good reports about prophets and trenchant dismissals of them as deceivers and idolaters'. All of this should make the modern interpreter beware of assuming that he or she knows what biblical prophecy was (Carroll 1989b: 209-15).

There is an obvious link here with the argument based on terminology. By stressing the distinction between the act of 'prophesying' and the social role 'prophet', Auld was able to argue both that Amos was not a prophet and that the book reveals nothing about Amos's attitude toward prophecy (Auld 1986: 25-35; cf. 1988: 246-50).

Carroll has suggested a third argument, namely that our association of texts with specific prophets is merely a matter of convention and cannot be substantiated with hard evidence. The poetic sections of the prophetic books, he reminds us, tend to be anonymous; they are associated with named individuals on the basis of the editorial frameworks, which serve to incorporate them into larger collections. The introductory colophons are very important in this respect, since in most cases they are the only place in a book where the prophet is named. The contents of the colophons cannot be substantiated historically, however, and 'we may equally regard them as part extrapolation [from tradition] and part invention' (Carroll 1988: 28; 1989a: 26). The persons who wrote these colophons thus 'helped to *invent* the ancient prophets as biographical figures' (Carroll 1988: 25).

Finally, it is relatively clear to students of the Hebrew Bible that many of its books are the result of a long and complicated process of editorial activity. The fourth argument for the 'poets not prophets' position focuses on two aspects of this editorial process. The first of these is that the texts of the prophetic books are products of literary activity. According to Carroll, we must think of the biblical books as conventional literary texts fabricated by their authors for particular purposes. Furthermore, 'prophecy was an oral phenomenon', and the writing down of prophecy severed the originally oral text from the speaker's situation and transformed it into a 'timeless reference... addressed to future generations'. So, unless there is 'considerable justification', to infer a social background from the text amounts to 'an illegitimate transfer of meaning from story to social background' (Carroll 1989b: 206-207).

The implications of this view may be seen in Carroll's interpretation of the book of Jeremiah. Since we are basically ignorant about the formation of that book, scholars have resorted to 'axiomatic assertions', for example, that the poetry contained in it had to be spoken by someone, and in view of 1.1-3 this someone must have been Jeremiah. But such assertions are 'very unhelpful'. In fact, it is reasonable 'to accept, for the sake of argument', the view 'that the book purports to be the work of a fictional character called Jeremiah and then to proceed from that point to treat the work *as if* such a figure behaved and spoke in the ways attributed to him in the book'. This is the way we understand Homer's Odysseus, Shakespeare's Macbeth, Swift's Gulliver, and Joyce's Bloom,

> and there is no good reason to treat biblical characters in a different fashion. What we would not do is to insist on a one-to-one correspondence between the fictional characters and any historical counterparts we might imagine of them... A similar approach must be advocated for reading Jeremiah. We should treat the character of Jeremiah as a work of fiction and recognize the impossibility of moving from the book to the real 'historical' Jeremiah, given our complete lack of knowledge independent of the book itself (1989a: 12).

At issue is not whether in their present form the prophetic books are products of a period of editorial activity, but how this activity is to be conceived. In his recent commentary on Jeremiah, William McKane proposed the idea of a 'rolling corpus' to explain the process of growth. According to this theory, poetry generally preceded prose, and expansions of the text were not systematic but were ad hoc and exegetical in intent. Auld and Carroll both embrace this idea, which allows them to focus on the motivations of the redactors of the books and play down the possibility that portions of the text may reflect an original (or at least earlier) message and social situation (Auld 1983a: 3-5). Furthermore, Carroll draws more far-reaching conclusions than does McKane, who like many others assumes that the poetry of Jeremiah 2–20 contains genuine words of the prophet. Although Carroll says this hypothesis is worth entertaining, he insists that 'there is no hard evidence to support it'. The identity of Jeremiah actually derives from the editorial framework of the book (1.1-3) and not from the poetry (Carroll 1989a: 37).

To speak of the motivations of redactors suggests a need to view the texts in terms of their ideological content. This is the second aspect of the argument from editorial activity. Carroll points out that within the book of Jeremiah one finds 'quite contrary, even contradictory' views on matters ranging from the social situation (society is totally corrupt; it is composed of both righteous and wicked persons) to the possibility of repentance (the people are incorrigible; repentance is possible) to the prophet himself (in the laments he is a 'depressed and depressing' figure; in the narratives he 'commands' and 'confronts'; 1986: 292-95). Such diverse views must have their origin in attitudes of the redactors.

Carroll's view of the laments indicates his inclination to look for *later* ideological developments. These poems, often interpreted as 'autobiographical utterances of the prophet Jeremiah', are neither collected into a single place nor 'given any editorial connections with Jeremiah's speaking', though the placement of 11.21-23 and 18.18 'suggests some connection between the laments and the life of Jeremiah'. Carroll suggests that 'the most natural way to read' those poems is as a stage in the development of the traditions in which the innocent who suffered at the nation's fall seek vindication—contradicting Jeremiah's blaming of the whole nation for the disaster (e.g. 5.1-5; 6.13; etc.; 1989a: 46-47).

In view of the Bible's differing attitudes toward prophecy, it is less problematic to refer to the canonical figures like Amos, Isaiah and Jeremiah as 'poets' rather than 'prophets'. The fact that later compilers of the 'anthologies' shared at least some of these poets' ideology may account for the development in the direction of correlating poet and prophet (Carroll 1983; Auld 1988: 246-50).

Prophets after All

Commenting on the organization of his study of the book of Amos, Auld says

> I have started near the end, with reports of Amos's visions and the discussion of his status, rather than at the beginning because I find that much reading of the Bible's prophetic literature is prejudiced since readers *know* in advance what a prophet or visionary *really* is—but are wrong (1986: 10).

A prominent feature of my attempt to rebut the Auld–Carroll position on prophets and prophecy will be this: historically and sociologically, religious intermediation is a very widely distributed phenomenon, and it conforms rather strictly to a particular pattern. On the basis of such comparative evidence we can indeed know in advance what 'prophets' are, and we will be *right*. Let me take up their lines of argumentation one by one.

1. *The 'History of Terminology'*

Amos 7, where 'the designation "prophet" is rejected but the activity of "prophesying" acceptable' (Auld 1984: 68), is a good place to begin a consideration of the linguistic evidence. Auld's only explanation for this locution is that here (and in Amos 3.8) we have a parallel with the books of Jeremiah and Ezekiel, in which the verb develops more rapidly than the noun 'in connection with the hero of a "prophetic" book' (1984: 73). The narrative of Amos 7.10-17, however, demonstrates clearly the weakness of concentrating on terminology. Although Amos denies he is a prophet, Amaziah recognizes his public activity as 'prophesying' (7.12-13) and Amos uses the same term to describe his commission from Yahweh (7.15). Würthwein (1950) has argued that Amos's refusal to accept the title 'prophet' was motivated by his desire to distinguish himself from official prophets whose primary task was intercession. This is a reasonable explanation. In any case, the important point is that regardless of what he and they were called, it is evident that both Amos and the 'prophets' to whom he refers were performing a recognizable social role.

Who, according to Auld, was Amos? It appears

> that he did not regard himself as a 'prophet', that he did not claim status as a 'religious' functionary, that he did not require a position in popular or official religion to say what he had to say... He appears rather to have held that *anyone* who had heard Yahweh speak should himself 'prophesy' [cf. Amos 3.3-6, 8]: that means, speak out with the freedom prophets use. He appears to have been an agriculturalist. Yet our main evidence for him is as a communicator: and he certainly was extraordinarily skilful in his use of words (1986: 73).

But this leaves unanswered the question of what role Amos was playing in society when he uttered his wonderfully poetic words. The definition of prophecy implied here—a prophet is someone to whom Yahweh has spoken and who freely communicates the contents of this revelation to an audience—describes precisely what, according to the narrative, Amos claimed he was doing. Therefore, Amos was a prophet!

Similarly, Auld notes about Ezekiel that he is never 'directly' given the title 'prophet', though twice he is indirectly called that (2.5; 33.33). Still, about 30 times his 'words are introduced...by a reported command to "prophesy". Perhaps during the period when attitudes were changing the verb was more acceptable than the noun "prophet" as a designation of acceptable 'prophetic' activity' (1983a: 5). It is not clear why the

noun should be unacceptable. In any case the use of the verb implies
some observable behavior. It follows that the prophetic role is being
performed and *recognized*. This presupposes that both the performers
and the audience had a certain view of what was transpiring.[1]

The same thing is true of Auld's discussion of how the terms develop
within Jeremiah. There the verb form occurs more often in the 'shorter
prose tradition' than it did in the poetry, and in these prose passages it
can refer to

> the activity of individuals who are not otherwise 'prophet' *in the
> immediate context of the passages concerned*: eight times of Jeremiah
> himself—11.21; 19.14; 20.1; 26.9, 11, 12; 29.27; 32.3; twice positively of
> others—26.18 (Micah of Moresheth) and 26.20 (Uriah); and five times
> negatively of others—20.6; 28.6; 29.21, 26, 31' (1984: 71; emphasis
> added).

The intent, of course, is to bolster the point that these individuals were
not yet designated as 'prophets'. But again, what sense does it make to
say audiences recognized that people were 'prophesying' but did not
understand them to be 'prophets'? The reference to the 'immediate (literary) context' is a smokescreen which obscures the fact that there must
certainly have been a social context in which the use of the verb made
sense. Notice the content of the eight references to Jeremiah: most
involve other persons identifying his activity as 'prophesying'; two have
the narrator making the reference (19.14; 20.1), and in one Jeremiah is
made to describe his own activity in this way (26.12).

There is a similar problem in his treatment of Jeremiah 28. The longer
prose (= MT) uses the title 'prophet' for both Jeremiah and Hananiah.
On the other hand, the shorter prose (= LXX) never gives Jeremiah the
title, and gives it only once (in the form *pseudoprophētēs*, 'false prophet'
[v. 1]) to Hananiah. Although admitting 'proof is impossible' (1984: 72),
Auld infers that the short prose does not consider Hananiah a prophet.
As evidence he cites the fact that elsewhere the short prose uses
'prophet' only of groups mentioned in conjunction with other groups
(6.13; 26.7, 8, 11; 27.9; 29.1, 8). But what sociological sense does it
make to assert that persons operating in groups can be recognized to be
prophets, while those operating (as far as we know) independently would
not be called by the same name? The use of the verb for both implies

---

1.   This applies also to Auld's denial that Elijah was a prophet (1984: 80).

that at the very least the individuals were recognized as performing the same social role.

As to the Jeremiah poetry, if it mostly criticizes prophets and does not refer to Jeremiah himself as a prophet, this seems only what one would expect. The poetry is preoccupied with a critique of Judean society; there is little opportunity for self-reference.

The major assumption in my rebuttal of Auld's argument from the 'history of terminology' is that the kind of religious intermediation we designate 'prophet' was a social reality in ancient Israel and Judah, presumably from very early times. Furthermore, I believe it was a social role which the population as a whole understood very well. To think that prophecy developed late in the Old Testament period, or that the canonical figures were only then identified as prophets, is incorrect.

My assumption is based upon evidence that prophetic intermediation is a widely distributed and precisely describable social phenomenon and the conviction that cross-cultural research on prophecy can contribute to our understanding of the Hebrew prophets.[2] Data from a number of cultures and historical periods show that prophetic intermediation is characterized by a regular and recognizable set of social behaviors, which are in turn made possible (and rendered plausible) by the societies' own assumptions about the relationships of the gods to the everyday world of human experience.[3]

Old Testament prophecy conforms to this pattern. It is not a unique phenomenon invented, so to speak, by the Israelites, let alone by a group of exiles late in their history. This is not merely a negative comment, since seeing the Israelite prophets within the broader context of the history of religions has the advantage of confirming and providing a clearer description of their role in Israelite society.

The pattern of behavior defined by my model of the prophetic process constitutes a kind of 'program' which allows members of a

2. I have discussed this at length in my book, *Channels of Prophecy* (1989). Because of vast differences in time, circumstances and geographic location, cross-cultural comparisons of prophecy require the use of a model which focuses on the social dynamics of the prophetic act itself, on how the prophetic process works. The model I have developed for this purpose contains two essential features: a set of three actors (a deity, an intermediary and an audience) and a pattern of interrelationships among them involving revelation, the proclamation of a message, and feedback (cf. pp. 17-25).

3. Cf. Overholt (1989: 157-59) and the discussion of 'social prerequisites of intermediation' in Wilson (1980: 28-32).

society to recognize and respond to persons who seem to have taken up a certain socio-religious role (Overholt 1989: 149-62). Both the ancient Israelites and Judeans (because they lived in a society hospitable to this kind of intermediation and with a tradition of such activity) and we (because on the basis of research we can recognize the presence of the pattern) do, contrary to Carroll, 'have knowledge independent of' the biblical accounts themselves.

The point is, conclusions about prophets in ancient Israel based on an examination of the use of words like 'prophet' and 'prophesy' err in failing to take into account a social reality clearly perceivable in (or behind) the texts.

2. *Consensus and Definition*

The second line of argumentation had to do with the supposed lack of unanimity within the Hebrew Bible on 'what a prophet is or should be'. The 'ancient Israelite writers', says Carroll, 'had no clear image' about the prophets and often dismissed them as undesirable (1989b: 209). The statement seems hyperbolic. I have already referred to a cross-cultural account of prophecy which identifies a process of intermediation that can be precisely described (Overholt 1989). The model employed in that study, it should be noted, accommodates the variety of terms used to gloss the role of this particular kind of religious intermediation, as well as conflicts between intermediaries themselves and between intermediaries and segments of their audiences. Such conflicts are a normal part of the process (cf. Long 1981). They may be disconcerting to audiences faced with the need to evaluate what a particular prophet is saying, but they should not be to us.

Etymologically, it may be true that 'the biblical word *nābî'*' has no 'definite meaning in Hebrew'. On the other hand, in ancient Israel and Judah it evidently glossed a rather well-recognized social role, a religious intermediary of a specific type. If the description of this type in terms of a cross-cultural model seems somewhat ideal, it has social reality nonetheless, incorporating functionaries ranging along a continuum from prophet to diviner.

According to Auld, the notion of prophecy, 'the idea of God speaking to or through mediators', came to be attached to approved figures like Amos and Jeremiah only during a late 're-formation of the prophetic traditions' (1988: 248). In his own time Amos

was a critic of the community of classic proportions…[but] he was not a
prophet till the descendants of his community made him one, nor did he
purvey the word of God till his successors discerned that quality in his
words… Poetic critics like Amos were deemed bearers of the divine word
even before they were redefined as 'prophets' (1988: 246-47).

Amos himself was not a prophet. He and others like him, Auld says

come across not as men of the word but as craftsmen with words. The
developed view of the prophet may be of the divine messenger or
ambassador… If that poetic succession from Amos to Jeremiah was later
re-presented as a series of 'servants' duly acknowledged by God then this
is in part a judgment that they had in fact been good advocates. It tells us
how their authority for a later scriptural age was understood; but leaves
unstated how they functioned in their own age. My submission is that
when later generations called Amos and Isaiah 'prophets', and received
their words as 'Word of God', they gave them an honour they had richly
deserved but did not claim (1988: 250).

There is some truth in this formulation, since ultimately prophets must
be recognized (authorized) by the communities in which they function;
one cannot perform a social role like 'prophet' unless at least some
members of the society validate that performance. It is no doubt also the
case that appreciation of the biblical prophets increased as time passed
and some of what they said was confirmed by events. But there are
problems. First, even if it could be established that Amos and the others
did not claim to be prophets, we would not be entitled to conclude that
no one understood them to be performing the role of prophets. Explicit
claims are not the only, or the most important, feature of prophetic
behavior.[4] Secondly, Auld does not seem to reckon with the possibility
that there existed in Israel from earliest times the assumptions that
Yahweh and humans could be in contact and that persons performing
certain recognized roles (generally glossed 'prophets' and 'diviners')
were the chief channels of this intercourse.

In the same context, Auld suggests the prophets

sought to convince by argument rather than compel by authority. Amos
makes his appeal to Israel not in terms of divine revelation old or new but
by an invidious point to point comparison of her behaviour with that of
her neighbours who she knew broke all natural norms (1988: 250).

This poet cannot be a prophet; he is too rational. But it is not clear why

---

4.   Cf. the account of the Melanesian prophet Yali in Overholt 1986: 295-308.

revelation and rational 'point to point comparison' should necessarily be incompatible. Intermediaries need not be considered mere megaphones through whom an emotional deity speaks.

3. *Identity and Invention*

The third line of argumentation for the 'poets not prophets' position entailed the claim that the identity of the figures after whom the prophetic books are named derives from the editorial material in those books and is as likely as not a late fiction. Carroll argues that the book of Jeremiah is 'a highly polemical text' made up of 'many different polemical pieces', coming from a variety of times and situations. It cannot, therefore, go back to a single author. Even the assumption that Jeremiah is at least responsible for the poetry depends for support upon taking secondary editorial material (e.g. 1.1-3) at face value. But 'good scholarship', he says, requires that 'nothing must be assumed without some evidence for it' (1986: 298-99).

The question is whether Carroll sets up a straw opponent and assaults it with too big a weapon. Who would claim that the whole book of Jeremiah goes back to a single person? Why is it necessary, in order to refute such a position, to completely dispose of the prophet Jeremiah as a human being about whom something can be known? One might just as well pose a different question about the book: Doesn't the fact that there is a major block of material bearing the name 'Jeremiah' make it plausible to assume that somewhere behind, and in, that tradition is a real historical person? Carroll admonishes us that 'nothing must be assumed without some evidence for it', but what passes for evidence? I am proposing that if the texts speak of behavior which confirms to a widely distributed pattern of intermediation, we should accept this as evidence that they attest in some way to actual social and historical phenomena.[5]

---

5.   It is difficult for any of us to be entirely consistent in our use of biblical evidence. So it is that in a study of the introductory colophons of the Old Testament prophetic books Carroll comments

> no named prophet in the prophetic traditions and no figure in the colophons is said to have come from Jerusalem! It would appear to be the case that no Jerusalemite prophet was accepted in the canon of the prophets—whether for ideological, cultural or political reasons must be left to scholarly speculation (1988: 30).

It seems to me that, contrary to his own position, this statement depends upon the

Carroll claims about the colophons of the prophetic books that without them we would neither 'read what follows as the utterances of specific persons', nor would we 'be tempted to read what follows as the output of prophets in the first place!' (since the collections condemn prophets and 'no prophet is praised' in them [1988: 33]). On the contrary, I think it quite likely we would. Thematic and stylistic coherence in prophetic books or sections thereof suggests the influence of some specific person, whether or not he or she could be identified. And if some of these texts tend to attack prophets, this should be no surprise. Prophecy is at home in times of crisis, and at such times differences of opinion are bound to arise. Polemics against prophets are easily understood as directed against *other* prophets. A response made by H.G.M. Williamson to one of Auld's papers is pertinent here: the pre-exilic prophets do not reject their opponents 'because they are *nebiʾim*, but because they are bad ones' (1983: 34).

4. *The Literary Character of Prophetic Texts*

Finally, there is the matter of the literary character of the Old Testament prophetic texts. For Carroll, the writing down of materials originally transmitted orally seems to imply a 'transformation' of content: 'The import of the words' has been changed, enabling them 'to change beyond their immediate context and to apply to circumstances far removed from their original setting' (1989b: 208). The argument seems to be: literary texts yield reliable data only about the situation and ideological purpose of their authors; since the authors of prophetic texts are not the prophets themselves, we cannot look to these texts for reliable data about the prophets.

Again, the position seems extreme. I am perfectly in agreement with the notions that a series of editors have in all likelihood shaped our present prophetic books to fit their own understandings and the needs of their time and that what these texts 'mean' does not so much reside in the books, like a precious pearl in its shell, as arise out of the process of persons ancient and modern hearing and reading them. The question is whether this on-going process of interpretation forecloses the possibility of deriving from the words themselves hints about the social situations that were the occasions for their utterance. In my opinion, it does not.

The larger issue is the extent to which a literary text (in this case a

assumption that the books and their colophons do indeed retain some historical information.

prophetic book) asserts some influence over readers' interpretations of it and yields useful information about the prophet and his time. This is a complex issue, much debated among recent literary theorists.

The crux of the problem lies in the peculiar relationship that exists between texts and readers. That the text of Jeremiah can be physically present on the desk in front of me like a coffee mug or a computer is obvious. But I am related differently to the Jeremiah text than to these other objects. In the words of Georges Poulet, the text offers itself to me to be read, and when I read it, its images and ideas come to reside in the 'interior world' of my 'consciousness' (Poulet 1972: 42-43). The result is a 'convergence of text and readers', in which the author's text stimulates a response in the reader and gives rise to a dynamic, dialectical process which 'brings the literary work into existence' (Iser 1974: 50). To be sure, subsequent readings by the same or different readers may yield differing 'realizations' of the text, but since 'the written text imposes certain limits on its unwritten implications', the process is not entirely arbitrary (Iser 1974: 51, 57).

This view, which acknowledges the role of the reader in creating the meaning of the text while seemingly preserving the text's independent status, has been challenged by Stanley Fish. For Fish it is not the author's 'intention' that determines a text's meaning. Rather, readers see in a text what the 'interpretive strategies' of the community to which they belong allow them to see (1976: 176). But it seems likely that Fish has given away too much. We ought to concede to him (and others) that the text (the collection of words that confronts us on the printed page or in some other medium) is not a self-sufficient entity which contains a single, true meaning that has only to be uncovered. The proposition that meaning arises out of the dynamic, dialectical process set in motion by the 'convergence of text and reader' (Iser) seems altogether reasonable. However, if the text is an occasion for the reader's experience, it also sets boundaries for that experience. Interpretations of it can be more or less warranted by the language it contains. Thus, if the aim is to interpret a text, it will be useful to be attentive to its language, for example, to the range of possible meanings of the words its author has selected.[6]

6.   J. Swift's essay, 'A Modest Proposal', has been understood by readers with a literalistic interpretative strategy to be a serious espousal of cannibalism, and it is possible to imagine a reader who becomes sexually aroused as a result of reading the U.S. Constitution. But most readers would agree that the warrant for such

On the other hand, if the text creates a boundary or horizon that marks off the proper realm for its interpretation, it is important that this horizon not be considered too close at hand. It must be wide enough to encompass more than a single reading of the text. The ideal, it would seem, is to avoid the two extremes on the reader–text continuum: the view that texts contain *a* meaning which one simply has to uncover, and the view that texts place virtually no limit on the meanings generated while reading them. Fish (who claims to have 'made the text disappear' [1976: 183]) seems close to the latter pole.[7]

Robert Scholes agrees with Fish that interpretation enters the reading process at an early point, but insists that texts do guide us in their interpretation. His argument has two main prongs, a rather minimalist statement of which would be that there is 'some reality in the texts and some freedom in the interpreter' (1985: 159). A text is always 'encoded in a particular language' and can exist 'as a text only in and through its language' (1985: 152). Interpretation, therefore, assumes 'familiarity with [its] linguistic code'.

Codes (such as language, or the rules of chess) set boundaries for behavior, but allow freedom within those boundaries. Scholes (1985: 161-62) uses the example of Pat Kelly, a Baltimore Orioles outfielder who attributes his home runs to divine intervention, to illustrate

> the major problem in Fish's theory: his refusal to see any difference between the primary system in which a text is encoded and secondary systems that can only be brought to bear by an interpreter who comprehends the primary system.

Both Kelly and the sports writer share a primary system, the rules of baseball by which home runs are perceived as home runs. It is not that for Kelly the Christian view has replaced the baseball view; rather, 'he grafts another interpretation onto the baseball interpretation'. The dispute between the two is over the proper hierarchy and the relevance of several codes. So, says Scholes

interpretations resides less in the language of the text itself than, say, in specific readers' own needs or the interpretative strategy of their community of like-minded readers.

7. Cf. the critique of Scholes (1985: 147-52), and also Moore (1986). B. Long offers a reader-response interpretation of 2 Kgs 4.8-37 which demonstrates a healthy balance: there are 'contrary tendencies' in the narrative, but both 'rest on one's response to items in the work' (1988: 174).

> Where Fish sees interpretive communities remotely controlling acts of
> interpretation by individuals suffering from the illusion of freedom, I see
> individuals with many codes, some more and some less relevant, trying
> to see which ones will serve best in dealing with structures that have their
> own necessities.[8]

But we must not forget that our readings of a text are never neutral
or innocent. Terry Eagleton's claim that every reading of a work is also
in some sense a re-writing of it does not refer simply to the fact that our
subjective value judgments somehow subvert the factual knowledge
conveyed by the text. While it is possible for 'factual knowledge...[to]
be distorted by particular interests and judgements', the more basic
point is that 'interests are *constitutive* of our knowledge, not merely
prejudices which imperil it'. We come to a literary text, as to everything
else in life, 'bearing a largely concealed structure of values', beliefs and
interests which as members of a society we are 'born into'. Our
interpretations and value judgments are not whimsical, but are informed
by an 'ideology' (1983: 1216).

I have no interest in claiming that my reading supplies the only—or
even the best—interpretation of the biblical texts concerning prophecy.
It is one of a number of useful ways of interpreting them. What prompts
me to argue so vigorously against the 'poets not prophets' hypothesis is
an interest in understanding a particular kind of human social behavior
to which we may give the rather general label 'prophecy'. I have
encountered the basic structures of this type of behavior in texts
produced by or about such a wide variety of societies—including those
of ancient Israel and Judah—that the attempt to eliminate it from certain
biblical texts seems to me to be a misinterpretation. The biblical texts

---

8.   See Eagleton's brief meditation on the word 'nightingale', the point of which
is that 'language is not in fact something we are free to do what we like with'.
Despite the fact that we can easily imagine inventing any number of contexts that
would permit us to make its words signify what we wished, we cannot make a
literary text mean whatever we want it to mean. 'For such texts belong to language as
a whole, have intricate relations to other linguistic practices, however much they
might also subvert and violate them' (1983: 86-88). It is true, of course, that one is
more constrained when reading a road sign, which supplies a ready-made context
that renders the language intelligible, than when reading a literary work, which
generally does not. But in no case can there be 'total interpretative freedom', because
'the social uses of words...govern my search for appropriate contexts of meaning'
(88). For a related criticism of the post-structuralist 'dogma that we [can] never
know anything at all' (cf. 144-45).

seem clearly to embody a 'code'—a pattern of social behavior quite analogous to Scholes's 'rules of baseball'—that was both expected and recognized as 'prophetic', and that persistently points the reader in the direction of social reality. This code was evidently firmly entrenched in the ideology of ancient Israel and Judah during the whole period of the texts' production and for centuries before. That these texts are considered Scripture by three major religious traditions does not privilege them, or the society in which they were produced, in the sense of placing them off limits to non-theological interpretations or comparisons with other cultures.

One can only speculate about the 'ideology' which informs the 'poets not prophets' position. It seems fair to observe that Auld's view of Amos as a great communicator has the effect of playing down spiritual claims and making him appear to be more an 'enlightened' social reformer than perhaps he was. And Carroll's choice of the phrase 'deconstructing the prophet' in one of his titles invites us to assume some level of commitment to a specific theoretical position.

There is another matter which relates to the literary character of the prophetic texts. Carroll, as we have seen, has argued that we ought to understand the prophet Jeremiah as a fictional character like Homer's Odysseus and Shakespeare's Macbeth, recognizing 'the impossibility of moving from the book to the real "historical" Jeremiah, given our complete lack of knowledge independent of the book itself' (1989a: 12). This proposal to treat the book of Jeremiah as fiction raises the issue of the role of *genre* in interpretation. Does the genre of a work allow us to infer anything about the intention of its author or put any constraints upon us as readers? For example, one assumes when reading a novel or a play, no matter how historically oriented (e.g. *Macbeth*), that the author is at liberty to create the story as he or she sees fit. One is, therefore, wary of reading history out of such texts, although there may in fact be historical information in them. One further assumes that the author intended freely to create a story; that is why the genre was chosen over another (say, a history of...). If, on the other hand, authors choose to write histories, we assume they intend to construct accounts of the past. This does not, of course, mean that such accounts are perfectly accurate and free from bias. Still, we will be inclined to look for historical information in them, and rightly so.

The idea that attention to genre might be relevant to biblical studies is not a new one. Since the pioneering work of Hermann Gunkel at the

turn of the century and of Karl Ludwig Schmidt, Martin Dibelius and
Rudolf Bultmann just after World War I, form criticism has been one of
the prominent methods employed in the critical study of the Bible.
Central to this approach is the idea that genres 'arise and become stereotyped because of recurring situations in human life' (Tucker 1971: 2). To
speak of the function, or intention, of a genre is to ask—both in general
and with respect to specific examples of the genre—about the particular
purpose it arose to fulfill in its ancient setting (Tucker 1971: 16).

Genre has thus been used as a tool for classifying biblical texts and
reconstructing the social and historical background out of which they
arose, but this is not its only significance. Genre is also important in the
process by which readers come to construct the meaning of particular
texts. Without it, texts would hardly be 'readable'. In the words of Mary
Gerhart, 'Genres are not only principles of categorization or identification; they are also principles of production. Understood retrospectively,
genres can be said to produce, as well as to identify meanings' (1988:
33-34; cf. Buss 1979: 10).

This position has been argued at length by the literary theorist,
E.D. Hirsch, Jr. Hirsch contends that interpretation must address itself to
the 'verbal meaning' of a text, which he defines as 'whatever someone
has willed to convey by a particular sequence of linguistic signs and
which can be conveyed (shared) by means of those linguistic signs'
(1967: 31). Verbal meanings are 'changeless' in the sense that they
remain 'the same from one moment to the next' (1967: 46). Language,
on the other hand, is 'two-sided and reciprocal', involving both the
expression and the interpretation of meaning. This confronts us with a
problem for which genre will offer the solution: the 'paradox' that
verbal meaning is individual but interpretations are variable is resolved
when we realize that in our acquisition of language all of us master
through repeated experience 'not only [its] variable and unstable
norms...but also the particular norms of a particular genre'.[9]

Our understanding of a text is powerfully influenced by our 'meaning
expectations', which in turn arise from our 'conception of the type of

9.   Hirsch (1967: 68-71); in his discussion he utilizes Saussure's distinction
between *langue* and *parole* and Wittgenstein's idea that one must know the rules of
the game being played to know the meaning of an utterance. Later in the book Hirsch
says, 'At the level of verbal meaning, all types, regardless of their earliest provenance,
are learned types—that is, they are type ideas which derive from previous experience
and can subsume later experience' (269).

meaning that is being expressed', that is, from our 'generic conception' of the text (1967: 76). Therefore, a 'genre conception is constitutive' of both speaking and interpreting. Verbal meaning is 'genre-bound', since both speaking and understanding 'must be governed and constituted by a sense of the whole utterance' (1967: 78).[10]

We can now see how genre provides the key to solving another problem: If meaning is (as Hirsch insists) 'an affair of consciousness', then how can an author mean more than he or she is conscious of meaning? The answer lies in 'typification': the author conceives meaning as a whole, and, within this whole, unintended meanings are possible (Hirsch 1967: 48). To conceive of verbal meaning as a 'willed type' allows us to see how it 'can be (as it is) a determinate object of consciousness and yet transcend (as it does) the actual contents of consciousness' (1967: 49).

Terry Eagleton strenuously objects to Hirsch's position on the grounds that (under the influence of Husserl's phenomenology) his conception of authorial intention is too purely mental[11] and his defense of that intended meaning too 'authoritarian', its aim being 'the protection of private property' (1983: 68). Because they are 'the products of language, which always has something slippery about it', authorial meanings can never be stable, and no 'complete distinction' can be made between a text's meaning and its meaning to me (1983: 69-70).

To show the flaw in Hirsch's argument 'that meaning is always the intentional act of an individual at some particular point in time', Eagleton develops an example (uses of the phrase, 'close the door') to make the point that 'the meaning of language is a social matter: there is a real sense in which language belongs to my society before it belongs to me' (1983: 7071). To ask about someone's intentions in using the phrase is not, as Hirsch would have it, to ask about a purely private mental act. The question is rather about the 'effects the language is

10. See his explanation of how 'generic expectations' help us understand the early parts of a text even before we reach its end (1967: 85). In the same vein, A. Fowler has argued that the recognition of genres is 'fundamental to the reading process... No work, however avantgarde, is intelligible without some context of familiar types' (1982: 259). Genre, then, 'primarily has to do with communication. It is an instrument not of classification or prescription, but of meaning' (1982: 21-22; he develops the idea of 'redundancy', taken over from communication theory).

11. According to Eagleton, Hirsch conceives of meaning as 'prelinguistic... something which the author *wills*: it is a ghostly, wordless mental act which is then "fixed" for all time in a particular set of material signs' (1983: 67).

trying to bring about'. To understand a speaker's intention is to grasp his or her

> speech and behaviour in relation to a significant context. When we
> understand the 'intentions' of a piece of language, we interpret it as being
> in some sense *oriented*, structured to achieve certain effects; and none of
> this can be grasped apart from the practical conditions in which the
> language operates (1983: 114).

One might say that Hirsch is asking for this criticism, but that in the end it is too harsh. Hirsch ultimately defines 'verbal meaning' as 'a *willed type* which an author expressed by linguistic symbols and which can be understood by another through those symbols' (1967: 49). The clue to the intended meaning of a text (despite even an author's subsequent change of opinion about what he or she has written) lies in the particular pattern of its language. Once written, both the language and its pattern are public. They provide both the clues and the restraints for the reader's construction of the work's meaning.

In any case, I should like to utilize Hirsch's theory in a weaker form than that attacked by Eagleton. Genre gives an indication of at least part of the meaning a text had for its author, but it does not guarantee that we can reconstruct the author's intention exactly. However, it is not crucially important that we do so, since what we need is only a broad indication of the context in which interpretation should take place. Hirsch is aware, no less than Eagleton, that there will always be a variety of interpretations of a given text. He also proposes criteria for judging how satisfactory various interpretations are. But ultimately, the constraints of genre can only be part of our judgment. To ask which of all the possibilities available for interpreting a text is likely to be the most fruitful is to raise, of course, the question, 'Fruitful for what?' 'Ideology' is not something we can, or should, aspire to escape.

But what is the genre of Jeremiah? If we were to consider it an *anthology*, that would assume the activity of one or more editors, who chose materials to preserve and 'edited' and arranged them. But what were the materials that the earliest editor(s) collected? Presumably, they were utterances of a prophet named Jeremiah. Clearly a great deal of the material in the book comes from persons other than Jeremiah, but the genre gives us license to believe that there was such a person as Jeremiah and that the book contains at least some evidence for his life and work. The existence of the prophet is on this account a more plausible assumption than his absence.

I am proposing that at least some of the prophetic books of the Hebrew Bible belong to a genre that we may call 'anthology'. Works in this genre have two prominent features: there is an opening colophon which announces that the work contains the words (or vision) of a named (male) individual and dates his activity within the reign of a specific king or kings.[12] Following the colophon is a body of material consisting of separate and discrete units which are homogeneous in neither form nor (in the judgment of many researchers) date. If we view the colophons as expressions of authorial intention, it should be immediately clear that what follows is to be understood as collections of material related to the life and work of historical figures who were active at specified times. We must not, of course, be too naive about this. The colophon to the book of Jeremiah opens with the phrase, 'the words of Jeremiah', but there are extensive narratives in the book that do not fit that rubric. We can safely assume that the editor of the present book of Jeremiah worked sometime after the prophet's death and had some freedom in the choice of materials to include in his or her anthology. It is even possible that the criteria by which 'words of Jeremiah' were identified for inclusion differed from those modern scholars would apply.

However, the issue is not whether some parts of the book accurately report the *ipsissima verba* of the prophet, or whether it is the prophet's biography—another genre altogether.[13] We are concerned, rather, with the verbal meaning of an editor's work. When the anthologist tells us in the introductory colophon that what follows pertains to the activity of a man named Jeremiah who was active during the reign of the last five kings of Judah and who he or she and, presumably, others understood to have been the recipient of revelations from Yahweh, there is no good reason to reject this broad characterization out of hand. On the contrary, there is a very good reason to accept it as a guide to our interpretation, since this is precisely what we expect of anthologies. By contrast, the genres implied in Carroll's own notion of the book's fictional nature are not appropriate to the text. The book as it stands (or even as it could conceivably be reconstructed by scholarly effort) is neither an epic nor a play nor a novel.

But is the book of Jeremiah an anthology? Unlike modern anthologies, it does not cite sources or bear the name of its editor. On the other

12. Isa. 1.1; Jer. 1.1-3; Ezek. 1.1-3; Hos. 1.1; Amos 1.1; Mic. 1.1; Zeph. 1.1; cf. Hag. 1.1; Zech. 1.1.
13. Cf. the discussion of biography in Overholt (1988: 601-603).

hand, the organization, although loose, is like many modern anthologies roughly thematic (poetry predominates in chs. 1–25 and narratives in 26–45; 46–51 is a collection of oracles against the nations). As Fowler points out, genres resist definition, and because they tend to change over time, we must guard against imposing our up-to-date conceptions of a genre's characteristics on older materials (1982: 40, 261).

If we recognize that the prophetic books are literary products, we also recognize that these anthologies have an ideological content. Carroll finds evidence for this in the conflicting, even incompatible, images of the prophet within the book of Jeremiah. For example, references to his speaking to (26.16), even commanding (19.1), the nation's leaders suggest that Jeremiah had great authority, but this contradicts the idea that the nation fell because these same leaders refused to listen to him. That he was both supported and rejected by the public are incompatible ideas that 'can only be sustained at a theoretical or *textual* level' they cannot be justified '*in real life*'. The contradiction stems from the editors' desire to do two things: show that Jeremiah was recognized as a true prophet and account for the fall of Jerusalem (1989a: 78-79). Certainly, this is a case of black-and-white reasoning and does not correspond to what we know both intuitively and from cross-cultural studies to be social reality. Prophets must have support groups, but these need not include the entire population. Nor need the membership of the groups remain constant. People can change their minds; their support can blow hot and cold. We need to keep *social reality* in perspective.

Carroll is preoccupied with later ideological developments that may be mirrored in the prophetic texts, so he claims that 'the most natural way to read' the laments in the book of Jeremiah is as an exilic attempt to vindicate the innocents among the people who suffered at the nation's fall. But if that were the intent of the laments, why would they speak of murder plots and commands not to prophesy (11.21), of the speaker's associations with Yahweh's word (15.16, 19; 17.15; 20.8-9), of intercession (18.20), and of childbirth (20.14-18)? The collective reading does not seem particularly 'natural' for these laments, taken as a group. At the very least, the personal reading seems equally 'natural'.

Clearly, there are many details of this argument from genre that remain to be worked out. What I want to argue here is that the 'meaning expectations' associated with the genre anthology, taken together with what cross-cultural research demonstrates about the social reality of prophecy, enable us to affirm that the named individuals of the Hebrew

Bible actually *were* prophets, both in their own eyes and in the judgment of at least some of their contemporaries. The Bible contains many things of which critical scholars can be skeptical, but this is not one of them. The radical skepticism of Auld's and Carroll's 'poets not prophets' position is unwarranted.

BIBLIOGRAPHY

Auld, A.G.
    1983a   'Prophets through the Looking Glass: Between Writings and Moses',
            JSOT 27: 3-23.
    1983b   'Prophets through the Looking Glass: A Response', *JSOT* 27: 41-44.
    1984   'Prophets and Prophecy in Jeremiah and Kings', *ZAW* 96: 66-82.
    1986   *Amos* (OTG; Sheffield: JSOT Press).
    1988   'Word of God and Word of Man: Prophets and Canon', in L. Eslinger
            and G. Taylor (eds.), *Ascribe to the Lord: Biblical and Other Studies
            in Memory of Peter C. Craigie* (JSOTSup, 67 Sheffield: JSOT Press):
            237-51.
Buss, M.J.
    1979   'Understanding Communication', in M.J. Buss (ed.), *Encounter with
            the Text* (Philadelphia: Fortress Press): 1-44.
Carroll, R.P.
    1983   'Poets Not Prophets', *JSOT* 27: 25-31.
    1986   'Dismantling the Book of Jeremiah and Deconstructing the Prophet',
            in M. Augustin and K.-D. Schunck (eds.), 'Wunschet Jerusalem
            Frieden': *Collected Communications to the XIIth Congress of the
            International Organization for the Study of the Old Testament,
            Jerusalem 1986* (Frankfurt am Main: Peter Lang): 291-302.
    1988   'Inventing the Prophets', *IBS* 10: 24-36.
    1989a   *Jeremiah* (OTG; Sheffield: JSOT Press).
    1989b   'Prophecy and Society', in R.E. Clements (ed.), *The World of Ancient
            Israel* (Cambridge: Cambridge University Press: 203-25.
Eagleton, T.
    1983   *Literary Theory: An Introduction* (Minneapolis: University of
            Minnesota Press).
Fish, S.E.
    1970   'Literature in the Reader: Affective Stylistics', reprinted in Tompkins
            1980: 70-100.
    1976   'Interpreting the Variorum', reprinted in Tompkins 1980: 164-84.
Fowler, A.
    1983   *Kinds of Literature: An Introduction to the Theory of Genres and
            Modes* (Cambridge, MA: Harvard University Press).

Gerhart, M.
1983   'Genric [sic] Competence in Biblical Hermeneutics', *Semeia* 43: 29-
             44
Hirsch, E.D., Jr
1967   *Validity in Interpretation* (New Haven: Yale University Press).
Iser, W.
1974   'The Reading Process: A Phenomenological Approach', reprinted in
             Tompkins 1980: 50-69.
Long, B.O.
1981   'Social Dimensions of Prophetic Conflict', *Semeia* 21: 31-53.
1988   'A Figure at the Gate: Readers, Reading and Biblical Theologians', in
             G.M. Tucker, D.L. Petersen and R.R. Wilson (eds.), *Canon, Theology,
             and Old Testament Interpretation: Essays in Honor of Brevard S.
             Childs* (Philadelphia: Fortress Press): 166-86.
McKane, W.
1986   *A Critical and Exegetical Commentary on Jeremiah*, I (Edinburgh: T.
             & T. Clark).
Moore, S.D.
1986   'Negative Hermeneutics, Insubstantial Texts: Stanley Fish and the
             Biblical Interpreter', *JAAR* 54: 707-17.
Overholt, T.W.
1986   Prophecy in Cross-Cultural Perspective (Atlanta: Scholars Press).
1988   'Jeremiah', in J.L. Mays (ed.), *Harper's Bible Commentary* (San
             Francisco: Harper & Row).
1989   *Channels of Prophecy: The Social Dynamics of Prophetic Activity*
             (Minneapolis: Fortress Press).
Poulet, G.
1972   'Criticism and the Experience of Interiority', reprinted in Tompkins
             1980: 41-49.
Scholes, R.
1985   *Textual Power: Literary Theory and the Teaching of English* (New
             Haven: Yale University Press).
Tompkins, J.P.
1980   *Reader-Response Criticism: From Formalism to Post-Structuralism*
             (Baltimore: Johns Hopkins University Press).
Tucker, G.M.
1971   Form Criticism of the Old Testament (Philadelphia: Fortress Press).
Williamson, H.G.M.
1883   'A Response to A.G. Auld', *JSOT* 27: 33-39.
Wilson, R.R.
1980   *Prophecy and Society in Ancient Israel* (Philadelphia: Fortress Press).
Wurthwein E.
1950   'Amos-Studien', *ZAW* 62: 10-52.

JSOT 48 (1990), pp. 31-32

PROPHECY IN BOOKS: A REJOINDER

A. Graeme Auld

Several of the issues raised by Overholt concerning the proper integration of textual study and sociological and anthropological research
are also addressed in a recent paper by Deist with which I much more
easily sympathize. I am puzzled that Overholt should write that the
major assumption in his rebuttal of my argument is 'that the kind of
religious intermediation which we designate "prophetic" was a social
reality in ancient Israel and Judah, presumably from ancient times'. I
have in fact no quarrel with such a statement; and indeed believe that
cross-cultural studies like those of Overholt may fairly be used to clarify
aspects of intermediation in ancient near eastern states.

What does give me pause is that distinctions readily maintained in
contemporary social anthropology between the self-understanding of
those observed and theoretical constructs of observers become blurred
as we move to the biblical sources. Overholt concedes that the prophetic
books are highly edited. He would agree that we find in them a blend of
fragments of the original (oral) performances of intermediaries and
possibly the responses of contemporaries on the one hand, and the
theorizing of (often very much later) followers and historians on the
other. It was my contention through the series of studies which he
reviews that we have some grounds for distinguishing between these
elements. Insofar as this is true, we have more immediate access to the
views of the observers than of the original intermediaries, and that
means to the later terminology than to the earlier.

I am quite as interested as Overholt in historical reconstruction.
Granted the absence from the biblical texts of manifest examples of
'prophetic' self-reference, for which he rightly notes there was little
opportunity, it is important to recognize just how little good evidence

there is even of the technical terms in which contemporary observation would have been stated. For the usage of expressions like 'prophet', 'seer', 'man of God', 'messenger of Yahweh', and the like is remarkably sparing outside redactional and late narrative contexts.

Overholt invites us to begin a history of terminology with Amos 7.10-17. But this is a bad place to start, not so much because of the long-standing dispute over how to translate vv. 14-15, but rather because the whole story is a late insert into the account of Amos's visions; and its sources are to be found in 1 Kings 13 and 2 Chronicles 25. My discussion of the historical implications (1986: 27-30) is unfortunately ignored by Overholt.

A second issue which I have not much previously discussed, but which I think Overholt needs to address, is the literary quality, as distinct from the literary history, of much of the material in the prophetic books. We are all familiar with shorter units edited more or less artistically into larger ones as a model of the development of the prophetic literature. However, some of the more recent critics have sought to persuade us of larger and more seamless literary creations within these books. Such are less likely to embody records of oral performances by prophetic intermediaries. If they do have a relation to these, it is much less immediate and much more filtered and imaginative and 'literary'.

BIBLIOGRAPHY

Auld, A.G.
  1986   *Amos* (OTG; Sheffield: JSOT Press).
Deist, F.E.
  1989   'The Prophets: Are we Heading for a Paradigm Switch?', in *Prophet und Prophetenbuch: Festschrift für O. Kaiser* (BZAW, 185; Berlin: de Gruyter): 1-18.

JSOT 48 (1990), pp. 33-49

WHOSE PROPHET? WHOSE HISTORY?
WHOSE SOCIAL REALITY?
TROUBLING THE INTERPRETATIVE COMMUNITY AGAIN
NOTES TOWARDS A RESPONSE
TO T.W. OVERHOLT'S CRITIQUE

Robert P. Carroll

Not a poet, not a prophet— a woodcutter am I.	‏—לֹא מְשׁוֹרֵר, לֹא נָבִיא‎ ‏הוֹסֵב עֵצִים אָכִי.‎ (Hayim Nahman Bialik)[1]

...for the sake of those who either could not or would not give themselves to this labour and toil by which they might deserve to be instructed in or to recognise things of such value and importance, to wrap up and conceal, as we said before, in ordinary language, *under the covering of some history and narrative of visible things*, hidden mysteries.

...so for that reason divine wisdom took care that certain stumbling-blocks, or interruptions, to the historical meaning should take place, by the introduction into the midst of the narrative of certain impossibilities and incongruities; that in this way the very interruption of the narrative might, as by the interposition of a bolt, present an obstacle to the reader, whereby he might refuse to acknowledge the way which conducts to the ordinary meaning; and being thus excluded and debarred from it, we might be recalled to the beginning of another way, in order that, by entering upon a narrow path, and passing to a loftier and more sublime road, he might lay open the immense breadth of divine wisdom (Origen).[2]

---

1. From Bialik's poem 'My Soul Has Sunk Down'; see *The Penguin Book of Hebrew Verse* (ed. T. Carmi; Harmondsworth: Penguin, 1981), pp. 515-16. The lines hardly need translating, but I have nudged them into English. The obvious echo of Amos 7.14 and Zech. 13.5 (1 Kgs 13.18 negates the negative) is its point as one of my epithets.

2. Origen, *De Principiis*, 4.1.14-15. From the Latin of Rufinus translated by

For one more accustomed to accusations of 'dogmatic scepticism'[3] or to
being almost set aside as an extremist[4] for my work on Jeremiah, it is
salutary to be informed by Thomas Overholt that there is at least one
area of the Hebrew Bible where radical scepticism is definitely unwarranted. Overholt and I have long been in correspondence on the subject
of prophecy and before commenting on his article, 'Prophecy in
History: The Social Reality of Intermediation', I would like to acknowledge that correspondence as a gracious contribution to my thinking
about biblical prophecy.[5] His work, especially in terms of the social
reality of prophecy,[6] has kept me constantly aware that there are other
fields and different ways of ploughing them than the ones I work. I
should, however, make it clear at the outset of this response that there is
no Auld–Carroll line on prophecy north of Hadrian's Wall. Graeme
Auld is a good friend and a colleague who works in the East of Scotland
and I work in the West. I admire his work as a scholar and have learned
much from him. Also, of course, it was his invitation to me to comment
on his original SOTS paper of 1983 that got me into this debate in the
first place. But I am an adult and cannot therefore blame him for my
saying 'yes' to his invitation. We may share some views in common but
we are really working on different issues and coming from very different
directions in our approaches to the prophets.[7] So in this response I shall

F. Crombie in A. Roberts and J. Donaldson (eds.), *The Writings of Origen*, I (Ante-
Nicene Christian Library, 10; Edinburgh: T. & T. Clark, 1869), pp. 311-13
(emphases added).

3.   'Carroll adopts a rather dogmatic scepticism over many aspects of the
Jeremiah tradition in his study entitled "From Chaos to Covenant"' (R.E. Clements,
'The Prophet and his Editors', in D.J.A. Clines, S.E. Fowl and S.E. Porter [eds.],
*The Bible in Three Dimensions: Essays in Celebration of Forty Years of Biblical
Studies in the University of Sheffield* [JSOTSup, 87; Sheffield: JSOT Press, 1990],
p. 213).

4.   Cf. J.M. Ward, 'The Eclipse of the Prophet in Contemporary Prophetic
Studies', *USQR* 42 (1988), p. 101; in fairness to Ward it should be said that he does
not set McKane and myself aside as extremists because our methodological
assumptions are supported by the textual history of Jeremiah (LXX and MT).

5.   Apart from acknowledging his correspondence I must express gratitude to
him for sending me an early copy of his *Channels of Prophecy* book.

6.   See *Channels of Prophecy: The Social Dynamics of Prophetic Activity*
(Minneapolis: Fortress Press, 1989); *Prophecy in Cross-Cultural Perspective: A
Sourcebook for Biblical Researchers* (SBLSBS, 17; Atlanta: Scholars Press, 1986).

7.   This difference can be seen in note 3 to his article, 'Word of God and Word
of Man: Prophets and Canon', in *Ascribe to the Lord: Biblical and Other Studies in*

be answering only for myself. Auld is old and clever enough to speak for himself.

I prefer to think óf myself as a struggling agnostic when it comes to reading the prophets rather than a dogmatic sceptic. I would admit to using a certain degree of epistemological scepticism in my essay on 'prophecy and society',[8] but even that approach had to do with the secondary literature and the models used by scholars to interpret biblical prophecy. The fact of the matter is that I really do not know how to read the prophets and so I am trying with every piece I write to make sense of *all* the data contained in the Bible on prophets. The traditional and conventional views on the prophets, both religious and scholarly, do not help me to make sense of the data. Therefore I am engaged in the task of trying to construct a model or a theory which will do the most work given the nature of the biblical text and the data contained therein. But because my approaches and conclusions are somewhat different from those operated by other members of the Guild (interpretative community of biblical scholars) I seem to attract the epithet 'sceptic' or even 'iconoclast'.[9] I know from lecturing to students of a conservatively religious bent that the charge of scepticism among scholars easily becomes one of cynicism at lower levels of the intellectual totem pole. So in my defence I must protest that the biblical data are such that they demand an approach which is sceptical of received wisdom. The central problems are in the text long before they appear in scholarly approaches. That prophecy in the Bible is problematic is so obvious and self-evident to the reader of the Bible that I wonder why its problematic status needs to be restated and argued for so often. Read 1 Samuel and try to answer the questions, 'Was Samuel a prophet?', 'Was Samuel a

Memory of Peter C. Craigie (JSOTSup, 67; Sheffield: JSOT Press, 1988), p. 240, where he expresses hope for a 'sounder approach' to Jeremiah than appears to emanate from my 1986 commentary.

8.   R.P. Carroll, 'Prophecy and Society', in R.E. Clements (ed.), *The World of Ancient Israel: Sociological, Anthropological and Political Perspectives. Essays by Members of the Society for Old Testament Study* (Cambridge: Cambridge University Press, 1989), pp. 203-25.

9.   In his review of the Clements volume ('Talking Points from Books', *ExpTim* 101 [1990], p. 194), C.S. Rodd writes, 'In a magnificently iconoclastic essay on prophecy Robert P. Carroll demolishes any easy sociological interpretation of the Old Testament'. All I had wanted to do in that essay was to make a clearing in the forest so that some serious work could be done on another occasion. Perhaps that is a good working definition of 'iconoclasm'.

ruler?', 'Was Saul a ruler?', 'Was Saul a prophet?', 'If a *nābî* was a *rōʾeh*, what then was a *rōʾeh*?' The problematical status of these terms is enshrined in the narratives of Samuel.[10] So my statement 'ancient Israelite writers had no clear image of what a prophet is or should be'[11] is not to be read as 'hyperbolic', as Overholt calls it, but as a shorthand way of summarizing what I think the book of 1 Samuel is saying in its narratives.

Now I must not try to reinvent the wheel nor should I simply restate the arguments of what I have written elsewhere in the articles which are the target of Overholt's critique. Overholt's main contention is that ethnographical data provide a paradigm of social reality which can be used to identify quite clearly in the Bible the status, character and activities of prophets. My initial response to Overholt's claim is less than enthusiastic because such an approach sacrifices the particular for the general and avoids close reading of the text in favour of loose readings of culture. I feel about it as many before me have felt about J.G. Frazer's monumental work, *The Golden Bough*. That multi-volume enterprise lumped everything together from all over the world without chrono-logical distinctions and paid little attention to the particularity of cultures or to how customs and rituals which superficially looked the 'same' functioned very differently in distinctive settings. To some extent Frazer may be defended on the grounds that he was just collecting raw data which merely illustrated certain patterns of thought and feeling.[12] But the tone and tenor of Overholt's article go beyond that illustrative function and assert that it is the case that Hebrew prophecy can be 'precisely described' by his model. In my opinion his model will function as a Procrustes' Bed in the analysis of biblical prophecy and will reduce or expand the text accordingly.

The extent to which models derived from the Seneca tribe of the

10. On Samuel see P.D. Miscall, *1 Samuel: A Literary Reading* (Indiana Studies in Biblical Literature; Bloomington: Indiana University Press, 1986); and the more recent R.M. Polzin, *Samuel and the Deuteronomist: A Literary Study of the Deuteronomic History*. II. *1 Samuel* (San Francisco: Harper & Row, 1989).

11. Carroll 'Prophecy and Society', p. 209; relevant discussion on pp. 209-15.

12. Cf. T.H. Gaster, *Myth, Legend, and Custom in the Old Testament: A Comparative Study with Chapters from Sir James G. Frazer's Folklore in the Old Testament* (New York: Harper & Row, 1969), pp. xxii-xxiii; 'But there is some molten gold in Frazer's volcanic overflow', so S.J. Tambiah, *Magic, Science, and the Scope of Rationality* (The 1984 Lewis Henry Morgan Lectures; Cambridge: Cambridge University Press, 1990), p. 53.

Iroquois League (the Handsome Lake material) and the Ghost Dance of 1890 in conjunction with models drawn from prophecy at Mari (c. 1800 BCE) will assist in the task of a close reading of the Hebrew Bible constitutes a complex analytical enterprise which space here does not allow me to investigate.[13] Like all models, the work this model will do is at best an approximation. It will provide a patterned background against which to read the biblical text, but it will not provide a sophisticated reading of that text. Furthermore, and this is important for Overholt's claims in his article, it will not even begin to address the central point of much of what Auld and I have been writing about. To avoid a long-drawn-out niggling set of arguments (in the context of this paper only!) let me accept for the sake of the argument that a pattern of prophetic behaviour can be established from all the wide ranging ethnographic data and that it can also be applied to the prophets in the Bible. So what? Both Auld and myself allow that there were prophets in biblical times. Our claim is not that there were no prophets in the Bible, but that the named *individuals* represented by the fully and finally redacted Bible *as* 'prophets' were not prophets at all. How does the model cope with that claim? It copes by using a blanket patterning process which insists that the redactional ploy of making these individuals prophets must be correct because the redaction reflects the pattern of the model. I find that a question-begging response.

Of course the redactional presentation of these characters reflects the pattern derived from the model. It would, wouldn't it! Any writer even half-competent could write a character *in character*. Literature is filled with realistic representations of characters who conform to whatever social model is appropriate. Sidney Carton is a lawyer, Thomas Gradgrind a teacher; they are modelled on social realities, no doubt, by Charles Dickens, but they are characters in fiction all the same. If a figure in a text conforms to a social reality model, what can be said about that figure? Well, it depends on what you wish to do by way of exposition. Describing or evaluating the poetics of Dickens's novels or the book of Jeremiah is one thing. Making assertions about the historical existence of the characters in these writings is quite a different thing. And I do not see this different thing being seriously addressed by Overholt's model of

---

13. Cf. Overholt, *Channels of Prophecy*, pp. 27-68; *Prophecy in Cross-Cultural Perspective*, pp. 309-31. My brief comments on Overholt's use of the Handsome Lake material in my essay 'Prophecy and Society' (pp. 219-20) express my disagreement with him but are too brief to be a serious commentary on the matter.

social reality for the prophets. What the model tells us is this: the representation of a character as a prophet is an accurate representation. It cannot tell us anything about whether the character is historical or not. Nor can it help us to differentiate between the character and the character's author.

Both Overholt and Robert Wilson, together with various other biblical scholars, like to redefine prophecy as 'intermediation' and then make use of ethnographic models of intermediation. But the redefinition is not unproblematic. Of course there are intermediaries in the Bible. They are called priests. These priests worked in the two spheres of the sacred and the profane, the holy and the unholy or this world and the other world. The combination of the roles of priest and prophet in the representation of various figures in the Bible (e.g. Abraham, Moses, Samuel, Elijah, Jeremiah, Ezekiel) complicates the matter considerably and raises tricky questions about intermediation in ancient Israel as represented by the Bible. The use of models drawn from shamanistic cultures which were oral rather than literate raises further problems for analysing the biblical data. I know Overholt (like many other biblical scholars) does not think that spoken oracles can be transformed by being turned into written forms, but it is that transformative process which lies behind the biblical presentation of prophecy rather than any original oral communication.[14] In my opinion it is a further complication of the topic. There is therefore a cluster of problems here which, in my opinion, will not be resolved by recourse to a social reality model. Mind you, I should point out in defence of both Overholt and myself that the pieces of mine criticized by Overholt in his article are all minor, occasional or inchoate pieces. Where they appear to be more substantial (the JSOT Guide and the SOTS volume article) they only touch on the problems of analysis mentioned in this paragraph. It is of course my own fault that lengthier and more comprehensive treatments of the problems have not yet seen the light of day and using Overholt's critique as a spur I shall in due course produce a much more detailed account of what I see as the central problems of interpreting biblical prophecy.[15]

14. The qualitative differences between the spoken and written word are part of my domain assumptions in studying prophecy and writing my Jeremiah commentary. Contributing to such assumptions are the work of Walter Ong (e.g. his *Orality and Literacy: The Technologizing of the Word*) and Jacques Derrida (e.g. his *Of Grammatology*); see also my 'Prophecy and Society', pp. 207-209.

15. Apart from my SOTS volume essay, I really need to rewrite for publication

Overholt defines a prophet as 'someone to whom Yahweh has spoken and who freely communicates the contents of this revelation to an audience'. *Quite so*. But many of the prophets represented in the Bible might be better defined as 'someone to whom Yahweh has *not* spoken but who freely communicates their own thoughts to an audience' (see Mic. 3.5-8; Jer. 14.13-15; 23.9-40; 27–28; Ezek. 13.1-19). The larger questions of whether there are gods and persons who might be regarded as speaking to and for them ought to be on the academic agenda for otherwise all our deliberations are simply question-begging activities which assume what ought to be demonstrated. It would, however, take up too much time and space to debate this foundational approach to the subject, so I shall accept for the sake of convenience biblical assertions about the existence of gods and prophets. That is, in this response I shall take an emic view of biblical statements rather than an etic view.[16] To return to Overholt's definition: prophets are speakers, but are they also intermediaries? They speak but do they speak *for* anything or anybody? In other words, do they intermediate?

The naive response to that is, undoubtedly, 'of course there are always good and bad prophets'. As I understand the biblical material on this question it seems to be more a case of 'they may be prophets but they do not speak for YHWH'. It is not that they are *bad* prophets, they are just prophets. In opposition to them are the speakers represented in the text. *These* are the people who speak for YHWH: for example, note how Mic. 3.5-8 is constructed ('...concerning the prophets...but as for me'), where a sharp distinction is drawn between the prophets and the (unknown) speaker (now identified by incorporation into a collection bearing the name Micah in 1.1). The defining of that speaker *as a prophet* is not part of the text but part of its *Rezeptionsgeschichte*. That then is the crux of the dispute between Overholt and me and it cannot be resolved by models of social reality. We shall just have to continue to differ in our *reading of texts*.

---

my 1985 SOTS paper, 'Central and Peripheral Prophets: An Anthropological Model for Biblical Prophecy', which was a critique of R.R. Wilson's *Prophecy and Society in Ancient Israel* (Philadelphia: Fortress Press, 1980).

16. For this distinction see M. Harris, *Cultural Materialism: The Struggle for a Science of Culture* (New York: Vintage Books, 1980), pp. 32-45; there is a useful summary account of the distinctions in J.W. Rogerson, 'Anthropology and the Old Testament', in R.E. Clements (ed.), *The World of Ancient Israel* (Cambridge: Cambridge University Press, 1989), pp. 31-35.

I have no quarrel with models or theories, be they anthropological, sociological, literary or whatever. I sometimes worry that theory may be prematurely applied to ancient texts or that the theory used may be inappropriate. Theories and models solve no real problems because they themselves become part of the problem of interpretation. Reading texts with the aid of theories and models just provides another set of problematized readings. The readings are still disputed, only on different grounds now. No real problem here if the readers recognize what they are doing—one of the major contributions of feminism to biblical scholarship has been its reminder to us that our interpretations are just readings (Mieke Bal makes the point regularly in her writings). A proliferation of readings, no doubt, but no longer can the Guild imagine that it is promulgating *the* reading of the text or even *the way* to read texts. Overholt speculates about my 'ideology' at one point. Well he might speculate. I often speculate myself about that, but never can find a coherent enough viewpoint which lasts long enough to be scrutinized for ideological holdings. I do possess shards of theory and fragments of values which I use to do my readings of texts, but they are changing and expanding all the time and so frustrate the construction of a thorough-going ideology. To construct a coherent account of the matter would take me years and many books to accomplish it and even then I would have doubts about the intensity and depth of my self-perception to have done it accurately. But let me address myself to the lengthy theorizing section of Overholt's paper as a way of expressing my current thinking here and as a means of providing a few clues about alternative approaches to reading biblical texts.

Much of the quarrel between Overholt and myself must centre on the book of Jeremiah because we have both written extensively on it. The more often I read that text and the more I read the secondary literature on it the more dissatisfied I become with how we read biblical texts in the Guild. That is why I have prefaced this response with a couple of fragments from Origen's celebrated writings on the divine inspiration of the scriptures (my added emphases are intended to focus on phrases which indicate the importance of knowing how to read biblical texts). In many ways Origen saved the scriptures for the churches by showing how the text could be read other than historically and literally and how in so doing its fictions and impossibilities could be handled. As I read Jeremiah I am struck by its ahistoricality and its intertextuality. Poem after poem has little reference outside the book itself and much of the prose is commentary on the Deuteronomistic History. There are parts of Jeremiah which read like commentary on, where they are not replications of, that History. Some of the laments are so much in the style of Psalms and there are so many citations from other parts of the Hebrew Bible that any reading of the book as history or the reportage of actual events in the period set by 1.1-3 strikes me as a complete misreading of the text. Social reality models are irrelevant here. The text is too convention-bound, too stereotypical for them to do sufficient work. The book is a supplementation of other books (a kind of *Erzänzungstext*)[17] and the social dynamics of its production will have to be found in terms other than historical reportage of the sixth century. That is how I read the text. While I do not know how the text came into existence, I find the models of Jeremiah offered by other commentators utterly unconvincing (I exclude from this judgment McKane's helpful notion of a 'rolling corpus'). I think the figure of Jeremiah *as a prophet* has been generated by certain levels of the book's production and Overholt's social reality models do not seem to me to have much to say at this point.

My reading of Jeremiah and my reconstruction of its dynamics may be rather different from what many scholars in the Guild regard as responsible exegesis and interpretation. But interpretative communities can be part of the problem too.[18] They can restrict vision and range as well as generate self-serving mechanisms of conformistic study. I would not claim for myself any great innovative approach to texts because I am aware of building on the work of others (e.g. Duhm and Torrey especially). Also I am deeply conscious that the Guild has many fine independent scholars within it, whose work is a constant inspiration and example to me. If a model outside the field of biblical studies is sought

17. This notion arises out of Bernhard Duhm's treatment of Jeremiah in his classic commentary *Das Buch Jeremia* (Tübingen: Mohr [Paul Siebeck], 1901); cf. C.C. Torrey's arguments in his 'The Background of Jeremiah 1-10', *JBL* 56 (1937), pp. 193-216. See also my 'Arguing about Jeremiah: Recent Studies and the Nature of a Prophetic Book', in J.A. Emerton (ed.), *Congress Volume, Leuven* (VTSup, 43; Leiden: Brill, 1991), pp. 222-35. The raw data for an *Ergänzungstext* approach to reading Jeremiah are usefully gathered together in W.L. Holladay's *Jeremiah 2: A Commentary on the Book of the Prophet Jeremiah Chapters 26–52* (Hermeneia; Minneapolis: Fortress Press, 1989), pp. 35-70, 80-91.

18. The notion of 'interpretative communities' is of course Stanley Fish's; see his *Is There a Text in This Class? The Authority of Interpretive Communities* (Cambridge, MA: Harvard University Press, 1980), especially pp. 167-73, 303-71.

for what I see myself as doing in Jeremiah studies, let it be Georges Dumézil's study of Marcus Furius Camillus, the putative second founder of Rome.[19] Dumézil's euhemeristic approach to reading Indo-European religion has the advantage of paying close attention to the conventions of language used so that the transformation of myth into the epic mode is 'perceived hermeneutically'.[20] Dumézil does not deny the probable existence of a Roman supreme commander in the past (sometime between 445 and 365 BCE), but he strips the epic of its status as a historical chronicle and recognizes its poetic qualities. Much of his analysis consists of reading the texts of Livy and Plutarch and reinterpreting their linguistic conventions so as to arrive at his transformed account of the saga of Camillus. Now, I am not claiming that the same can be done for the biblical book of Jeremiah, though if it could it might meet Auld's demand for 'a sounder approach'.

My purpose here in introducing Dumézil's work into the discussion is to broaden the debate in cross-disciplinary terms (like Overholt's use of social dynamics models but in a different direction). But it is equally to enlarge it in relation to the ancient literary historians who wrote about their past in ways which cannot just be read as ancient history *simpliciter*, whether the comparative historians are Herodotus or Thucydides, Xenophon, Livy, Plutarch or Homer, the so-called Yahwist or the Deuteronomistic Historian. If it is a commonplace in classical and ancient historical studies that such writers are a mixture of history, myth and inventive writing, why should biblical scholars imagine that the Bible escapes such classifications? Here I have to disagree with Overholt's assumption that the biblical writers 'intend to construct accounts of the past' and his inclination 'to look for historical information in them, *and rightly so*' (my emphases). I would like to see some argument here about the historiographic intentions of the biblical writers as well as some evidence against alternative suggestions that they might have been writing for ideological or propagandist purposes (not to mention inventive literary or epigonic commentary reasons). In other words, 'Who killed Goliath?' remains a question to be addressed by any reader of the Bible interested in treating the book as if it were a modern history book.

Overholt makes much of genre as an important consideration in

---

19. G. Dumézil, *Camillus: A Study of Indo-European Religion as Roman History* (ed. with an introduction by U. Strutynski; Berkeley: University of California Press, 1980). The book is an amalgam of a number of Dumézil's writings.

20. This phrase is from Strutynski's 'Introduction' to *Camillus*, p. 17.

reading the Bible. I agree with him. Generic analysis is an important element in reading texts. But it is hardly a problem free notion. If we could all agree on the genres contained in biblical texts we might make some progress, but try determining the genre of Isa. 5.1-7! As for the genre of a prophetic book as a whole, who will agree on deciding what that might be? Is the book of Jeremiah an anthology, as Overholt seems to believe? Well, it contains an anthological section in chs. 2–20, 30–33 and 46–51, but it cannot be said to be an anthology per se. What genre shall we assign to chs. 26–29, 32–36, 37–44? Biographical narratives, the passion of Jeremiah, legends of the prophets? All these genres suggest themselves but none of them does enough work to warrant its acceptance. Even if we agree on the genres, how far does that get us? For example, is the anthology one of anonymous poems, hymns, psalms and laments or should it be regarded as an anthology of the utterances of the speaker described in 1.1-3? Perhaps the (final) writer of 1.1-3 intends (writer's intention forsooth!) us to read the anthology as a selection of Jeremiah's best work. Fine! We may read it as such. Just as we would read the poems included at the end of Boris Pasternak's novel *Doctor Zhivago* as the poems of Zhivago. But it is a long jump from that mode of reading to arguing that Zhivago and Jeremiah were historical persons who actually did write poetry. How does genre help here? Of course genres produce meaning but we have no access to what genres the writers of Jeremiah imagined they were using, so the discussion must remain open to the decisions of individual readers of Jeremiah.

Overholt discusses the theories of a number of well-known literary critics on genre and meaning. While I am familiar with all these critics and might wish to add a few more of my own (e.g. Fredric Jameson, Harold Bloom, Jacques Derrida, Paul de Man, Roland Barthes, Edmond Jabès, Hans Robert Jauss, to mention but a few) I really do not see what they contribute to the point over which Overholt and I disagree. The theoretical underpinnings of these various writers would serve my position as well as his. For it really is not the case that the interpretation of the Bible is unproblematic, with its genres all agreed on and its historicity universally accepted. The groundwork has still all to be done and the issues which divide Overholt and me also divide many scholars in the Guild. They cannot be resolved by appealing to a set of critics who are discussing something else. To be told then that there is no good reason for rejecting the 'broad characterization' of the opening colophon 'out of hand' and that the genre of the book is that of 'anthology' strikes me

as involving some question-begging moves. Obviously here Overholt
and I must agree to differ, but I am not convinced that his theoretical
witnesses have added anything of substance to his viewpoint.

As I read Overholt's article and pondered whether I should or should
not respond to it, it occurred to me that I should reply to him by
instancing Jonathan Swift's *A Modest Proposal*. Now there's a text
which many a modern reader has completely misread because irony and
satire are not always easy to detect and generic recognition is often a
tricky business. However, Overholt had forestalled me by referring to
the celebrated work in his footnote. I just wish he was not always so
sanguine about what 'most readers' (a phrase which reminds me of e.e.
cummings's wonderful word 'mostpeople') would agree on. Give a
modern class of students *A Modest Proposal* to read and the responses
will be quite mixed. Why shouldn't they be? Cannibalism is a standard
myth in our world: peasant cultures will talk about people from other
areas in terms of 'sure they eat their dead there' (I know, I come from
Ireland; my Scottish students assure me that they know similar sayings
for their part of the world). Good grief, I know biblical scholars who
write monographs proving that the Israelites practised human sacrifice
because they have read about it in classical authors. So why should
people not read Swift's satire as if it had been intended (oh dear,
writer's intention again) as a serious solution to England's Irish problem?
Generic recognition really is not as easy as some scholars may think it is.

Again I must have recourse to cross-disciplinary matters. Whatever
may be said about *A Modest Proposal* and the problem of reading
Swift's irony, I would like to draw Overholt's attention to the reception
of Daniel Defoe's pamphlet *The Shortest Way with the Dissenters* (1702
I think is the date of it; but dating Defoe's writings is far from easy).
When the anonymous author of the pamphlet was discovered to be
Defoe he was sent to Newgate Gaol and to the pillory. His advocacy of
the suppression of dissenters using the very language of the Anglican
sermons preached against them outraged the politicians, though at least
one High Churchman wrote to a London bookseller to say that next to
the Holy Bible and Sacred Comments the pamphlet was the most
valuable thing he had.[21] Now, this is not just a case of some fool
misreading irony or satire—when he wished to indicate that he was
writing a satire Defoe usually made it obvious (e.g. his poem 'The True-

---

21. See F. Bastian, *Defoe's Early Life* (London: Macmillan, 1981), pp. 270-301
for a general treatment of the controversy.

Born Englishman: A Satire'—it is much more a case of a writing that defies easy generic recognition. Defoe had to write another pamphlet to explain what he had meant by his late pamphlet! Even today scholars debate the genre of the pamphlet and wonder about 'an irony that neither friend nor foe could recognise'.[22] Whether the prophetic books come into the same category as Defoe's pamphlets I do not know, but to be honest I must admit that I do not regard Overholt's remarks about genre analysis as solving any of the problems constituted by our different readings of the prophets. Discerning the genre of prophetic books is the problem of reading them—in another form.[23]

My article on the colophons to the prophetic books could be read as making a sharp distinction between historical and ideological facts.[24] On the other hand, 1 would wish to point out that I am not arguing at any stage of my work for the proposition that 'there is absolutely no historical material in the Bible'. What I do hold to be the case is the difficulty (extreme at times) of determining which elements in a given text of the Bible have a claim to be regarded as historical and which as literary, ideological or fictional. It is not nearly so easy to make such a determination as so many members of the Guild seem to believe it to be (and so practise). The fact that the colophons never register a 'prophet' as coming from Jerusalem just might be a historically accurate piece of information or there again it might be ideological control of the material.

22. Bastian, *Defoe*, p. 280. See M.E. Novak, 'Defoe's Shortest Way with the Dissenters: Hoax, Parody, Paradox, Fiction, Irony, and Satire', *Modern Language Quarterly* 27 (1966), pp. 402-17 for a discussion of the subtleties of generic analysis. On Swift and Defoe see M.E. Novak and H.J. Davis, *The Uses of Irony: Papers on Defoe and Swift Read at a Clark Library Seminar, April 2, 1966* (Los Angeles: William Andrews Clark Memorial Library, 1966). A thought-provoking treatment of irony is Stanley Fish's essay, 'Short People Got No Reason to Live: Reading Irony', in his collection *Doing What Comes Naturally: Change, Rhetoric, and the Practice of Theory in Literary and Legal Studies* (Oxford: Clarendon Press, 1989), pp. 180-96, 568.

23. I will forego the pleasure of citing Derrida on genre, but see J. Derrida, 'The Law of Genre', *Critical Inquiry* 7 (1980), pp. 55-81.

24. R.P. Carroll, 'Inventing the Prophets', *IBS* 10 (1988), pp. 24-36. The distinction between historical and ideological facts may be stated simply in terms of objective and subjective information: e.g. who invented the telephone system is a historical fact, whereas the claim that Soviet communism invented all the major technological advances of the twentieth century belongs to ideological facts. If some biblical 'prophets' did actually come from Jerusalem then the silence of the Bible on that fact must have an ideological explanation.

But I do not know how to show which it is. This failure is due to agnosticism (i.e. lack of concrete knowledge) rather than to scepticism. In my opinion we simply do not know in any historical sense of the word 'know'. We lack external, reliable data to use as controls on the biblical sources. Even Overholt's patterns of social intermediation have no bearing on this point. We must read the colophons according to our own hermeneutic principles for reading texts. Every judgment we make about the text vis-à-vis history will always remain open to serious questioning and is hedged about with many problems. But this is not something peculiar to biblical studies; it is the nature of all textual interpretation, especially of texts from the alien past.[25] Historians have been described as 'merely prophets in reverse',[26] and I guess that description nicely conjoins the historians who study the biblical prophets with the subject of their study. Overholt and I share a common discipline but I think we probably are divided, to some extent, by a Berlin Wall of hermeneutic differences. He has marshalled an impressive array of social reality models to explain the biblical texts *as if* they were the

---

25. A vast bibliography exists on this subject, but the following are worth using as an introduction to a complex topic: *History as Text: The Writing of Ancient History* (ed. A. Cameron; London: Gerald Duckworth, 1989); M.I. Finley, *Ancient History: Evidence and Models* (London: Chatto & Windus, 1985); J.H. Hexter, *Doing History* (London: Allen & Unwin, 1971); J.R. de J. Jackson, *Historical Criticism and the Meaning of Texts* (London: Routledge, 1989); P. Veyne, *Did the Greeks Believe in their Myths? An Essay on the Constitutive Imagination* (ET of *Les Grecs ont-ils cru à leurs mythes?* [Paris: Editions du Seuil, 1983]) (Chicago: University of Chicago Press, 1988); T.P. Wiseman, *Clio's Cosmetics: Three Studies in Greco-Roman Literature* (Leicester: Leicester University Press/Rowman & Littlefield, 1979). Also I would like to remind biblical scholars of Mario Liverani's important article 'Memorandum on the Approach to Historiographic Texts', *Orientalia* 42 (1973), pp. 178-94. Further on generic analysis see T. Kent, *Interpretation and Genre: The Role of Generic Perception in the Study of Narrative Texts* (Lewisburg: Bucknell University Press, 1986).

26. The phrase is Paul Veyne's

> Historians are merely prophets in reverse, and they flesh out and animate their post eventum predictions with imaginative flourishes. This is called 'historical retrodiction' or 'synthesis', and this imaginative faculty furnishes three-fourths of any page of history, with documents providing the rest. There is more. History is also a novel containing deeds and proper names, and we have seen that, while reading, we believe that what we read is true. Only afterward do we call it fiction, and even then we must belong to a society in which the idea of fiction obtains (*Did the Greeks Believe in their Myths?*, p. 103).

productions of prophets. I, on the other hand, think that we are seeing a paradigm switch in the understanding of the so-called 'writing prophets' and am therefore busily trying to find my feet in such a vertiginous period.[27] If my reading of the situation is right (a large 'if', I will grant) then we are all about to be plunged into the hermeneutic maelstrom. I wonder if Overholt and I just have different reading strategies for trying to get out of it or is there more to this dispute than meets either of our eyes?

27. See F.E. Deist, 'The Prophets: Are We Heading for a Paradigm Switch?', in V. Fritz, K.-F. Pohlmann, H.-C. Schmitt (eds.), *Prophet und Prophetenbuch: Festschrift für Otto Kaiser zum 65. Geburtstag* (BZAW, 185; Berlin: de Gruyter, 1989), pp. 1-18.

JSOT 48 (1990), pp. 51-54

'IT IS DIFFICULT TO READ'[1]

Thomas W. Overholt

The foregoing papers address the question of what can be known about
the prophets of the Hebrew Bible. Their focus is the important underlying issue of why particular claims are made about the prophets and the
prophetic books and how these claims can be justified. It is, I hope, clear
from my paper that I found the original studies of Auld (1983a, 1984)
and Carroll (1983) challenging in the best sense of that word. The idea
that figures like Amos and Jeremiah were really not prophets seemed to
me counterintuitive, but forced me to consider the grounds for claiming
that they were. I am therefore in debt to both Auld and Carroll for the
stimulation that their studies have provided, as well as for the seriousness
with which they have responded to my paper printed above. I am under
no illusions that the following response will settle any issues, but I want
to make a few observations, nevertheless.

Auld apparently considers biblical figures like Amos and Jeremiah to
have been real historical persons, although they were poets, not prophets.
The issue here is the role such persons played in Israelite and Judean
society. Carroll goes a step farther, at least in the case of Jeremiah, whom
he considers the fictional creation of some later compiler. This raises the
additional issue of the historicity of individual persons mentioned in the
text.

One part of my response to such claims goes roughly as follows. A
systematic analysis of data from a variety of cultures suggests that the
type of intermediation we can conveniently refer to as 'prophecy' entails

1. The quotation is from the beginning of W. Stevens's poem, 'Phosphor
Reading by his Own Light' (*The Collected Poems of Wallace Stevens* [New York:
Vintage, 1982], p. 267). The complete couplet: 'It is difficult to read. The page is
dark./ Yet he knows what it is that he expects.'

a definite pattern of behavior. This pattern is well known to members of the societies in which such figures are found. Despite some ambiguity in terminology, the 'classical' prophets of the Old Testament are reported to have behaved in this manner. (These indications of behavior are, in my opinion, much more revealing than the presence or absence of certain terms by which the behavior is glossed.) Therefore, they were prophets, that is, they were recognized by at least some members of their societies as performing that particular social role.

Carroll claims that this argument is too general, that it begs the question of the role of figures like Jeremiah. I note, however, that his argument contains as an assumption one of the points under contention, namely that the identification of these individuals as prophets is a 'redactional ploy'. He asserts the belief that 'the figure of Jeremiah *as a prophet* has been generated by certain levels of the book's production'; but what would be the *point* of such fictionalizing? It is obviously the case that we can identify 'ideological or propagandist purposes' in the book of Jeremiah, but it is not clear to me how the invention of a fictional prophetic figure (Jeremiah) can be said to contribute to these. Indeed, Carroll's recourse to modern novels and plays as a model for the fictionalizing of the figure 'Jeremiah' seems to me anachronistic in a way that my use of comparative materials is not.

What puzzles me is why someone would collect material and then assign it to a fictional character, 'Jeremiah' (Carroll), or alternatively, falsely attribute a real social role, 'prophet', to a historical person like Amos (Auld). The question is: How would the growing collection of materials which in its final form came to be called 'Jeremiah' have been understood? My remarks on 'genre' were meant to suggest one possible answer to this question. The point was not to recover the *ipsissima verba* of the prophets or, as Carroll imagines, 'to explain the biblical texts *as if* they were the productions of prophets' (notice particularly the last four words). Nor was it to propose a definitive reading of the text or any of its parts. The point was rather to suggest that there may be some warrant in the final form of the texts themselves for seeing in the collected traditions a reflection of the activity of actual prophets named Amos and Jeremiah. I am aware that while calling the book of Jeremiah an 'anthology' suggests solutions to some problems, it raises others. However, to assert that 'the book as a whole cannot be said to be an anthology *per se*' implies a certainty about the definition of that genre that seems to me unwarranted.

On another matter, I think it incorrect to limit the term 'intermediary' to priests, as Carroll appears to do. Not only are those biblical figures we conventionally call 'prophets' intermediaries, but diviners are as well (cf. Overholt 1989: 117-47). Furthermore, to cite the 'false prophecy' pericopes in Micah, Jeremiah and Ezekiel as evidence that prophets do not 'speak *for* anything or anybody', and therefore do not 'intermediate', is to miss an important sociological point. In whose opinion were these prophets not prophets? In the opinion of Micah, Jeremiah and Ezekiel (and/or the editors of those collections), of course. I think it reasonable to say that in their own opinion and that of at least some of the people who heard them most of the prophetic figures of the Old Testament were speaking for Yahweh. They were not, however, speaking with one voice. There was rivalry and conflict among them. This is common in societies which accredit 'prophetic' intermediation. One can see it today (cf. Overholt 1989: 163-83). But here is the main point: it is not particularly relevant whether Carroll or I or anyone else believes that a given figure is an intermediary (believes that a god exists who cares about and has the power to act in human affairs, that in this particular case that god has actually spoken through a human being to a particular audience, and so on). In point of fact, intermediation is real for those who acknowledge (authorize, accredit) it. I can recognize that persons in a given socio-historical situation acknowledged the existence of intermediaries without myself believing that such divine–human communication either has taken or could have taken place.

Carroll's complaint throughout is that my rather 'loose' reading of culture avoids a 'close reading' of the texts. It is not altogether clear what is being prescribed here, although I must assume, by his own account, that 'close reading' cannot refer to a method of studying the text which is privileged over all others. One gathers that a properly 'sophisticated' reading would be attentive to the contradictions and other problems generated by the texts and constantly be on the lookout for 'hard evidence' outside the text which might be helpful in their resolution. I presume that many who study the biblical texts (including Origen) would claim they were engaged in a similarly 'close' reading. The argument is over what constitutes 'evidence' and 'sophistication'.

I don't know anyone, at least not in 'the Guild', who thinks 'the interpretation of the Bible is unproblematic'. The ferment in biblical studies over the past decade or so has provided more than one occasion to reexamine old positions, and reading the works of Carroll can be a particularly effective way of coming to conscious awareness of how precarious is our 'knowledge' about the texts we study. I am conscious of 'knowing' less than I used to, although I continue to have the feeling that Carroll, a scholar of broad and impressive learning, admits to 'knowing' too little.

JSOT 57 (1993), pp. 39-60

NO PROPHETS? RECENT DEVELOPMENTS IN BIBLICAL PROPHETIC RESEARCH AND ANCIENT NEAR EASTERN PROPHECY

Hans M. Barstad

'Es ist gleich tödlich für den Geist, ein System zu haben, und keins zu haben. Er wird sich also wohl entschliessen müssen, beides zu verbinden'[1]

I

Despite the vast amount of scholarly interest in the prophetic literature of the Hebrew Bible during the last hundred years or so, surprisingly little consensus has been reached in this field. Evidently, most of the questions that were raised when the scientific study of biblical prophecy was first introduced upon the scholarly scene appear to remain as unanswered today as they were then. However, notwithstanding the lack of any consensus, at least one tendency appears to be characteristic of recent developments in prophetic research. A few examples may serve to illustrate this particular trend.

O. Kaiser has claimed that the nucleus of Isaiah 1–39 consisted of a handful of prophetic sayings from the beginning of the fifth century, the purpose of which was to come to terms with the collapse of the kingdom of Judah. The so-called 'Isaiah of Jerusalem', supposed to have been active in the middle of the eighth century, thus disappears into legend.[2] Likewise, J.M. Vincent has argued that there is no such thing as

---

1. 'It is equally fatal for the mind to have a system as it is to have no system. Consequently, it [the mind] should rather decide to combine the two'. *Charakteristiken und Kritiken I (1796–1801)* (Kritische Friedrich-Schlegel Ausgabe; ed. E. Behler, II.1; Munich, 1967), p. 173.

2. O. Kaiser, *Das Buch des Propheten Jesaja: Kapitel 1–12* (ATD, 17; Göttingen: Vandenhoeck & Ruprecht, 5th edn, 1981).

a 'Second Isaiah'. All of Isaiah 40–55, for the most part originating from cultic prophecy in the temple in Jerusalem, consists of material handed down during several generations and subsequently made into one composite work by several authors and redactors in post-exilic times.[3] A similar view has been proposed by J.H. Eaton, who, in accordance with his earlier work on the Psalms and the autumnal New Year Festival, attempted to demonstrate that the text of Isaiah 40–55, ultimately stemming from this very festival, is the work of an 'Isaian circle' of 'festal prophets'.[4] Apparently, these different approaches cohere well with another recent development in Isaian research, where a growing (and in my view justified) dissatisfaction concerning the classical Duhmian tripartite division of the Book of Isaiah, and its failure to do justice to the theology of the final editorial framework, has already produced a sizable amount of secondary literature.[5]

Moreover, in his excellent commentary on Jeremiah, R.P. Carroll shows that the Book of Jeremiah has rather little to do with any pre-exilic prophet Jeremiah, and that what we find in this book is an anthology produced by Deuteronomistic redactors in the exilic and post-exilic eras, and a 'prophetical book' of the kind that these redactors believed, or wished, that a prophetic book should look like.[6] Finally, in a

---

3.   J.M. Vincent, *Studien zur literarischen Eigenart und zur geistigen Heimat von Jesaja, Kap. 40–55* (Beiträge zur biblischen Exegese und Theologie, 5; Frankfurt am Main: Peter Lang, 1977). I am grateful to Dr Vincent for providing me with a copy of his important work.

4.   J.H. Eaton, *Festal Drama in Deutero-Isaiah* (London: SPCK, 1979).

5.   The literature in this field is growing rapidly. See, for instance, M.A. Sweeney, *Isaiah 1–4 and the Post-Exilic Understanding of the Isaianic Tradition* (BZAW, 171; Berlin: de Gruyter, 1988). To Sweeney, the whole of the book of Isaiah has been conceived as an answer to the problems of the Jewish community in the second half of the fifth century. See also J. Vermeylen, 'L'unité du livre d'Isaïe', in *idem* (ed.), *The Book of Isaiah: Le Livre d'Isaïe: Les oracles et leurs relectures: Unité et complexité de l'ouvrage* (BETL, 81; Leuven: Leuven University Press, 1989), pp. 11-53. Apparently, this particular development should not be viewed in isolation from another recent trend, commonly referred to as 'inner-biblical exegesis'. See, for instance, M. Fishbane, *Biblical Interpretation in Ancient Israel* (Oxford: Oxford University Press, 1985), and J. Koenig, *Oracles et liturgies de l'exil babylonien* (Etudes d'histoire et de philosophie religieuses, 69; Paris: Presses Universitaires de France, 1988).

6.   R.P. Carroll, *Jeremiah: A Commentary* (OTL; London: SCM Press, 1986). For the view that the book of Jeremiah in its final form is basically the work of a redactor writing under the influence of 'Ezekiel traditions', see C.R. Seitz, *Theology*

recent work on the book of Micah, K. Jeppesen has put forward the thesis that the book of Micah should be read as a coherent composition from the time of the exile, its purpose being to explain to its readers why Jerusalem was destroyed and the people taken into exile, as well as to show that there is now good reason for future hope. The purpose of the Micah work, then, is rather similar to what we may find with regard to Isaiah 40–55. Jeppesen even suggests that the editor of Micah and the editor of Isaiah 40–55 may be the same person. As a post-exilic literary creation, the work has little to do with any pre-exilic prophet Micah.[7]

In addition to these, and similar works, mention should here be made of A.G. Auld, who, in a series of studies, has attempted to demonstrate that the designation 'prophets' for the biblical 'prophets' is very late ('it was only after the exile that such figures became termed "prophet"'),[8] and that 'both parts of the "prophetic canon" of the Hebrew Bible received much of their distinctive and positively intended "prophetic" vocabulary over a briefer and in a later period of the biblical tradition than is regularly supposed',[9] leaving it, however, to 'another study to clarify what about these writings let them become prophetic...'[10] Auld bases his thesis primarily on a statistical and terminological study, attempting to show that the term נביא in the so-called 'prophetic books' was editorially attached to the 'prophets' only in late, post-exilic times.[11] Jeremiah, Isaiah, Ezekiel and 'the minor prophets' were not 'prophets' but 'poets'. Thus, the prophet Amos 'only became a good prophet when he was a dead one'.[12] In fact, they all 'denounced' and 'abhorred' prophets, and 'would hardly have been seen dead in their company'.[13]

---

in Conflict: Reactions to the Exile in the Book of Jeremiah (BZAW, 176; Berlin: de Gruyter, 1989).

7. K. Jeppesen, *Græder ikke saa saare: Studier i Mikabogens sigte* (2 vols.; Aarhus: Aarhus Universitetsforlag, 1987).

8. A.G. Auld, 'Prophets through the Looking Glass: Between Writings and Moses', *JSOT* 27 (1983), pp. 3-23 (7).

9. Auld, 'Prophets through the Looking Glass', p. 16.

10. Auld, 'Prophets through the Looking Glass', p. 20.

11. A.G. Auld, 'Prophets and Prophecy in Jeremiah and Kings', *ZAW* 96 (1984), pp. 66-82.

12. A.G. Auld, 'Word of God and Words of Man: Prophets and Canon', in L. Eslinger and G. Taylor (eds.), *Ascribe to the Lord: Biblical and Other Studies in Memory of Peter C. Craigie* (JSOTSup, 67; Sheffield: JSOT Press, 1988), pp. 237-251 (247).

13. Auld, 'Word of God and Words of Man', p. 245.

Likewise, such prophetic 'paraphernalia' as the phrase 'the word of YHWH' was inserted editorially into the texts at a late stage.[14] Unlike Carroll, however,[15] Auld is concerned with the *persons* Jeremiah, Isaiah, *et al.* He believes that we should attempt to find out more about these historical poets from the texts.[16] So, even though he would warmly support the views put forward by Auld, Carroll clearly also radicalizes them.[17]

Even if the different views referred to above remain far from presenting any uniform appearance, they apparently do share the common belief that there is little or nothing to be learnt about pre-exilic prophecy on the basis, for example, of the books of Isaiah, Jeremiah, Ezekiel and the minor prophets. Despite some critical voices (among them notably

---

14. Auld, 'Word of God and Words of Man', p. 246. This, in my view, is the weakest part of Auld's argument. Ever since L. Köhler in his work (strongly influenced by Gunkel), *Deuterojesaja (Jesaja 40–55) stilkritisch untersucht* (BZAW, 37; Giessen: Töpelmann, 1923), pp. 102-109, made the discovery that the formula used by the Hebrew prophets, כה אמר יהוה, originated from the profane messenger formula, studies on the prophets as 'divine messengers' have belonged to one of the more established accomplishments of prophetic research, and it certainly takes more than mere allegations to disintegrate this and related vocabulary from the 'prophetical' books. On the messenger, see most recently S.A. Meier, *The Messenger in the Ancient Semitic World* (HSM, 45; Atlanta: Scholars Press, 1989), and, less good, but with a large section on 'the prophet as messenger' (pp. 137-266), J.T. Greene, *The Role of the Messenger and Message in the Ancient Near East: Oral and Written Communication in the Ancient Near East and in the Hebrew Scriptures: Communicators and Communiques in Context* (BJS, 169; Atlanta: Scholars Press, 1989). Again, Mari provides us with some interesting evidence (see J.-M. Durand, *Archives épistolaires de Mari*, I.1 [ARM, 26; Paris: Editions Recherche sur les Civilisations, 1988], pp. 377-81). Compare also the following prophetic declaration from Mari: 'Dagan has sent me' (*Archives épistolaires*, p. 449 = no. 220, l. 19). Below, the work by Durand is abbreviated *AEM*, I/1.

15. In addition to the works by Carroll mentioned elsewhere in this article, one should also note his important paper on the superscripts of the prophetical books, 'Inventing the Prophets', *IBS* 10 (1988), pp. 24-36, where Carroll claims that whoever wrote these colophons containing the different names actually 'invented' the prophets.

16. Auld, 'Word of God and Words of Man', p. 240 n. 3. Cf. also his 'Poetry, Prophecy, Hermeneutic: Recent Studies in Isaiah', *SJT* 33 (1980), pp. 567-581 (567).

17. Cf. R.P. Carroll, 'Poets not Prophets. A Response to "Prophets through the Looking Glass"' (appearing in this volume).

Williamson,[18] Ringgren[19] and Overholt[20]), and judging also from the fast growing tendency to date more and more of the biblical material to very 'late' periods, as well as from the ever increasing interest in 'redactional layers' and 'inner-biblical exegesis', there are good reasons to suspect that the trend described above in the rather sketchy survey of recent developments may soon turn into more than a general tendency, and eventually change completely the very nature of prophetic research.[21]

Apparently, the trend in recent scholarship to which I have been referring does not deny that that there were such things as prophets in ancient Israel. However, by reducing what we find in the 'prophetic writings' of the Hebrew Bible to post-exilic literary creations with little or no connection at all back into the history that went before, it may seem that recent scholarship has postulated an impassable tradition gap, and made whatever pre-exilic prophetic activity there was quite unavailable to us.

Are then the prospects for future prophetical studies so bleak? Are the prophets of ancient Israel really completely lost to us? Is it not at all possible, on the basis of the texts found in the Hebrew Bible, to gain access to the phenomenon of ancient Israelite prophecy in the period prior to the exilic era?

In spite of the obvious value of much recent scholarship on the prophets, and despite the perhaps even greater merit of the works of scholars like Auld and Carroll, I find it difficult to see that all of their views can be easily accepted. Since the field involved is a fairly large one, however, and the space limited, I shall, in the present context, have to refrain from treating the problems involved in any great detail, and will have to restrict myself to a few provisional remarks.[22]

18. See his essay in this volume, 'A Response to A. Graeme Auld'.

19. H. Ringgren, 'Israelite Prophecy: Fact or Fiction', in *Congress Volume, Jerusalem 1986* (VTSup, 40; Leiden: Brill, 1988), pp. 204-10.

20. See his essay in this volume, 'Prophecy in History: The Social Reality of Intermediation'.

21. Cf. also J.M. Ward, 'The Eclipse of the Prophet in Contemporary Prophetic Studies', *USQR* 42 (1988), pp. 97-104, and in particular F.E. Deist, 'The Prophets: Are we Heading for a Paradigm Switch?' in V. Fritz, K.-F. Pohlmann and H.-C. Schmitt (eds.), *Prophet und Prophetenbuch: Festschrift für Otto Kaiser zum 65. Geburtstag* (BZAW, 185; Berlin: de Gruyter, 1989),pp. 1-18.

22. I would like to add here that I am far more in sympathy with the works of Auld and Carroll than one might perhaps come to suspect from the following remarks. For my own part, I do not hesitate to say that I have probably learnt more

Tentatively speaking, Carroll may well be correct in his claim that the book of Jeremiah is a post-exilic creation based on what its author believed pre-exilic prophecy looked like, and that we cannot really know anything about whether there ever existed a prophet Jeremiah. Also, his stand against certain trends is basically sound and certainly necessary, forcing biblical scholarship to reconsider its historical positivism and naive empiricism, and it should, consequently, be warmly welcomed in a branch of the humanities where positivism, if far advanced in decrepitude, is nevertheless still with us.

Following this eulogy of Carroll's healthy methodological approach, however, I should also mention some of the weaknesses in his approach. Here, I am not referring primarily to such 'minor matters' as, for instance, the fact that his epistemological scepticism appears sometimes to be arbitrary and selective,[23] nor to his occasionally troubled notion of 'history',[24] where it sometimes may be a problem to the reader of

---

from the reading of Carroll's stimulating works than from any other scholar in his generation. It is a delight to read Carroll because he is knowledgeable also about the intellectual debate in the humanities in general, a capacity rarely to be found in exegetes on a level beyond the customary dilettantism, which is perhaps motivated by a chronic inferiority complex. This same inferiority complex tends to make biblical scholars look up to somewhat outmoded trend-setting theoreticians (more often than not of the French persuasion) who take a very little scholarship a very long way in order to make biblical research look more 'philosophical'.

23. Carroll's 'epistemological scepticism', strangely enough, appears to be less impassioned vis-à-vis the works of Dumézil or Ong, for example (cf. below notes 38 and 53).

24. Occasionally, Carroll's view of 'historical' even appears to be of a good old-fashioned positivistic variant. See, for instance, his attempt to make a distinction between 'historical' on one side and 'literary, ideological and fictional' on the other ('Whose Prophet?', p. 44.) For someone who is apparently well aware that the 'historical fact' debate is methodologically *passé*, Carroll remains rather obsessionally concerned with the 'fact' that the book of Jeremiah is not historical: 'As I read Jeremiah I am struck by its ahistoricality and its intertextuality. Poem after poem has little reference outside the book itself and much of the prose is commentary on the Deuteronomistic History' ('Whose Prophet?', p. 40). However, it is *not* possible to claim that the texts of the Hebrew Bible are 'ahistorical'. No text coming out of the past can be. No one, I suppose, would refer to the works of Jane Austen or Thomas Hardy as 'historical' books. But this does not at all mean that we cannot learn a lot about the societies in which these writers lived from the reading of their books. Even if the ancient Israelite society is long gone, and thus definitely a thing of the past (not available to our senses), this does not mean that the written remains from this society do not yield 'historical' information. In my attempt to

Carroll's always stimulating writings that he sometimes appears to take sides with the anti-empiricists.

Far more open to criticism is, for instance, his claim that we are facing serious difficulties evaluating the biblical prophets because there are two different perceptions of prophecy in the Bible: one very positive and one equally negative.[25] In a similar manner, Carroll holds the opinion that the prophets cannot be mediators because the priests were, so severely complicating 'the combination of the roles of priest and prophet in the representation of various figures in the Bible (e.g. Abraham, Moses, Samuel, Elijah, Jeremiah, Ezekiel)'.[26] Such strange, self-inflicted problems reveal a curious cognitive aporia, inconsistent with Carroll's otherwise sound theoretical principles.

Without denying that there were such personages as 'prophets' in ancient Israel, Carroll shows himself unwilling to grant the biblical writers much interest in the phenomenon. It is not surprising, then, that Auld and Carroll are both rather vague and reticent over what terms like 'prophet' and 'prophecy' can or should mean.

Since any discussion of the term 'prophecy' is bound to spark off endless new discussions, I shall here be content to introduce a definition proposed by a third, 'neutral' party. M. Weippert has described a 'prophet' in the following manner

> A prophet(ess) is a person, male or female, who (1) through a cognitive experience, a vision, an audition, a dream or the like, becomes the subject of the revelation of a deity, or several deities, and (2) is conscious of being commissioned by the deity/ deities in question to convey the revelation in

choose *my* version of the biblical past, I should in fact be far more worried about to what extent *we* share a common intellectual universe with the authors of the book of Jeremiah than the 'tradition gap' between the view on prophecy in the book of Jeremiah and pre-exilic notions of prophecy. The best treatment I have seen on some of the problems involved here is found in the recent book by H.B. Brichto, *Toward a Grammar of Biblical Poetics: Tales of the Prophets* (New York: Oxford University Press, 1992).

25. 'Poets not Prophets: A Response to "Prophets through the Looking Glass"', in this volume. For some of the issues of prophecy involved here, see J.J.M. Roberts, 'Does God Lie? Divine Deceit as a Theological Problem in Israelite Prophetic Literature', in *Congress Volume, Jerusalem 1986* (VTSup, 40; Leiden: Brill, 1988), pp. 211-20, with references to the ancient Near Eastern material.

26. 'Whose Prophet? Whose History? Whose Social Reality?', in this volume.

speech, or through metalinguistic behaviour, to a third party who constitutes the actual recipient of the message'.[27]

I am aware that several objections, including a few of my own, could be raised against this definition,[28] but since it is introduced here purely for heuristic reasons, where any 'reasonable' definition would be helpful, Weippert's contribution will have to do.

The major problem, in my view, with recent trends in prophetic research, including such weighty contributions as those of Auld and Carroll, is that they tend to be too theoretical and take little or no heed of what is actually *to be found* in the biblical texts,[29] above all lacking any serious attempt to relate the *contents* of the prophetical books to the phenomenon of biblical and ancient Near Eastern prophecy in general. It is possible to steer clear of Carroll's anti-historicism by approaching the problem of biblical prophecy from a purely phenomenological angle. By doing so, I believe in fact that we can really learn a good deal about ancient Israelite prophecy from the so-called prophetical books of the Bible, even if the phenomenon found here is not identical with the phenomenon of prophecy in ancient Israel, which will have to be reconstructed. What I want to plead in the present context is a positive rather than a negative scepticism.

II

The corpus of ancient Near Eastern 'prophetical' texts is growing fast, and we now have at our disposal materials that enable us to understand fairly well the important role played by the phenomenon of divination in the ancient Semitic world, and the prevalent need to consult deities concerning the future fate of the various undertakings of day to day life, above all in times of crisis. Typically, one may refer to the kings of

27. M. Weippert, 'Aspekte israelitischer Prophetie im Lichte verwandter Erscheinungen des Alten Orients', in G. Mauer and U. Magen (eds.), *Ad bene et fideliter seminandum: Festgabe für Karlheinz Deller zum 21. Februar 1987* (AOAT, 220; Neukirchen–Vluyn: Neukirchener Verlag, 1988), pp. 287-319 (289-90).

28. So, in his definition of 'prophet', Weippert makes a distinction between 'intuitive' prophecy and different forms of 'inductive' divination by the means of signs, omen, prodigies and the like.

29. Interestingly enough, this is the same kind of criticism Carroll would raise towards Overholt, for example (see 'Whose Prophet?', p. 35).

Mesopotamia, who apparently hardly ever went to battle without prior consultation with higher powers.[30] In a similar manner, prophecies from Mari and from the time of Esarhaddon and Ashurbanipal also are not meant for the distant future, but concern some contemporary national crisis.[31]

Traditionally, scholars have made a clear distinction in the literature between 'prophecy' and 'divination', the former supposedly of a 'free' and 'inspired' kind, whereas the latter has been regarded as purely technical. This distinction, having its background in, among other things, a wish to place biblical prophecy on a 'higher level' than the divination of Israel's more 'primitive' surroundings, ought not to be stressed too much.[32] A sharp differentiation between the role of 'priests' and that of 'prophets', accordingly, is not always practical or feasible, neither in ancient Israel nor in the surrounding cultures. Divination in the ancient Near East should be studied as a whole. Whenever attempts have been made in the literature to distinguish between 'intuitive' and 'provoked' prophecy, this has been done under the influence of biblical studies, where scholars have wanted to place the prophets of ancient Israel 'higher up' on the evolutionary ladder. The difference between what is commonly referred to as 'prophecy' and what is called 'divination' is therefore often an unnatural and ideological one, and bears not so much on the phenomenon as such as upon the different techniques applied.[33]

30. How heavily, for instance, the later Sargonids depended upon consulting the gods in connection with their warfare activities, can now most conveniently be seen from the recently published *Queries to the Sungod: Divination and Politics in Sargonid Assyria* (ed. I. Starr, with contributions by J. Aro and S. Parpola; State Archives of Assyria, 4; Helsinki: Helsinki University Press, 1990).

31. *AEM* I.1 (1988), p. 399; M. Weippert, 'Assyrische Prophetien der Zeit Asarhaddons und Assurbanipals', in F.M. Fales (ed.), *Assyrian Royal Inscriptions: New Horizons in Literary, Ideological, and Historical Analysis: Papers of a Symposium Held in Cetona (Siena) June 26–28, 1980 (Orientis antiqui collectio,* 17; Roma: Istituto per l'Oriente, 1981), pp. 71-116 (71-72).

32. In the same manner, the former, often sharply made, distinction between the 'earlier prophets' (mentioned in the 'historical' parts of the Hebrew Bible) and the 'later prophets' (whose surviving writings we supposedly have at our disposal) is quite artifical and cannot any longer be upheld.

33. Even if divination of a more technical kind apparently was not popular among those responsible for the final form of the Hebrew Bible, there is enough evidence left to suggest that the phenomenon must have been known in ancient Israel. Among the more conspicuous traits we find the references to 'Urim' and 'Thummim' (see Num. 27.21; 1 Sam. 14.36-42; 23.9-13; 28.5-6; 30.7-10). Of great

However, the problem of Mesopotamian divination in general can only marginally concern us here.[34]

Perhaps the most important single new insight concerning a comparison of the ancient Near Eastern prophetic material with the biblical is that the earlier claim, that the Mesopotamian world only knew of inductive divination through technical interpretations of different kinds, and not oracles spoken directly to a person or groups of persons, is no longer tenable. Even if this point, of course, was apparent after the publication of the Mari texts, it remains important to realize that it is now further attested also by other texts.[35] In the present context, however, I shall restrict myself to making a few remarks with regard to Mari.

There already exists a literature of rather considerable extent, both of the primary and the secondary kind, on the relationship of 'Mari prophecy' to the 'prophets of the Hebrew Bible'.[36] In recent years,

interest also is the story of Elisha and the arrows in 2 Kgs 13 (cf. Ezek. 21.21-22). All of these references, moreover, concern warlike situations. The harsh words in Mic. 3.6-7 are not directed against divination as such, but must be viewed in the light of the words against 'false' prophets in general. Following the discovery of clay liver models at Hazor, we must now also consider the possibility that hepatoscopy was in use in ancient Israel (cf. B.O. Long, 'Divination', *IDBSup*, pp. 241-43 (242).

34. An excellent introduction to ancient Mespotamian divination as such is found in J. Bottéro, 'Symptômes, signes, écritures en Mésopotamie ancienne', in J. Vernant *et al.* (eds.), *Divination et rationalité* (Recherches anthropologiques; Paris: Editions du Seuil, 1974), pp. 70-197. The most recent review of Akkadian prophetic texts, rich in bibliographic references, is M. deJong Ellis, 'Observations on Mesopotamian Oracles and Prophetic Texts', *JCS* 41 (1989), pp. 127-96.

35. M. Weippert has pointed to similarites between several Assyrian prophecies from the seventh century BCE and the prophecies of the Hebrew Bible (M. Weippert, 'Assyrische Prophetien', in Fales [ed.], *Assyrian Royal Inscriptions*, pp. 71-116). About half of these very interesting prophecies (14) concern the goddess Ishtar of Arbela (p. 75). Mention should also be made here of the recently published texts from Emar, containing several references to 'prophetesses', which will have to be studied more closely in the future with regard to the topic here discussed (see D. Arnaud, *Recherches au pays d'Ashtata: Emar VI:1-4* [Paris: Editions Recherche sur les Civilisations, 1985], *passim*).

36. For a very complete survey of the literature on Mari, see J.-G. Heintz, *Bibliographie de Mari—Archéologie et Textes (1933–1988)* (Wiesbaden: Otto Harrassowitz, 1990), with 'Supplement I (1989–1990)', *Akkadica* 77 (1992), pp. 1-37. A balanced survey of 'Mari and the Bible' is provided by A. Lemaire, 'Mari, la Bible et le monde nord-ouest sémitique', *MARI* 4 (1985), pp. 549-58. In the literature we find large variations over how to relate Mari prophecy to that of Israel. The

however, many new texts have been published, and today we have access to three times as many prophetic texts from Mari as when the major monographs on Mari prophecy were written. So, in his recent, excellent edition of the Mari 'letters', J.M. Durand lists as many as 30 texts, both new and formerly published, under the heading of 'prophetic texts'.[37] In addition, there is a large quantity of other texts of a divinatory and oracular kind, including dreams, which are, in accordance with the above claim, also of relevance. Undoubtedly, the time has now come for a larger study of Mari prophetic texts, and the immediate future will hopefully see more and more works within this interesting and important area, both with regard to Mari prophecy as a phenomenon

pioneering work of F. Ellermeier, for instance, claims direct influence: 'Each of the features of Mari prophecy that we can recognize in Israelite seers could have ben transmitted via Canaanite, Phoenician and Philistine channels' (F. Ellermeier, *Prophetie in Mari und Israel* [Theologische und Orientalistische Arbeiten, 1; Herzberg: Verlag Erwin Jungfer, 1968], p. 167). Another representative of this kind of old-fashioned 'comparativism' is the author of the most recent monograph on the subject, A. Schmitt. Schmitt seems to assume that we may find in Mari the 'Vorgeschichte der atl. Prophetie', subscribing to the somewhat obsolete myth of the 'unchangeable orient': 'In view of the persistence and robustness of certain traditions in the ancient Near East, it would be no surprise if in an area as important as prophecy a kernel of forms and structures endured over a long period of time and exerted an influence on neighbouring regions' (A. Schmitt, *Prophetischer Gottesbescheid in Mari und Israel: Eine Strukturuntersuchung* [BWANT, 114; Stuttgart: Kohlhammer, 1982], pp. 13-14; editor's translation). Much sound judgment is found in, for example, E. Noort, *Untersuchungen zum Gottesbescheid in Mari: Die 'Mariprophetie' in der alttestamentlichen Forschung* (AOAT, 202; Neukirchen–Vluyn: Neukirchener Verlag, 1977). Noort, however, is too sceptical when he claims that 'Phenomena that display similarities between Mari and Israel are, considering the background of all the textual material, too unspecific to permit a historical reconstruction' (p. 109; editor's translation). Also, Noort has a very narrow view on prophecy as such, and his presupposition, based on his views on ancient Israelite prophecy, that 'A collective "prophecy" term as a systematic category of divine communication is unknown of Man' (*Untersuchungen*, see also pp. 18ff.), fails to make the necessary distinction between prophecy as depicted ideologically by the biblical writers and the historical phenomenon 'prophecy in ancient Israel' (which has to be reconstructed on the basis of the sources we have available). Close to Noort is A. Malamat (despite the title of his article), 'A Forerunner of Biblical Prophecy: The Mari Documents', in P.D. Miller, D. Hanson and S.D. McBride (eds.), *Ancient Israelite Religion: Essays in Honor of Frank Moore Cross* (Philadelphia: Fortress Press, 1987), pp. 33-52 (37).

37. *AEM*, I.1.

worthy of study in its own right, as well as in relation to biblical studies.

Here, however, we shall have to be wary. There was a time in biblical scholarship when comparative studies were quite common, and rather uncritical. These times, hopefully, are long past. Notwithstanding this development, the former—sometimes uncritical—historical diachronic approach appears to have been replaced by a 'structuralist' one, and I am not so sure that this form of 'neo-comparativism' is always sounder than its somewhat less elegant predecessor.[38] Comparative studies, it appears, still have some way to go before their value to biblical studies can be fully appreciated.[39]

For instance, despite such apparently self-evident knowledge that every culture has to be assessed for its own value, there still is no lack in Mari studies of scholars who complacently regard the Mari 'prophets' as the 'forerunners' of the Hebrew prophets. We should realize, once and for all, that what we are dealing with are manifestations of similar phenomena within a much greater cultural context. Obviously, there is no *direct* connection between Mari and ancient Israelite prophecy. Also there is a considerable gap in time. Nevertheless, the obvious phenomenological similarities, witnessed by contemporary documents from Mari, *are* very important for the assessment of 'historical' prophecy in ancient

---

38. It is somewhat curious to read how Carroll, criticizing the use of models taken from 'outside' biblical studies ('Whose Prophet?', pp. 40-41), introduces the name of G. Dumézil. Even if Dumézil most certainly has his followers (especially in North America), it is probably difficult to find a more controversial theoretician in the comparative field today (for some samples of the negative Dumézil critique, see the evaluation of the linguistic basis of Dumézil's thesis in J. Haudry, 'Linguistique et mythologie comparée', *L'Information Grammaticale* 34 [1987], pp. 3-8. For a critique of his attempt to impose his theorizing for Indo-European cultures on the study of Roman society, see A. Momigliano, 'Premesse per una discussione su Georges Dumézil', *Rivista Storica Italiana* 95 [1983], pp. 245-61 [another version: 'Georges Dumézil and the Trifunctional Approach to Roman Civilization', *History and Theory: Studies in the Philosophy of History* 23 (1984), pp. 312-30]. And for a solid critique of Dumézil's Indo-European theory in general, see J.-P. Demoule, 'Réalité des indo-européens: Les diverses apories du modèle arborescent', *RHR* 208 [1991], pp. 169-202). I am aware that it may seem strange to refer only to negative reviews of Dumézil's theories, but my point here is not to claim that Dumézil in any way is wrong, but only that he is too controversial to serve the study of biblical prophetical texts well.

39. The recent book by M. Malul, *The Comparative Method in Ancient Near Eastern and Biblical Legal Studies* (AOAT, 227; Neukirchen–Vluyn: Neukirchener Verlag, 1990), has some interesting observations.

Israel. Even if Carroll's scepticism concerning 'models' is basically
sound, we cannot, and should not, close our eyes to what have the
appearance of being strongly related phenomena within cognate cultures.

In sum, comparing Mari prophecy with ancient Israelite prophecy is
not as unproblematic as some scholars may seem to believe, not least
because there exists no scholarly consensus about ancient Israelite
prophecy in the first place. Then, of course, there is the matter of a
considerable distance both in time and culture. Yet, the parallels are so
many and so striking that we simply cannot disregard them. From a
methodological point of view, it is also of considerable importance that
what information we may find concerning prophecy at Mari is supported
not only by the Hebrew Bible, but also by other ancient Near Eastern
'prophetical' texts. Altogether, this makes it in fact possible to see a
'pattern' or to make a 'model', or whatever one choses to call it. I am,
of course, not claiming that we here have 'identical' phenomena. What
we find in these different contexts are strongly related phenomena within
connected cultures, showing us that 'prophecy' was a widespread phenomenon in the different ancient Near Eastern cultures.

III

The theses of Auld and Carroll are, in my view, established on a basic
misunderstanding of what prophecy 'is'. Thus, the prophetic writings
are not prophetic because 'it was onto these books and not to others
that 'prophetic' or 'visionary' terminology was grafted',[40] but because
the *contents* of these books are to be regarded as prophetic when
viewed within the broader context of (biblical and) ancient Near Eastern
prophecy in general. The different phenomena described in Jeremiah and
the other prophets reflect the phenomenon of prophecy in the ancient
Near East as such. It is really not possible to reject biblical prophecy, for
example, on the grounds of statistical use of terminology. Such an
approach *may* establish whether or not the later editors regarded these
books as 'prophetic', but it does not necessarily follow from this that the
materials found in these books were not 'prophetic' in the first place. For
the present purpose it is only of secondary interest what the 'prophets'
are called; it is their function, their role in society, that is of interest to us
here. Carroll is quite right in pointing out to us that this society (similar

40. Auld, 'Prophets through the Looking Glass', p. 16.

to all historical societies) is long lost to us,[41] and he is possibly justified in his claim that the superscriptions may be late additions to the prophetical books, and, following Auld, even that נביא (and related terminology) may be editorially inserted in the prophetic books; I may even grant him the point that the book of Jeremiah has fairly little to do with any historical pre-exilic prophet Jeremiah, and so on, but none of this is really very important compared to the fact that what we find described phenomenologically in the book of Jeremiah largely corresponds to what we find elsewhere in the Bible *and* in the ancient Near East. The fact that the biblical prophets are not identical with the historical prophets of ancient Israel (in the same way as the religion of the Hebrew Bible is not identical with the religion of ancient Israel), which entails that the latter have to be reconstructed, does not mean that we cannot know *anything* about ancient Israelite prophecy (or religion).

For a moment feigning ignorance concerning the vast amount of scholarship invested in the so-called 'basic forms of prophetic speech', we may classify, very roughly and very superficially, but not without good cause (and not taking the prose sections into consideration), most of what we find in the books of Isaiah, Jeremiah, Ezekiel and the minor prophets as words proclaiming prosperity ('salvation'), or calamity ('doom'), as well as words of accusations and words of consolation, addressed to the nations of Israel or Judah, or to some foreign nation, or to individuals of Israel or Judah, or of some foreign nation. When we read the 'historical' books of the Bible, we will further find that similar functions are richly attested whenever prophecy is being referred to. One very striking feature in prophetic poetry is its preoccupation with warlike situations.

Wars in the ancient Near East were so-called 'holy wars'.[42] It was

---

41. That this complicates very much the use of sociological and social-anthropological models for the relationship between the prophets and their contemporary society has been seen correctly by Carroll in his article 'Prophecy and Society', in R.E. Clements (ed.), *The World of Ancient Israel* (Cambridge: Cambridge University Press, 1980), pp. 203-25. In my view, this article represents one of the most important contributions to the study of biblical prophecy in recent years. Nevertheless, I cannot share several of the viewpoints found in this article. A statement such as the following, 'Ancient Israelite writers had no clear image of what a prophet is or should be' ('Prophecy and Society', p. 209; cf. also 'Whose Prophet?', p. 35), is, in my opinion, in itself a very strange claim.

42. Again, the literature on this subject is overwhelming. One of the most important contributions is still M. Weippert, '"Heiliger Krieg" in Israel und Assyrien:

commonly believed that the gods conducted war affairs, and that they also played an active role on the battlefield. Since priests and prophets had access to the will of the deity, they played an important role in time of war (as well as during other communal crises such as drought and the like). This situation is demonstrated throughout the whole of the Hebrew Bible, and I can here only give some examples. In Judges 6 we read how YHWH sent a prophet to help the Israelites when they were in danger of losing the war against the Midianites. Illustrative is also the story in 1 Samuel 15, where Samuel intervenes in the war against the Amalekites. In 1 Samuel 7 there is an interesting description of Samuel, prophet and judge, acting as intercessor and mediator between YHWH and the people before the battle with the Philistines. Yet another illustrative story is found in Judges 20, where the priest Phinehas asks YHWH whether to go to war or not before the battle with the Benjaminites, and is given the following answer by YHWH: 'Go up! For tomorrow I will give them into your hand'.

Obviously, we cannot and should not regard these texts as 'historical' in the sense that they tell us 'what actually took place'. On the other hand, it is wrong to classify these stories as 'ahistorical'. Sprung from historical environments long lost to us, all of these stories *reflect* the historical and social surroundings that created them, and illustrate to us the significance of war in ancient Near Eastern societies, and of the role of 'prophets' in times of crisis.[43] This should not surprise us, for we may find the same phenomenon richly attested also outside of the Hebrew Bible, for instance in the Mari texts. The distance from mediator to counsellor, apparently, is not a very great one, and this seems to have given the prophets a high position in society. For instance, in the story of the war between Ben-hadad and King Ahab in 1 Kings 20 we are introduced to a prophet as military advisor. In this rather fascinating story we may also learn not a little about the role of the gods in war activities.

Kritische Bemerkungen zu Gerhard von Rads Konzept des "Heiligen Krieges im Alten Israel"', *ZAW* 84 (1972), pp. 460-93.

43. The immense significance of war, the most important single threat to human existence in the ancient Near East, can hardly be exaggerated, and is reflected on 'almost every page' of the Hebrew Bible. This, of course, does not mean that there were not other threats to ancient society (crop failure, epidemic disease, drought), where prophets also played a role. We find numerous examples of 'war language' in prophetic poetic texts (for a few examples, see Isa. 9.3; 14.5; 14.29; Jer. 48.17; 49.35; 51.56; Ezek. 39.3; Hos. 1.5; 5.8, Joel 2.1-11; Amos 5.3; Mic. 5.8; Zeph. 1.13; Zech. 9.10; 10.11).

Following the overwhelming victory of the Israelites, Ben-hadad's men can inform the king that the reason for their being defeated is that the gods of the Israelites are mountain gods, and had the battle only taken place on the plain, the Aramaeans would no doubt have been the victors! The act of defeating the enemy is at the same time a demonstration of power by the gods.

The interesting thing, now, is that the phenomena that I have just referred to concerning biblical prophecy are reflected also in the so-called prophetical books of the Bible (not least in the book of Jeremiah) as well as in other ancient Near Eastern 'prophetical' texts[44] (in particular in prophetical texts from Mari). This can hardly be a coincidence.

When, for instance, in the prologue to the Book of Jeremiah (Jer. 1.5) Jeremiah is made a נביא לגוים, 'a prophet to the nations', rather than to Judah, this is typical. In his excellent commentary Carroll relates this passage to the words against the nations in the book of Jeremiah, but feels that the 'force of the term' is less clear.[45] The passage, however, should be viewed in the context of the general role of prophetic activity, and should also be connected with Jer. 28.8, where we may learn something about the role of prophets as such: 'The prophets who were before me and before you [Hananiah] from the old days prophesied against many countries and great kingdoms war, famine and pestilence'.

In a class of their own we find the so-called 'oracles against the nations' in the prophetical books. Unfortunately, these have not attracted the interest they deserve in recent research. Whereas earlier scholarship regarded these oracles as important, and even as the basic form of prophetic activity (e.g. H. Gunkel), recent scholars have paid little or no attention to them (e.g. C. Westermann). However, we can hardly disregard the simple fact that oracles against the nations do occupy very large parts of *all* (with the exception of the book of Hosea) the prophetical books (cf. for instance Isa. 13–23, Jer. 46–51, Ezek. 25–32, Amos 1.1–2.3). In fact, three of the 'minor prophets', Obadiah, Jonah and Nahum, consist almost *solely* of oracles against foreign nations. Apparently, these oracles are there for some reason, and I have earlier suggested that we have in these texts reminiscences of a historical context of holy war and of 'divine cursing' of the enemy before going

44. See most conveniently the two articles on ancient Near Eastern prophecy by Weippert referred to above, notes 27 and 35.

45. Carroll, *Jeremiah*, p. 95.

to battle, or possibly even in the midst of battle.[46] Why should not the same apply for the book of Jeremiah? Prophets were heavily depended upon in times of war and crisis,[47] so why should this have been any different in the greatest war of all, Nebuchadnezzar's siege of Jerusalem? It is my conviction that what we find in the book of Jeremiah, strongly edited and worked over as it may appear, nevertheless reflects prophetic activity in the period prior to the fall of Jerusalem.[48] After all, as Weippert has most convincingly demonstrated, holy war continued to exist as long as wars existed in ancient Israel, and, moreover, there are no reasons whatsoever to assume that Israel should behave in any way differently from the rest of the ancient Near Eastern nations in this particular respect. It is interesting to note that the genre 'words against the foreign nation', so typical of prophetic activity, is also well attested at Mari.[49]

It is in the very nature of prophetic behaviour, then, to encompass not only the role of intermediator, but also that of intercessor.[50] Again, this

46. See H.M. Barstad, *The Religious Polemics of Amos: Studies in the Preaching of Am 2:7b-8, 4:1-13, 5:1-27, 6:4-7, 8:14* (VTSup, 34; Leiden: Brill, 1984), pp. 103-108. Obviously, we must here also reckon with the possibility of a non-cultic, but nevertheless religiously founded, conventional 'boosting of morale', something which is bound to have been a side effect of this kind of prophetic oracles in any event. Nor can we, of course, completely disregard the possibility suggested by Auld and Carroll that the 'prophets' of the biblical texts *in their present form* actually do represent mere poets, reusing older genres in a 'decontextualized' manner for their own rhetorical and poetical purposes, and writing a kind of religious 'national literature'. This, however, we shall never be able to find out. Also, this is not so important. As long as the genres used reflect the well-known phenomenology of ancient Near Eastern prophecy, these texts may nevertheless be used for the reconstruction of pre-exilic prophetic activity, no matter what their present character and nature are.

47. Cf. the typical statement in Ps. 74.9, a text lamenting the destruction of Jerusalem: 'Our signs we do not see. There is no longer any prophet, or anyone among us who knows for how long (it will last).'

48. Cf. also my article, 'Lachish Ostracon III and Ancient Israelite Prophecy', forthcoming in *Eretz-Israel* (1993).

49. For several prophetic words from Mari against foreign nations (including Babylon and Elam), as well as words of disaster addressed to the foreign king, followed by words of prosperity to the local king, see *AEM* I.1, pp. 435-43.

50. Thus, I am not at all convinced by the otherwise solid study by S.E. Balantine, 'The Prophet as Intercessor: A Reassessment', *JBL* 103 (1984), pp. 161-73.

is demonstrated in the book of Jeremiah. In Jer. 21.2 we may read how Zedekiah sends two of his priests to Jeremiah with the following message: 'Ask (דרש) YHWH for us, for Nebuchadnezzar king of Babylon is making war against us. Maybe YHWH will do with us according to all his wonderful deeds, and make him go away from us'. This text quite clearly reflects the intercessory role of the prophets in times of crisis,[51] a feature characteristic of ancient Near Eastern and of biblical prophecy in general.

IV

If the so-called prophetical texts are not post-exilic 'fiction' or 'pure poetry', but, as the parallels from ancient Near Eastern prophetical texts seem to indicate, in fact represent edited and worked over collections of prophetical sayings the way most scholars believe, we should also have to ask, to what circumstances do we owe the very existence of such texts?

Again, the mere fact that we do have in our possession a large quantity of ancient Near Eastern divinatory texts suggests that the taking down in writing of 'prophetic' texts must have been a rather widespread phenomenon. We may wonder why this was done to such a large degree, as we may today witness from the Akkadian sources—especially since most of the 'prophetic' texts were not meant to be reused—but the fact remains that such texts *were* written down. Also, we should here remind ourselves that, despite the fairly large quantity of texts that have been brought to light, the proportion of such texts compared to the total amount of texts that were once in existence is very modest indeed.

I am not so sure that the taking down in writing did change very much *the nature* of the original prophecies, as some scholars of today seem to believe. The unmistakable parallels between the biblical and the ancient Near Eastern prophetic material clearly attest the contrary. Apparently, because some importance was attached to these words, it became important to secure the message from the deity in the most accurate way possible, or the message had to be taken down in order that it might be delivered to the correct addressee. It is hardly likely that

51. Other texts in the book of Jeremiah reflecting prophets as intercessors are the description of the drought in Jer. 14 (see Carroll, *Jeremiah*, pp. 306-10), and the reference in Jer. 15 to Moses and Samuel as the greatest of intercessors (cf. Carroll, *Jeremiah*, pp. 319-21).

the writing down took place in order to secure the words for posterity.

The same, we should assume, would apply also for ancient Israelite prophetical texts. There is little cause to believe that the ancient Israelites behaved in any way differently from their neighbours in this respect, and, again, there are indications in the biblical material itself suggesting that prophetical texts were written down after they had been delivered.[52]

Since by nature oral poetry involves the possession of a certain vocabulary combined with certain compositional techniques, two oracles of the same prophet are not likely to have been completely identical. For this reason, it is probable that prophecies were written down at a very early stage and later collected. Because prophetic oracles were given in the form of oral poetry, their genuine form most certainly would very soon have been lost to posterity, had they *not* been written down. The scholarly myth, earlier favoured in Scandinavia in particular, that oral material could be handed down through several generations without this process leaving its mark on the tradition, is totally unfounded.[53]

---

52. That the ancient scribes took great care to write down prophetic words has been noted also by A.R. Millard ('La prophétie et l'écriture: Israël, Aram, Assyrie', *RHR* 202 (1985), pp. 125-45), who claims the prophetic texts of the Bible were written down straight away and were not changed at all. Because such an extreme view does not take into consideration even the simple fact that we may often find material from different periods and of different kinds put together in the books ascribed to single prophets, it cannot be taken too seriously.

53. The futile Scandinavian discussion on the reliability of oral tradition has been replaced by the more acceptable theory that this mode is not really very reliable unless supported by written documents.

It was the great merit of Hermann Gunkel and Gustav Hölscher to realize that the prophets were not writers, but *speakers*. In the meantime, however, it seems to have been forgotten that the words of these speakers ultimately *were* taken down in writing, and present day prophetic research is remarkably little concerned with any discussion of that process from oral to written which must have taken place, or the relationship between written and oral prophetic activity in general (among the exceptions in recent scholarship we find H. Utzschneider, *Künder oder Schreiber: Eine These zum Problem der 'Schriftprophetie' auf Grund von Maleachi 1,6–2,9* (Beiträge zur Erforschung des Alten Testaments und des antiken Judentums, 19; Frankfurt am Main: Peter Lang, 1989), which, however, appears not to break any new ground.

When it comes to the problem of oral literature in general, both inside and outside the Hebrew Bible, the secondary literature, of course, is enormous. It is worth noticing that Carroll ('Whose Prophet?', p. 37) subscribes to the views of W. Ong and others concerning a qualitative difference between the spoken and the written

We know that literacy, if not a widespread phenomenon, was certainly extant in ancient Israel.[54] Clearly, reflections of this may be found also in the prophetic books. One may here compare such texts as Isa. 8.1; 30.8; Jer. 36; Ezek. 2.10; 37.16-17; Hab. 2.2. Again, even if we are not dealing with 'historical' texts, there is, on the basis of the ancient Near Eastern analogies, little reason to doubt that these texts reflect historical reality.

As an example, we may here single out Jeremiah 36. This well-known story, where Jeremiah the prophet dictates his message to Baruch the scribe, *may* actually reflect the way the words of prophets sometimes were taken down in writing. This, however, is not the same as saying that what we find in Jeremiah 36 is a 'historical' account of what really happened, or that the book of Jeremiah as we have it today is largely the result of the writing down of Baruch the scribe as attested by Jeremiah 36! But then again, this is not so important. Thus, it is doubtful that this story of the turning of the spoken word into writing should be regarded as 'only' a symbolic act.[55] The event would not have been used to portrait a symbolic act in the first place if it had not been meaningful to the readers of the story, who would be able to relate the episode to some known phenomenon. Carroll has put forward the thesis that what

word. There is, apparently, no need to underestimate the changes in societies passing from orality to literacy, but it is important to be aware of the fact that in the ancient Near East both modes existed side by side for centuries. Also, I do not at all believe that literacy in itself causes such dramatic cognitive changes in the way that it has until recently become fashionable to believe. For a recent critique of the positions of scholars like E.A. Havelock, J. Goody, I. Watt, W. Ong or D.R. Olson, see now, among others, R. Thomas, *Oral Tradition and Written Records in Classical Athens* (Cambridge Studies in Oral and Literate Culture, 18; Cambridge: Cambridge University Press, 1989), pp. 24-34; R. Narasimhan, 'Literacy: Its Characterization and Implications', in D.R. Olson and N. Torrance (eds.), *Literacy and Orality* (Cambridge: Cambridge University Press, 1991), pp. 177-97: R. Finnegan, *Oral Traditions and the Verbal Arts: A Guide to Research Practices* (ASA Research Methods; London: Routledge, 1992), p. 6. Valuable observations are also to be found in G. Mazzoleni, 'Oralità "mitica", oralità "storica"', *Studi e materiali di storia delle religioni* 49 (1983), pp. 303-307 and 50 (1984), pp. 293-318.

54. This, of course, does not mean that writing and reading belonged to the 'common man' (cf. M. Haran, 'On the Diffusion of Literacy and Schools in Ancient Israel', in J.A. Emerton [ed.], *Congress Volume, Jerusalem 1986* [VTSup, 40; Leiden: Brill, 1988], pp. 81-95, and the similar conclusions reached by E. Puech, 'Les écoles dans l'Israël préexilique: Données épigraphiques', VTSup, 40, pp. 189-203).

55. Carroll, *Jeremiah*, p. 665.

we find in the book of Jeremiah is what a post-exilic writer believed or wanted his readers to believe that prophetical behaviour looked like, and that there is no connection whatsoever between this literature and what pre-exilic Israelite prophecy there was. Apparently a more correct way of viewing the whole matter is found in a phenomenological approach to the problem where 'the truth' is to be found somewhere in the middle of the line between Carroll's cognitive reticence and other scholars' historical positivism. What is important is that the *phenomenon* is 'historically' correct.

Some attention should here be directed towards the Lachish shards. Stemming from the 'same' historical setting as the book of Jeremiah, these materials also present interesting evidence concerning the writing down of prophetic words.[56]

Finally, even if what we find in Jeremiah 36 may reflect how the post-exilic author thought, or wanted his readers to think, prophets behaved, once more we have here an interesting 'parallel' from Mari. Again, I do not believe that it is a coincidence. With the story of Jeremiah and Baruch in mind, we may read the join A.431 with the earlier published ARM II, 108: 'Another matter: Atamrum, the *âpilum* of Shamash came to find me, and he said: Send me a very competent scribe in order that I can make him write down the message that Shamash has sent me for the king...'[57]

---

56. See my article, 'Lachish Ostracon III and Ancient Israelite Prophecy'.

57. D. Charpin, F. Joannès, S. Lackenbacher and B. Lafont, ARM I.2 no. 414 [A. 431 + A. 4883], pp. 294-295.

THE COMPOSITION OF PROPHETIC BOOKS

JSOT 31 (1985), pp. 95-113

BEYOND TRADITION-HISTORY:
DEUTERO-ISAIANIC DEVELOPMENT OF FIRST ISAIAH'S THEMES

R.E. Clements

1. *An Analysis of Methods and their Underlying Assumptions*

The book of Isaiah has come down to us as a work of 66 chapters and it is noteworthy that our earliest complete Hebrew manuscript of an Old Testament text of this size, namely the famous Isaiah Scroll found at Qumran (1Q15[a]), is of this book, and presents it to all intents and purposes in the form in which we know it. Yet concerning this book, unlike many Old Testament literary works, there has emerged something akin to a consensus among critical biblical scholars that the book does not derive from a single author, the eighth-century Isaiah of Jerusalem, and that the presence of material from much later than the eighth century BCE is unmistakably evident. Earlier scholars, such as the mediaeval commentator Ibn Ezra and the seventeenth-century Dutch philosopher B. Spinoza (1632–77), had inferred that chs. 40–66 of the book derive from a sixth-century BCE Babylonian background and firm arguments for this were set out in 1788 by the German scholar J.C. Doederlein in a critical review.[1] This theory gained for itself a modest following, but with the publication of Berhard Duhm's famous commentary of 1892 the case, both for this and for the futher separation of chs. 56–66 as of still later origin, became widely accepted. So a kind of rough and ready

---

1. For J.C. Doederlein's work on Isaiah a critical assessment is made by J.M. Vincent, *Studien zur literarischen Eigenart und zur geistigen Heimat von Jesaja, Kap. 40–55* (Beitrage zur biblischen Exegese und Theologie, 5; Frankfurt am Main: Peter Lang, 1977), pp. 17ff. Doederlein's hypothesis was advocated in a review of the commentary by G. Hensler, *Jesaier neu übersetzt mit Anmerkungen* (Hamburg und Kiel, 1788), published in *Auserlesenen theologischen Bibliothek*, 4.8 (Leipzig, 1788), pp. 554-79.

characterization of the book as deriving from at least three prophets—First Isaiah, Second Isaiah (Deutero-Isaiah) and Third Isaiah (Trito-Isaiah)—has arisen, although this was never more than a very marginal and improbable explanation of the origin of the book. The extent to which the last eleven chapters (56–66) had a united origin in themselves has consistently been seriously questioned, as has also the extent to which these chapters evidence a relationship of some kind to those ascribed to 'Second Isaiah'.[2] Some scholars have upheld the claim that at least some parts of chs. 56–66 share a common authorship with 'Second Isaiah'. Nevertheless, within this overall critical break-up of the assumption of the unity of the book based on a common historical setting and single prophetic author, the view that the 16 chapters that form the present 40–55 of the book are a literary and historical unity has been widely adopted. In fact so confident has scholarship felt in its identification of the work and activity of the unnamed author of these chapters that, not only have commentaries been published on them alone, isolated from the remainder of the book,[3] but it has become customary in reconstructing the overall chronology of prophetic activity in ancient Israel and Judah to describe the work of the unnamed prophet of the exile to whom we owe Isa. 40–55 as quite independent of its preserved literary setting.

Nevertheless we may note some significant points which have remained unresolved questions concerning this critical reconstruction of the work of the so-called 'Second Isaiah'.

In the first place there have always been some scholars who have challenged the hypothesis altogether on the grounds of a very conservative literary and theological approach to the Old Testament, pointing to a number of thematic and stylistic connections which link the various parts of the book of Isaiah together. So, in spite of the difficulties so carefully noted by scholars, a unity based on common authorship has been defended by, among others, O.T. Allis[4] and E.J. Young.[5]

This approach has convinced few critical minds for the clear reason that the difficulties do not lie with matters of vocabulary and style, but

2. Cf. F. Maass, 'Tritojesaja?', in *idem* (ed.), *Das ferne und nahe Wort: Festschrift L. Rost* (BZAW, 105; Berlin: de Gruyter, 1967), pp. 156-63.

3. So especially C.R. North, *The Second Isaiah* (Oxford: Clarendon Press, 1964).

4. O.T. Allis, *The Unity of Isaiah* (London: Tyndale Press, 1951).

5. E.J. Young, *Studies in Isaiah* (London, 1954).

rather with even more important issues relating to the very nature of prophecy and its historical relationships. The sixth-century Babylonian background of chs. 40–55 is so explicit that to deny its relevance for an understanding of their contents is to ask for a totally different understanding of prophecy from that which clearly pertains elsewhere in the Old Testament prophetic books. We can cite even so important a figure as Martin Luther himself for a recognition of this important 'historical' context to prophecy.[6] More attractive, therefore, has appeared the argument that the connection of chs. 40–55 with the work of the eighth-century Isaiah of Jerusalem may be explained by positing the existence of a group of 'disciples' of this prophet, among whom eventually 'Second Isaiah' emerged.[7] Yet this approach seems to claim more than it properly explains, since it retains the idea of a connection based on authorship, only now it is a 'school' of authors, without requiring any truly intrinsic connection of content between the various blocks of material. So far as it goes, it may be correct, but it does not really explain anything very much; it merely projects a hypothesis to account for the fact that chs. 40–55 of the book of Isaiah now appear as part of a larger work.

We may pause now to note the attraction that has been given afresh to the unique literary problems of the book of Isaiah by the method of 'canon criticism' advocated by B.S. Childs.[8] This recognizes that, alongside the evident historical context which has a bearing on the interpretation of Isa. 40–55 there is also a literary context in which chs. 1–39 form for the reader an indispensable part of the context of meaning by which they should be interpreted. When 'Second Isaiah' speaks of 'former things' therefore (Isa. 41.21; and elsewhere), the

6.   Cf. M. Luther, *Lectures on Isaiah Chapters 1–39* (ed. J. Pelikan and H.C. Oswald; St Louis: Concordia, 1969); *Chapters 40–66* (1972). Luther strongly stressed the importance of a historical knowledge of the prophet's background for the interpretation of his message (cf. Preface to *Chapters 1–39*, p. 3) and noted that 'we rightly divide Isaiah into two books' (*Chapters 40–66*, p. 3). The references to Cyrus, king of Persia in the sixth century, however, were interpreted by Luther as prophecies concerning him. In this way the later historical background is fully recognized as important, but it is explained in a distinctively prophetic manner.

7.   Cf. D.R. Jones, 'The Traditio of the Oracles of Isaiah of Jerusalem', *ZAW* 67 (1955), pp. 226-46. Further suggestions along this line are made by J.H. Eaton, 'The Origin of the Book of Isaiah', *VT* 9 (1959), pp. 138-57.

8.   B.S. Childs, *Introduction to the Old Testament as Scripture* (London: SCM Press, 1979), pp. 311-38.

reader will naturally recognize that things prophesied in chs. 1–39 are being referred to.[9] I should not wish here to comment upon the many wider issues raised by the whole approach which Childs advocates under the name of 'canon criticism'. From the perspective of the book of Isaiah it seems highly improbable that the process of 'canonization' had anything at all to do with the reasons why the book of Isaiah acquired its present shape. From the evidence, not only of the Qumran manuscript and the references in the New Testament, but also from the intrinsic contents of the book, it is virtually certain that those who ultimately adopted the book of Isaiah into the canon, along with the other prophetic books of the Old Testament, already found them in their present form and that their intentions in establishing the shape of the canon cannot, and should not, be assumed to have been identical with the intentions of those who shaped the present book of Isaiah.[10] Our problem is a literary and theological one of redaction-criticism, not the larger and more problematic one of canon criticism, which we may set aside for discussion in the realm of hermeneutics. The most that we can properly say in regard to canon criticism is that, only when we can resolve some of the problems concerning how the book of Isaiah acquired its present shape, may we have something to contribute towards the larger issues relating to the canon. We should assume that the problems of the book of Isaiah need to be clarified and resolved first of all in relation to that book, rather than in relation to a wider set of questions concerning the canon of the Old Testament.

We may conclude this part of the broader survey of modern critical

9. Childs, *Introduction to the Old Testament*, p. 328.

10. This appears to me to represent an important misdirection in the work of Childs, with which in many of its aspects I am in agreement. So far as a book such as Isaiah is concerned, with its unique historical and literary problems, it appears to be methodologically wrong to attempt to resolve these problems by an all-embracing hermeneutical appeal to the perspective of the canon. The book of Isaiah had acquired its present shape by the time the limits of the canon were determined. No doubt the understanding of prophecy inherent in the way in which the book was given shape bore some relationship to the interests of those who finally endorsed the canon. Yet the redactional shaping of the book took place first, and it would appear to be an entirely proper and valuable field of enquiry to examine this, quite apart from a hermeneutical interest in the 'canon' in its larger compass. Furthermore the varied interests which contributed to the shape of the book may then, incidentally, provide a better insight into the reasons why the whole corpus of the Former and Latter Prophets acquired the shape it did in the canon of the Old Testament.

approaches to the book of Isaiah by noting some relevant points, if only to remove them from clouding our discussion. The first of these is that to assume that ancient scrolls needed to be of a certain length; that nothing more than a question of literary convenience (and a saving of expensive materials) accounts for the current length and shape of the book of Isaiah must be looked upon as a counsel of despair. More than this certainly appears to have been at issue, and there are sufficient signs of a deeper concern with questions of meaning and interpretation that stretch across all 66 chapters to rule out such an approach based on purely external, material factors.

It is also very striking that ch. 35, for instance, which H. Graetz[11] and C.C. Torrey[12] thought belonged along with chs. 40ff., consciously anticipates and summarizes the major themes of chs. 40–55 This fact seems best explained as a conscious attempt to introduce later themes at this point in the book for some deliberate editorial and interpretative function. It is all of a piece with the fact, which I have myself drawn attention to elsewhere, that ch. 39 serves as an important editorial 'bridge' between the threat to Jerusalem posed by the Assyrians and that which was later posed by the armies of Babylon.[13]

It is also in order for us to bear in mind that no simple process of simply 'adding on' more and more prophecies to the Isaiah scroll can account for its present shape. By a wide scholarly consensus chs. 24–27 are regarded as the latest chapters in the book, later even than chs. 56–66, and other late material is to be found in chs. 3–35, and is certainly also scattered in other parts of chs. 1–21. Some process of editorial shaping has taken place, however much we may also be led to recognize that sometimes more arbitrary factors may have served to form the book into its final sequence of material.

So far, this survey of scholarly methods and their underlying assumptions has had the rather negative intention of showing that little has up till now been achieved in explaining the purpose and shape of the book of Isaiah as comprising the material which makes up the 66 chapters it now possesses. It is, I firmly believe, one of the most complex literary structures of the entire Old Testament. The ascription of it to

11. H. Graetz, 'Isaiah xxxiv and xxxv', *JQR* 4 (1891), pp. 1-8.

12. C.C. Torrey, *The Second Isaiah* (Edinburgh, 1928), pp. 279ff

13. Cf. my study *Isaiah and the Deliverance of Jerusalem* (JSOTSup, 13; Sheffield: JSOT Press, 1980), pp. 90ff; also 'The Unity of the Book of Isaiah', *Int* 36 (1982), pp. 117-29.

Isaiah has created a rather dangerous assumption that it is a unity because it derives from a single author. Such a view prevailed both in Judaism and Christianity down to the end of the eighteenth century, although in practice it had very little impact upon the book's interpretation, which was governed by other considerations than the more strictly historical ones. It was not until the work of Doederlein and those who came after him that a rigidly historical approach led, of necessity, to the break-up and abandonment of the idea of a unity of the book based on single authorship. Yet questions remain, since the book does not have a common author: What were the literary factors which gave rise to its present overall shape? Does this overall shape offer anything that might properly be called the message of the book of Isaiah? What we are concerned with is then quite properly an essay in editorial history, or more technically, an essay in redaction criticism. Given that the extant work is a unity, if only in the sense that it is a unified 'collection', we shall be asking whether it does not also possess a unity of theme and content. After all, even an anthology of texts such as we may produce in the modern world may usually be expected to display some overarching unity of background and theme.

We may pause over a further couple of general points. The method that has come to be known as 'redaction criticism' has initially arisen in biblical studies in relation to narrative texts, such as the Gospels of the New Testament or the supposed Yahwist source of the Hexateuch. Where such narrative texts are concerned we may expect the chief redactional interests to show themselves in relation to an overarching 'plot' by which much shorter narrative units are brought together. It is less clear that anything of this nature can, or should, be looked for in relation to a prophetic text. Rather, we may start our investigation here with a prior assumption that the redactional elements will show themselves in regard to the way in which the prophecy was believed to have been fulfilled, or to be awaiting fulfilment.[14] It is this aspect of an

---

14. The conception of a prophetic 'fulfilment' would appear to have been central to the understanding of the concerns which motivated the various editors of the book of Isaiah. Cf. Childs, *Introduction to the Old Testament*, pp. 336ff. Yet Childs argues from this that, in shaping the material in the book, the tradents have consistently divorced it from its original 'historical' setting and given to it another 'thematic' or 'theological' setting. This can only be conceded with considerable modification, since, so far as Isaiah 40–55 is concerned, it is quite clearly the historical Babylon of the mid-sixth century BCE that is envisaged as Israel's oppressor and the historical Cyrus of Persia who appears as its deliverer. Only later was such a historical

expected fulfilment of prophecy which lends to the question about what prophecy 'means'—a peculiar, but fascinating, difficulty. The fulfilment was understood in relation to events, but these events were merely alluded to, often under the guise of vague symbols or word imagery, so that we cannot now recover a very clear picture of what precise events they were, or were expected to be. The second general point lies in the problems relating to the whole method of redaction criticism and the kind of text that it was designed to deal with. Religious texts of many kinds have an extraordinary multi-dimensioned and multi-faceted character, but none more so than the Old Testament books of prophecy. Just as they have been centuries in being formed, so, during that time, many different interpretations, and kinds of interpretation, have been woven into them. Much recent discussion has centred, in part sparked off by B.S. Childs's method of canon criticism, upon whether the earliest, or the latest, level of meaning is the most important and authoritative for us. I do not wish to take sides over this broad issue, except insofar as it is very markedly evident that such a scholar as B. Duhm, with his analytical method, was entirely, and almost obsessively, concerned with the problems of original meaning. Such would be in order if the books of prophecy were merely collections, or anthologies, in which the original sense has been retained and the role of the editor, or editors, reduced to a minimum. On the other hand, if the work of the editors has been substantially more than this, then we may expect that they will themselves have injected a great degree of their own understanding into the work. Even at a *prima facie* level it would certainly appear that the very complexity of the final shape given to the book of Isaiah points us to this latter conclusion. The later, redactional, stages in the formation of the book have contributed more to an understanding of what it means than can usefully be gleaned by modern attempts to reconstruct the story of the 'life and times' of Isaiah of Jerusalem in the eighth century BCE.

My purpose from this point on is a relatively straightforward one: accepting that chs. 40–55 of the book of Isaiah originated from the sixth century BCE, when Judah and Jerusalem were under the domination of Babylon, what have these chapters to do with the earlier prophecies of Isaiah of Jerusalem preserved in chs. 1–39 of the book? Three broad possibilities present themselves: (1) The prophetic author of chs. 40–55

background veiled by the superimposing of a more complex set of interpretative guidelines, such as we find in the *pesher* techniques of Qumran.

had nothing to do with the original Isaiah and neither did his prophecies. For unknown reasons a later scribe came to associate them with the earlier sayings of Isaiah and thus they came to be linked in a literary fashion. Only later, at a level that we might relate to the period of canonization of the prophetic literature, were serious attempts made to understand the book as a whole. (2) A second possibility would, more plausibly, offer a modification of this and would arise if once the quite independent author of chs. 40–55 had left his material in literary form, a scribe recognized its eminent suitability to form a sequel to the earlier prophecies of Isaiah. So the two parts of the book—the 'Assyrian' part and the 'Babylonian' part—would have become linked together and, from this time onwards, further material would have been added developing the sense of interconnectedness still further.[15] (3) Yet a third possibility, however, should also be considered. This is that, from the outset, the material in chs. 40–55 was intended to develop and enlarge upon prophetic sayings from Isaiah of Jerusalem. In this case the later material was intended to supplement the earlier and to influence the way in which it was understood. In this case a further consideration arises, although I shall not deal with it in the course of the present examination. It will have to remain as an issue for further investigation. This is the question whether the contents of chs. 40–55, if they were not at one time an independent body of prophecies from the person of the otherwise unknown 'Second Isaiah', should be regarded as forming the unity that has so widely been maintained during the present century?

My present concern is to try to show that this third possibility concerning the origins of the so-called 'Second Isaiah' material is the most probable one, and that it calls for fuller and more serious investigation than it has hitherto received. This position is that, from the time of their

15. Childs, *Introduction to the Old Testament*, pp. 328ff., points out the central position occupied by the question of the nature of the connections with the contents of the prophecies of the eighth-century Isaiah. This still leaves unresolved, however, the extent to which such connections may be thought to have been present at the compositional stage of Isaiah 40–55, or whether they were simply perceived by the redactors of the book. To a considerable extent the lack of clarity on this point stems directly from the prior assumption that such connections are essentially a feature of the 'canonical' shape of the book. Against this we must insist that it was not the 'canon' which established the connections within the material; they occurred at a very much earlier period in the process of forming the book of Isaiah. It then requires to be asked whether such connections existed in the material at the primary compositional stage of Isaiah 40–55.

origin, the prophetic sayings of Isa. 40–55 were intended as a supplement and sequel to a collection of the earlier sayings of the eighth-
century Isaiah of Jerusalem. I shall certainly not be able to argue that all
the material of Isa. 40–55 can be explained in this fashion, but this is not
of itself necessary. Rather I should wish to proceed along the lines of
separating the more certain from the less certain aspects of such a
conclusion. A few concluding remarks may then be in order concerning
what further direction of research such deductions may be pointing us to.

2. *Two Fundamental Themes*

We may begin our more detailed investigation by looking at two
prominent and fundamental themes to be found in Isa. 40–55 where a
conscious allusion back to themes from the collection of Isaiah's prophecies appears to be intended. The first of these concerns *Israel's blindness
and deafness*; three passages call for immediate attention, and a fourth
will need to be looked at. The first of these is in Isa. 42.16:

> Then I will lead the blind along the road [...][16]
>> I will guide them in paths they have not known. (Isa. 42.16).

A few verses later a much longer section expressing the same contention appears, making it clear that 'spiritual' blindness is what is being
referred to:

> Hear, you deaf;
>> and look, you blind, that you may see!
> Who is blind except my servant,
>> or deaf as my messenger whom I send?
> Who is blind as the one with whom I am at peace [or, 'who fulfils
>> my purpose']
> or blind as the servant of Yahweh? (Isa. 42.18-19).

The following verses (42.21-25) then elaborate further upon this
deafness as a failure to listen to, and obey, Yahweh's *tôrâ*.
A third passage with the same theme of blindness and deafness then
follows in 43.8:

> Bring forth the people who are blind, yet have eyes,
> who are deaf, yet have ears! (Isa. 43.8).

The following section which enlarges upon this theme then concerns

---

16. This omits 'which they have not known' as a dittography. Cf. BHS.

Israel's role as Yahweh's witnesses. This is followed by a kind of 'excursus' on the theme of the folly of idolatry in vv. 9-20 during the course of which the fourth reference to those who are blind and those who are deaf appears:

> They do not know; nor do they understand; for he has covered over their eyes, so that they cannot see, and their hearts, so that they cannot understand (Isa. 44.18).

This verse clearly intends the reader to understand that the practice of idolatry is a major consequence of the blindness and deafness which has befallen Israel and raises the possibility that we should understand the entire prose excursus on the folly of idolatry as an elaboration of the theme of blindness. It is, in effect, a homiletical discourse showing how spiritual blindness affects people, and could very well be a subsequent elaboration upon the original prophetic text.

The theme of Israel's blindness and deafness, understood in a metaphorical and spiritual sense, is clearly of central importance to Isa. 40–55. Not only so, but it makes its point in a way which assumes that this deafness and blindness are already known to be the case. Nor do I think that we can properly doubt its source of origin, since it derives from the call narrative of Isaiah and the terms by which he was commissioned with a divinely given task towards Israel:

> And he [God] said, 'Go and say to this people:
> Listen carefully, but do not understand;
> look intently, but do not perceive.
> Make the mind of this people deaf,
> and their ears deaf,
> and cover over their eyes;
> lest they see with their eyes,
> and hear with their ears,
> and understand with their minds
> and repent and be healed' (Isa. 6.9-10).

Not only do we have here language so strikingly related to the otherwise unanticipated references to blindness and deafness in chs. 42 and 43 that we should not doubt that the later instances are dependent on the earlier, but the central importance of the original occurrence in the call narrative must further confirm this conclusion. In case we should remain in any doubt that this is an instance where later prophetic sayings have been modelled on an earlier one, the further taking up and development of the theme of blindness and deafness in still later prophecies introduced into the book should assist still further in persuading us. The most notable instance of this is to be seen in Isa. 35.5. We have already had occasion to mention that, seen from an editorial perspective, this chapter serves as a kind of summary anticipation of themes and assurances which are found more fully set out in chs. 40–55. Nor can there be very much doubt, I believe, that, in spite of its location within chs. 1–39, the material of ch. 35 is later than, and dependent on, the contents of chs. 40ff. We read in Isa. 35.5:

> Then [in the coming time of salvation] the eyes of the blind shall be opened,
>> and the ears of the deaf unstopped.

It proceeds further to declare the great life-enriching healing and vitality which will mark this new age by affirming that the lame man will leap like the hart and the dumb will speak. All of this rather suggests that the imagery of deafness and blindness is being understood in a literal, and not a metaphorical, sense.

A higher, and possibly even later, development of the theme of the ending of the era of blindness and deafness appears in 29.18:

> On that day the deaf shall hear the words of a book,
>> and out of their gloom and darkness
>> the eyes of the blind shall see (Isa. 29.18).

A point of further interest in this is that the reference to gloom and darkness appears to allude back to Isa. 8.23, thereby linking this imagery with that of blindness. Certainly, if we can reconstruct the chronology of the development of this theme in the book of Isaiah we arrive at the following picture. First Isaiah's call account used the imagery of Israel's blindness and deafness to signify the refusal of the people to listen and respond to the prophet's message. In chs. 42 and 43 the unknown exilic prophet has taken up this imagery to affirm that it describes a condition which still prevails, but in spite of it God's salvation will quickly come. Further development of the imagery in 35.5 and 29.18 then uses the idea that the ending of (physical) blindness and deafness will characterize the coming great era of salvation. It would seem here that we have a very strong case indeed for regarding the prophetic author of Isa. 42–43 as familiar with the actual words recorded of Isaiah's call in a section which is usually ascribed to the 'Isaiah Memoir'.

I should like now to turn to another group of passages in chs. 40–55, which are usually reckoned as the work of 'Second Isaiah', where a conscious allusion back to the language of Isaiah of Jerusalem appears intended. This concerns the varied expressions which are employed to affirm *the divine election of Israel*; to stress that Yahweh really has chosen it, in spite of all appearances to the contrary, and to make plain that God has not rejected it. So we find the following:

> Comfort, comfort my people,
>   says your God (Isa. 40.1).

> But you, Israel, are my servant,
>   Jacob, whom I have chosen,
>   the descendants of Abraham, my friend;
> you whom I took from the ends of the earth,
>   and called from its remotest parts,
> saying to you, 'You are my servant,
>   I have chosen you and not rejected you' (Isa. 41.8-9).

> I will say to the north, Give up,
>   and to the south, Do not withhold;
> bring my sons from afar
>   and my daughters from the end of the earth,
> every one who is called by my name,
>   whom I created for my glory,
>   whom I formed and made (Isa. 43.6-7).

> But now hear, O Jacob my servant,
>   Israel whom I have chosen!
> Thus says Yahweh who made you,
>   who formed you from the womb and will help you:
> Do not be afraid, Jacob my servant,
>   Jeshurun whom I have chosen (Isa. 44.1-2).

We could easily go on to multiply many more instances of this theme which is such a prominent one in chs. 40–55 of Isaiah (cf. especially 42.1-4; 43.20-21; 44.1-5, 21-22; 45.4, 9-10; 51.4, 16; 52.5). So in fact scholars have usually written concerning the distinctive doctrine of Israel's election which is to be found as a new feature in the teaching of Second Isaiah.[17] But, we must ask, is it only the circumstances of the plight of those exiled and imprisoned in Babylon which has given rise to the idea that Yahweh appeared to have reflected his people? This might be sufficient reason for the development of a special doctrine of Israel's divine election by the supposed Second Isaiah. Yet I think that we

---

17. Cf. T.C. Vriezen, *Jahwes Eigentumsvolk* (ATANT, 37; Zürich-Stuttgart, 1960), pp. 109ff.; H. Wildberger, *ThWAT*, I, cols. 290-91.

cannot set aside the evidence that it is precisely in the prophecies of the earlier Isaiah of the eighth century that language is used which clearly affirms that Israel no longer is God's people and that he has indeed rejected her. So it is a distinctive feature of the language of Isaiah, one which has received perhaps insufficient attention from the commentators, that Israel is described as 'this people', in a manner which is designed to show that Yahweh is no longer prepared to speak of it as 'my people' (so Isa. 6.9-10; 8.6, 12; 28.14; 29.13; cf. further 30.9). Isa. 10.6 describes Israel as 'the people with whom I am angry' (literally 'people of my wrath'). Most prominently Isa. 2.6, which commences the admittedly difficult and heavily overworked unit of 2.6-22, asserts:

> For thou hast rejected thy people,
> the house of Jacob (Isa. 2.6).

Can there be any real doubt here, in view of the clear nature of the original language in Isaiah affirming that God has rejected his people, that this highly distinctive aspect in the teaching of Deutero-Isaiah has arisen in conscious awareness that the opposite had earlier been affirmed? The later prophecy is making unmistakably plain that the time of rejection is now past and that a new age is about to dawn in which the closeness of Yahweh's relationship to his people will be especially evident.

That the prophecies of Isa. 40–55 should have arisen in a situation where access to a written collection of the prophetic sayings of Isaiah of Jerusalem was possible should in no way surprise us. Hermann Barth has made out a very good case, which I have elsewhere given written support to, that a carefully edited and compiled edition of Isaiah's prophecies had been prepared during the age of Josiah (639–609 BCE).[18] In this the ending of the time of Assyrian domination over Israel and Judah, which had been central to the historical understanding of Isaiah's prophecies, was affirmed. Yet, it would appear that the view here presented, that particular themes from chs. 40–55 have arisen in conscious development of and response to earlier Isaianic sayings, indicates rather more than a peripheral feature of their origin. It strongly suggests that the concern to carry forward the message of Isaiah of Jerusalem was a significant part of the intention of these chapters from the beginning. All the more is this so in view of their highly distinctive

18. H. Barth, *Die Jesaia-Worte in der Josiazeit* (WMANT, 48; Neukirchen–Vluyn: Neukirchener Verlag, 1977).

lyrical and psalm-like quality. This would appear to represent more than a rather unusual degree of influence from the tradition of cultic psalmody and to belong closely to the way in which these lyrical sayings were designed to counterbalance the more traditional forms of prophecy which are to be found in chs. 1–32. In any case it certainly suggests that chs. 40–55 should no longer be regarded as the self-contained and independent body of material that it has so widely been thought to be in recent years. The 'life and times of Second Isaiah' would appear to be a highly problematic reconstruction on the part of the modern critic!

3. *Other Themes Possibly Developed from Isaiah*

So far we have considered only two fundamental themes where a prominent saying from the tradition of Isaiah's prophecies has occasioned developments of them in chs. 40–55. We now come to consider some other possible themes where this feature is also present. In order to establish the general method of approach it seems important that we should endeavour to keep the more certain examples apart from those which are less clear. In general we should note in regard to 'First Isaiah' the quite extraordinary way in which individual themes based on particular words and verbal images in Isaiah are given later interpretative treatment. So we find that the 'briars and thorns' from Isaiah's Song of the Vineyard (Isa. 5.1-7) is a verbal image which is taken up several times subsequently (the original occurrence in Isa. 5.6, followed by 7.23-25; 9.18; 10.17; 27.4). Other images are similarly dealt with, of which probably the most important is that of the 'Remnant' implicit in the name of Isaiah's child, Shear-jashub (Isa. 7.3; cf. further 10.20-22; 11.11, 16). Yet other verbal imagery is given interpretation in this fashion and it is open to explore whether some of 'Second Isaiah's' language may not display similar characteristics. Here there immediately comes to mind that of Yahweh's 'witnesses' which appears in Isa. 43.10, 12 and 44.8, and most enigmatically so far as its proper significance is concerned, in Isa. 55.4 in a retrospect on the role of David among the nations. We may consider seriously also whether the reference in the 'Isaiah Memoir' regarding the conferring of a sign-name on the prophet's son Maher-shalal-hash-baz has not been an influence here. From a reference to those whose task it was to act as 'reliable witnesses' (Isa. 8.2) to the inscribing of the child's intended name upon a tablet, the idea has developed that the whole of Isaiah's prophecy is a 'witness' to God's action and intentions towards his people. From this has then arisen further the idea that all Israel, which is in possession of this prophetic word of testimony from God, can serve as his witnesses (cf. especially 43.10-13). Such an idea might appear far-fetched and unnecessary were it not for the fact that the concern with 'witnesses' in Isa. 43.9ff. occurs in immediate sequence to the reference to the blind and the deaf in 43.8.

A further possibility also presents itself in that in Isa. 8.16 the child's name, Maher-shalal-hash-baz, is described both as a 'testimony' (*t^e‘ûdâ*) and a 'teaching' (*tôrâ*). In 42.4 and 21 the term *tôrâ* = 'teaching' is used in a very unusual fashion, since it can hardly be intended as a reference to Yahweh's 'law' in the later sense. Rather it appears to refer to Yahweh's 'purpose', which is shortly to be realized and which has been declared beforehand by the prophets. With such a wide-ranging and important term such as *tôrâ* it might seem to be special pleading to suggest that an allusion back to Isa. 8.16 may have been intended. Yet it certainly seems to be the case that, so far as its meaning is concerned, a connection with the earlier prophetic usage serves greatly towards a better understanding of its significance in ch. 42.

We may note some further possibilities. It is in Isa. 44.26 that the message of 'Second Isaiah' takes on a truly prophetic character where it makes a clear pronouncement about God's future action:

> [He it is]
> who confirms the word of his servant,
>   and performs the counsel of his messengers;
> who says of Jerusalem, 'She shall be inhabited',
>   and of the cities of Judah, 'They shall be built,
>   and I will raise up their ruins' (Isa. 44.26).

Such a saying might appear to be wholly explicable from within the historical context which has been reconstructed for the origin of Isa. 40–55. Yet once again a most striking counterbalance is achieved to the central terms of the prophetic commission that was given to Isaiah at his call:

> Then I said 'How long, O Lord?' And he said:
> 'Until cities lie waste without inhabitant,
>   and houses without men,
>   and the land is utterly desolate...' (Isa. 6.11).

The later passage achieves a very clear effect of declaring that the terms of the original prophetic commission given to Isaiah have been fulfilled, so that the time to restore and rebuild can now begin. Once again it is not merely the fact of interesting verbal connections that catches our attention, but that, both in the terms of the original threat and of the subsequent reversal of it, its centrality to the overall message that is being declared is so evident. In this case too we cannot let pass unnoticed that the later prophecy is insisting that God does 'confirm the word of his servant', which may here then refer not simply to the message that is being given but to that which has already been given and is now fulfilled.

One further possible instance may be looked at. In the close redactional structure of Isaiah ch. 5 the pronouncement of how Yahweh intends to carry out his punitive purpose upon his people is declared in a passage which pictures him summoning a hostile army from afar, in which there can be no doubt that a reference to the army of Assyria is intended. This act of divine summoning is to be carried out by Yahweh's raising a 'signal', or 'flag', to them:

> He will raise a signal to a distant nation,
>   and whistle to it at the ends of the earth;
> then behold, swiftly, speedily, it comes! (Isa. 5.26).

This has a very close counterpart in the unit of Isa. 49.22-23 which declares that Yahweh will raise a signal to the nations to send back his scattered people from among them. The very leaders of the nations, their kings and queens, will assist Israel to make their return. We might have considered this imagery of the raising of a signal flag to have been so established a part of contemporary military practice that it could easily have provided a suitable image for two quite independent prophetic speakers to have adopted it. Yet the theme of this 'signal flag' evidently became one of importance to the later, more deeply eschatological development, of the prophetic theme of the great 'return' from the nations. Isa. 11.10 interprets it of the house of David and then 11.12 uses it to designate the time when Yahweh will act to bring about the great return of his people from among the nations. Since these two later developments appear, with near certainty, to be developments based upon the imagery used in 49.22, is it not logical to suggest that, in turn, the usage there has been based upon the original Isaianic saying in 5.26?[19]

It could be argued that, even if all that I have said regarding the conscious allusions back to Isaianic prophecies in chs. 40–55 of the book

19. Childs, *Introduction to the Old Testament*, p. 328.

of Isaiah is conceded, this still does not dislodge the secure position of
the widely adopted hypothesis of an unknown prophet, the so-called
'Second Isaiah', who was active in Babylon during the years between
546 and 538 BCE. This is indeed possible, for it is certainly to be
reckoned with that such a prophet may have been in possession of a
collection of Isaiah's sayings. Yet such a hypothesis would appear to be
less and less likely the more closely the material is investigated. Since the
work of J. Begrich showed the heavy dependence of 'Second Isaiah'
upon the forms and language of psalmody,[20] the distinctive literary
characteristics of this material have been widely remarked upon. The
distinctive form of address to 'Zion', even apparently for those who
were in Babylon, has elicited special comment and attention.[21] Persistently too questions have arisen whether scholarship has been correct in
positing for all of chs. 40–55 an origin in Babylon. The place of origin
would seem to be a question that is not so readily capable of resolution
as may at first appear. In any case my own purpose will have been
achieved if a strong case can be made to show that the evidence that the
prophecies of 'Second Isaiah' reveal a conscious dependence on earlier
sayings of Isaiah of Jerusalem is firm and reliable. This in itself would be
sufficient cause for those who have preserved the material to have
combined the material of chs. 40–55 with the earlier prophecies.[22] In
turn this can be shown very clearly to have had a profound influence
upon the shaping of the book, since a number of themes, as I have
already mentioned, are then taken up still further in its later contents.

A further point deserves mention at this juncture. Since the studies of
G. von Rad, a great deal of attention has been given to the so-called

20. J. Begrich, *Studien zu Deuterojesaja* (BWANT, 4.25; Stuttgart, 1938; repr.,
ed. W. Zimmerli; TBü, 20, Munich: Kaiser Verlag, 1963).

21. Cf. G. Fohrer, 'Zion-Jerusalem im Alten Testament', *Studien zur
alttestamentlichen Theologie und Geschichte (1949–1966)* (BZAW, 115; Berlin: de
Gruyter, 1969), pp. 195-241, esp. pp. 221-22.

22. The issue here appears to me to be a deeper one than simply whether the so-
called Deutero-Isaiah was familiar with, and alluded to, sayings of Isaiah of
Jerusalem. Rather it raises the question whether the existence of the earlier Isaianic
prophecies has not provided the primary stimulus in the shaping of much of the
contents of chs. 45–55. On this point also the attempt of S. Mowinckel and others to
explain the presence of an 'Isaianic connection' in chs. 40ff. on the basis of an
'Isaianic School' must be regarded as weak. Instead of serving to explain the
meaning and intention of the material, it explains only the author's connections with
the tradents of Isaiah's prophecies.

'traditio-historical' method of approach to such a book as that of Isaiah. So, in his interpretation, the presence of elements of the 'Zion' and 'David' traditions in chs. 40–55 can be explained on the prominence of both within the cultic tradition of Jerusalem upon which both Isaiah, and the later 'Second Isaiah', drew.[23] No doubt in the latter case this was at some remove on account of his time of exile in Babylon. Yet what I have been arguing for is essentially of a rather different nature from such an influence from established cultic and political traditions which may be assumed to have had a long and widespread influence in Israel. The distinctive connections that are observable in the formation of the book of Isaiah, where one prophetic saying provides a basis for the development of further sayings related to it, appears as a distinctively prophetic feature. It related to the very nature of prophecy itself. in which particular words and images could be regarded as fraught with special power and significance. So they could be re-applied, re-interpreted and even re-cast altogether, so as to provide further images of God's purposes for his people. In time the more intricate and elaborate consequences of this type of prophetic interpretation gave rise to apocalyptic, which cannot properly be isolated from prophecy itself.

If we are also to press the questions concerning the origin of the material in Isa. 40–55, which has come conventionally to be ascribed to 'Second Isaiah', then it would seem that the case for recognizing the contribution made by cultic personnel, the so-called cult-prophets, from Jerusalem is very strong. This has been argued for by J. Vincent, and it appears to be an increasingly probable deduction to make from so much of the recent research into the origin of these enigmatic chapters.[24] Whether this must imply an actual origin in Jerusalem appears to be less certain, and the possibility of a Babylonian setting, as so widely advocated, may be correct for at least some of the material.

A further consequence also appears to be worthy of further consideration and investigation. If the 16 chapters which have usually been ascribed to 'Second Isaiah' are really the work of one person, then they stand unique within the otherwise intricate web of prophecy and prophetic interpretation which constitute the remainder of the book.

23. G. von Rad, *Old Testament Theology*, II (trans. D.M.G. Stalker; London: SCM Press, 1965), pp. 239-40.

24. J.M. Vincent, *Studien zur literarischen Eigenart und zur geistigen Heimat von Jesaja, Kap. 40–55* (Beiträge zur biblischen Exegese und Theologie, 5; Frankfurt am Main: Peter Lang, 1977).

Nowhere else do we have such a solid and undisturbed block of material left intact. This is not in itself a reason why it should not be the case here. Nevertheless there do appear to be indications that in respect of some material, as in the admonitory rejections of idolatry, later hands have been at work. Overall the formation of the Old Testament books of prophecy has been a remarkably complex sequence of literary and theological developments of ancient written texts. The assumption, which was really never more than an assumption until the end of the eighteenth century, that the unity of these books can be explained as a unity of authorship is clearly mistaken. Yet they do possess a certain kind of unity which belongs to the nature of prophecy itself and the various ways in which it was applied to historical events, which alone could provide its fulfilment, and so, in a real sense, which alone could establish its true meaning.

We might be disposed to describe the processes of unravelling the intertwined threads by which such a book as Isaiah has taken shape as 'redaction criticism'. Yet, if this is to be so, it behoves us to keep in mind that this is concerned with very different kinds of redactional operations from those which pertained to narrative texts, where the combination of smaller units and themes has been undertaken from quite different perspectives from those which belong to prophecy.

JSOT 57 (1993), pp. 81-98

ISAIAH 1.1–2.4 AND 63–66, AND THE COMPOSITION
OF THE ISAIANIC CORPUS

Anthony J. Tomasino

I

In recent years, the 'unity' of the canonical book of Isaiah has once
again become a legitimate object of critical biblical study.[1] Scholars have
well recognized that there are several themes and ideas that may be
found in all three sections of the book of Isaiah, such as the 'Holy One
of Israel', or the 'blindness and deafness' of God's people.[2] Furthermore, many connections have been observed between certain chapters
in one section of the book and the ideas found in other sections.[3] These

---

1.   The current interest in this question is often traced back to B.S. Childs's
Introduction to the Old Testament as Scripture (Philadelphia: Fortress Press, 1979),
as well as the almost simultaneous publication of P.R. Ackroyd, 'Isaiah I–XII:
Presentation of a Prophet', in J.A. Emerton (ed.), *Congress Volume, Göttingen 1977*
(VTSup, 29; Leiden: Brill, 1978), pp. 16-48. But interest in the question could
certainly be traced back much farther, for scholars have long been asking why the
various sections of the canonical Isaiah were brought together in the first place (e.g.
in the proposal of an Isaianic 'school').

2.   Some of these features have long been recognized by scholars who would
use them as a basis for arguing for a single author for the entire book (see, e.g.,
O.T. Allis, *The Unity of Isaiah* [Philadelphia: Presbyterian and Reformed Publishing,
1950]). Critical scholars, however, have been slower to appreciate their significance.
For an excellent treatment of several of these themes, cf. R. Rendtorff, 'Zur
Komposition des Buches Jesaja', *VT* 34 (1984), pp. 295-320; R.E. Clements,
'Beyond Tradition-History: Deutero-Isaianic Development of First Isaiah's Themes',
JSOT 31 (1985), pp. 95-113.

3.   A major example of this kind of connection is Isa. 34–35, which connections
to Deutero-Isaiah have long been recognized (Cf. H. Graetz, 'Isaiah XXXIV and
XXXV', *JQR* 4 [1891], pp. 1-8). More recently, R. Rendtorff has pointed out many

observations have led most scholars to conclude that the canonical book of Isaiah is not the product of thoughtless amalgamation, but rather a carefully crafted work of literature. Yet, there is some difficulty with this assessment. A work of literature is not characterized by thematic unity alone, but by some kind of coherent structure, as well. So far, there has been dubious success in discerning the structure of Isaiah, and little agreement.

This study of Isa. 1.1–2.4 and the last section of Trito-Isaiah (chs. 63–66) is a small step toward piecing together one part of the puzzle of the macro-structure of canonical Isaiah. Several scholars have noted that ch. 1 and chs. 65–66 share too many vocabulary items and themes for it to be a mere coincidence.[4] While the importance of these observations cannot be diminished, they capture only part of the relationship between the opening and closing chapters of Isaiah. My approach differs from these significantly. To begin with, I have defined the first unit of the book of Isaiah not as ch. 1 alone, but as 1.1–2.4, adopting Fohrer's observations on the structure of the unit.[5] I have also defined the final section of Trito-Isaiah differently: not as chs. 65–66, but as 63.7–66.24.[6]

connections between Isa. 6 and Isa. 40 ('Jesaja 6 im Rahmen der Komposition des Jesajabuches', in J. Vermeylen [ed.], *The Book of Isaiah—Le Livre d'Isaïe* [BETL, 81; Leuven: Leuven University Press, 1989], pp. 73-83).

4.   The corresponding vocabulary items are listed by L.J. Liebreich, 'The Composition of the Book of Isaiah', *JQR* 46 (1955–56), pp. 259-77, and *JQR* 47 (1956–57), pp. 114-38. While Liebreich's list is impressive, it is not entirely persuasive as a case for literary dependence. A study of the distribution of the vocabulary of ch. 1 in the book of Isaiah shows that nearly the same amount of overlap can be shown for other chapters of Isaiah as well (e.g. chs. 43–44, 59, and even ch. 53). R. Lack goes further than Liebreich, noting also the thematic parallels between the chapters (*La symbolique du livre d'Isaïe* [AnBib, 59; Rome: Biblical Institute Press, 1973], pp. 139-41). M.A. Sweeney (*Isaiah 1–4 and the Post-Exilic Understanding of the Isaiah Tradition* [BZAW, 171; Berlin: de Gruyter, 1988], pp. 21-24) builds on Lack's observations and strengthens them considerably, particularly by bringing compositional considerations to bear on the issue.

5.   G. Fohrer, 'Jesaja 1 als Zusammenfassung der Verkündigung Jesajas', *ZAW* 74 (1962), pp. 251-68. The insertion of a second 'introduction' at 2.1 plays an important part in shaping the final form of Trito-Isaiah, as will be seen later in this article.

6.   This delimitation is similar to that made by O.H. Steck, 'Tritojesaja im Jesajabuch', in Vermeylen (ed.), *The Book of Isaiah*, pp. 361-406. The problem lies in what we are to do with 63.1-6, which is difficult to place with either 63–66 or with 60–62. For a recent discussion of this question (as well as many other questions on the redaction of Trito-Isaiah not treated in this paper), cf. S. Sekine, *Die*

Most significant of all, however, the main focus of this article is not on vocabulary, or even on themes alone, but rather on the structure of the passages. As will be seen, the final chapters of Trito-Isaiah have drawn not only their content from Isaiah 1.2–2.4, but their form as well.[7]

II

There seem to be two factors at work in the relationship between Isaiah 1.2–2.4 and the final group of oracles in Trito-Isaiah. First is the parallelism between 1.2–2.4 and 63.7–66.24.[8] In these two sections, similar themes are presented in the same order, using much of the same vocabulary. Secondly, there is a more specific similarity between the structure of Isa. 1.2-31 and that of Isa. 66.1-24, based on the occurence of the same vocabulary items at the beginning and end of each chapter, as well as some other features. As I proceed through my analysis of the thematic units of 1.2–2.4,[9] it will become apparent how both of these factors have shaped chs. 63–66 in different and even competing ways.

First Unit: 1.1-9

The first verse of Isaiah is the formulaic introduction of the prophet. While it may be of interest to speculate on how much of the canonical book of Isaiah this verse was designed to introduce, it is of little relevance at this place in my study.[10] My interest begins with v. 2, the actual

Tritojesajanische Sammlung (Jes. 56–66) redaktionsgeschichtliche untersucht (Berlin: de Gruyter, 1989), pp. 140-47.

7. A similar claim was made by J. Vermeylen for Trito-Isaiah as a whole, arguing that Isa. 1 served as a pattern for Isa. 56–66 (*Du prophète Isaïe à l'apocalyptique*, II [Paris: Gabalda, 1978], pp. 504-11). For Vermeylen, 63.7–66.24 is an appendix, which does not follow the pattern of Isa. 1.

8. Actually, 66.24 departs significantly from the pattern of 1.2–2.4, and represents an addition to the section. I will explain the function of the verse, and how it came to be in its current position, later in this article.

9. By 'unit', I do not mean the originally separate oracles that have been combined in order to form Isa. 1.2–2.4. Rather, my interest is in the thematic units of the passage, which may themselves consist of smaller independent units of only a few verses or so. For a more detailed discussion of the compositional units of Isa. 1, cf. Fohrer, 'Jesaja 1', or Sweeney, *Isaiah 1–4*, pp. 101-33.

10. The question is addressed by Sweeney (*Isaiah 1–4*, pp. 28-32), whose argument that the verse introduces the book as a whole is persuasive. It does not prevent us from asking, however, what the author of the book thought of as the 'book as a whole'. This question is obviously linked to the issue of when ch. 1 was produced, which will be dealt with later in the paper.

oracle. The oracle starts off in the form of a *rîb*, a charge presented by
YHWH against his people.[11] Verse 2 calls the witnesses and sums up the
basis for the dispute.

The witnesses in YHWH's lawsuit are the heavens and the earth. This
phrase, of course, functions as a merismus, calling everything in creation
to heed YHWH's words. But after the summons, the passage quickly
turns from these witnesses, and begins to address Israel directly. The
merismus does not reappear in Proto-Isaiah. It is used in Deutero-Isaiah
(49.13; 51.6), but these occurrences have no obvious connection to its
usage in 1.2. In Trito-Isaiah, the word pair appears three times. Both
65.17 and 66.22 refer to 'new heavens and a new earth' that YHWH
will create, symbolic of a totally new state of affairs about to be
initiated.[12] The other occurrence of the merismus, in 66.1, is completely
unrelated to these: 'Heaven is my throne, and the earth is my footstool.
What kind of house, then, would you build for me?' In this case, the
merismus is invoked to illustrate YHWH's immensity—the fact that he
fills all things.

From this survey, it would appear that the various occurrences of the
'heaven and earth' merismus are largely unrelated to one another. One
might see some significance in the fact that 1.2 personifies the pair,
which could lead to the mistaken impression that the heaven and earth
are some kind of deities, while 66.1 minimizes their status considerably,
precluding any misinterpretation of 1.2. But in this particular case, the
meaning of the merismus in these passages is not as significant as its
position. It is important to note that the same word pair appears at the
beginning of the first oracle of the book, in 1.2, and the beginning of the
last oracle, in 66.1. The use of this merismus constitutes the first
parallelism between 1.2-31 and 66.1-24.

With the next line of the verse, the thematic parallelism between 1.2–
2.4 and 63.7–66.24 begins, 'Sons I have reared and brought up, but
they have rebelled (פשעו) against me.' Here, YHWH presents himself as
an aggrieved father, disowned by his wicked children. This 'father–son
metaphor' appears in v. 4, as well: 'Evil offspring, corrupt sons!' But the
metaphor is soon dropped, and YHWH is not presented as Israel's father

---

11. Cf. K. Nielsen, 'Das Bild des Gerichts (Rib-Pattern) in Jes. I–XII', *VT* 29
(1979), pp. 309-24.

12. This is one of the many 'incidental' vocabulary overlaps between ch. 1 and
chs. 65–66. While it does strengthen the perception of literary dependence, such
vocabulary overlap alone does not make a case for inclusio. Cf. n. 2 above.

again until Isa. 45.9-11. Even here, however, the theme is only touched upon. It is not until Isaiah 63 that the metaphor is 'fleshed out'.

There is a clear break in the flow of Trito-Isaiah at 63.7. After Trito-Isaiah's many promises of restoration and glory, the narrative breaks into a lengthy prayer for divine intervention, stretching from 63.7 to 64.11. The basis for this appeal is the relationship between YHWH and his people. The 'father–son metaphor' appears at once, in 63.8. The verse reads, 'For he said, "Surely, they are my people; sons who would not be false". So he became their savior.' The passage goes on to recount how the people rebelled and caused YHWH to turn against them (63.10).[13] But the speaker prays for forgiveness and divine intervention on the people's behalf. He appeals to the family imagery: 'You are our father, even though Abraham does not know us, and Israel does not recognize us. You, YHWH, are our father; our redeemer from eternity is your name' (63.16).[14]

As the prayer continues, further connections between Isa. 1.2-9 and Isa. 63.7–64.11 become apparent. Some of these are almost incidental; for instance, in 1.3, Israel is compared to livestock in an unfavorable manner: domesticated oxen and donkeys know their master, but Israel does not. Isaiah 63.13-14 makes a similar comparison, with Israel likened to a horse and to cattle that YHWH had led to a resting place. Other parallels between the passages are more explicit and significant. Isa. 1.4 describes the nation as 'sinful' (חוטא), and laments that the people are laden with iniquity (עון). In 64.4, as well, the speaker confesses that the people have sinned (נחטא), and their iniquity (עון) is acknowledged in 64.6-7, but the passage pleads with YHWH not to remember the iniquity forever (64.9). In 1.7, the results of Israel's sin are graphically depicted:

> Your land is a desolation (שממה), your cities burned with fire.
> Strangers are devouring your farmland before you,
> And it is a desolation, as if overthrown by strangers.

In 64.9-10, the state of the land is described in very similar terms:

> Your holy cities have become a wilderness; Zion has become a wilderness; Jerusalem is a desolation (שממה).

---

13. The verb used here is מרד; cf. 1.20, which uses the same term.

14. One might even see a 'pun' on 1.2 in this verse: 'Abraham does not know us; Israel does not recognize us' (63.16). 'Israel does not know; my people do not understand' (1.2).

> Our holy and beautiful house, where our fathers praised you, has been
> burned with fire.

Thus, Isa. 1.2-9 and 63–64 describe the same situation: they presuppose
that YHWH is the people's father; but the people have become sinful,
and therefore the land has been devastated. The difference between the
passages lies in purpose. Isa. 1.2-9 is addressed to the people, essentially
as a call for repentance, while Isaiah 63–64 is a prayer for mercy. It does
not deny that the punishment is well-deserved, but it pleads with YHWH
to put away his anger and take action against those who defile his
sanctuary.[15]

Before we leave this unit, there is yet another feature of 1.2 which is
worth noting: its use of the term 'rebelled' (פָּשְׁעוּ). This word appears
twice in Isaiah 1, first in 1.2 and again in 1.28. It is also used in 66.24,
the last verse of the book: 'They will go out and look on the corpses of
those who rebelled (פֹּשְׁעִים) against me...' The appearance of the same
term in the first full verse and the last verse of the Book of Isaiah is
irrelevant to the question of the parallelism between 1.2–2.4 and 63–64,
but it does accomplish the very important end of giving the book a
sense of closure. The rebels of the first verse of the book are dealt with
once and for all in its final verse.

Second Unit: 1.10-20[16]
The next section, Isa. 1.10-17, contains a polemic against cultic
observances without righteous behavior:

> What is the number of your sacrifices to me?, says YHWH.
> I am sated with burnt offerings of rams, and the fat of fatlings.
> And I take no delight in the blood of bulls, lambs, and goats.
> When you come to see my face,
> Who has sought this from you—trampling of my courts?
> Do not continue to bring worthless *minḥâ*.
> Your incense is an abomination to me (vv. 11-13).

The passage goes on to condemn solemn assemblies and prayers,
because the people continue to practice sin (vv. 13b, 15). It ends with a
call for repentance and purification (vv. 16-20). This is certainly not the
only place in the Hebrew Bible that one could find such a polemic (cf.

---

15. The prayer seems to assume that the people's rebelliousness is somehow
God's doing (63.17)—thus probably presupposing Isa. 6.

16. The unit is clearly defined by its opening and closing phrases: 'Hear the word
of YHWH' at the beginning, and 'Surely, the mouth of YHWH has spoken' at the end.

Jer. 6.20). But in the entire corpus of Isaiah, only one other such condemnation of the cult may be found. Isa. 66.1-6 begins with a passage that questions the importance of the temple, stressing instead humility and respect for YHWH's word. It goes on to say,

> He who kills an ox is as one who smites a man;
> One who sacrifices a lamb is as one who breaks a dog's neck;
> One offering up a *minḥâ* like one who offers swine's blood;
> The one offering a memorial of incense like one who blesses an idol (66.3).

This oracle actually surpasses that in ch. 1. For 1.11-12, sacrifice was unnecessary, a mere 'trampling of the courts'. YHWH had grown tired of it. In 66.3, this condemnation is strengthened, and sacrificial rites, performed by unrighteous individuals, are actually identified as sinful.

These parallel condemnations of the cultus are the clearest indication of the relationship between 1.2–2.4 and 63.7–66.24. No other portions of Isaiah express these sentiments. In fact, Isa. 43.22-24 criticizes Israel because they have failed to bring sufficient sacrifices and offerings. Thus, the presence of these indictments in the first and last sections of Isaiah serves as further evidence for the relationship between the oracles.

In Isaiah 1, this polemic is followed by an appeal for repentance (vv. 16-20). YHWH invites his people to set things right, and promises blessings for those who repent: 'If you consent and listen (root שמע), you will eat the good of the land.' Yet, the verse ends with a threat: 'If you refuse and rebel, you will be eaten by the sword. Surely, the mouth of YHWH has spoken (root דבר).' In Isaiah 66, the polemic against cultic practice is followed by a promise of judgment, because the people have failed to heed YHWH's call: 'Because I called, and no one answered; I spoke (root דבר), and no one listened (root שמע)' (66.4). It then gives a somewhat cryptic promise to those who 'tremble' at the word YHWH (66.5). The final verse of the section (66.6) anticipates the judgment about to come upon the enemies of YHWH. It may be a bit adventurous to try to identify YHWH's unanswered 'call' in 66.4 with the call for repentance in 1.16-20, but there is an undeniable similarity between the structure of 1.10-20 and that of 66.1-6:

1.10-20		*66.1-6*	
10-14	Condemnation of cult	1-3a	Condemnation of cult
16-18	Call for repentance	3b-4	Judgment of unrepentant
19	Blessings for obedience	5	Comfort for obedient
20	Promise of judgment	6	Anticipation of judgment

This suggestion may stretch the credulity of some readers of this article, but the many significant parallels between the structure of 1.1–2.4 and that of 63.7–66.24 make it reasonable to consider the possibility that 1.10-20 and 66.1-6 have been composed according to the same pattern—particularly so in light of the very significant parallel that follows this section.

Third Unit: 1.21-26

In 1.21-26, we have the first occurrence in Isaiah of a very important metaphor: Zion is personified as a woman. The same personification appears in 66.7-13, with quite a different significance. In the structure of both passages, however, the metaphor occurs in the same place: the polemic against the cultus is followed by a threat of judgment, then the Zion metaphor. Such a parallelism could hardly be accidental. But the correspondence may not be immediately apparent, because of the very different form of the personification in the two passages—a harlot in ch. 1, and a mother giving birth in ch. 66. In order to understand the relationship between these two images of Zion, we must trace the metaphor through the entire book of Isaiah.

In Isa. 1.21, Zion is compared to a wayward wife: 'How she has become a harlot (זוֹנָה), the once-faithful city!' The passage then proceeds to talk about the sorry state of the city, and how YHWH will purge it of evil. Not until v. 26 does the metaphor resurface: 'Afterwards you shall be called "The Righteous City", "Faithful City".' The personification does not reappear in Proto-Isaiah. In fact, it is not until Isaiah 49 that the image is taken up again. In 49.14 we read, 'But Zion said, "YHWH has abandoned me; the Lord has forgotten me".' This passage then assures Zion that she has not been forgotten. Indeed, she is promised a glorious future. The personification is developed further in vv. 20-21:

> Once again the children of whom you were bereaved will say in your
>   hearing,
> 'This place is too cramped for me; give me more room so I may live in it.'
> Then you will say to yourself, 'Who has borne these to me, since I am
>   bereaved, and barren, and an exile and wanderer?
> And who has raised these? See, I was left alone; where did these come
>   from?'

The reason that Zion was so abandoned is found in 50.1:

> Thus says YHWH:
> Where is your mother's divorce certificate, whereby I sent her away?
> Or to whom among my creditors did I sell you?

> See, you were sold on account of your iniquity (עָוֹן), and because of your
> rebellion (פֶּשַׁע) your mother was sent away.

These verses may link the personification of chs. 49–50 with that of
ch. 1. Zion bemoans her abandoment, but the reason for this abandonment is the rebellion (cf. 1.2, 28) and inquity (cf. 1.4) of her inhabitants.
Clearly, the sin of Zion's inhabitants constitutes the city's harlotry in ch.
1, as well. In ch. 49, the results of the harlotry are made manifest in
terms of the personification: like a wayward wife, Zion is abandoned by
YHWH.

But this is not to be the end of the matter. In 54.1-8, Zion is promised
that she will bear many children, even though she has not travailed
(v. 1). Her husband, YHWH, had put her away in his anger (v. 7), but he
promises to have compassion on her again (v. 8). Trito-Isaiah, too, takes
up this idea, in 62.1-5. Once again, Zion is assured of YHWH's favour, in
spite of her present abandonment. Verses 4-5 promise,

> No longer will it be said of you, 'Abandoned',
> Or of your land, 'Desolation (שְׁמָמָה)',
> For you will be called, 'My Delight is in Her',
> And your land, 'Married';
> For YHWH delights in you,
> And your land will be married.
> For as a young man marries a virgin,
> So will your sons marry you.
> And as the bridegroom exults over the bride,
> So your God will delight in you.

The woman Zion, once a faithful wife, became a harlot. Because of her
harlotry, she was put away by her husband (YHWH) and bereaved of
children. But YHWH had not abandoned her entirely. In spite of her
previous harlotry, he promises to take her back, as a man takes a virgin
bride. This process comes to its climax in Isa. 66.7-13. Now, the newly-
married Zion is with child, bearing sons to replace those whom she had
lost:

> Before she goes into labour, she gives birth;
> Before the travail comes upon her, she brings forth a male.
> Who has heard such a thing? Who has seen such things?
> Can a land give birth in one day? Can a nation come forth at one time?
> Yet as soon as Zion goes into labour, she brings forth her sons (66.7-13).

Thus we may see the correlation between the metaphor in Isaiah 1 and
that in Isaiah 66. In the case of this metaphor it is necessary to read the

book of Isaiah as a whole, if we are to understand its significance. Only when we trace the metaphor through the entire corpus can the parallelism between its usage in these chapters be appreciated.

Fourth Unit: 1.27-31

Following the personification, both the first and last sections of Isaiah have a passage of mixed blessing and cursing (1.27-31; 66.14-17). The redemption of Zion is to be a two-part process, wherein the righteous are saved, but the wicked are destroyed:

> Zion will be redeemed with justice,
> And those returning with righteousness;
> But rebels (פשעים) and sinners will be shattered as one,
> And those who abandon YHWH will be destroyed completely (1.27-28).

A similar statement is found in 66.14. The verse acts as a hinge between promises of blessing for Zion, and threats of judgment for YHWH's enemies:

> You will see it, and your heart will exult,
> You will flourish like the grass.
> The power of YHWH will be made known to his servants,
> And he will act indignantly toward his enemies (66.14).

It is noteworthy that in both of these sections one particular group is singled out as deserving of punishment:

> For you (MT: 'they') will be put to shame on account of the oaks you have desired,
> And you will be abashed on account of the gardens (גנות) you have chosen (1.29).
> Those who sanctify themselves and purify themselves for gardens (גנות),
> going after one in its midst (66.17).

The end of these evildoers is spelled out quite explicitly. In Isa. 1.31, their end will be fire:

> The strong man will be tinder, and his deeds a spark.
> Both shall be consumed together;
> There shall be none to quench (מכבה).

Isa. 66.16 also believes that fire will be the tool of judgment, but it adds yet another:

> For with fire YHWH executes judgment,
> And with his sword against all flesh.
> Many will be slain by YHWH.

This verse may well combine both of the punishments mentioned in Isaiah 1, for in 1.20, the call for repentance, there is a threat that those who continue in apostasy will be devoured by the sword. In any case, the two passages, 1.27-31 and 66.14-17, end with very similar words: Isa. 1.31 says, 'Both shall be consumed together', while 66.17 says, 'They shall come to an end together.'

In 1.31, we can also observe evidence of the attempt to impose a similar structure on 1.2-31 and 66.1-24. The root כבה ('quench'), which appears in the last verse of ch. 1, also appears in the last verse of ch. 66:

> And they will go out and look on the corpses of those who rebelled
> against me,
> For their worm shall not die,
> Nor shall their fire be quenched (תכבה)
> And they shall be an abhorrence to all flesh (66.24).

Thus, ch. 1 and ch. 66 not only begin with the same word pair ('heaven and earth'), but they also end on the same note, even employing the same verb to describe the punishment of the evil-doers.

The 'misplacement' of these verbal parallels in chs. 1 and 66 reveals that the two aspects of the structural parallelism between the sections (the thematic parallelism between 1.2–2.4 and 63.7–66.24, and the verbal parallelism between chs. 1 and 66) are not compatible. The first unit of Isaiah 1 does not correspond thematically with the first verse of ch. 66, but with 63.7–64.11. Thus, the 'heaven and earth' merismus should have been found at 63.7. Likewise, the use of the root כבה should have been found in 66.17, not 66.24. Both of these verbal parallels, then, are 'out of place' in terms of the thematic correspondence of 1.2–2.4 with 63.7–66.24. Thus, we find a tension between a tendency to follow the thematic development in 1.2–2.4, and the tendency to establish verbal parallels between the first and last chapters of Isaiah. I will give this problem further attention below.

Fifth Unit: 2.2-4

Following the promise of judgment in 1.27-31, 2.2-4 brings a promise of universal salvation, in which all the nations of the world shall make their way to the mountain of YHWH in Jerusalem, in order to learn the word of YHWH.[17] The author of Isaiah 63–66 was not unaware of the fact

---

17. This unit was identified as part of the first section of Proto-Isaiah by Fohrer, 'Jesaja 1'. P.R. Ackroyd ('A Note on Isaiah 2, 1', *ZAW* 75 [1963], pp. 320-21) has

that this promise seems to be a part of the first section of Proto-Isaiah. After the prophecy of judgment in 66.14-17, vv. 18-23 predict a glorious future for Zion, where all the nations of the world shall come to YHWH's holy mountain in order to see his glory. Yet, in ch. 66, the emphasis is somewhat different from that in ch. 2. Ch. 2 is more universalistic in tone—the nations come for their own sake, in order to learn of YHWH. In 66.18-23, the nations gather primarily for Israel's sake, in order to bring back her exiles to Jerusalem (perhaps revealing the different *Sitz im Leben* of ch. 66). But even so, the final verses of ch. 66 are not without universalistic implications. The primary thrust of vv. 18-19 is the gathering of the nations in order that they might behold the glory of YHWH—just as in 2.2-4.

Summary

As stated at the beginning of this section, there are two considerations at work in the parallel constructions of Isaiah 1.1–2.4 and 63–66. First, there are parallels between the broader thematic units. Isaiah 1.2–2.4 and 63.7–66.24 (or, better, v. 23) both treat the same themes in the same order, using much the same vocabulary. The only departure from this pattern, as the reader may have noticed, is ch. 65. The role of this chapter in the unit will be addressed in Section III of this paper. The other factor is the verbal and structural parallelism between 1.2-31 and 66.1-24. This is particularly obvious in the addition of 66.24, an oracle of judgment appended to a promise of a glorious future for Zion. The verse seems quite out of place in its present setting, but it accomplishes two important ends: (1) it establishes a sense of closure for the book of Isaiah as a whole, by vividly depicting the fate of the 'rebels' (פשעים) of the opening line of the book (1.2) in the closing line of the book (66.24); and (2) it draws a verbal parallelism between the last verse of ch. 1 and the last verse of ch. 66, just as the 'heaven and earth' merismus draws a parallel between the first verses of each chapter.

The following diagram summarizes these parallels:

expanded on this idea, explaining the introduction at 2.1 as an intrusion, designed to alert the reader that the following oracle (which also appears in the book of Micah) originated with the prophet Isaiah.

Theme	1.2–2.4	63.7–66.24
Heaven and Earth Merismus	*1.2*	*66.1*
'Sons' metaphor; Judah devastated	1.2-9	63.7–64.11
Anti-cultic polemic	1.10-20	66.1-6
Personification of Zion	1.21-26	66.7-13
Redemption/Judgment of Zion	1.27-31	66.14-17
Gathering the Nations to Zion	2.2-4	66.18-24
Wicked consumed by unquenchable fire	*1.31*	*66.24*

There are yet other parallels between Isaiah 1 and the final chapters of Trito-Isaiah that could be mentioned;[18] but these, while strengthening the case for a connnection between the two sections, add little to my observations concerning the structure of the passages. In the next section of this article, therefore, I will explore some possible ways that the structural similarities of Isaiah 1 and Isaiah 63–66 might be explained.

III

Accepting that the structural parallels that we have observed are real and are not mere accidents, there are basically three ways in which we might account for them:

1. Isaiah 1 has been composed with Isaiah 63–66 in mind.[19]
2. Isaiah 63–66 has been composed with Isaiah 1 in mind.
3. Both Isaiah 1 and Isaiah 63–66 have been composed in the same mind (i.e. by a single author).

There may be no way that we can determine with certainty which of these processes actually occurred, if any. But we can, on the basis of connections between these passages and others in Proto-, Deutero-, and Trito-Isaiah, form a workable hypothesis.

The first scenario suggested above would require that Isaiah 1 had been composed in some sense separately from Proto-Isaiah as a whole (unless we regard all of Proto-Isaiah as later than Trito-Isaiah). If such

18. E.g. the use of the term בחר in 1.29 and 66.3-4, or the parallelism between 1.30, 'You shall become like a tree whose leaves whither', and 64.6, 'All of us are withered like a leaf.' Cf. the studies under n. 4 above for further examples.

19. This hypothesis, which might sound outlandish at first, actually accords well with the idea that Isa. 1 was composed to serve as an introduction to the entire book of Isaiah, rather than Proto-Isaiah, or even Isa. 1–12. Thus J. Becker, *Isaias—Der Prophet und sein Buch* (SBS, 30; Stuttgart: Katholisches Bibelwerk, 1968), pp. 45-47.

were the case, we would not expect to find many connections between
Isaiah 1 and the rest of Proto-Isaiah. But there are actually many such
connections, for example:

1. Isaiah 1.2 and 30.1, 9 both refer to 'rebellious sons'. Even though ch. 30 is
    referring to 'sons of Jacob' rather than 'sons of YHWH', the verbal connec-
    tions between the chapters are obvious.
2. The reference to a vineyard in 1.8 seems to be related to the vineyard song of
    5.1-6.
3. The idea of the remnant in 1.9 is taken up in 4.2.
4. The allusions to Sodom in 1.9-10 reappear in 3.9.
5. The reference to blood in 1.15, and the call to 'wash yourselves' in 1.16, are
    both taken up in a new context in 4.4.

Several other possible connections could also be observed. These are
sufficient, however, to indicate that Isaiah 1 was not composed separately from the rest of Proto-Isaiah, and then transported to its present
position. If it was composed apart from the rest of Proto-Isaiah, it was
done so by an author with a full knowledge of Proto-Isaiah, and with a
clever hand at weaving together themes and emphases from two
different parts of Isaiah into a single chapter.

There are also connections, however, between Isaiah 1 and Deutero-
Isaiah. Such catchwords as צדק, עון, קדוש ישראל, and particularly the
treatment of Zion/Jerusalem, demonstrate that Isaiah 1 and Deutero-
Isaiah derive somehow from the same tradition.[20] But there are some
central themes in Deutero-Isaiah that do not appear at all in Isaiah 1: the
polemic against idolatry, for example, or divine sovereignty and fore-
knowledge, or the extremely important 'comfort' (נחם) theme. These
facts make it appear unlikely that Isaiah 1 was composed by an author
who possessed a verbal knowledge of the work of Deutero-Isaiah.

Our next area of inquiry should be the literary affinities of Isaiah 63–
66. Do these chapters stand in the tradition of Trito-Isaiah? This is a
more difficult question, considering that many scholars have questioned
the very existence of Trito-Isaiah as a separate composition.[21] But there
does seem to be some continuity between 63–66 and the rest of those
chapters termed Trito-Isaiah (56–66). For instance, there is the centrality
of Zion/Jerusalem theme, with a particular interest in cultic affairs

20. Cf. Rendtorff, 'Zur Komposition'.
21. E.g. Steck, 'Tritojesaja im Jesajabuch'. A detailed linguistic study of Trito-
Isaiah vis-à-vis Deutero-Isaiah may be found in A. Murtonen, 'Third Isaiah: Yes or
No?', *AbrN* 19 (1980–81), pp. 20-42. His answer is 'no'.

evident in 66.1-6 and 21, as in 56.3-7.[22] The description of the return in 66.18-20 is quite reminiscent of that in 60.4-9. Also, the idea that the nations will see the glory of YHWH, which appears in 62.2, reappears in 66.19. Finally, there is Zion's bringing of sons to birth in 66.7-9, which seems to be connected to 62.1-5. Yet, the much more obvious connection for 66.7-9 is 54.1-8—not Trito-Isaiah, but Deutero-Isaiah.

This last example underlines the major problem with Trito-Isaiah— sorting it out from Deutero-Isaiah. But, besides the passage just mentioned, there is yet another in Isaiah 66 which clearly has affinities with Deutero-Isaiah: 'As one whom his mother comforts, so will I comfort you, and you shall be comforted in Jerusalem' (66.13). The 'comfort' theme is a hallmark of Deutero-Isaiah. Its presence here in Isaiah 66 is strong evidence that the author of Isaiah 66 had a knowledge of Deutero-Isaiah. The 'creation' theme, too, in Isa. 65.17-25 and 66.22, is quite reminiscent of Isa. 40.25-28, 45.18, and other Deutero-Isaianic passages.

In the light of these various links between the sections of the book, we may draw the following inferences. First, there is no reason to suppose that the composer of Isaiah 1 had any knowledge of Deutero-Isaiah. This makes it difficult to believe that this chapter was composed after the rest of the book, as an introduction to the book as a whole, or that it was composed by the author of chs. 63–66. Second, the author of Isaiah 63–66 knew Isaiah 1 and Deutero-Isaiah. Given these data, a reasonable explanation for the structural parallelism between 1.2–2.4 and 63.7–66.24 would be that the final chapters of Isaiah were composed based on the pattern of the first oracle of Proto-Isaiah, as it was received by their author. Indeed, Isaiah 1 may have been the first chapter in an early Proto-Isaianic collection, just as scholars have suspected for many years. When Trito-Isaiah, or whoever authored these last chapters, brought together the book of Isaiah, he or she wanted to give the collection a sense of unity and closure. This was best achieved by thematically and structurally linking the first and last oracles of the book.

While this hypothesis explains the structural parallelism between the first and last oracles of the canonical book of Isaiah, there are two phenomena for which it does not account: (1) the insertion of ch. 65 in

---

22. However, one may well argue that chs. 56 and 66 express very different opinions on the importance of the cult. In 66.1-6, the cult does not seem to be held in much regard; but this must be balanced against 66.20-21, which seems to express a more moderate opinion.

the section, which clearly breaks up the thematic parallelism between 1.2–2.4 and 63.7–66.24, and (2) the structural similarity between chs. 1 and 66 (i.e. the 'heaven and earth' merismus at the beginning, and the use of the root כבד at the end). There may be several ways to account for these features of the text,[23] but my suspicion is that there was a 'double redaction' of the last chapters of Trito-Isaiah. The original composition (i.e. the redaction based on ch. 1) may not have contained ch. 65 at all. Rather, it probably moved from 64.11 to 66.1 like this:

> Our holy and beautiful house, where our fathers praised you, has been
>   burned with fire...
> Will you restrain yourself at these things, YHWH?
> Will you remain silent, and afflict us heavily? (64.11-12).

> Thus says YHWH:
> Heaven is my throne, and the earth is my footstool.
> What kind of house would you build for me?
> And in what kind of place would I rest? (66.1)

The principal concern of the passage at this point was the restoration of the temple and the cult. The author, while perhaps not actually opposed to the cult, wished to de-emphasize the temple and its rituals, stressing instead righteousness and humility.

Isaiah 65, along with 66.22-24, was added to the text by the second redactor. By this time, the temple may already have been reconstructed, and the anti-cultic polemic may have rung a bit hollow. Ch. 65 was designed to expand the focus of the final oracle of the book of Isaiah from a primarily cultic interest to a more general concern for the restoration of Israel. It has a great deal of verbal similarity to ch. 1, as other scholars have noted; but it draws much material from elsewhere as well, even quoting verbatim from 11.6. Thus, the parallels between Isaiah 1 and Isaiah 65 may not have been intentional. Rather, its similarities to ch. 1 could derive from its connections with ch. 66.

The verbal similarities between 1.2, 31 and 66.1, 24 also derive from the work of the second redactor. Apparently, by this author's day, the secondary introduction had already been inserted at Isa. 2.1 (or perhaps the author made the insertion him- or herself). This addition practically redefined the first section of Isaiah, and allowed the second redactor to view ch. 1 as a self-contained unit. Since ch. 1 ended on a note of

---

23. E.g. the author of chs. 63–66 may have broken from the pattern of ch. 1 as an 'emphatic' device, in order to draw even more attention to ch. 66.

judgment, Isaiah 66 had to end on a similar note in order to maintain the parallelism between the first and last sections of the book. This explains the addition of 66.24, which is quite out of place in the flow of the section. Verse 22 also was a product of this second redaction, composed to link ch. 66 to the newly-created ch. 65. Verse 23, on the other hand, may have already existed as the original conclusion for the final section of Isaiah.

IV

In conclusion, a few general remarks about the composition of the book of Isaiah seem to be in order. In the course of this study, two long-recognized features of the Isaianic corpus have been reaffirmed: the dependence of Trito-Isaiah on Deutero-Isaiah, and the relative independence of at least certain sections of Proto-Isaiah. While there can be no denying that many connections exist between Isaiah 1 and the rest of the book of Isaiah, there are not enough explicit connections with the later material to establish a case for the late composition of ch. 1. Rather, it is likely that Isaiah 1.1–2.4 existed as a unit before either Deutero- or Trito-Isaiah came into being.

It is difficult to say much more about the shape of Proto-Isaiah, if such a book ever existed. Sections such as ch. 12 and chs. 13–14 so strongly echo the language of Deutero-Isaiah that it is reasonable to suppose that they were created much later than some other Proto-Isaianic material. Given this fact, it is likely that Proto-Isaiah attained its final form after the composition of Deutero-Isaiah—perhaps by the same hand that was responsible for Trito-Isaiah.[24] Yet, it is not impossible to suppose that Proto-Isaiah was not the product of composition so much as evolution. Proto-Isaiah may have come together like some celestial body, attracting a few chapters here, a few verses there, until the process was brought to an end by the authoritative hand of the final redactor. If such was the case, we would be quite brash to think that we might be able to unravel the process with any degree of certainty.

24. Thus Rendtorff, 'Zur Komposition'.

JSOT 57 (1993), pp. 61-80

REACHING FOR UNITY IN ISAIAH

David Carr

This article is not just about the book of Isaiah.[1] It is also about the increasing tendency in biblical studies to search for some kind of 'literary' or 'canonical' coherence in the final form of biblical texts. In recent years, studies of the book of Isaiah have been deeply influenced by the trend in biblical studies to emphasize treatment of the final forms of biblical texts as 'unities'.[2] Whereas previous generations of historical

---

1.   An earlier version of this article was read and discussed in the 'Formation of the Book of Isaiah' Consultation of the 1990 Annual SBL meeting in New Orleans. This study benefited substantially from the input by the participants in that consultation. In addition, I want to recognize the gracious assistance I received from the following individuals who read and responded to earlier drafts of this essay: M.A. Sweeney, R. Melugin, G. Stansell and R. Tannehill. I thank all for their help, and bear full responsibility for this final product.

2.   For a bibliography of literary studies see M.A. Powell, *The Bible and Modern Literary Criticism: A Critical Assessment and Annotated Bibliography* (Bibliographies and Indexes in Religious Studies, 22; New York: Greenwood, 1992). The continuing preoccupation of many of these studies with establishing the unity of biblical texts draws on literary theories that were prevelant decades ago (especially 'New' Literary Criticism and Structuralism). The resulting constellation of emphases and methods is somewhat distinctive vis-à-vis contemporary literary theory. On this see in particular S.D. Moore's excellent discussion of the background of similar forces in 'literary' studies of the New Testament Gospels: 'Are the Gospels Unified Narratives?', SBLSP 26 (1987), pp. 443-58.

Similarly, the claim of many studies for some kind of special 'canonical' status for approaches that focus on the shape of entire books is hardly borne up by the evidence of preceding centuries of pre-critical canonical interpretations. Although some pre-critical interpretations reconstrued diverse biblical materials into a non-textual typological historical framework (H. Frei, *The Eclipse of Biblical Narrative: A Study in Eighteenth and Nineteenth Century Hermeneutics* [New Haven: Yale

critics tended to emphasize the distinctions between 'first', 'second' and 'third' Isaiah, scholars have begun to recognize the benefits of starting by studying the book as a whole. This essay is a critical review of some of their major proposals. In it I will attempt to show that the book of Isaiah provides us with a unique opportunity to realize some of the possibilities and limits of this more general search for unity in biblical texts. We will find that the contemporary tendency to search for unity in Isaiah builds on and parallels attempts within the tradition itself to 'reach for unity' in a diverse tradition not amenable to final closure.

In these discussions 'unity' can mean quite different things. For example, many recent studies have focused on the thematic and inter-textual unity of the overall Isaiah tradition. This has produced a number of productive insights into distinctive themes occurring across various strata of the book,[3] correspondences between traditio-historically

University Press, 1974]), they also frequently atomized and recombined Biblical texts to make their theological points. For some examples, see surveys by M. Fishbane, *Biblical Interpretation in Ancient Israel* (Oxford: Clarendon Press, 1985) and J.L. Kugel and R.A. Greer, *Early Biblical Interpretation* (Library of Early Christianity, 3; Philadelphia: Westminster Press, 1986). In their focus on the coherence and unity of large swathes of biblical texts, many 'canonical' studies share more with 'New' Literary Criticism and Structuralism than with the pre-critical interpretation that they often invoke.

3.   J.H. Eaton, 'The Origin of the Book of Isaiah', *VT* 9 (1959), pp. 153-54; P.-E. Bonnard, *Le Second Isaïe, son disciple et leur éditeurs: Isaïe 40–66* (EBib; Paris: Gabalda, 1972), pp. 74-75; J. Jensen, *The Use of tôrâ by Isaiah: His Debate with the Wisdom Tradition* (CBQMS, 3; Washington, DC: Catholic Biblical Association, 1973), especially pp. 131-32; R. Melugin, *The Formation of Isaiah 40–55* (BZAW, 141; Berlin: de Gruyter, 1976), p. 178; J.F.A. Sawyer, *From Moses to Patmos: New Perspectives in Old Testament Study* (London: SPCK, 1977), pp. 113-18; P.R. Ackroyd, 'Isaiah I–XII: Presentation of a Prophet', in J.A. Emerton *et al.* (eds.), *Congress Volume, Göttingen, 1977* (VTSup, 29; Leiden: Brill, 1978), p. 22; W.L. Holladay, *Isaiah: Scroll of a Prophetic Heritage* (Grand Rapids: Eerdmans, 1978), pp. 17, 151, 215-16; J.J.M. Roberts, 'Isaiah in Old Testament Theology', *Int* 36 (1982), pp. 131-42; R. Rendtorff, 'Zur Komposition des Buches Jesaja', *VT* 34 (1984), pp. 297-312; R.E. Clements, 'Beyond Tradition History: Deutero-Isaianic Development of First Isaiah's Themes', *JSOT* 31 (1985), pp. 101-109; J.D.W. Watts, *Isaiah 1–33* (WBC, 24; Waco, TX: Word Books, 1985), pp. liii-liv; J. Jenson, 'Yahweh's Plan in Isaiah and in the Rest of the Old Testament', *CBQ* 48 (1986), pp. 443-55; D.G. Meade, *Pseudonymity and Canon* (WUNT, 39; Tübingen: Mohr [Paul Siebeck], 1986), pp. 27-43, particularly pp. 32-34; J.F.A. Sawyer, *Prophecy and the Prophets of the Old Testament* (Oxford Bible Series; Oxford: Oxford University Press, 1987), p. 76; C.T. Begg, 'Babylon in the Book of Isaiah',

The Prophets

disparate parts of the book,[4] and places where certain parts of the book
seem to allude to other parts of the book.[5] Whereas earlier in historical
scholarship all of these types of observations would have been used to
argue for unity of authorship or school behind the book as a whole, this

in J. Vermeylen (ed.), *Le Livre d' Isaïe: Les oracles et leurs relectures, unité et complexité de l'ouvrage* (BETL, 81; Leuven: Leuven University Press, 1989), pp. 121-
25; G.I. Davies, 'The Destiny of the Nations in the Book of Isaiah', in Vermeylen
(ed.), *Le Livre d' Isaïe*, pp. 98-106; A.K. Jenkins, 'The Development of the Isaiah
Tradition in Isa. 13–23', in Vermeylen (ed.), *Le Livre d' Isaïe*, pp. 249-50;
K. Nielsen, *There is Hope for a Tree: The Tree as Metaphor in Isaiah* (trans. C. and
F. Crowley; JSOTSup, 65; Sheffield: JSOT Press, 1989); J.F.A. Sawyer, 'Daughter
of Zion and Servant of the Lord in Isaiah: A Comparison, *JSOT* 44 (1989), pp. 89-
107; J. Vermeylen, 'L'unité du livre d'Isaïe', in *idem*, (ed.), *Le Livre d'Isaïe*, pp. 29-
31; R. Albertz, 'Das Deuterojesaja-Buch als Fortschreibung der Jesaja-Prophetie', in
E. Blum, C. Macholz and E. Stegemann (eds.), *Die Hebräische Bible und ihre
zweifache Nachgeschichte: Festschrift für Rolf Rendtorff zum 65. Geburtstag*
(Neukirchen–Vluyn: Neukirchener Verlag, 1990), pp. 248-51; W.A.M. Beuken,
'The Main Theme of Trito-Isaiah: The "Servants of YHWH"', *JSOT* 47 (1990), pp.
67-87.
    4.   H. Brownlee, *The Meaning of the Qumrân Scrolls for the Bible* (New York:
Oxford University Press, 1964), pp. 247-59; P.R. Ackroyd, 'Presentation of a
Prophet', pp. 41-42; *idem*, 'Isaiah 36–39: Structure and Function', in W.C. Delsman
(ed.), *Von Kanaan bis Kerala: Festschrift J.P.M. van der Ploeg* (AOAT, 211;
Kevelaer: Butzon & Bercker; Neukirchen–Vluyn: Neukirchener Verlag, 1982),
pp. 17-21; C.A. Evans, 'On the Unity and Parallel Structure of Isaiah', *VT* 38
(1988), pp. 129-47; M.A. Sweeney, *Isaiah 1–4 and the Post-Exilic Understanding
of the Isaianic Tradition* (BZAW, 171; Berlin: de Gruyter, 1988), pp. 13-17;
E. Conrad, 'The Royal Narratives and the Structure of the Book of Isaiah', *JSOT* 41
(1988), pp. 67-81.
    5.   Eaton, 'Origin', p. 154; Ackroyd, 'Presentation of a Prophet', p. 22; Sawyer,
Moses to Patmos, pp. 113-18; Childs, *Introduction to the Old Testament as
Scripture* (Philadelphia: Fortress Press, 1979), p. 330; R.E. Clements, 'The Unity of
the Book of Isaiah', *Int* 36 (1982), pp. 121-25; *idem*, 'Beyond Tradition History', pp.
101-109; G. Sheppard, 'The Anti-Assyrian Redaction and the Canonical Context of
Isaiah 1–39', *JBL* 104 (1985), pp. 212-13; Meade, *Pseudonymity*, pp. 38-41;
Davies, 'Destiny of the Nations', pp. 115-16; C.A. Evans, *To See and Not Perceive:
Isaiah 6.9-10 in Early Jewish and Christian Interpretation* (JSOTSup, 64; Sheffield:
JSOT Press, 1989), pp. 17-46; and E. Conrad, *Reading the Book of Isaiah*
(Overtures to Biblical Theology; Minneapolis: Fortress Press, 1991). Brueggemann's
work resembles this approach in its focus on the sequence of 'social intentionality' in
the (traditional) three major parts of Isaiah: W. Brueggemann, 'Unity and Dynamic
in the Isaiah Tradition', *JSOT* 29 (1984), pp. 89-107.

is not the aim or achievement of most recent studies in this area.[6] Instead, these studies have simply established the interpretative possibilities opened up by looking at traditio-historically disparate parts of the book in relation to one another.

At some points, recent studies have gone on to imply a stronger concept of 'unity'. These studies propose that the book as a whole is a literary unity, united by a common structure that is the context for making sense of the book's individual parts. This is primarily evident when scholars argue not only that individual texts *may* be illuminated through correlation with other individual parts of the Isaiah tradition (so implying a thematic and inter-textual unity), but that they *must* be understood in the literary context of the book as a whole. So, for example, Clements introduces his essay on 'The Unity of the Book of Isaiah' in the following way:

> The Book of Isaiah comes to us as a single literary whole, comprising sixty-six chapters, and this given datum of the form of the book must be regarded as a feature requiring explanation. It establishes a basis for the interpretation of the individual sayings and units of which it is made up and provides a literary context which must inevitably affect the interpretation of the several parts of the whole.[7]

This claim can not be adequately supported by arguing that certain individual parts of the book can be productively compared with other individual parts of the book. Rather, this stronger claim for the *necessity* for a prior focus on the book as a whole must be supported through arguments for some kind of overarching macrostructure, a structure that is the necessary literary context for interpretation of the book's individual parts. Many recent studies have pointed to texts that might signal the existence and shape of such a structure. The following is a critical review of some of their most important proposals.

---

6.   See particularly C.R. Seitz, 'The Divine Council: Temporal Transition and New Prophecy in the Book of Isaiah', *JBL* 109 (1990), pp. 229-47.

7.   Clements, 'The Unity of the Book of Isaiah', p. 117. This quotation is but an example of a much wider phenomenon. For example, Sweeney argues that 'Analysis must begin with a synthetic procedure, a detailed examination of the final form of the entire book, including its structure, genre, setting and intent'. Sweeney, *Isaiah 1–4*, p. 8. Cf. also C. Seitz, 'Isaiah 1–66: Making Sense of the Whole', in *idem*, (ed.), *Reading and Preaching the Book of Isaiah* (Philadelphia: Fortress Press, 1988), p. 107.

Critical Review of Macrostructural Proposals

Isaiah 40.1-8 along with Isaiah 35 and 36–39

From pre-critical interpreters like Rashi and Luther to recent interpreters like Sweeney and Albertz, scholars have recognized that Isaiah 40.1-8 initiates one of the overall book's most prominent divisions.[8] This is particularly clear because this text is a meta-communicative statement, that is, a statement that introduces a major block of material through describing that material's context, origin and aim. More specifically, this chapter is a particular type of biblical meta-communicative statement, a prophetic commission report. It sets the stage for a decisive shift in the prophetic message through describing that shift as being divinely authorized.[9]

---

8.   Rashi observes concerning 40.1, 'from here to the end of the book are words of comfort'. Before commenting on Isaiah 40.1, Luther begins his lectures on 'The Second Book of Isaiah' (covering Isa. 40–66) in the following way:

> We rightly divide Isaiah into two books. We have heard the first one, in which the prophet has functioned as a historical prophet and leader of the army, because so far he has prophesied concerning Christ and concerning the defeat of the king of Assyria. Then he has both comforted and reproved the people. In the following book the prophet treats two matters: Prophecies concerning Christ the King and then concerning Cyrus, the king of Persia, and concerning the Babylonian captivity (*Lectures on Isaiah, Chapters 40–66* [Luther's Works, 17; trans. H.J.A. Bouman; St Louis: Concordia, 1972], p. 3).

Recent scholars making similar observations have included Melugin, *The Formation of Isaiah 40–55*, pp. 82-86, 177-78; Childs, *Introduction to the Old Testament as Scripture*, pp. 328-30; Clements, 'The Unity of the Book of Isaiah', pp. 126-27; Rendtorff, 'Komposition', pp. 298-305; *idem*, 'Jesaja 6 im Rahmen der Komposition des Jesajabuches', in Vermeylen (ed.), *Le Livre d' Isaïe*, pp. 79-81; Sweeney, *Isaiah 1–4*, pp. 92-99; Seitz, 'Divine Council', pp. 243-47; Albertz, 'Das Deuterojesaja-Buch als Fortschreibung der Jesaja-Prophetie', pp. 243-48.

9.   The term 'commission report' is used here (rather than 'call report') to leave open the possibility that we do not have a new prophetic figure in Isa. 40.1-8, but a continuation of the same divine–human interaction initiated in 6.1-13. Otherwise, in this context, the shape and function of call reports and commission reports are taken to be similar. Previous scholars who have identified 40.1-8 as a call or commission report have included: N. Habel, 'The Form and Significance of the Call Narratives', *ZAW* 77 (1965), pp. 314-16; L. Krinetski, 'Zur Stilistik von Jes. 40.1-8', *BZ* 16 (1972), pp. 57-58; Melugin, *The Formation of Isaiah 40–55*, pp. 82-84 and Sweeney, *Isaiah 1–4*, pp. 66-67. For further discussion, including arguments regarding the meta-communicative function and generic identification of 40.1-8, see my

The text opens with a command in the divine council to comfort Jerusalem and Judah, proclaiming the following pivotal message (40.2):

> Her time of forced labor is completed;
> her bloodguilt has been paid for;
> She has received from the hand of the LORD
> double for all her sins.

To the extent that parts of chs. 1–39 proclaimed Jerusalem's bloodguilt, those parts are now superseded by this proclamation of expiation. This proclamation then becomes the basis for the following announcement in 40.3-5 of a new Exodus (now presented as a New Year's Procession), out of the 'forced labor' of exile in Babylon:

> A voice calling:
> Prepare in the wilderness
> the LORD's way,
> Make straight in the wasteland
> a highway for our God.
> Let every valley be filled in
> and every mountain and hill be leveled.
> May the canyon become flat
> and the ridges become a plain.

forthcoming article, 'Isaiah 40.1-11 in the Context of the Macrostructure of Second Isaiah: A Text-Linguistic Approach', in W. Bodine (ed.), *Discourse Analysis of Biblical Literature* (Semeia Studies; Atlanta: Scholars Press, 1993).

Seitz ('The Divine Council', pp. 236-237) argues that 40.1-8 can not be a call report because it lacks a clear statement of the prophet's acceptance of the commission, particularly after the prophet's objection in 40.6-7. Yet, Seitz does not present compelling reasons why 40.9-11 cannot be taken as the prophet's implicit acceptance of his commission through its initial execution. This objection seems to be based on an excessively stringent definition of the call report form and of what constitutes parallels to its parts. For other arguments against identification of Isa. 40.1-8 as a call report, see E. Nielson, 'Deuterojesaja: Erwägungen zur Formkritik, Traditions- und Redaktionsgeschte', *VT* 20 (1970), pp. 190-205; K. Kiesow, *Exodustexte im Jesajabuch: Literarkritische und motivgeschichtliche Analysen* (OBO, 24; Göttingen: Vandenhoeck & Ruprecht, 1979), pp. 38-41, 61-62; C. Westermann, *Das Buch Jesaja: Kapitel 40–66* (ATD, 19; Göttingen: Vandenhoeck & Ruprecht, 1966), pp. 30-31; J.M. Vincent, *Studien zur literarischen Eigenart und zur geistigen Heimat von Jesaja, Kap. 40–55* (BEvT, 5; Frankfurt am Main: Peter Lang, 1977), pp. 209-17, 245-48; and R.P. Merendino, *Der Erste und der Letzte: Eine Untersuchung von Jes 40–48* (VTSup, 31; Leiden: Brill, 1981), pp. 59-60.

> The glory of the LORD will be revealed,
> and all flesh shall see it together,
> For the mouth of the LORD has spoken.

Up to this point, these announcements have been directed at God's heavenly council.[10] Then in 40.6-7 an unspecified figure is commissioned to proclaim a message:

> A voice saying: 'Call',
> and he [or I] said,[11]
> 'What shall I call?
> All flesh is grass,
>   and its loyalty like a wildflower;
> The grass dries, the flower fades
>   When the LORD's wind blows on it.
> Surely the people is grass

And this figure receives the following reply in v. 8, emphasizing the timelessness of God's message:

> The grass dries, the flower fades,
>   but the word of our God stands forever.

10. H.W. Robinson, 'The Council of Yahweh', *JTS* 45 (1945), p. 155; F.M. Cross, 'The Council of Yahweh in Second Isaiah', *JNES* 12 (1953), pp. 274-77; and K. Elliger, *Deutero-Jesaja* (BKAT, 11.1; Neukirchen–Vluyn: Neukirchener Verlag, 1970), pp. 5-7. Also cf. J.M. Vincent, *Studien*, pp. 209-17, 245-48.

11. The textual problem here has played some role in discussion of the form and function of Isa. 40.1-8. In the above translation the third person reading of the Masoretic text, Targum and Peshitta is given in the text, while the first person reading of the Old Greek, 1QIsa[a] Scroll, Vulgate (possibly dependent on the Old Greek at this point) and some of Kennicott's manuscripts is given in parentheses. On the form in 1QIsa[a], see E. Qimron, *The Hebrew of the Dead Sea Scrolls* (HSS, 29; Atlanta: Scholars Press, 1986), p. 44.

D. Barthélemy (*Critique Textuelle de l'Ancien Testament* [OBO, 50/2; Göttingen: Vandenhoeck & Ruprecht, 1986], p. 279) and Seitz ('The Divine Council', pp. 236-37) argue that the first person reading of the Old Greek and others is an assimilation of Isa. 40.6-7 to call reports such as Isa. 6.5 and Jer. 1.6. Yet it is more likely that it is modern scholars—not the ancient scribes—who are preoccupied with parallels between Isa. 40.6 and call reports such as Isa. 6.5 and Jer. 1.6. Especially since Habel's article on call reports, this kind of connection has been taken for granted (N. Habel, 'Call Narratives', pp. 297-323). The ancient readers of the text, however, would have been more likely to subsume an original first person reading to a third person reading, thus blending 40.6 into its surroundings (which lack any first person references).

Seen in terms of its present position in the book of Isaiah, this commission report can be seen to have a crucial affirming, yet modifying role vis-à-vis the preceding Isaianic tradition. As Seitz, Rendtorff and Albertz have observed, this affirming yet modifying stance is particularly highlighted by the parallels and contrasts of Isa. 40.1-8 with Isa. 6.1-13, the description of the eighth-century Isaiah's call. Point by point, the commission report in Isa. 40.1-8 parallels 6.1-13, even as it sets a decisive new tone for the following part of the book.[12] In Isa. 6.6-7 a seraph pronounces Isaiah's sins 'turned away' and his bloodguilt 'atoned for', while in Isa. 40.1-2 all of Zion/Jerusalem experiences this same process. In 6.3 the seraphim sang praises to God's glory, a glory that fills the earth. In 40.5 the new exodus allows 'all flesh' to see God's glory. Then, just as Isaiah was commissioned to bring a message of judgment in 6.8-10, so 40.6-8 describes the commissioning of a figure to bring the message of the new exodus.

What is most significant, however, is that this idea of a shift in Isaiah's message at ch. 40 is not confined to just the commission report in Isa. 40.1-8. Instead, to some extent, the commission report in 40.1-8 introduces a profound shift in treatment of themes shared by many other parts of the book. Melugin and Rendtorff have been foremost in describing how this happens with regard to the themes of sin and bloodguilt.[13] First, Jerusalem's sin and/or bloodguilt are specifically proclaimed at (at least) four points in Isaiah 1–39 (1.4; 5.18; 22.14; 30.13). Forgiveness for this sin and bloodguilt is predicted in 27.9 and 33.24, but this forgiveness does not actually happen until the beginning of Isaiah 40. Then this forgiveness is reaffirmed in a couple of later texts (43.25; 53.5-11).

In general, texts in Isaiah 40–66 tend to take up earlier themes of Isaiah in order to proclaim an end to the judgments given in the first half

---

12. Rendtorff, 'Jesaja 6', pp. 79-81; Albertz, 'Das Deuterojesaja-Buch als Fortschreibung der Jesaja-Prophetie', pp. 244-48; Seitz, 'The Divine Council', pp. 238-43. For earlier less systematic observations of this parallel, see Brownlee, *The Meaning of the Qumrân Scrolls*, pp. 248-49; Habel, 'Call Narrative', p. 314; Cross, 'The Divine Council', p. 276; Melugin, *The Formation of Isaiah 40–55*, pp. 83-84; Sawyer, *Moses to Patmos*, pp. 113-15; Vincent, *Studien*, pp. 245-46; Kiesow, *Exodustexte*, p. 66; Ackroyd, 'Isaiah 36–39', pp. 5-6; O. Loretz, 'Die Gattung des Prologs zum Buche Deuterojesaja (Jes. 40.1-11)', *ZAW* 96 (1984), p. 220.

13. Melugin, *The Formation of Isaiah 40–55*, p. 177; Rendtorff, 'Komposition', pp. 302-305.

of Isaiah (1–39). Whereas Isaiah was commissioned in ch. 6 (6.9) to 'see and not understand', God's servant in chs. 40 and following (especially 42.7) is commissioned to 'open the eyes of the blind'; the judging 'holy one of Israel' of Isaiah 1–39 becomes a saving 'holy one of Israel' in 40–66; Jerusalem is no longer being punished and purged as in 1–39, but is restored in chs. 40 and following.[14]

Furthermore, this overall transition from judgment to restoration seems to be thematized in the body of chs. 40–48 through several texts that refer to 'former things' (Isa. 41.21-23; 42.9; 43.9-12; 44.6-8; 45.21-22; 46.9-11; 48.3-8; cf. 43.19). These texts argue that Yahweh's new word of restoration can be trusted because Yahweh (and not the pagan gods) has previously proclaimed and fulfilled some words about 'former things'. *In their present context*, these references to 'former things' now seem to refer to Isaiah of Jerusalem's prophecies of judgment. Jones, Becker, Childs, Clements, Seitz and Meade have proposed that these texts now make the following argument from prophecy: just as God proclaimed and then fulfilled eighth-century Isaiah's 'former things' message of judgment, so God can be counted on to execute the new message of restoration given in chs. 40 and following.[15] In making this argument, these texts now provide one view of thematic shifts in Isaiah: chs. 1–39 are construed as a reliable and now fulfilled 'former' message of judgment, while all or part of chs. 40 and following are taken as a 'new' message of promised liberation and restoration.

Having recognized the importance of Isa. 40.1-8, it is important to observe that it is not the only text in this portion of Isaiah that plays an important role in discussion of the structure of the book. One of the most significant insights of recent macrostructural studies of Isaiah has been the way chs. 35 and 36–39 play a transitional role along with the commission report in 40.1-8. For example, Steck has exhaustively argued that ch. 35 was composed as a transition between chs. 33–34 on

14. For more discussion of transitions in treatment of themes, see Rendtorff, 'Komposition', pp. 297-314 (pp. 310-12 on the transition in treatment of the 'holy one of Israel' figure).

15. D. Jones, 'The Traditio of the Oracles of Isaiah of Jerusalem', *ZAW* 67 (1955), pp. 245-46; J. Becker, *Isaias—der Prophet und sein Buch* (SBS, 30; Stuttgart: Katholisches Bibelwerk, 1968), pp. 37-38; Childs, *Introduction*, pp. 328-30; Clements, 'The Unity of the Book of Isaiah', p. 125; Meade, *Pseudonymity*, pp. 35-36; C.R. Seitz, 'Isaiah 1–66', p. 110; *idem*, 'The Divine Council', p. 244. This reinforces the theme of the reliability of God's word that was sounded in 40.8, 44.26 and 50.11.

the one hand and ch. 40 on the other.[16] Likewise, starting with Ackroyd's articles on chs. 36–39, there has been an increasing recognition of the crucial transitional role of the Isaiah–Hezekiah narratives in chs. 36–39.[17] Most importantly, these chapters explain the delay in punishment of Judah/Jerusalem so that it is executed by Babylon and not Assyria. In this way, this set of narratives about Isaiah and Hezekiah eases the transition to chs. 40–66, parts of the book which presuppose a destruction of Judah and exile at the hands of Babylonia. Thus, both Isaiah 35 and 36–39 prepare in crucial ways for the transition completed in the commission report in Isa. 40.1-8.

In sum, there is an apparent macrostructural shift at this point in the book of Isaiah. This shift, embodied in the overall transition in treatment of themes (e.g. 'Holy one of Israel', 'Zion/Jerusalem'), prepared for in chs. 35–39, completed through the commission report in 40.1-8, and now referred to by the texts that compare the 'former' with 'latter/coming/new things', is among the most prominently marked structural shifts in the book of Isaiah.

Nevertheless, even this highly marked and often recognized shift is a good example of how structuring texts in Isaiah only incompletely organize the material which they govern. For not all of Isaiah 1–39 is a message of judgment, nor is all of 40–66 a message of comfort. Restoration is already proclaimed early in the book in texts like the 'swords into plowshares' vision (2.2-4), the prophecies of a royal savior in 9.1-6 and 11.1-9, the thanksgiving for forgiveness and restoration in ch. 12, and so on.[18] Then, particularly in chs. 56–66, proclamations of judgment once again appear: the proclamation against blind watchmen in 56.9–57.13a, the judgment against seeking the LORD through contentious fasting in 58.1-4, or the harsh descriptions of the fate of sinners in chs. 65 and 66 (65.1-7, 11-15; 66.3-5, 6, 17, 24).[19]

---

16. O.H. Steck, *Bereitete Heimkehr: Jesaja 35 als redaktionelle Brücke zwischen dem ersten und dem zweiten Jesaja* (SBS, 121; Stuttgart: Katholisches Bibelwerk, 1985).

17. P.R. Ackroyd, 'An Interpretation of the Babylonian Exile: A Study of 2 Kings 20; Isaiah 38–39', *SJT* 27 (1974), pp. 329-52; *idem*, 'Isaiah 36–39', pp. 3-21; Clements, 'The Unity of the Book of Isaiah', pp. 120-21; Sweeney, *Isaiah 1–4*, pp. 32-34.

18. Cf. also Isa. 4.2-6; 10.20-23; 25.6-8, 9; 27.6; 30.18-26; 32.1-8, 15-20; 33.5-6 and the anticipatory transition in 35.1-10.

19. Cf. also Isa. 50.10-11; 59.1-19. Also compare the references to past judgment and the present unworthiness of the audience for redemption in Isa. 40.12-31;

In some cases the restoration texts in chs. 1–34 and judgment texts in 56–66 traditio-historically precede the transitions in Isa. 35.1–40.8 (e.g. Isa. 9.1-6 and 11.1-9); in other cases they seem to have been inserted later than those transitions (e.g. Isa. 2.2-4; 56.9–57.13a). But the main issue at hand is not the exact shape of the traditio-historical process that produced the book, but the complex literary shape that resulted. Whatever the intentions of the author/editors of Isaiah 35, 36–39 and 40.1-8, it is clear that not all of the overall book of Isaiah agrees with the macrostructural conceptions implicit in these transitional texts. Instead these texts represent related attempts to construe the quite varied textual materials that surround them, materials not amenable to being encompassed by any redactor or set of redactors' conception of the whole.

In conclusion, insights into the macrostructural perspectives of these texts is essential to understanding the nature and full interpretative potential of the texts themselves. Moreover, such insights can add to our knowledge of the early interpretation history of some of the materials these transitional texts govern. None of these transitional texts, however, reflect a single macrostructural perspective that can be found in the book as a whole. The most these texts can tell us is how certain final redactors understood the whole, even if the whole does not completely conform to their understanding.

Isaiah 1 and 65–66

The same can be said about other proposals about the macrostructure of the book of Isaiah. For example, since Fohrer's 1962 article on Isaiah 1 as a summary of Isaiah's preaching, the introductory character of this chapter has been widely recognized.[20] The superscription in 1.1 can be seen as introducing the whole book. Then, as Sweeney points out, the rest of the verses of the chapter (1.2-31) can be seen as an exhortatory survey of the significance of the following book.[21] It includes the following elements:

41.14; 42.18-25; 43.8, 22-28; 45.9-10; 46.8, 12; 48.1-8. Despite this, in Isa. 40–48 it is clear that these texts only highlight God's sovereignty over Judah's previous defeat on the one hand, and God's exclusive responsibility for Judah's redemption on the other.

20. G. Fohrer, 'Jesaja 1 als Zusammenfassung der Verkündigung Jesajas', *ZAW* 74 (1962), pp. 251-80. See for example Clements, *Isaiah 1–39*, pp. 28-29, and Seitz, 'Isaiah 1–66', pp. 112-13. But cf. Ackroyd, 'Presentation of a Prophet', pp. 31-32.

21. Sweeney, *Isaiah 1–4*, pp. 97-99.

1. A pair of oracles in vv. 2-9 describing Judah and Jerusalem's sin and justified punishment.
2. An exhortation in vv. 10-17 to repent and be truly righteous.
3. A final collection of oracles in vv. 18-31 that focus on the consequences for the Judaean audience of a decision either way. These oracles especially emphasize the negative consequences of failure to repent.

Finally, the superscription in 2.1, whatever its original more limited function, now marks the end of introductory material and the beginning of the body of the book.[22]

In addition to these proposals regarding the introductory character of Isaiah 1, an increasing number of scholars have begun to see chs. 65–66 as a concluding inclusio with ch. 1. Liebreich pointed out a number of individual words in common,[23] and Lack and Sweeney have substantially strengthened the case through looking at specific themes that the chapters hold in common.[24] Such themes include the following:

1. The negative consequences of cultic infidelity (specifically worship in gardens [1.29-31; 65.3; 66.17]).
2. Separation of wrongdoers from the righteous prior to the restoration and renaming of the righteous (renaming 1.26 [Jerusalem]; 65.15 [God's servants]).
3. Wrongdoers being 'put to shame' (1.29; 66.5; cf. 65.15) and punished with fire (1.31; 66.15-16, 24).

22. Sweeney (*Isaiah 1–4*, pp. 30-31) argues that this superscription relates to the more limited text block in chs. 2–4. His most salient argument is that this block focuses on the 'Judah and Jerusalem' mentioned in the superscription, while ch. 5 begins a section that includes Israel, and subsequent chapters focus on other nations. Nevertheless, though much of the material in chs. 2–66 concerns nations other than Judah, it is becoming increasingly clear that the nations focus in Isaiah interacts closely with the cosmic implications of Zion theology (on this see, in particular, Davies, 'Destiny of the Nations', pp. 119-20). Therefore, even focus on the nations is a reflection on God's work with Jerusalem, the true center of the world. Sweeney's other arguments regarding דבר ('word') versus חזון ('vision') and הדבר ('the word') by itself rather than דבר־יהוה ('the word of the LORD') are not compelling.

23. L.J. Liebreich, 'The Compilation of the Book of Isaiah', *JQR* 46 (1955–56), pp. 276-77; *JQR* 47 (1956–57), pp. 139-41.

24. R. Lack, *La Symbolique du livre d'Isaïe* (AnBib, 59; Rome: Biblical Institute Press, 1973), pp. 139-41; Sweeney, *Isaiah 1–4*, pp. 97-98.

These parallels suggest that just as Isaiah 1 introduces the book, so the corresponding pair of chapters in Isaiah 65–66 conclude it. In sum, both texts are conceived as playing a macrostructural role in the book as a whole.

To some extent, this set of observations is contradicted by the failure of Isaiah 1 and 65–66 to anticipate or summarize (respectively) much of the intervening material. For example, as Seitz has observed, the focus on the prophet Isaiah in Isa. 1.1 is lost through much of the material this superscription governs, and it is openly contradicted by elements in 'Second Isaiah' such as the 'former'/'latter things' dichotomy or the mention of Cyrus (Isa. 44.28).[25] Similarly, the introductory exhortation in 1.2-31 fails to introduce many elements crucial in the following book—themes such as God's plan for the nations (see chs. 13–27, 34 and 47, for example), the new exodus out of Babylon in 40–48, the restoration of Jerusalem in 49–66, and the struggle in 56–66 about what constitutes the true community.[26] To the extent that the case for 1.2-31 being an introduction is based on just such thematic observations, these counter-observations are pertinent. Nevertheless, no introduction can completely summarize the contents of the material it introduces. Aside from textual placement (at the beginning of a text), the claim for something being an introduction is difficult to disprove. And the same is true for conclusions.

Perhaps more pertinent is the observation of a fundamental conflict between the exhortatory focus of 1.2-31 and the rhetorical presuppositions of other parts of the book, particularly Isaiah 65–66. Whereas the 1.2-31 exhortation depends for its existence on the possibility of repentance (note in particular 1.18), chs. 65–66 presuppose that, though it may not yet be obvious, the groups of sinners and righteous have already been determined. Chapter 65 is directly addressed to the sinners, even though they hear about the fate of the righteous. The sinners hear directly about their punishment in 65.7, 11-12, and only indirectly about the reward of God's servants in 65.8-10, 17-25.[27] The contrast between these groups is particularly clear in 65.13-16, where the sinful audience's punishment is contrasted with God's reward of the righteous. In contrast, in ch. 66 it is the righteous God-fearers (66.5) and not the sinners who

25. Seitz, 'Isaiah 1–66', pp. 116-22.
26. Cf. Sweeney, *Isaiah 1–4*, pp. 97-98.
27. Isa. 65.7 is second person in the MT. Note that in 65.8-10 and 17-25 the righteous ones are described exclusively in the third person.

are directly addressed (see particularly Isa. 66.10-14, 20, 22). By this point the sinners are being described exclusively in the third person (66.3-4, 6, 15-21, 24).

All this suggests that the respective audiences for these two chapters have already been determined: sinners for Isaiah 65 and righteous for Isaiah 66.[28] Here the past tense is important. This is not an exhortation to be on the right side of a division that is about to be made. Instead, Isaiah 65–66 is a pronouncement of the consequences of a choice that *has already been made*. The exhortation in Isa. 1.2-31 focuses on the consequences of future decisions in order to influence those decisions. In contrast, Isaiah 65–66 describes the consequences of decisions that have already taken place. Though the sinners are fictively addressed in Isaiah 65, the overall aim of Isaiah 65–66 is to strengthen an already faithful audience (the 'righteous') in the face of the apparent present success of their opponents (the 'sinners').

In sum, recent insights into the cross-book perspective offered by Isaiah 1 and Isaiah 65–66 have increased our knowledge of these texts and of the ways other parts of the Isaianic tradition are construed by them. Nevertheless, Isaiah 1 and 65–66 are diverging conceptions of the significance of that tradition. Chapter 1 extracts themes from Isaiah's message in order to exhort the Judaean audience to repent. In contrast, chs. 65–66 draw together themes of the preceding material (including ch. 1) to describe a situation where repentance is no longer a prominent possibility. There is not a place in Isa. 1.2-31 for the rhetorical situation in Isaiah 65–66, nor does Isaiah 65–66 allow room for the exhortation to repentance in Isa. 1.2-31. This is not just a thematic conflict, but a conflict in rhetorical aim, a conflict that makes it difficult for 1.2-31 and 65–66 to function cohesively as a paired introduction and conclusion to the book as a whole.

28. Compare the concluding accusation in 65.12b (sinners in second person) with the similar one in 66.4b (sinners in the third person). To be sure, this scheme is not completely tidy. For example, the sinners are referred to in the third person in 65.1-7 (except for part of 65.7 in the MT). In addition, on first glance, the final part of ch. 65 (Isa. 65.17-25) seems an odd section to be addressed to the sinners, especially the call to rejoice over the joyous future of the righteous in 65.18. Nevertheless, compare this call in Isa. 65.18 with Isa. 66.10, a similar call to rejoicing, but one that explicitly specifies that this time it is the righteous who are being called to rejoice.

Concluding Observation: Early versus Late Redaction

To be sure, there are some cases where there is evidence that materials have been organized according to an editor's macrostructural conception, and this has made a difference in the structural cohesiveness of certain smaller portions of Isaiah. For example, Barth has presented a persuasive analysis of just such an editorial rearrangement of two sets of oracles in Isaiah 5 and 9.7–10.4. For a long time scholars have recognized that the there are two sets of connected oracles here: the woe oracles in 5.8-24 originally began with 10.1-4a, and the oracles in 9.7-20 originally were concluded with 5.25-29. Barth argues that these oracles have been rearranged by a seventh-century redactor so that now they lead up to the following elements focused on Assyria: the woe oracle against Assyria in 10.5-15, a taunt song (originally directed) against Assyria in 14.4b-23, and a summary appraisal in 14.24-27.[29] As Anderson subsequently proposed, the *Denkschrift* of 6.1–9.6 now shows how God can be 'with' Judah even in the violent storm of God's judgment against Israel, Judah and then Assyria.[30] In sum, at one time, the materials in Isa. 5.1–10.19 and 14.4b-19 were rearranged to show how God is not only behind present judgment of Judah and Israel, but can also be trusted to punish the Assyrians.

Nevertheless, this rearrangement occurs relatively early in the redaction history of the book. Subsequent redactors modified the shape of this section through adding the thanksgiving song in ch. 12, beginning a new 'nations' section with the addition of ch. 13, and redirecting ch. 14 to focus on Babylonia. Moreover, this example of early redactional rearrangement should not necessarily be taken as a model for how the final form of the book was put together. On the contrary, examples such

---

29. H. Barth, *Die Jesaja-Worte in der Josiazeit: Israel und Assur als Thema einer produktiven Neuinterpretation der Jesajaüberlieferung* (WMANT, 48; Neukirchen–Vluyn: Neukirchener Verlag, 1977), pp. 109-17. Cf. C. L'Hereux, 'The Redactional History of Isaiah 5.1–10.4', in W. Barrick and J. Spencer (eds.), *In the Shelter of Elyon* (JSOTSup, 31; Sheffield: JSOT Press, 1984), pp. 99-119. For further proposals regarding intrusive editing by the same redactor, see G. Sheppard, 'The Anti-Assyrian Redaction', pp. 198-211. Also, both Sheppard and L'Hereux emphasize the double inclusio formed by this seventh-century redactor through rearranging earlier materials.

30. B.W. Anderson, '"God with Us"—In Judgment and in Mercy: The Editorial Structure of Isaiah 5–10 (11)', in G.M. Tucker, D.L. Petersen and R.R. Wilson (eds.), *Canon, Theology and Old Testament Interpretation: Essays in Honor of B.S. Childs* (Philadelphia: Fortress Press, 1988), pp. 239-244.

as chs. 1 and 35–39 suggest that the final set of redactors seem to have confined their efforts to insertions on the edges of or between blocks of material, insertions that often imply a certain conception of the structural significance of those blocks. Moreover, these blocks of previous material were somewhat amenable to, but not completely conformed to, the redactors' various conceptions of the whole.

The above reflections apply particularly to materials in chs. 56–66 of Isaiah, traditionally termed 'Third Isaiah'. Here several different individuals or communities seem to have reflected on the Isaiah tradition as a whole, adding at the end of the Isaiah collection their unique configuration of Isaiah themes relevant to them. Clearly, once again, understanding of the connections of this material to earlier chapters is essential to understanding this material at all. Moreover, these latter chapters of Isaiah are crucial examples of early interpretation of Isaiah traditions.[31] They do not, however, necessarily represent the perspective of a redactor or redactors who structured the earlier materials, whether by arrangement or insertion. Rather, the placement of these chapters at the end, rather than throughout, the Isaiah collection is *prima facie* evidence that these redactors understood the preceding materials to have a certain

---

31. A. Zillessen, '"Tritojesaja" und Deuterojesaja: Eine literarkritische Untersuchung zu Jes 56–66', *ZAW* 26 (1906), pp. 231-276; W. Zimmerli, 'Zur Sprache Tritojesajas', *Schweizerische Theologische Umschau* 20 (1950), pp. 110-22, reprinted in *Gottes Offenbarung* (Munich: Chr. Kaiser Verlag, 1963), pp. 217-33; D. Michel, 'Zur Eigenart Tritojesajas', *Theologia Viatorum* 10 (1965–66), pp. 213-30; P.D. Hanson, *The Dawn of Apocalyptic* (Philadelphia: Fortress Press, 1979), pp. 60-70; U. Mauser, 'Isaiah 65.17-25', *Int* 36 (1982), pp. 181-82; Meade, *Pseudonymity*, pp. 37-42; O.H. Steck, *Bereitete Heimkehr*, pp. 66-71; *idem*, 'Der Grundtext in Jesaja 60 und sein Aufbau', *ZTK* 83 (1986), pp. 261-96, particularly pp. 292-96; *idem*, 'Heimkehr auf der Shulter oder/und auf der Hüfte: Jes 49.22b/60.4b', *ZAW* 98 (1986), pp. 275-77; *idem*, 'Der Rachetag in Jesaja LXI 2: Ein Kapitel redaktionsgeschichtlicher Kleinarbeit', *VT* 36 (1986), pp. 323-38; W.A.M. Beuken, 'Isa. 56.9–57.13: An Example of the Isaianic Legacy of Trito-Isaiah', in J.W. van Henten (ed.), *Tradition and Reinterpretation in Jewish and Early Christian Literature* (Festschrift J.C.H. Lebram; SPB, 36; Leiden: Brill, 1986), pp. 48-64; *idem*, 'Trito-Jesaja: Profetie en schriftgeleerdheid', in F.G. Martinez, *et al.* (eds.), *Profeten en profetische geschriften* (Festschrift A.S. van der Woude; Kampen: Nijkerk, 1986), pp. 71-85; *idem*, 'Servant and Herald of Good Tidings: Isaiah 61 as an Interpretation of Isaiah 40–55', in Vermeylan (ed.), *Le Livre d' Isaïe*, pp. 411-42; Davies, 'The Destiny of the Nations', p. 118; O.H. Steck, 'Tritojesaja im Jesajabuch', in Vermeylan (ed.), *Le Livre d' Isaïe*, pp. 361-406, especially pp. 367-79.

integrity that they were reluctant to modify through massive, direct rearrangement of and addition to those earlier materials themselves.

Results of the Survey

Much more could be said about the potential macrostructural role played by various parts of the book[32] and the lack of integration in the book's treatment of certain themes, such as the role of the nations in God's plan.[33] Nevertheless, the preceding survey is sufficient to indicate some of the possibilities and limits of macrostructural study in a book like Isaiah with such a complex tradition history. On the one hand, the studies that I have discussed have increased our understanding of crucial texts in Isaiah and of the interpretation history of the materials they now aim to organize. On the other hand, it is clear that not just one, but several redactors have introduced their macrostructural conceptions into the book of Isaiah.

Though at early stages some redactors seem to have systematically rearranged earlier materials, later redactors did not completely integrate their materials into their overall macrostructural conception. Of course it is possible that these editors simply elegantly drew upon the already existing semiotic potential of the material that preceded them, in casting all of the material in a new light without having to reorganize or rewrite it. The preceding survey, however, suggests that the complexity of the Book of Isaiah's tradition history meant that it was not amenable to such an elegant, complete redactional rereading. Instead, later editors merely added their texts to the margins of earlier units, allowing the diverse perspectives of the different materials to clash and complement each other.

Concluding Reflections

All of this calls into question whether observations of the macro-structural *perspective* of some of the texts in Isaiah establish that the book is governed by some kind of overall 'conceptual structure', whether

32. Cf. for example: Steck, *Bereitete Heimkehr*, pp. 62-64; and Rendtorff, 'Komposition', particularly p. 315.

33. Texts describing God as destroying the nations or making them vassals include the bulk of Isa. 13–23 along with Isa. 24; 34; 47; 49.22-26; 60.1-18; 61.5-7; and 63.1-6. Texts describing a more positive role for the nations include Isa. 2.2-4; 19.18-25; 22.1-19; 25.6-9; 56.1-8; and 66.18-21. For a more complete survey, see Davies, 'The Destiny of the Nations', pp. 93-106.

intentional or unintentional.[34] Not only does it seem that no editor intervened deeply enough into the book to make it all conform to an overall conception, but the materials are diverse enough that the Isaianic tradition did not end up unintentionally coalescing into a coherent literary statement. As a result, the book of Isaiah displays the kind of fractured thematic and inter-textual unity that might be expected in a text whose authors/editors did not generally subsume the book's earlier parts into a larger whole.

Given the complexity of the unity produced by this process, we need to scrutinize the kinds of images we choose for describing the book of Isaiah as a whole. On the one hand, texts like journals, for example, may have very little cohesion across their various parts. On the other hand, texts like this essay aim for more cohesiveness. As we turn to characterize the book of Isaiah as a whole, we must consider the full range of possibilities here. To follow Seitz and Sweeney in considering Isaiah as a 'drama' or 'exhortation' may be to presuppose more structural integration than actually exists in the book.[35] Further, we have certain textual analogies, such as that of 'collection' for example, that may better exemplify the type of thematic and inter-textual unity that does occur in Isaiah, a unity without overall macrostructural integration.

In addition, the above arguments for the weakness of the case for literary unity in Isaiah raise some questions about our contemporary

34. This term is taken from Sweeney, *Isaiah 1–4*, p. 25.

35. 'Drama' is proposed in Watts, *Isaiah 1–33*, pp. xliv-lii, and Seitz, 'Isaiah 1–66', p. 122. 'Exhortation' is proposed by Sweeney, *Isaiah 1–4*, pp. 96-98.

Seitz ('Isaiah 1–66', pp. 107-109) also proposes the example of a farmhouse, bearing clear marks of prior additions over the years yet still one house, as an example of a basic unity, despite seams created by growth over time. This example, however, likewise presupposes a degree of unity not necessarily found in texts that have been added to over the years. A builder adding to a house makes sure the final result is coherent enough to be livable.

Yet someone inserting a text into a larger work might not necessarily feel the same compulsion to make the final result such a coherent whole. On the contrary, as indicated in the preceding critical survey of texts in Isaiah, there is significant evidence that the book's editors often carefully preserved the integrity of the traditions that preceded them. So, to some extent, the perspectives of the earlier materials resisted the reconceptualization of their role in the redactional additions. Rather than subsuming or reorganizing the materials into their new redactional conception of the whole, the editors allowed the early materials to stand over against the perspective implicit in their redactional additions.

compulsion to find literary unity in Isaiah and throughout the rest of the Bible. This tendency has emerged at just the time when attempts to recover the original words of the prophets have proven a less and less reliable guide for interpretation. Faced with such a crisis, the search for literary coherence of the 'final form' of the biblical text has seemed a godsend. Thus, for example, after describing how historical criticism 'divided' the biblical text and so 'conquered' it, Seitz introduces his essay on 'Isaiah 1–66: Making Sense of the Whole' in the following way:

> What I offer, then, is not a complex new literary theory. I hope that by demonstrating something of the Book of Isaiah's own efforts at unity and coherence, I might make our point of standing, as preachers, readers, and hearers of the Word of God in Isaiah, more stable and coherent.[36]

So Seitz presents his efforts at demonstrating unity in Isaiah as an attempt to reconstruct its authority over against us after the dissolution of the text effected by historical criticism.

Here is an important way in which our hermeneutical presuppositions have exegetical consequences. For if we believe that we must begin our interpretation with understanding of the unitary literary shape of the text's final form, we will be impelled to find such shape in texts whether or not it is there. Having surveyed in this article the limited success of previous attempts to find unity in Isaiah, this is the point to ask, to what extent is the search for unity in Isaiah truly a reflection of semiotic potentialities in the text itself?

Perhaps texts like the book of Isaiah can teach us the limits of so generally emphasizing a search for structural or literary coherence in biblical texts. As indicated in the above survey, such a search can have great heuristic value, leading us beyond a focus on individual pericopes to see how texts like Isaiah 1, 35.1–40.8 and 65–66 'reach for unity', synthesizing the varied materials surrounding them, if only partially. Yet excessive confidence in the existence of a more complete unity in biblical texts—and our need to find it—can blind us to the unresolved, rich plurality built into texts like Isaiah. Just as in its parallel process within the formation of the book, such scholarly 'reaching for unity' can achieve only limited success. At best such study can productively, yet only

---

36. Seitz, 'Isaiah 1–66', p. 107.

partially, construe and reconstrue the significance of varied materials not amenable to final closure.[37]

37. For the purposes of this essay, this conclusion is limited to showing how the book of Isaiah can be a textual opportunity to recognize the limits of an absolute generalization of the search for literary coherence. For some helpful, more general reflections on the political background of this search for literary coherence, see T. Eagleton, *Literary Theory: An Introduction* (Minneapolis: University of Minnesota Press, 1983), particularly pp. 46-51; *idem*, 'Macherey and Marxist Literary Theory', *Against the Grain: Essays 1975–1985* (London: Verso, 1986), pp. 14-17. See also Sheppard's suggestive critique of B.S. Childs's approach in 'The Anti-Assyrian Redaction', pp. 213-16.

PROPHETIC IDEOLOGY

JSOT 41 (1988), pp. 83-103

SECOND ISAIAH—PROPHET OF UNIVERSALISM

J. Blenkinsopp

One of the most widely accepted assumptions in Old Testament studies is that the exilic Isaiah and his disciples, active during and for some time after the exilic age, proclaimed for the first time that knowledge of the one true God revealed to Israel was to be shared with the nations of the world. It is often added, as a more or less self-evident corollary, that in this respect Second Isaiah provided the model for early Christianity's openness to the Gentile world, an openness which stands in glaring contrast to the ethnic and religious particularism of Second Commonwealth Judaism.[1] The purpose of this paper is not to refute this interpretative schema—which, in any case, is no longer representative of the best scholarship—but to take another look at Isaiah 40–66 from this point of view, to argue to a rather different conclusion from the one commonly held, and to suggest in the light of that conclusion an alternative way of

---

1. E.g. H.H. Rowley, *The Missionary Message of the Old Testament* (London, 1955), p. 65; *The Biblical Doctrine of Election* (London: Lutterworth, 1950), pp. 62-63; on universalism in Second Isaiah see, in addition, H. Halas, 'The Universalism of Isaiah', *CBQ* 12 (1950), pp. 162-70; U.E. Simon, *A Theology of Salvation* (London: SPCK, 1953); S.H. Blank, *Prophetic Faith in Isaiah* (London: Black, 1958); R. Martin-Achard, *Israel et les nations, la perspective missionnaire de l'Ancien Testament* (Neuchatel, 1959); R. Davidson, 'Universalism in Second Isaiah', *SJT* 16 (1963), pp. 166-85; A. Gelston, 'The Missionary Message of Second Isaiah', *SJT* 18 (1965), pp.308-18; P.-E. Dion, 'L'Universalisme religieux dans les différentes couches rédactionelles d'Is. 40–55', *Bib* 51 (1970), pp. 161-82. I have dealt with the issue of early Jewish particularism in 'Old Testament Theology and the Jewish-Christian Connection', *JSOT* 28 (1984), pp. 3-15 and 'Yahweh and Other Deities: Conflict and Accommodation in the Religion of Israel', *Int* 40 (1986), pp. 354-66.

posing the issue of universalism–particularism in Second Commonwealth Judaism inclusive of early Christianity.

Isaiah 40–48

Since the end of the eighteenth century critical scholarship has agreed to date chs. 40–66 of the Isaiah scroll some two centuries later than the *floruit* of the Judean prophet Isaiah whose name is on the title leaf. The further distinction between chs. 40–55 and 56–66, the former exilic and the latter mostly post-exilic, was first argued by Bernhard Duhm in his commentary of 1892. It too has been widely accepted, as has Duhm's singling out of the four 'Servant Songs' (a curious title, since whatever else they are, they are not songs) for special consideration. All of this is well known and part of the critical consensus. Like most 'assured results of modern scholarship', however, these conclusions could do with an overhaul from time to time. To begin with, the break between Isaiah 1–39 and 40–55 is more apparent than real. Chapters 36–39, taken from 2 Kings 18–20 and appended to the scroll, break the connection with ch. 35 which clearly belongs with Second Isaiah.[2] The break between 40–48 and 49–55 is also at least as clear as that between 40–55 and 56–66. Chapters 40–48 deal with the political situation created by the victories of Cyrus and have as their centerpiece his commissioning as YHWH's anointed (45.1-7). They begin and end with the theme of exodus from Babylon and return to Zion (40.1-5; 48.20-22). Chapters 49–55, on the other hand, deal with internal Jewish affairs, we hear no more of Cyrus and the downfall of Babylon, there is no more satire directed at the Babylonian imperial cults, and the language of servant-hood, so important and problematic in this second part of Isaiah, is used in a significantly different way.[3] As for the final section (56–66), while there are significant new developments, there is also much in common with the preceding chapters. It is also difficult to decide where exactly it begins, since 56.1-5 ends in the same way as the preceding passage

2. It offers words of consolation, speaks of the vision of the glory of YHWH, the healing of the blind, deaf and so on, miracles in the wilderness, a highway prepared for the return to Zion. This last theme (35.8-10) runs on uninterruptedly into 40.1-5.

3. In 40–48 the term 'servant' (*'ebed*) refers to the community with the probable exception of 42.1 and the possible exception of 42.19 and 44.26. In 49–55 all occurrences refer to an individual with the exception of 49.7 and 54.17.

(55.13), and ch. 57 has the same ending as 40–48. One could argue the matter further, but for practical purposes we may take the three sections (40–48; 49–55; 56–66) in sequence with the provisional but reasonable expectation that they represent distinct stages of development.

Read politically, Isaiah 40–48 is propaganda for Cyrus and the Persians which circulated during the last decade of the last Babylonian king Nabonidus (556–539 BCE), probably after Cyrus's conquest of Lydia in 547 (Isa. 45.3). The author, whose name is unknown,[4] belonged to the Babylonian *golah*. He may even have been in the entourage of Cyrus himself,[5] although this would not be necessary to explain the harsh anti-Babylonian invective (e.g. 43.14; 47; 48.14), the satire directed against the Babylonian imperial cults (e.g. 40.19-20) and against the religious and intellectual tradition of Babylon in general (e.g. 44.25; 47.9-10, 12-13). Much of the symbolic language can also be explained as countering the ideology of power encapsulated in Babylonian myth, especially the canonical creation myth, recited during the *akitu* festival, which must have been familiar to the deportees. This would help to explain the closely related themes of cosmogonic victory, creation of the world and divine kingship in Second Isaiah, which can be read as a kind of Jewish mirror image of the ideology of *enuma elish*.[6] The claim that YHWH (not Marduk, of course) is the only god, that (unlike Marduk) he is not begotten of other gods (43.10-11), and that therefore he is the only source of salvation, can be understood in the same context. It is therefore not surprising that the language of 'monotheïsm' in Second Isaiah mirrors the Babylonian claim to supremacy: 'I am, and there is no one beside me' (47.8, 19).

These claims made on behalf of the Jewish God imply a drastic relativizing of current assumptions about political power. For if the ultimate source of power resides with the god worshipped in the *golah* community, the political power of the dominant nation is no more than a drop in the bucket, a grain of dust on the scales (40.12-17). And since it

---

4.   It has been suggested that the name was Meshullam, based on Isa. 42.19, read as 'who is blind like Meshullam?' (*mî ʿiwwēr kimʿšullām*) but this half-verse is very obscure and is in any case probably a gloss on v. 19a; see the commentaries and C.R. North, *The Suffering Servant in Second Isaiah* (Oxford: Clarendon Press, 2nd edn, 1952), pp. 89-90.

5.   Suggestion of M. Weinfeld, 'Universalism and Particularism in the Period of Exile and Restoration', *Tarbiz* 33 (1963/64), p. 231 (Hebr.).

6.   For details see my *A History of Prophecy in Israel* (Philadelphia: Fortress Press, 1983), pp. 212-14.

was believed that YHWH had mysteriously chosen this people as the instrument of his purposes in history, current events, especially the conquests of Cyrus which were then making the headlines, and even projected future events such as the conquest of Egypt,[7] must be interpreted from the perspective of this externally negligible people, 'the servant of rulers' (49.7), all indications to the contrary notwithstanding.

In this respect Isaiah 40–48 reads like a Jewish version of the propagandistic manifesto of Cyrus on his famous cylinder published shortly after the conquest of Babylon in 539.[8] There is in both texts religious polemic against the impious Nabonidus, the accusation that he had condemned his subjects to forced labor (40.2; 47.6), and the charge that he had treated their cults with contempt. In consequence of which YHWH (not Marduk) chose Cyrus as his agent, made the vast populations of the Babylonian empire subject to him, and inspired him to exercise rule without the violence and brutality characteristic of the Babylonians (42.1-4, if it referred originally to Cyrus). Above all, Cyrus reversed the policy of his predecessors by restoring the cults of the subject peoples (44.28) and repatriating those who had been deported (44.26-28).

So far, Second Isaiah has not moved significantly beyond the theological range of the great pre-exilic prophets, including the original Isaiah, who provided a religious interpretation of international events and designated foreign peoples and rulers as YHWH's agents (e.g. Isa. 10.5). In fact, the pressing needs of religious polemic against foreign cults and culture, and especially the need to speak in the idiom of power, even divine power, were even less calculated to encourage a universalistic perspective. Yet in one all-important respect the situation is quite different: Israel is no longer a nation state but a confessional community. Some of the implications of this transformation are detectable in Second Isaiah, although not yet by any means fully developed. They can be picked up in the following passages which require comment. The first is

7. Cyrus may have planned the conquest of Egypt, but it was carried out by his son Cambyses in 525 BCE.

8. *ANET*, pp. 315-16. M. Smith, 'II Isaiah and the Persians', *JAOS* 83 (1963), pp. 415-21, argued that the first part of the inscription, which provides a theological justification of the conquest of Babylon and speaks of Cyrus in the third person, was put together by the Babylonian priesthood before the conquest of the city and provided the model for the pro-Cyrus propaganda in Isa. 40–48.

addressed to the congregation under the names of Israel, Jacob, Jeshurun:[9]

> I will pour water on the thirsty land,
> Streams of water on the parched land;
> I will pour out my spirit on your descendants,
> My blessing on your offspring.
> They shall spring up like verdure amid waters, (?)
> Like willows by flowing streams.
> This one will say, 'I belong to YHWH',
> Another will receive the name Jacob,
> Yet another will write on his hand, 'belonging to YHWH',
> And adopt the name Israel (44.3-5).

The prophet has in mind the blessing on Abraham which is to make of him a great nation (Gen. 12.1-3), but he gives it a decisively new slant by interpreting the blessing of the nations (reading 'by you all the families of the earth *shall be blessed*') as adherence to the religion of Abraham's descendants. In other words, a well-known text is reinterpreted with prophetic authority in light of a new situation, that of a confessional community adherence to which can come about by personal decision. For the prophetic author, therefore, the YHWH-cult is already in principle a religion which accepts proselytes. Adherence is sealed by certain external and symbolic acts which, perhaps significantly, do not include circumcision. As in Christian baptism, there is the taking of a new name, a practice deducible also from Second Temple onomastics.[10] The writing of the deity's name on the hand signifies a change of ownership or allegiance, reminiscent of the custom of tattooing slaves.[11] For later readers it would inevitably recall the phylacteries or *tefillin* bound on the hand and the forehead, indicative of Jewish identity.[12]

All of this is couched in the future tense, and we have no way of

9.   Isa. 44.1-2. With the following passage cf. the somewhat similar Ps. 89.4-6.

10.   RSV's translation of *kinnâ* as 'surname' is anachronistic. On the relation between names and cults in the Neo-Babylonian and Persian periods see M. Smith in W.D. Davies and L. Finkelstein (eds.), *The Cambridge History of Judaism*, I (Cambridge: Cambridge University Press, 1984), pp. 220-33.

11.   Which, however, did not prevent YHWH from reciprocating the gesture; 'Behold, I have graven you on the palm of my hands', Isa. 49.16.

12.   Deut. 8.6. The Isaiah targum has nothing about writing on the hand but speaks of 'YHWH fearers' and 'drawing near in the name of Israel', language associated with proselytism; see J.F. Stenning, *The Targum of Isaiah* (Oxford: Clarendon Press, 1949), pp. 148-49.

knowing what it corresponded to in terms of sociological realities in the Babylonian diaspora. Our next passage is well-known and much quoted in this context:

> Assemble and come, draw near all together,
> You survivors among the nations!
> (Those who carry around their wooden idols and pray to a god who
>   cannot save are ignorant.)
> State your case, present it; let them consult together;
> Who announced this of old, declared it long ago?
> Was it not I YHWH? There is no other god beside me,
> None victorious and saving, there is none but me.
>
> Turn to me and be saved, all the ends of the earth,
> For I am God and there is no other.
> By myself I have sworn,
> Victory has gone forth from my mouth,
> A word which shall not return.
> For to me every knee shall bend,
> By me every tongue shall swear,
> 'In YHWH alone', it shall be said of me, 'is victory and strength'
>   (45.20-25).

The summons is addressed to survivors of, or among, the nations. The gloss which follows (in parenthesis) suggests that these survivors are Gentiles, not diaspora Jews;[13] and indeed this kind of summons is regularly addressed to Gentiles in Second Isaiah, itself a noteworthy indicator of a new situation. The prophet may have had in mind the defeated, or about to be defeated, Babylonians among whom the deportees lived,[14] but the invitation to be saved goes out to the ends of the earth. All Gentiles are invited to turn to YHWH to accept salvation from him as the only one able to confer it. Since the ability to save is the test of divine reality, the existence of other deities is, for all practical purposes, negated.

What, then, does this 'turning to YHWH' as the precondition of salvation imply? One could turn to a deity and offer acts of cult in return for favors received without making a complete break with one's past. To use A.D. Nock's well-known distinction, adhesion was possible without conversion.[15] The sequel, however, suggests something more than

13. P.A.H. de Boer, *Second Isaiah's Message* (Leiden: Brill, 1956), p. 90.
14. Weinfeld, 'Universalism and Particularism', p. 175.
15. A.D. Nock, *Conversion* (repr.; Oxford: Clarendon Press, 1952 [1933]), p. 7 and throughout.

this. The bending of the knee (*proskynesis*) and the confession of faith in YHWH alone seem to imply abandonment of the worship of other gods and therefore a more radical re-orientation of one's religious life.

This is a point of quite exceptional importance; for we now have, in addition to the taking of a new name and other symbolic indicators of a new allegiance, the essential element of a *confession of faith*. Such a confession appears in a somewhat different form earlier in the same chapter: 'God is with you and there is no other; no other god' (45.14). The situation here is certainly different, since it is predicted that Egyptians and other foreigners will come in as slaves.[16] Another example of this typical 'fantasy of the oppressed' occurs in Isa. 14.1-2, a prose insertion which is certainly post-exilic, and which foresees proselytes (*gērîm*) as part of the reconstituted Israel of the future. While we have little to go on, it makes sense to suggest that such confessions as these, in the mouth of new adherents to the YHWH cult, the Jewish religion, draw on actual praxis and experience as early as the neo-Babylonian and Persian periods. Other examples which should be taken into consideration, all of which exemplify the process of conversion in later Jewish tradition,[17] are the following:

1. Jethro, father-in-law of Moses, is catechized by Moses, the instruction dealing with the previous history of YHWH with his people; he makes a confession of faith: 'Now I know that YHWH is greater than all gods...'; and he offers sacrifice (Exod. 18.8-12).

2. Rahab of Jericho recites what sounds like a similar piece of catechetical instruction; she then makes the confession, 'YHWH your God is he who is God in heaven above and on earth beneath' (Josh. 2.9-11).

---

16. C. Westermann, *Isaiah 40–66* (Philadelphia: Fortress Press, 1969), p. 169, is probably correct in his view that these verses are out of place.

17. As far as I have been able to discover, no comprehensive historical study of proselytism has appeared since B.J. Bamberger, *Proselytism in the Talmudic Period* (New York, 1939) and W.G. Braude, *Jewish Proselytizing in the First Five Centuries of the Common Era, The Age of the Tannaim and Amoraim* (Cambridge, MA: Harvard University Press, 1946). G.F. Moore, *Judaism in the First Centuries of the Christian Era* (New York, 1971 [1927]), I, pp. 323-53 can still be read with profit.

3. On being healed, Naaman the Syrian makes the extraordinary confession of faith, 'Now I know that there is no god in all the earth except in Israel' (2 Kgs 5.15).

The list is not, of course, exhaustive. Rabbinic tradition, which traces the history of proselytism, by a remarkable paradox, back to Abraham, has no difficulty finding prototypes in biblical narrative for every kind of proselyte.[18] The suggestion offered here is that the indications in Second Isaiah, few as they are, can be explained with references to the beginnings of proselytism in the Babylonian diaspora.

Since the claim of universalism has generally relied heavily on a certain interpretation of the Servant poems, we cannot leave Isaiah 40–48 without taking note of the only one of the four which occurs in this section (42.1-4). Here YHWH addresses an audience, not specified but probably, as elsewhere, in the Gentile world. The purpose of the address is to recommend an individual whom he has chosen, whom he supports, who is endowed with the divine spirit, and whose mission is to establish law and order among the nations, but without the violence and brutality generally assciated with this task. The identity of this individual has always been, and will no doubt continue to be, the subject of inconclusive speculation.[19] As has just been noted, however, this is the only one of the four 'songs' which occurs in this first section of Isaiah 40–66. It may therefore call for an interpretation quite different from the other three, one more in keeping with the thematic of the section as a whole. It does not seem likely that this designated individual is a prophetic

18. In his undertaking a journey of faith out of paganism and idolatry, Abraham exhibited the characteristics of the ideal proselyte. In both Philo and Hebrews Abraham is represented as a journeyer, a traveller, in keeping with a supposed derivation of the word 'Hebrew'; one who 'passes over', *peratēs* in Philo: *De Migr. Abr.* 4.20, Cf: Heb. 11.9, 13; followed by Origen (*Patrologia Graeca* 12.725). Philo also speaks of the proselyte in language reminiscent of Gen. 12.1-3; it is therefore as an imitator of Abraham that the proselyte is entitled to respect, *De Spec. Leg.* 1.51. Rabbinic texts distinguish between the *gēr ṣedeq*, who is circumcised, and the *gēr tôshab*, who observes the Noachic laws but is not yet circumcised (for references see Bamberger, *Proselytism*, pp. 134-35). Other categories include the Gibeonites (Josh. 9) who became *gērîm* by sleight of hand and are therefore known as *gērîm gᵉrûrîm* which can perhaps be translated as 'hangers on', and the inhabitants of the north after the fall of Samaria who had to be frightened into it by lions (2 Kgs 17.24-28), and are therefore known as *gērē ʾarāyôt*, lion proselytes.

19. The broad array of options is catalogued by C.R. North, *Suffering Servant*. Others have been added since.

figure. The prophetic commissioning does not call for witnesses, and prophets are not called to establish law and order, least of all among the Gentiles. Comparison with the designation of David by Samuel resulting in the conferring of the spirit (1 Sam. 16), the Isaian poem about the ideal ruler, also endowed with the spirit and charged with establishing order non-violently (Isa. 11.1-9), and similar allusions to the ideal dynast (e.g. Isa. 55.34; Jer. 33.15), points unmistakeably to a royal figure. In that case the general context of Isaiah 40–48, and the unit immediately preceding (41.25-29), would strongly support the candidacy of Cyrus as the one charged by YHWH with this responsibility. And, if that is so, the idea that the author and his support-group cherished the dream of a world mission by Israel or a representative of Israel would not find support in this passage.

Isaiah 49–55

Throughout Second Isaiah we sense a certain ambiguity in the *golah* community's perception of the Gentile world and their relations with it. Here and there we have intimations of a community prepared to serve as the humble instrument of God's purposes in the world. With at least equal frequency, however, we hear the voice of an oppressed and resentful people, the dream of a reversal of fortune which will bring the great powers into subjection to Israel and its God. It must seem strange that this way of thinking, which reaches its most extreme expression in the so-called Isaian apocalypse (chs. 24–27), should be mistaken for universalism. In the present section we hear much of the subjection of foreign peoples and their rulers (49.7; 54.3). They will perform menial labor, bow down before the elect, and lick the dust of their feet (49.23). If the nations are to be saved, it will be at the price of subjection; the basic metaphor is imperium (e.g. 51.4-5). The universal domination of YHWH is a prominent theme throughout the section. Already implicit in creation (51.9-11), it will be inaugurated in Zion witnessed by the nations of the world (52.7-10). Return to Zion is therefore a precondition of this reversal of fortune, and it is the principal task of the Gentiles to see to the repatriation of Jewry dispersed throughout the vast Babylonian empire (49.22).

If we recall that this task was first assigned to Cyrus (44.28; 45.13), we may have a clue to the interpretation of the second of the servant poems which opens this section (49.1-6). It begins, as does the first, with an address to the nations, but this time by the one commissioned. He is set aside from the womb to be a chosen instrument. His mission is, in the first place, to re-assemble dispersed Israel. He feels that it has not succeeded, but is told not only to persevere in it but to undertake a further mission to the Gentile world. He is to be a light to the nations, the means by which the saving power of YHWH will reach to the ends of the earth.

This second 'song' is no more forthcoming on the identity of this agent than the first. The text testifies to an early identification with Israel (v. 3), a solution which has remained standard in Jewish interpretations of the servant passages. But it then goes on to speak of a mission to Israel, and therefore implies an individual or plurality within the *golah* community convinced of the need to undertake the mission. Since it is no longer a question of a public installation requiring witnesses, and since the task is to be accomplished by speaking (49.2), we are probably to think of a prophetic individual and his following, especially in view of the language of prophetic revelation used in the third servant poem (50.4-5). We are not told how the Gentile world is to be enlightened, whether by example alone or, as understood in early Christianity (Acts 13.47; 26.23), by a mission of preaching. In one passage (Isa. 51.4-5), the 'light to the nations' is identified with YHWH's *torah* (law) and *mishpat* (justice), in other words, his jurisdiction. If our interpretation of the first servant poem is correct, these were to be the characteristics of Cyrus's rule as mandated by YHWH. But after it became clear that Cyrus had failed to discharge this task, the responsibility reverted to the *golah* community and its prophetic representatives.

If this line of interpretation is correct, it will help to explain why there is no further mention of Cyrus in this section. It is a common experience that promises made to supporters during political campaigns often go by the board once the candidate is in power. The *golah* community, or that part of it represented by the Isaian prophet, had backed Cyrus to the hilt. Despite the fact that he permitted the repatriation of Jews and other deportees, the more idealistic of the prophet's support-group must have felt let down. He did not, after all, restore the native dynasty. Far from acknowledging the role of YHWH in his spectacular success, he claimed to rule in the name and by favor of Marduk, restored the great *akitu* festival which Nabonidus had neglected, and had his son Cambyses play the leading role in it.[20] The ensuing disillusionment is reflected in the

20. J.M. Cook, *The Persian Empire* (London: Dent, 1983), p. 32.

unequal struggle between vision and reality recorded in the remaining chapters of the book.

Before leaving Isaiah 40–55 we will reformulate the question at the head of this paper: To what extent does Second Isaiah—leaving aside for the moment the matter of singie or multiple authorship—mark a break with the past and initiate new developments in the relation of Israel (nascent Judaism) to the Gentile world? The concentration on international affairs—*the* characteristic of Israelite prophecy according to Max Weber[21]—certainly continues to be in evidence, but the *raison d'être* is still Israel and its destiny. In addition, interest in the nations is not particularly benign.[22] Cyrus is greeted with exalted language, he is even described as YHWH's messiah, but the new order which he is to institute is of interest only insofar as it affects his Jewish subjects. Disillusionment with Cyrus after the collapse of the Babylonian empire made way for the idea of direct divine intervention and encouraged an apocalyptic view of politics. None of this was calculated to promote a positive approach to the Gentile world and its ultimate destiny.

The point has often been made that Second Isaiah was the preacher of monotheism, and that monotheism entailed religious universalism. Belief in the cosmic power and incomparability of Israel's God was not a discovery of the exilic age, although in Second Isaiah it achieved a degree of consistency unknown earlier.[23] It is also formulated in terms of a unique power to save, even of a universal will to save, although the conditions under which this could come about are not entirely clear. The negative side is the correlation between triumphant monotheistic faith and political domination, restricted to the realm of aspiration and fantasy in exilic prophecy, translated into reality during much of the history of Christendom and Islam. The positive side, as widely understood, is to be

21. M. Weber, *The Sociology of Religion* (Beacon, 1963 [1917–1919]), p. 51.

22. In this respect I agree with the cautious approach to the issue of P.A.H. de Boer, *Second Isaiah's Message*, pp. 120 and N.H. Snaith, 'The Servant of the Lord in Deutero-Isaiah', in H.H. Rowley (ed.), *Studies in Old Testament Prophecy* (Edinburgh: T. & T. Clark, 1950), p. 191; see also R.N. Whybray, *The Second Isaiah* (Sheffield: JSOT Press, 1983), pp. 62-65.

23. See, *inter alios*, J. Morgenstern, 'Deutero-Isaiah's Terminology for "Universal God"', *JBL* 62 (1943), pp. 269-80; M. Smith, 'Second Isaiah and the Persians', pp. 418-21, who argued for Zoroastrian influence on Second Isaiah's formulations. Following the Scandinavian school, J.H. Eaton, *Festal Drama in Deutero-Isaiah* (London: SPCK, 1979), exaggerates the bearing of the New Year festival and the ancient Near Eastern ideology of kingship on these chapters.

found especially in the Servant Songs.[24] To the extent that servanthood is the expression of the prophetic idea of instrumentality in Second Isaiah, and is in the service of a wider public than Israel, we would have a breakthrough of great significance for the future. It seems to be the case, however, that only the second of these four passages (49.1-6) alludes in any way to a mission or even an aspiration of this kind originating in the *golah* community. Perhaps the most we can say, therefore, is that Second Isaiah laid the foundations for later developments by making it possible to think of a role for Israel in the salvation of humankind.

In the last analysis, the most interesting result of our reading of Second Isaiah is that it allows us to see the emergence of a confessional community open on principle to outsiders. One indication is the reinterpretation of the promise to Abraham to include proselytes. Much, of course, remained to be worked out with regard to the conditions under which outsiders could become insiders—a subject which occasioned controversy, as we shall now see, from the beginning of the second temple period.

Isaiah 56–66

Since the late nineteenth century the last eleven chapters of Isaiah have been taken by most commentators to form a distinct literary unity of post-exilic origin. A closer determination of date is complicated by the presence of much liturgical and parenetic material (e.g. 58–59; 63.7–64.12) and the suspicion that some of the prophetic diatribe (e.g. 56.9–57.13) may be originally pre-exilic.[25] Making all due allowance for these factors, and for the likelihood of additions and expansions to meet new situations as they arose, we note that the temple is still in ruins (63.18-19), Jerusalem is still an unwalled city (58.12; 60.10), and the rest of the country has not yet recovered from the effects of the Babylonian

24. E.g. 'Behind the figure of the servant stands the idea of the mission of Israel and here it is a prophetic mission', S.H. Blank, *Prophetic Faith in Isaiah*, p. 149; cf. P. Altmann, *Erwählungstheologie und Universalismus im Alten Testament* (Berlin: de Gruyter, 1964), pp. 30-48.

25. On the pre-exilic basis for 56.9–57.13 see C. Westermann, *Isaiah 40–66*, pp. 301-302. The communal lament in 63.7–64.12 is perhaps exilic and Palestinian; see R.N. Whybray, *Isaiah 40–66*, p. 256; P.D. Hanson, *The Dawn of Apocalyptic* (Philadelphia: Fortress Press, 1975), p. 87.

devastation (61.4; 64.10-11). The wretched economic and social conditions attested to are matched by similar allusions in Haggai and Zechariah from the early Persian period.[26] The close correspondence between the criticism of contemporary attitudes to fasting in 58.1-9 and Zech. 7.1-14 and 8.18-19 points in the same direction,[27] and leads to the conclusion that the nucleus of the collection originated in the province of Judah during the first two decades of Persian rule before the rebuilding of the temple (completed about 515 BCE).

The close connections between chs. 56–66 and 40–55, which appear at times as commentary related to text,[28] suggest further an origin of some of the dicta in Isa. 56–66 among disciples of the exilic Isaiah who were attempting to come to terms with the disconfirmation of the hopes raised by his preaching.[29] Such an association would explain not only the obvious fact that 56–66 have been added to 40–55, but also the designation 'servants of YHWH' by which a prophetic-eschatological group in the province referred to itself (65.8-9, 13-16).[30]

As it happens, most of this section is concerned with the internal affairs of Jews in the province and only incidentally with international concerns. It is generally assumed that the nucleus of the collection is the compendium of eschatological teaching in 60–62, where continuity with the thought of the exilic Isaiah is most in evidence. According to this teaching, Jerusalem is the political and religious center of the world, a circle of bright light surrounded by darkness in which the nations languish (60.1-3). The Gentiles will be drawn to that light as to a magnet in order to *witness* YHWH's triumphant intervention on behalf of his people (62.1-2). Their role will be to bring tribute (60.5-7, 11, 16),

26. Hag. 1.6, 8-11; 2.16-17; Zech. 8.10; cf. Joel 1–2 and Neh. 5.1-5.

27. In both texts ritual observance is contrasted with the practice of social justice and works of mercy. With Zech. 7.13 ('as I called and they would not hear, so they called and I would not hear'). Cf. Isa. 58.9 ('then you shall call and YHWH will answer; you shall cry and he will say, 'Here I am'). The Zechariah passage is dated 518 BCE.

28. 62.10-12 appears to be a revised version of 40.1-3; Cf. also 57.14 with 40.3-5; 61.14 with 42.1 and 49.6-9.

29. This particular instance of cognitive dissonance is studied by H.-J. Kraus, 'Die ausgebliebene Endtheophanie. Eine Studie zu Jes. 56-66', ZAW 78 (1966), pp. 317-32.

30. On these 'servants' or 'quakers' (*hᵃrēdîm*) see my *A History Of Prophecy in Israel*, pp. 248-51 and 'The "Servants of the Lord" in Third Isaiah', *Proceedings of the Irish Biblical Association*, 7 (1983), pp. 1-23.

analogous to the tithes which Israelites bring to their priests (61.6).[31] They will also supply the labor for the rebuilding of the temple and serve as *Gastarbeiter* in a range of menial capacities (60.10, 12-14; 61.5-6; etc). The whole world will stand in awe, the kings of the nations will be led to Jerusalem in triumphal procession (60.11), the supremacy of Israel will be universally acknowledged (60.14), and so on. It all sounds as if the nations are being made an offer they can't refuse.

Also symptomatic is the interpretation of the Abrahamic blessing in terms not of proselytism but of imperium (60.21-22; 61.8-9). Following an older pattern of interpretation, the same text (Gen. 12.1-3) is associated with the Davidic dynasty, the promise of its eventual revival, and nostalgia for the Greater Israel of the Davidic-Solomonic epoch (Isa. 55.3-5).[32] This fantasy of an Israelite empire on which the sun never sets represents one form of universalism, but not the kind usually associated with Second Isaiah. In the opening and closing passages or 'book ends' of the so-called Trito-Isaiah, however, there finds expression a very different approach to 'the others'. Isa. 56.1-8 may be translated more or less literally as follows:

> Thus says YHWH:
> Preserve justice and do righteousness,
> For soon my salvation will come,
> And my triumph will be revealed.
> Blessed is the man who does this
> The son of man who holds it fast,

31. The description of the people as 'priests of YHWH' is therefore metaphorical, and there is consequently no 'astonishing democratization of the formerly exclusive sacerdotal office' as claimed by Hanson, *The Dawn of Apocalyptic*, pp. 67-68.

32. The 'great nation' theme, based on Gen. 12.1-3, underlies passages like Isa. 60.21-22 and 61.8b-9. The transfer of the Abrahamic covenant to the Davidic dynasty is assumed in 55.3-5, on which see O. Eissfeldt, 'The Promises of Grace to David in Isaiah 55.1-5', in B.W. Anderson and W. Harrelson (eds.), *Israel's Prophetic Heritage* (London: SCM Press, 1962), pp. 192-207; it also appears in a number of exilic prophetic texts—Jer. 23.5-6; 33.14-26; Ezek 34.23-24; 37.24-28. Post-exilic texts testify to a kind of crypto-messianism, understandable in the circumstances, exemplified by the codename Branch (*ṣemaḥ*) used of the Davidite Zerubbabel (Zech. 3.8; 6.12), cf. Jer. 33.15 (*ʾaṣmiaḥ lᵉdāwid ṣemaḥ ṣᵉdāqāh*). Isa. 61.8-9 alludes to blessings in the form of an everlasting covenant; and although the dynasty is not mentioned, associations already well established suggest that the author has the Davidic covenant in mind. The passage is rounded off with a psalm (61.11) which plays on the stem *ṣmḥ* (*ṣemaḥ taṣmîaḥ yaṣmâḥ*); cf. Isa. 45.8.

Who keeps sabbath without profaning it,
Who refrains from doing evil of any kind.

Let not the foreigner, the convert to YHWH, say,
'YHWH will surely separate me from his people';
Nor let the eunuch say, 'See, I am a withered tree'.

For thus says YHWH:
'To the eunuchs who observe my sabbaths,
Who choose what pleases me and hold fast to my covenant,
I will give a monument and a name in my house and within my
        wall,
Better than sons and daughters;
I will give then an everlasting name which shall not be cut off:

And the foreigners who have converted to YHWH,
To minister to him, to love his name, and to be his servants;
All who observe sabbath without profaning it,
Who hold fast to my covenant;
These I will bring to my holy mountain,
And make them glad in my house of prayer;
Their burnt offerings and sacrifices will be accepted on my altar;
For my house shall be called a house of prayer for all peoples.'

Oracle of the Lord YHWH
Who gathers the outcasts of Israel:
'I will gather yet others to him besides those already gathered'.

Arguably, the passage betrays a basic rhetorical and thematic unity despite the many efforts made to break it down into chronologically diverse components.[33] It begins and ends with the assurance of salvation consisting in the ingathering of the outcasts who are to form the future Israel. In its central part it speaks of two classes of these 'dubiously belonging' people, gives expression to their fears, and sets those fears at rest. The sense runs over from one saying to the next; the conditions for blessing laid down in the first are applied in the second, and the third places the foreigners and eunuchs among those in good standing in the community of Israel.

The first part of the saying (vv. 1-2) is a prophetic admonition to observe justice and righteousness *in view* of the imminent parousia. The

---

33. E.g. the analysis of J. Vermeylen, *Du Prophète Isaïe à l'Apocalyptique* (Paris: Gabalda, 1978), II, pp. 455-58 (vv. 1-2, 3-7, 8); J.D. Smart, *History and Theology in Second Isaiah* (Philadelphia: Fortress Press, 1965), p. 237; R.N. Whybray, *Isaiah 40–66*, p. 199

injunction is further expressed in specific forms (sabbath observance) and generic terms (avoidance of evil). The underlying idea, expressed here for the first time and taken up in early Christianity, is that fidelity can advance and sin retard the advent of salvation (cf. also 59.1-2). There follow the complaints of foreigners who have joined themselves to YHWH and of eunuchs. The identity of these two categories is not in doubt. To 'join oneself' (the verb *lwh* in niphal) to YHWH means to embrace the YHWH cult, to become a proselyte.[34] 'Eunuch' would apply to those Jews or proselytes who had been sexually mutilated to qualify them for certain positions in the imperial service, especially in the harem.[35] Their misgivings are met with an assurance of good standing in the cult community, one way of saying which is that their prayers and sacrifices are declared acceptable.[36] Since competence to participate in and, of course, support the cult, also determined civic status, including title to real estate (cf. Ezek. 11.14-17), the importance of this assurance can hardly be exaggerated.

The observation was made earlier that passages in Isaiah 56–66 can be shown to relate to passages in Isaiah 40–55 as commentary to text. It is worth noting, for example, that the opening words of our passage (v. 1) take up the eschatological teaching of Second Isaiah (46.13; 51.5), and take it further by associating ethics with eschatology.[37] Equally interesting is the last 'oracle' (*nᵉʾum*) which paraphrases very closely an earlier saying about the ingathering of the Jewish diaspora (Isa. 11.12), but updates it by adding recruits from the Gentile world (56.8). This process of adaptation, further 'revelation' drawn out of the traditum in the light of new experience, corresponds to developments of great interest:

---

34. Therefore the term *hannilweh ʾel YHWH* is practically synonymous with *gēr*; see Isa. 14.1; Zech. 2.15 [Eng. 2.11]; Est. 9.27. Est. 8.17 has the only occurrence in biblical Hebrew of the verb *hityahēd*, to become Jewish (or, perhaps, to pretend to be Jewish?).

35. One must suppose that the punning use of *yád*, monument but also phallus, together with *ʾᵃšer loʾ yikkārēt*, 'which shall not be cut off', is deliberate.

36. The connection between good standing and the ability to offer acceptable gifts is still detectable in the use of cultic terminology in the New Testament; e.g. *prosagōgē*, Rom. 5.2.

37. The same connection has long been the subject of debate in the context of early Christian faith.

1.   Incorporation and membership are determined not on ethnic or national considerations but on a profession of faith and a level of moral performance compatible with it. In this respect the sayings advocate an open admissions policy of remarkable liberality.

2.   This policy is in function of eschatological faith, belief in the reality of a final decisive intervention of God. The ingathered Israel of the future is to include both ethnic Judeans (Jews) and recruits from the Gentile world.

It would be natural to go on to ask on what grounds the status of these foreigners and eunuchs was threatened. One might think of certain prescriptions in the Ezekielan 'law of the temple' which take a dim view of the presence of foreigners in the sanctuary (Ezek. 44.4-14). Both the Ezekiel text and Isa. 56.1-8 seem to refer back to the cultic stipulation in Num. 18.1-7 (P) which defines the respective spheres of priests and of Levites who join them and minister to them—the same verbs as are used of foreigners in Isa. 56.1-8. While Ezek. 44.4-14 and Isa. 56.1-8 can hardly be described as contrasting prophetic interpretations of Numbers 18,[38] they both appear to take off from this text, and move in opposite directions in defining qualifications for participation in the cult at different levels: according to Ezekiel, those of foreign descent in Israel are debarred from the temple and, *a fortiori*, from service in the sanctuary; according to Isaiah, foreigners already incorporated in Israel are assured of their good standing in the cult community and are even eligible to serve in the sanctuary.[39] While we do not know the date of the Ezekiel text,[40] we appear to have the interesting situation of contrasting adjudications of an extremely important point of law on the basis of prophetic revelation.

Comparison with the Ezekiel text raises the issue of ethnic qualification or disqualification but not that of physical integrity. As is well known, the latter was an essential prerequisite for ordination to the priesthood (Lev. 21.16-24, especially v. 20). A set of stipulations in Deuteronomy known as 'the law of the assembly' (23.2-9) lists both

38. As argued by M. Fishbane, *Biblical Interpretation in Ancient Israel* (Oxford: Clarendon Press, 1985), pp. 138-43.

39. This would seem to follow from the verb *lᵉšārtô* Isa. 56.6, cf. Num. 18.2. Isa. 66.21 says it more clearly.

40. Fishbane (*Biblical Interpretation in Ancient Israel*, p. 119) seems to assume without argument that Ezek. 40–48 is roughly contemporary with Ezra.

ethnic and physical disqualifications for membership in the *q^ehal YHWH* (LXX: *ekklēsia tou theou*). The date of this series of laws is unknown. If genuinely ancient, a conclusion by no means certain,[41] it could be appealed to as authoritative by Nehemiah in the fifth century BCE (Neh. 13.1-9) and by the Qumran community some three centuries later (4QFlor 1.4). It debars from membership in the cult community the following categories of males:

1.   The sexually mutilated, those with crushed testicles or excised male organ;
2.   Bastards (*mamzerim*), either those born of incestuous union or, more likely, those of mixed Jewish-Gentile descent;[42]
3.   Ammonites and Moabites *in perpetuum*;
4.   First and second generation Edomites and Egyptians.

The combination of foreign proselytes and the sexually mutilated suggests very strongly that the misgivings expressed in Isa. 56.1-8 arose from the threatened application of this law. In which case, as suggested earlier, we would have an example of the abrogation of a point of *torah* on prophetic authority, an interesting and potentially very important precedent.

It may be possible to determine more precisely the circumstances which detemined this prophetic reassurance. During his first administration, Nehemiah attempted to enforce this law, which apparently was not being observed, and excluded from the community all those of mixed descent (Neh. 13.1-3).[43] During his subsequent absence at the

41.   G. von Rad (*Deuteronomy* [Philadelphia: Westminster Press, 1966], p. 145) thinks it is 'a splendid piece of ancient Yahwistic legal matter'. Most commentators seem to follow K. Galling, 'Das Gemeindegesetz in Deuteronomium 23', in *A. Bertholet Festschrift* (Tübingen: Mohr, 1950), pp. 176-91, who traces it back into the cult of the pre-state period.

42.   The former alternative, assumed in later Jewish halakic teaching, is defended by C.M. Carmichael, *The Laws of Deuteronomy* (Ithaca, NY: Cornell University Press, 1974), pp. 173-74 and by A. Phillips, *Deuteronomy* (Cambridge: Cambridge University Press, 1973), p. 154, *inter alios*. However, it may be noted that the only other occurrence of the word in biblical Hebrew, at Zech. 9.6, refers to the mixed population of Ashdod, recalling Nehemiah's violent reaction to marriage with Ashdodite women (Neh. 13 23-24).

43.   *kol-^cereb*, v. 3. Even if the original meaning of *^cereb* was different (= 'immigrant' according to W.A. van der Weiden, *VD* 44 [1966], pp. 97-104), at the

court in Susa, however, the high priest gave accommodation in the temple precincts to Tobiah, an Ammonite, in defiance of the law, a situation which Nehemiah on his return lost no time in rectifying (13.4-9). He also took decisive measures against Jews who had married Ashdodite, Ammonite and Moabite women,[44] this time following a certain interpretation of Deut. 7.3 (Neh. 13.23-27). Nehemiah's memoir is silent on the subject of eunuchs. If, as cupbearer and winetaster of the Persian king, he was one himself, the silence would be understandable, but this is by no means certain.[45]

Since it is possible that similar rigorist measures may have been advocated earlier, we cannot be sure that the prophetic utterances in Isa. 56.1-8 and Ezek. 44.4-9 either directly precipitated or were precipitated by the rigorist measures of Nehemiah in the second half of the fifth century BCE. In fact, tension and occasional conflict between integrationist elements and those who advocated a more open admissions policy can be assumed for the entire period of the Second Commonwealth, an obvious but important point for students of early Christianity to bear in mind. It is, at any rate, clear from Isa. 56.1-8 that Jewish communities had already begun to attract proselytes, and that the conditions under which they could be incorporated constituted a problem patient of very different solutions.

We must now turn to the other 'book end', the *finale* of Third Isaiah and therefore of the Isaiah scroll. The final verses (66.22-24) repeat the eschatological vision of the new heavens and the new earth and of the temple as the center of the remade cosmos. A later hand has rounded this off with the dark scenario of the survivors of the final struggle between good and evil going out of the city to inspect the corpses of the enemy. The wording is meant to recall the opening oracle of Isaiah (1.1-2), so rounding off the book with an *inclusio*.[46]

time of writing it clearly referred to a mixed population; cf Exod. 12.38; Jer. 25.20; 50.37 and the corresponding verbal form at Ezra 9.2.

44. The text may have spoken originally only of Ashdodites, though there are no pressing reasons for taking 'Ammonitesses and Moabitesses' as a gloss; see D.J.A. Clines, *Ezra, Nehemiah, Esther* (Grand Rapids: Eerdmans, 1984), p. 246.

45. Neh. 1.11. Not all cupbearers were eunuchs; and if Nehemiah had been such, and it was known in the province, we would have expected his enemies to have used it against him; it would also have rendered their allegations of messianic pretensions on his part quite implausible (Neh. 6.7).

46. *pošꜥîm bî* (66.24), cf. *pāšꜥû bî* (1.2). The word *dērāʾôn*, abhorrence, which occurs only here and at Dan. 12.2 where it describes the fate of the opponents of the

The preceding prose passage is the one which concerns us; it runs as follows:

> For I am coming[47] to gather all nations and races, so that they may come and see my glory. I will set a sign[48] among them, and I will send some of them, survivors, to the nations—Tarshish, Put, Lud, Meshech, Rosh, Tubal, Yavan, the far islands—[49] who have not heard tell of me or seen my glory; they shall declare my glory among the nations.
>
> [They shall bring all your brethren from all the nations as an offering to YHWH, on horses, in chariots, on waggons, on mules and dromedaries, to my holy mountain Jerusalem, says YHWH, just as Israelites themselves bring the offering in a pure vessel to the house of YHWH.] And I will also take some of them to be priests and Levites, says YHWH (66.18-21).

The opening sentence places the events described in the context of the end time, and therefore parallels Isa. 56.1-8. It is the old theme of the ingathering, but this time to be preceded by the sending out of emissaries or missionaries to the Gentiles[50] to preach the religion of YHWH, the Jewish religion. The missionaries are certainly Jews from the homeland or the diaspora, the designation 'survivors'—if it is not a gloss—alluding to those who had come through the trauma of exile with their faith intact. Nothing is said in explanation of the sign which is to be set up among the Gentiles. However, the same Isaian text which we have seen to be reinterpreted at Isa. 56.8 also speaks of a rallying point for the assembly and homeward journey of dispersed Jews, and in much the same terms (Isa. 11.11-12). It has therefore served as a starting point, a traditum interpreted at both the beginning and the end of Third Isaiah to accommodate a new situation and a new possibility, that of converts from the Gentile world.

The central 'message' of Isa. 66.18-21, therefore, is that there is to be a mission to the Gentiles as a necessary prelude to the parousia, the final decisive manifestation of God in human history. Indeed, the final sen-

maśkîlîm, gIves some indication of the milieu in which this final statement in the Isaiah scroll originated.

47. MT adds 'their deeds and their thoughts' which may have strayed from 66.17b; see Westermann, *Isaiah 40–66*, p. 422.

48. *'ôt*; 1QIsa has pl. *'ôtôt*.

49. 'Put' for MT 'Pul'; 'Meshech, Rosh' (still sometimes identified with Moscow and Russia!) for MT *môškê qešet*, drawers of the bow. The location of these places is not our concern. The writer has drawn on Gen. 10 and Ezek. 27 and 38.

50. 'All nations and races [literally, tongues]' is not restricted to the Jewish diaspora; cf. Zech. 8.23; Dan. 3.4; 6.25; 7.29.

tence even contemplates Gentiles being admitted to the priesthood and Levitical office, which once again implies the abrogation of ritual law by virtue of prophetic authority.[51] It is hardly surprising if moves of such boldness and liberality met with resistance. The sentence which we have placed in parentheses (v. 20) provides immediate confirmation. It deals with a quite different theme, that of the repatriation of diaspora Jews— responsibility for which is charged to the Gentiles (cf 59.18-19; 60.4-14). Since it does not make a good fit with the context, we follow those who take it to be an attempt to correct the remarkable claim that a Gentile mission must precede the final showdown in Jerusalem.[52]

To speak of a Gentile mission does not, of course, mean that we are dealing with actual proposals and strategies. What these texts express are attitudes, even dreams and fantasies, entertained in one segment of post-exilic Judaism. That such attitudes can be self-deceptive, self-serving and self-defeating goes without saying. But it is also true to our experience to affirm that projections of a possible future, especially when emitted with the passion and power of conviction often attested in these chapters, can actually create a future, even if the reality is never quite the same as the projection.

51. It is certainly a question of Gentiles, since there would be nothing remarkable about Jews, even diaspora Jews, exercising these functions; see Westermann, *Isaiah 40–66*, p. 426; Whybray, *Isaiah 40–66*, pp. 291-92; Smart, *History and Theology in Second Isaiah*, p. 291.

52. Westermann (*Isaiah 40–66*, p. 423) speaks of 'an abrupt confrontation between universalism and particularism'.

JSOT 43 (1989), pp. 95-107

JEREMIAH AS PROPHET OF NONVIOLENT RESISTANCE

Daniel L. Smith

In Robert Carroll's work, *From Chaos to Covenant: Uses of Prophecy in the Book of Jeremiah*,[1] there is a spirited criticism of attempts to moralize on the basis of Jeremiah's advice to exiles, advice summarized in Jeremiah's 'letter' in ch. 29: 'seek the Peace of the city where you live'. Arguing in a manner reminiscent of Henry J. Cadbury's *The Peril of Modernizing Jesus*, Carrol warned against 'modernizing' Jeremiah's advice in order to derive a mandate for what could be a simplistic appeasement or pacifism. While I agree that such a simplistic pacifism cannot be derived from the ethics of Jeremiah, much less the intention of Jeremiah's 'Letter' in ch. 29, it will be the purpose of this study to show that the advice, although nonviolent, was anything but simplistic. From an understanding of the critical and literary details of ch. 29, we will discover that the intention of the letter was to recommend a strategic posture for exilic existence that is best described as 'nonviolent social resistance'.

Jeremiah 29 is written in prose, and much debate taken place over the date and origin of the prose sections. Since this material specifically mentions Baruch the scribe as involved in writing some of the sayings of Jeremiah, the traditional view was that Baruch wrote down Jeremiah's own words, and then himself composed the prose material in an almost biographical work about Jeremiah. Mowinckel[2] separated out three layers of tradition: (1) the poetic prophetic words, (2) prose narrative, and finally (3) prose sermons, upon which many have noted a formal and literary resemblance to the Deuteronomic speeches. Wanke believed that chs. 27–29 were composed together, because of the similarity

1. R.P. Carroll, *From Chaos to Covenant* (London: SCM Press, 1981), pp. 275ff.
2. S. Mowinckel, *The Composition of Jeremiah* (Kristiania: Dybward, 1914).

in method and theme, and then attached to ch. 26.[3] Others, like Giesebrecht, are confident in assigning this section to the hand of Baruch.[4] T. Seidl,[5] in two meticulously detailed volumes, has argued against the compositional unity of chs. 27–29, but many reasons may be cited for their unity and their differentiation from ch. 26.[6]

Is there a Letter in Chapter 29?

Since Duhm, most commentators attribute to the original 'letter' only vv. 5-7.[7] The first few words of v. 1 are probably the earliest redactional

3. G. Wanke, *Untersuchungen zur sogenannten Baruchschrift* (BZAW, 122; Berlin: de Gruyter, 1971), pp. 43ff.

4. F. Giesebrecht, *Das Buch Jeremia* (HKAT; Tübingen: Mohr, 1907), p. xx.

5. T. Seidl, *Texte und Einheiten in Jeremia 27–29* (Arbeiten zu Text und Sprache im Alten Testament, 2; Munich, 1977), and *Formen und Formeln in Jeremia 27–29* (1978).

6. Chapter 26 is set in the time of Jehoiakim, while 27.1ff is in the time of Zedekiah. The MT has 'Jehoiakim' in 27.1, but this is clearly an error, in view of 27.3 and 12, and the fact that v.6 assumes Nebuchadnezzar's conquest. The Syriac (seventh-eighth century CE) and Arabic texts have corrected the text to 'Zedekiah' in 27.1.

Jeremiah is in the third person in ch. 26, while most often in the first person in chs. 27–29. The spelling of Jeremiah is ירמיה in 28.5, while it is the fuller ירמיהו in ch. 26. Chapters 27–29 contain Nebuchad*n*ezzar rather than 'Nebuchad*r*ezzar' elsewhere. Finally, the theme of yoke, yoke-bars, prison and restraint are connectors for chs. 27–28 especially. Prophetic conflict is more the theme of chs. 27–29 than of ch. 26, and it is clearly the internal thematic principle.

7. It is interesting to note that the LXX has already caught the significance of the theme of chs. 27–29, because the 'prophets' are called, in 29.1, and again in 29.8, 'pseudoprophets', ψευδοπροφητας.

The most important variant, however, is the omission of vv. 16-20 altogether from the LXX text. Most commentators therefore speculate that vv. 16-20 should be omitted from critical consideration of the earliest forms of ch. 29. It is clear that vv. 16-20 are Deuteronomic in influence, if not origin. To begin with, the concept of the 'Throne' הכאת of David, as a symbol of authority, is Deuteronomic (cf. 1 Kgs 1.13, 17, 20; 2.12, 24; 8.20—Throne of Israel, 2 Kgs 10.3, but cf. Jer. 17.25 which talks of Kings and Nobles on the throne of David. But MT has שׂרים as doubtful). Where the concept of Throne of David turns up in Jeremiah, there is obviously the presence of a formulaic sentence; cf. 17; 22; 29.16; 36.30.

The 'trilogy' of sword, famine and pestilence, and the figurative use of תאנה = figs, both relate directly to the prose section ch. 24, and obviously were either introduced at the same time as ch. 24 (although this is doubtful if the LXX does not

introduction to the letter, since the list of people depends on later additions. Further, much of v. 2 is deleted as being influenced by 2 Kgs 24.12. The most interesting variation at this point, however, is that the LXX has 'bound and free' rather than the MT 'craftsmen [woodworkers?] and smiths', in the list of exiles.

Duhm believed that ch. 29 contained portions of a real letter, consisting of vv. 4a, 5-7 and 11-14.[8] Within vv. 5-7 itself, he also believed that the addition of ותלדנה בנים ובנות ('so that these can bear sons and daughters in their turn') came from an exilic concern to lengthen the generations in keeping with the (in his view, late) tradition of a length of stay of '70 years'.

Volz also believed the letter to be genuine, and accepted the basic limits of the text reconstructed by Duhm. Seidl, too, believes that 8-10, with its great hope for the future, is *'unjeremianisch'*. Rudolph, on the other hand, disagreed over the secondary nature of v. 10 accusing Volz of wanting to read Jeremiah's letter as advising a permanent settlement and religious life without Temple and holy 'Land', a desire which Rudolph suspected to have faintly 'protestant' motives.[9]

Despite the significance of the 70 years theme for late generations,[10] it seems most likely to me that the 'original letter' did not contain the hoped for return; for had it done so, it would have had the effect, as Volz argued, of undercutting the impact of Jeremiah's advice. The original letter could even have come to serve other purposes entirely; as Duhm commented, one can easily see in v. 7: '...the desire of one of the Babylonian Jews to justify his and his compatriots' remaining in Babylonia by means of the authority of the prophet Jeremiah...'[11]

---

have vv. 16-20) or 16-20 was composed on the basis of ch. 24. Giesebrecht thought that they were from the same hand. (I do not accept this.) The fig imagery, it may be interesting to note, is used elsewhere only in Jotham's fable, in Judg. 8.7-8.

Finally, the charge of disobeying the many prophets that God sent (v. 19) is a common Deuteronomic theme, frequent in Deuteronomic sermons (noted by Nicholson, pp. 99-100).

Verses 16-20 are thus not considered integral to the message to the exiles by commentators such as Nicholson, Weiser, Duhm, Volz, Giesebrecht and Rudolph.

8. B. Duhm, *Das Buch Jeremia* (Kurzer Handkommentar zum Alten Testament; Tübingen and Leipzig, 1901), pp. 229-30.

9. W. Rudolph, *Jeremiah* (HAT, 12; Tübingen: Mohr, 1947), p. 155.

10. See M. Knibb, 'The Exile in the Literature of the Intertestamental Period', *HeyJ* 27 (1976).

11. Duhm, *Das Buch Jeremia*, pp. 229-30

Furthermore, the anger expressed in the 'response' to the letter (v. 28) was that Jeremiah had claimed that the stay would be long, quoting only the content of v. 5. One would have presumed some mention of a return if Jeremiah had mentioned one.

We are left with vv. 3-7 as the essence of the letter from Jeremiah. There is virtual unanimity among commentators that this letter is authentic, or based on an authentic tradition. The most cautious note, however, is Seidl's view that the economy of language, its '*Konzentration*', probably derives from an editor who is working on the basis, and perhaps authority, of a Jeremianic prophetic tradition with pro-Babylonian tendencies.[12]

But do we, in fact, have a letter in vv. 5-7? Recent analysis of Aramaic letters from the time of Jeremiah reveals common forms for the 'letter type'. As recently, and conveniently, enumerated by Pardee, they are as follows:

1.   Praescriptio–Address formula—Sender-Recipient, Greeting
2.   Transition to body (usually וֹאֵת)
3.   Body of letter
4.   Closing formula (late)[13]

With the sole exception of the term מֵפֶר in v. 1, nothing suggests a letter form. But, by including v. 23 in the original letter, Holladay has recently suggested that the mention of God as 'witness' suggests a '...technical term for "counter-signatory"...'[14] Further, in 29.4, Holladay believes he has found the typical 'From PN to PN' portion of the 'Praescriptio' (however, as a reference to Westermann's *Basic Forms of Prophetic Speech* will confirm, this is part of a standard messenger formula for prophetic pronouncements). Lastly, Holladay notes that some form of מֵפֶר is typical of greetings in the letters, and suggests that since the mention of 'peace' is not found until further in the letter, the letter is 'rude'; instead of the sender wishing peace, the sender is saying that peace is up to them! I consider Holladay's attempts to be somewhat strained, and at best one can say that the tradition which included this material as a מֵפֶר may have been aware of letter forms.

Duhm did not doubt that we have portions of a real letter, and Volz

---

12. Seidl, *Texte und Einheiten*, p. 301.

13. D. Pardee, 'Formulaic Features of the Hebrew Letters', *Handbook of Ancient Hebrew Letters* (SBLSBS, 15; Chico, CA: Scholars Press, 1982), ch. 4.

14. W.L. Holladay, 'God Writes a "Rude Letter"', *BA* 1983 (summer).

added that such a letter, sent by authority (or certainly with the permission) of King Zedekiah, would have served good propaganda purposes in assuring the Babylonians of Jewish cooperation. Further, Rudolph assumed that the writing of such a letter in the first place proves that we do not have to understand their condition as a 'life in prison', or even a 'concentration camp', but rather a circumstance with a certain freedom of movement within the areas where they were assigned.[15]

Volz assumed the letter's purpose was to advise on an ordered, settled existence on the land from which God would still hear their prayers, despite the view expressed in Amos 7.17 and Hos. 9.1ff. that foreign land was unclean and impious. Weiser considered the letter's purpose to be twofold. Noting first its context in chs. 27–29, where prophetic conflict is the theme, he said:

> He turned against the easy hope of a quick return home which was being fed by fanatic prophets in Babylon as well as in Palestine...but he also turned against a despondent, gloomy desperation of those in the new situation who could not cope, either inwardly or outwardly...[16]

Because it is contained in material that is considered highly controversial from a literary point of view, it is difficult, as we have seen, to determine what the letter of Jeremiah contained. But if we are able to assign ch. 29 to the period of exile at all, then it matters little whether it is a 'genuine letter' of Jeremiah—since the circumstances that it represents are of interest in any attempt to illuminate the experience of exile, and the historical message of Jeremiah.

The Meaning of Jeremiah's Letter: Nonviolent Resistance

If the letter refers to a genuine exchange of ideas between Palestine and Babylonia, then aspects of ch. 29 represent an important political document. This is particularly clear when one notes that chs. 27–29 are concerned mainly with prophetic conflict, between those prophets who advocated God's sure and quick end to the exile, and Jeremiah's teaching of long endurance.

But was the issue of chs. 27–29 merely one of true and false prophecy? In a very interesting article on chs. 27–29, Overholt argues

---

15. Rudolph, *Jeremiah*, p. 155.
16. A. Weiser, *Das Buche des Propheten Jeremia* (ATD, 4; Göttingen: Vandenhoeck & Ruprecht, 1960), p. 253.

that Hananiah must be seen as a prophet who stood firmly in the traditional role of preaching an orthodox message containing allusions both to the inviolability of Zion, and God's trustworthy protection and aid through a quick return from exile. Hananiah then, was not perceived as a false prophet by the people during his confrontation with Jeremiah. Indeed, the message of the prophets in the exilic community proves, if not Hananiah's own influence, then the wide range of similar prophetic views. As Overholt comments:

> The message of Hananiah had its roots sunk deep in the promises of security of Yahweh's positive action on behalf of his people, embodied in the nation's cultic establishment...[17]

While making interesting observations on the specific details of Hananiah's conflict with Jeremiah, Overholt is interested in the wider question of 'false prophecy' and its determination.

This is also the subject of Crenshaw's survey and analysis in his work, *Prophetic Conflict*.[18] Crenshaw detailed the many attempts to determine biblical criteria for 'false prophecy', but ended up supporting the notion that true and false prophecy are two sides of the same coin—they cannot be easily separated because of the nature of prophecy itself

One of Crenshaw's most helpful generalizations, however, is the fact that biblical 'true' prophets inevitably found themselves in conflict with the 'standard religion of the people'. Aspects of this standard religious view included, according to Crenshaw:

1.   confidence in God's faithfulness (Jer. 5.12; 23.17)
2.   satisfaction with traditional religion
3.   defiance of prophets who disagree
4.   despair when hope seems dead
5.   doubt of the justice of God (Ezek. 12.22f.; 18.25)
6.   historical pragmatism (Jer. 44.16-19)[19]

17. T.W. Overholt, 'Jeremiah 27–29: The Question of False Prophecy', *JAAR* 35 (1967), p. 245.

18. J.L. Crenshaw, *Prophetic Conflict: Its Effect upon Israelite Religion* (BZAW; Berlin: de Gruyter, 1971).

19. Crenshaw, *Prophetic Conflict*, pp. 24ff. Davidson, similarly also believed that Jeremiah was actually criticizing the generally held Deuteronomic 'tests' as themselves inadequate

> There is no reason to doubt the religious sincerity of the men who opposed Jeremiah on these issues. Viewed in the light of Deut. 8.1-6, Jeremiah was a false prophet inviting his people to 'go after other gods' (Deut. 13.3) a politico-religious fifth

The important thing to note, especially regarding point 1, is that many of the attitudes here enumerated could, in other circumstances, be orthodoxy in the strict sense; so justifying Buber's insight (echoed by Overholt) that false prophecy is simply 'the right word for the wrong time'.

I think it is fair to observe, however, that comments on prophetic conflict do not focus enough attention on the historical occasion for this particular conflict, the exile and the response to it. This is the specific issue which divided Jeremiah and Hananiah.

Most commentators assume that Hananiah was preaching some form of non-cooperation and resistance to the Babylonian conquerors, perhaps with the assumed support of Egypt. This is then considered similar to the message of Ahaz, Shemiah and Zedekiah in the exilic communities. Similarly, B. Lang[20] has argued that Ezekiel, far from having little political perspective, was actually preaching against Zedekiah's planned revolt in Jerusalem. Was Jeremiah, therefore, preaching against revolt or resistance in Babylon? The answer comes from focused attention on vv. 5-7 which relates the essence of Jeremiah's message to the exiles.

Build, Plant and Marry

In 1961, Bach analyzed the images of 'build and plant', as a well known theme in Old Testament tradition, in order to find the probable *Sitz im Leben* of this image.[21] Since it is usually in the context of future well-being, and it represents landed existence, and refers to one-time activities in a man's life (as connected with houses and Vines, or olive trees on rare occasions), Bach suggested that the phrases originated as parts of a 'wish' for future success at the birth of a son; '...for children, one wishes for what is considered most worthwhile in their lives...'[22] This was confirmed in Bach's thinking by the fact that another 'one-time life

columnist proclaiming treason against the noblest reformed tradition of his people... (R. Davidson, 'Orthodoxy and the Prophetic Word', *VT* 14 [1964], p.412).

20. See B. Lang, *Kein Aufstand in Jerusalem* (Stuttgart: Verlag Katholisches Bibelwerk, 1981).

21. R. Bach, 'Bauen und Pflanzen', in R. Rendtorff and K. Koch (eds.), *Studien zur Theologie der alttestamentlichen Überlieferungen* (Berlin, 1961). The varied instances used by Bach are helpfully set out on p. 16 of his work.

22. Bach, 'Bauen und Pflanzen', p. 22.

activity' was occasionally added to 'build houses' and 'plant garden/
vines', namely marriage.[23]

S. Paul also believes that this phrase is traditional and agrees that these
words of encouragement are 'no more than a well-known stereotypical
formula for future bliss'.[24] Paul is particularly interested, however, in
Jeremiah's relationship with Deutero-Isaiah, and relates ch. 29 of
Jeremiah to Isaiah 65, where 'build, plant and marry' is also found. Even
God's hearing of his people when they call, is common to both passages
(Isa. 65.23, 24).

While Paul does not relate the three images to Deuteronomy 20 and
28, neither does Bach relate Jeremiah 29, Deuteronomy 20 and 28 to
Isaiah 65. Bach considers his three occurrences of the three images to be
different enough in context to justify his assumption that the 'birth wish'
probably came to have marriage associated with it in some traditions.

But I disagree with Bach's view that Deuteronomy 20, 28 and
Jeremiah 29 are three different contexts, and I would also add Paul's
inclusion of Isaiah 65, so that we must consider the context of all four
occurrences of the three images of build, plant and marry. 'Build' and
'plant' is a well known combination and Bach's idea of a birthwish may
be granted as a feasible etiology for these two images. When 'marriage'
is added, however, to make a three point image, the context is always
warfare; that is, these relate to three things that are protected, or lost, in
warfare.

The context of Deuteronomy 20 is clear. Here are the Deuteronomic
military 'exemptions' from Holy War. Von Rad, Weinfeld and Dion have
commented on the Holy War language of this passage, such as the
bracing call to 'fear not'. 1 Macc. 3.55-56 attests to the continued tradition of these exemptions:

> Next Judas appointed leaders for the people, to command a thousand, a
> hundred, fifty or ten men. He told those who were building houses, or
> about to be married or planting vineyards, or who were simply afraid, to
> go home, every one of them, as the law allowed...

Carmichael comments that the dedication upon building a house

---

23. Bach speculated that houses and vineyards are typical of landed existence,
which may be significant in the light of the traditions, e.g. Deut. 6.10-11; Josh.
24.13; and in regard to Rechabites, Jer. 35.7.

24. S. Paul, 'Literary and Ideological Echoes of Jeremiah in Deutero-Isaiah', in
Peli (ed.), *Fifth World Congress of Jewish Studies* (Jerusalem: Magnes, 1969),
p. 119.

symbolized and anticipated an individual Israelite's residence in the land in a secure place.[25] Regarding the planting of vines, in Lev. 19.23-25 it is clear that the ritual process of purification of fruit takes five years, which would make it by far the longest exemption implied in Deuteronomy 20, unless house dedication took a length of time we are not now aware of. Deut. 24.5 implies that the marriage exemption was one year. Keil and Delitzsch's summary of these exemptions is instructive:

> The intention of these instructions was neither to send away all persons who were unwilling to go into the war, and thus avoid the danger of their interfering with the readiness and courage of the rest of the army in prospect of the battle, nor to spare the lives of those persons to whom life was especially dear, but rather to avoid depriving any member of the covenant nation of his enjoyment of the good things of this life bestowed upon him by the Lord.[26]

Deuteronomy 28 involves the punishment of not living according to the law given by God. The punishment includes not being able to live in one's house; not being able to enjoy one's vineyard; or not being able to marry one's wife because of defeat in war by the enemy (Deut. 28.25). Furthermore, Isaiah 65, with its parallels (although not as striking as the other three) concludes the section with a typical Isaianic motif of peace:

> 'The wolf and the lamb will feed together, the lion eat straw like the ox, the dust will be the serpent's food. They will do no hurt, no harm on all my holy mountain, says Yahweh...' (Isa. 65.25) (cf. Isaiah 11 regarding the return from... esp. vv. 10ff.).

On the basis of these parallels, and their context in warfare, and especially the cessation or exemption from warfare, it is clear that Jeremiah is not simply advising a settled existence, but using the Deuteronomic exemptions from warfare to declare an 'armistice' on the exilic community. This is confirmed by the martial language of Hananiah, who proclaimed God's deliverance in decidedly militaristic terms, 'I have broken the yoke of the king of Babylon... I will bring back Jehoiachin the son of Jehoiakim king of Judah' (28.3-4). 'I will break the yoke of Nebuchadnezzar king of Babylon from the neck of all the nations within

25. C.M. Carmichael, *The Laws of Deuteronomy* (Ithaca, NY: Cornell University Press, 1974); G. von Rad, *Studies in Deuteronomy* (London: SCM Press); Weinfeld, *Deuteronomy and the Deuteronomic School* (Oxford: Oxford University Press, 1972); P.-E. Dion, 'The "Fear Not" Formula and Holy War', *CBQ* 32 (1970).

26. C.F. Keil and F. Delitzsch, *Biblical Commentary on the Old Testament*. III. *The Pentateuch* (Grand Rapids: Eerdmans, 1951).

two years' (v. 11). If Jeremiah's advice is read in the traditional context of warfare, then we are quite clearly dealing with a prophetic conflict on the issue of the appropriate action towards Babylon. Jeremiah's call to seek the 'shalom' of the city/country would then be a direct call to abandon revolt in Babylon and Palestine, and would be as appropriate to this section as is Isaiah's ending to the section of that book where the same three elements are mentioned; both are in the context of holy war. This explanation supports Volz's suggestion that Zedekiah allowed the message to be sent to reassure the Babylonians of his sincerity and loyalty. The issue is not God's action, but the exiles' response to God's plan as announced by the prophets, either Jeremiah or Hananiah.

Once the issue is seen in terms of conflicting advice on strategy for exilic existence, then the division between Hananiah and Jeremiah is an example of a split between two political spokespersons in a community under domination and control. The split is between those who advocate limited cooperation and social resistance and those who advocate open and frequently violent rebellion. The frequency of this split appears to be in the nature of the social configurations resulting from domination and minority existence.[27] This debate, and the emotional power behind it, is a strong indication that the circumstances of the exile could hardly be described as 'not so bad' (even if the strong terms of Jeremiah 50ff. are ignored as unhistorical, as often in modern analysis).

So, I would argue that vv. 5-7 reflect Deuteronomy 20 and 28, and less dramatically, Isaiah 65. This conclusion, however, raises the question of whether the 'letter' is artificial, from the Deuteronomic redactor of Jeremiah, rather than a real letter. Certainly, if Nicholson's thesis is that strong Deuteronomic language in Jeremiah invariably signals an actual Deuteronomic hand as the author, I fail to see why the letter itself, vv. 5-7, should not be a prime candidate for such assignation. Thus, Jeremiah the prophet finally disappears from the entire chapter, and at best we have a faithful retelling of attitudes which are no doubt historically to be attributed to Jeremiah himself and his work. The enigmatic Lachish Letters at least indicate such a partisan conflict regarding the war against Babylon, even if the prophet in question is not Jeremiah.[28]

But I have no doubt that vv. 5-7 represent a tradition about Jeremiah from a Deuteronomic hand. The chronological sequence of the latter additions to ch. 29, and how they develop the thoughts of vv. 5-7, the

27. See my *The Religion of the Landless* (New York: Meyer-Stone, 1989).
28. See D.W. Thomas, *The Prophet in the Lachish Ostraca* (London, 1946).

addition of a hoped for return (ex eventu?), the 70 years time span, the traditions regarding Ahab and Zedekiah suggest this. Finally, the section containing vv. 16-20 represents an addition which connects with the dramatic imagery of ch. 24, and was added at a time when the split between the exiles and those remaining behind was growing, which I tentatively place before the destruction of 587, when hope for a return would have added to the animosity of those who wanted something to return to.

However, this dating must be qualified by insights on the continued social conflict in the Exilic period, noted in Ezekiel's reference to property rights and disagreements, even the derogatory use of 'thieves' in a document as late as Zechariah. Hence, an addition like vv. 16-20 could be dated virtually at any time during the exile, at about the same time that an idea of a '70 year' stay was current.

The whole of Jeremiah 29 gives us insights into the social psychology of a group under stress. We hear in this chapter about rumours, emotional upheaval, and divisions of leadership with their conflicting strategies for survival and faithfulness. Indeed, it may be that the additions to vv. 5-7 in ch. 29 give us a chronological 'history' of the ideological development of the attitude of the exiles to their fate, beginning with the advice to seek the peace of the city, progressing to the upheaval of occasional rumours of imminent freedom such as '70 years', and finally the word about the treatment of property 'back home'.

As contemporary attitudes inevitably enter into the issues surrounding the interpretative work on Jeremiah, a brief discussion of this matter is permissible. Hananiah's opposition to Jeremiah was the opposition of a Zealot, the violent revolutionary who called on Israel to draw their swords to end the yoke of Babylon. The argument between Jeremiah and Hananiah was both political and theological: how to be the people of God in a foreign land. In his Anchor Bible commentary, John Bright goes to great pains to acquit Jeremiah of the charge of 'pacifism' and 'cowardice':

> How one's country is best to be served is a question upon which men may at any time legitimately disagree...[Jeremiah]...advised submission to Babylon, but to mark him down as a Babylonian sympathizer, or a collaborationist, would be to do him a grave injustice... to suppose that Jeremiah spoke as he did because of pacifistic leanings, or from personal cowardice, would be, if possible, even more unfair...[29]

Despite the fact that those who advocate violent resistance consider other options to be 'unpatriotic' 'unfaithful' or ineffective, we can see that the other means of resistance, for example nonviolent social resistance (which represented Jeremiah's strategy) are not prescriptions for suicide or acceptance of evil, but alternative means of faithfulness and mechanisms for survival. The intent of Jeremiah's advice was to ensure that the Jewish community '...multiply there: do not decrease!' That this was taken as a significant model of Jewish nonviolent resistance is clear from the themes of 'spiritual' resistance to foreign influence (especially idolatry) which later traditions associated with Jeremiah, the books of Baruch and the Epistle of Jeremiah (parts of which date as early as the fourth century BCE).[30]

What we have in Jeremiah's advice to the exiles is further evidence of an emergent Jewish ethic of nonviolence that is also evident in Daniel[31] and later, in early Pharisaic practice (most notably in the teachings of R. Yolianan ben Zakkai),[32] and, of course, in early Christianity. It is a militant nonviolence that has very little in common with an appeasing liberal pacifism because it is an engaged, strategic position towards authority and power that is cannily aware of the requirements for success and survival.

29. J. Bright, *Jeremiah* (AB, 21; Garden City, NY: Doubleday, 1965), pp. cviii-cix.

30. See C. Moore, 'Toward the Dating of the Book of Baruch', *CBQ* 36 (1974), pp. 312-13, and his Anchor Bible Commentary, *Daniel, Esther and Jeremiah: The Additions* (AB, 44; Garden City, NY: Doubleday, 1977).

31. On Daniel, see J.J. Collins, 'The Tradition of Non-violent Resistance', in *The Apocalyptic Vision of the Book of Daniel* (Missoula, MT: Scholars Press, 1977), pp. 215ff.; J. Licht, 'Taxo, or the Apocalyptic Doctrine of Vengeance', in *JJS* 12 (1961).

32. The pacifistic teachings of R. Yoḥanan ben Zakkai reflected the well-established distaste of the Pharisaic law for capital punishment, even when it appeared to be called for according to strict interpretations of the Mosaic law. But ben Zakkai went considerably further than this with his nonviolence. See J. Neusner, *A Life of Rabban Yoḥanan Ben Zakkai* (Leiden: Brill, 1962), and *The Development of a Legend: Studies on the Traditions Concerning Yoḥanan Ben Zakkai* (Leiden: Brill, 1970). A critical comparison of these teachings with Gospel accounts of Jesus awaits a thorough analysis.

JSOT 56 (1992), pp. 85-99

SECOND ISAIAH: PROPHET TO PATRIARCHY

Bebb Wheeler Stone

A woman, reading, sees words on paper narrate and interpret an experience that is different because of her gender: rape. Suddenly she hears a woman's voice 'speaking' to her from the printed text. The voice speaks not only of the female experience of sexual violence, but also of childbirth. Having heard a woman's voice speaking in a text where no woman is expected to speak, the reader begins to 'hear' with new attentiveness. Just so, as H. Bloom remarks in *The Book of J*, 'I began to wonder whether the voice I encounter in the text is that of a woman'.[1]

Human suffering accompanied Nebuchadrezzar's victories over Jerusalem from 597 to 586 BCE (e.g. Jer. 52 and Lamentations). But the experience of suffering that Second Isaiah presents is uniquely woman's suffering. Listen to the implicit description of rape in Isa. 51.22b–52.2, where initially YHWH is the speaker:

> I will put it [that is, the cup of staggering] into the hands of your tormentors, who have said to you, 'Bow down, that we may pass over' (שחי ונעברה); and you have made your back like the ground and like the street for them to pass over.

> Awake, awake, put on your strength, O Jerusalem, put on your beautiful garments, O Jerusalem, the holy city; for there shall no more come into you (יבא־בך) the uncircumcised and the unclean. Shake yourself from the dust, arise, O captive Jerusalem; loose the bonds from your neck, O captive daughter of Zion.[2]

Jerusalem/Zion, addressed as woman, is told to rise and dress herself.

1. D. Rosenberg and H. Bloom, *The Book of J* (New York: Grove Weidenfeld, 1990), p. 34.
2. All biblical quotations are from the RSV unless otherwise indicated.

She has been lying naked in the street, and the uncircumcised and unclean have 'come into' her. The verbs עבר 'pass over' and בוא 'come into' in other contexts (עבר in *piel* in Job 21.10 and בוא more commonly)[3] have explicit sexual connotations. The poems of Lamentations, said to have emerged from and to describe the destruction of Jerusalem in 586 BCE have reference to rape in 5.11—the RSV uses the word 'ravished' to render ענו, but the JB and TEV translate it unequivocally as 'rape'.

Rape was customary behavior for conquering invaders.[4] It was not customary experience, however, for the women who suffered it. Could it be that this shattering experience became the source of insight for the woman (or women) behind Second Isaiah's anonymous voice? Could it be that rape 'conscientized'[5] a woman into her own oppression as a woman?

The thesis of this paper is that a woman, or women, of the sixth century BCE, experiencing misogyny, criticized her (their) own culture by that knowledge; in other words, a woman became a self-conscious prophet to patriarchy in the sixth century BCE. Either the prophet herself or her sisters have experienced rape. It is precisely the historical experience of suffering in a gender-specific form, of being a victim of sexual oppression in addition to the political oppression of her nation that disclosed a different meaning to her suffering. The now-clichéd phrase, 'the personal is political', describes fresh truth in Second Isaiah. For Second Isaiah the experience of a woman raped is heuristic—with new consciousness, a woman prophet has interpreted the meaning of the sociopolitical reality of exiled Israel and has directed her prophetic voice against institutionalized patriarchy for the sake of human consolation and redemption.

---

3. See for example Judg. 15.1; 16.1; Gen. 38.8, 9; Deut. 22.13; Ezek. 23.44; 2 Sam. 12.24.

4. S. Brownmiller, *Against our Will: Men, Women, and Rape* (New York: Simon & Schuster, 1975), p. 21.

> Protecting wellborn daughters of Israel from rape by threat of massive retribution was obviously serious business, but, as the story of Dinah shows, men of the Hebrew tribes, like their neighbors, had no compunction against freely raping women of tribes they had conquered, for in this way they prospered and grew.

5. P. Freire, *Pedagogy of the Oppressed* (New York: Seabury, 1973), pp. 54-55.

P. Trible's rhetorical critical methodology 'uncovered neglected traditions to reveal countervoices within a patriarchal document'.[6] These 'countervoices', taken together, comprise what Trible calls 'a remnant theology that challenges the sexism of scripture'.[7] Her work has established the presence of a nonpatriarchal tradition in which a contemporary hermeneutic of feminism (defined as 'a critique of culture in light of misogyny')[8] can identify the prophetic spirit. But this requires 'moving across cultures and centuries...[as] the Bible informed a feminist perspective and correspondingly a feminist perspective enlightened the Bible'.[9]

R.R. Ruether wrote, in *Sexism and God-Talk*:

> Those male prophets who were aware of oppression by rich urbanites or dominating empires were not similarly conscious of their own oppression of dependents—women and slaves—in the patriarchal family. Only the emergence of women conscious of their oppression could have applied the categories of protest to women. This did not happen in Yahwism.[10]

This essay is an attempt to suggest that—in one specific instance—it did. Stated most boldly, Second Isaiah, by P. Trible's definition, is at least in part a feminist text.

The method of this paper requires a cauldron, a three legged vessel in which feminists 'reconstitute'[11] history by the addition of large quantities of a missing ingredient: women. The first leg of the cauldron is the spirit of 'ludic cerebration',[12] a spirit of play unleashed by M. Daly. Daly defines ludic cerebration as 'the free play of intuition in our own [women's] space. Ludic cerebration is thinking out of experience.'[13]

The second leg of the cauldron is the process of 'seeing–naming–

---

6. P. Trible, *God and the Rhetoric of Sexuality* (Philadelphia: Fortress Press, 1978), p. 202.

7. P. Trible, *Texts of Terror* (Philadelphia: Fortress Press, 1984), p. 3.

8. Trible, *God and the Rhetoric of Sexuality*, p. 7.

9. Trible, *God and the Rhetoric of Sexuality*, p. 202.

10. R.R. Ruether, *Sexism and God-Talk: Toward a Feminist Theology* (Boston: Beacon Press, 1983), p. 63.

11. E. Schüssler Fiorenza, *In Memory of Her* (New York: Crossroad, 1983), p. 29.

12. M. Daly, *The Church and the Second Sex* (Boston: Beacon Press, 1985), p. 49.

13. Daly, *The Church and the Second Sex*, p. 49.

reconstituting'[14] (or perhaps in this case, hearing–naming–reconstituting), so described by Elizabeth Schüssler Fiorenza. I have used the process of 'seeing–naming–reconstituting', part of the formulation of a 'feminist heuristic paradigm',[15] as a model for reconstruction of women's past history as well as our historical agency.

The third leg of the cauldron is the goal of 'changing the recipe', a purpose made explicit by R.R. Ruether: 'women do not want a larger slice of the pie; women want to change the recipe'.[16] In this cauldron has been brewed a sixth-century exilic prophet who, although anonymous, has traditionally been referred to as 'he', who is outraged with the men of Israel, and who has prophesied against the patriarchy of Israel itself as evil.

This is an example of 'engaged scholarship',[17] that is, of feminist scholarship that rejects the possibility of 'objective' scholarship. Engaged scholarship admits its goals. It posits a hypothesis as a way of sharing a vision, or, in this case, as a way of sharing a voice. We begin to locate a woman's voice by listening for it. If a vision is successfully described, or if that voice is successfully heard, the verification comes from the experience of the viewers or auditors as they encounter a different reality.

This paper suggests that to listen to Second Isaiah's voice is to hear numerous reflections from gendered reality. The judgment as to the truth of the voice becomes an ontological judgment, the verification of which comes from an appeal to intelligent recognition, as Tillich expressed it.[18] The authority of the voice resides in those who are enabled to hear it.

Listen to a woman breaking silence:

> For a long time I have held my peace, I have kept still and restrained myself; now I will cry out like a woman in travail. I will gasp and pant (42.14).

While the first person speaking here is YHWH, the poet/prophet who crafted this message of theological presence to the exiles chose a simile from another uniquely female experience: childbirth. And the experience of restraining one's speech, holding one's peace, and keeping still is also

14. Schüssler Fiorenza, *In Memory of Her*, p. 1.
15. Schüssler Fiorenza, *In Memory of Her*, p. xv.
16. R.R. Ruether, AAR/SBL Address, Chicago, Illinois, December 1984.
17. Schüssler Fiorenza, *In Memory of Her*, p. xx.
18. P. Tillich, *Love, Power and Justice* (New York: Oxford University Press, 1954), p. 24.

familiar to women—the now-familiar, woman-identified phenomenon of cultural silence.[19] But childbirth is involuntarily noisy: in the midst of giving birth a woman wonders at the cries, curses and shrieks she hears, and then realizes those distant sounds are her body language, literally. After hearing a woman's voice in the text narrating female experience, the reader 're-searches'[20] the text expecting to find additional evidence of womanpresence. Such evidence, which will be presented, points to a consistent pattern of naming in Second Isaiah that not only sets up a gender dichotomy, but also places salvific power with the women.

In Isa. 51.22-23, 'captive Jerusalem' and 'captive daughter of Zion' suffered sexual violence. Jerusalem/Zion, historically the destroyed city/Temple and center of pre-exilic Israel, is in Second Isaiah female. Jerusalem is addressed in 51.17-20:

> Rouse yourself, rouse yourself,
> Stand up, O Jerusalem,
> you who have drunk at the hand of the LORD
> the cup of his wrath,
> who have drunk to the dregs
> the bowl of staggering.
> There is none to guide her
> among all the sons she has borne;
> there is none to take her by the hand
> among all the sons she has brought up.
>
> These two things have befallen you—
> who will console you?—
> devastation and destruction, famine
> and sword;
> who will comfort you?
>
> Your sons have fainted,
> they lie at the head of every street
> like an antelope in a net;
> they are full of the wrath of the LORD,
> the rebuke of your God.

Jerusalem has been drugged by God in God's anger. The woman is presented as a victim, and she is not blamed as the cause.

Zion and Jerusalem as symbols are consistently positive. In abrupt

---

19. T. Olsen, *Silences* (New York: Delta/Seymour Lawrence, 1965).

20. M. Daly, *Webster's First New Intergalactic Wickedary of the English Language* (Boston: Beacon Press, 1987), p. 222.

departure from the prophetic tradition of symbolizing apostasy as
women's sexual infidelity, Zion/Jerusalem is never accused of unfaithfulness or harlotry in Second Isaiah. Compare and contrast the metaphors of Israel/Judah's downfall: the faithless woman of Jeremiah 3, the
harlot of Hosea 2, the harlotry of Ezekiel 16 and 20, and the uncleanness
in the skirts of Jerusalem in Lamentations 1. In fact, there are no negative
images of women in Second Isaiah, with the possible exception of
ch. 47, with its 'daughter of Babylon', and I think even she, a woman of
the oppressor culture, is empathetically treated as woman and sister
victim, transcending the cultural separation, as I will discuss later.

As a control comparison, and an admittedly arbitrary one,
Deuteronomy 1–15, Jeremiah, Ezekiel, Lamentations and Isaiah 56–66
(that is, Third Isaiah) were examined for evidence of similar imagery
drawn from women's socio-sexual role. Only in Jeremiah was the frequency of simile and metaphor sufficient to analyze the usage, and of
that body of imagery more than half were negative socio-sexual role
images of women:

2.33	the wicked woman
3.6	the false sister Judah
3.20	faithless wife
4.30	prostitute
6.7	Jerusalem as wicked woman
13.22	Jerusalem deserves to be raped

This shift in Second Isaiah away from negative evaluation of women in
the imagery, which is the more usual pattern of the prophetic tradition,
should at least be noted at this point. Zion/Jerusalem has been a victim;
she has been raped, and she is not accused of harlotry.

Repeatedly the names 'Zion' and 'Jerusalem', the mountain of the
Lord and the city of the Lord, respectively, both of which are feminine
gender nouns, function in Second Isaiah as collective symbols for the
women of Israel. Parallel to the corporate female symbols named Zion
and Jerusalem are the corporate male symbols named Jacob and Israel.
Israel, the nation in tradition history descended from Abraham, Isaac and
Jacob, is male. Jacob, it will be remembered, is re-named Israel by
YHWH in Gen. 35.10.[21] For Second Isaiah, Jacob is the collective symbol
for the men within the exilic community, and Israel is the corporate

---

21. J.J. Schmitt, 'The Motherhood of God and Zion as Mother', *RB* 92 (1985),
pp. 557-69.

symbol of the nation now in exile. Examination of these symbols discloses that Second Isaiah lays the responsibility for the plight of Israel-in-exile squarely at the feet of the 'men of Israel' (41.14). It seems to me that this responsibility is purely masculine and is not meant to be inclusive for the following reasons:

1. The description of the sin of the 'men of Israel' is interwoven throughout chs. 40–48: they have continued to transgress against YHWH by confessing YHWH and claiming to be Yahwists, while making and worshipping idols and neglecting covenant rituals. This apostasy is the immediate situation provoking Second Isaiah's prophetic critique. The description of their apostasy is found in Isa. 48.1-2:

> Here this, O house of Jacob,
> who are called by the name of Israel,
> and who come forth from the loins of Judah;
> who swear by the name of the LORD,
> and confess the God of Israel,
> but not in truth or right.

There are several passages in which the making and worshipping of idols is raised as an issue (see 40.19-20; 41.7, 21-24, 29; 42.17; 44.9-20; 45.20; 46.1-2, 5-7; 48.4-5). Passages like the following directly connect the idol worshippers with Israel (48.4-5):

> Because I know that you are obstinate,
> and your neck is an iron sinew
> and your forehead brass,
> I declared them to you from of old,
> before they came to pass I announced them to you,
> lest you should say, 'My idol did them,
> my graven image and my molten image commanded them'.

It seems probable that the men of Israel have accommodated themselves to the dominant cultural religious behaviors. Further evidence of their religious apostasy is found in 43.22-24:

> Yet you did not call upon me, O Jacob;
> but you have been weary of me, O Israel!
> You have not brought me your sheep for burnt offerings,
> or honored me with your sacrifices.
> I have not burdened you with offerings,
> or wearied you with frankincense.
> You have not bought me sweet cane with money,
> or satisfied me with the fat of your sacrifices.

> But you have burdened me with your sins,
> you have wearied me with your iniquities.

Yet after Jacob's redemption is proclaimed (48.20), and thereby effected, the idols are not mentioned again.

2. The sins of Israel that eventuated in the fall of Jerusalem were, according to the prophets, the sins of religious apostasy and political injustice practiced by the leaders of the cult and the nation. In patriarchal Israel it is clear that that leadership was predominantly male.[22] What Second Isaiah has seen is the power that males had in that patriarchal structure, and she holds them responsible and accountable for the apostasy and the injustice that led to the exile. The prophet denies the appropriateness of the traditional prophetic metaphor of woman's sexual impropriety for the fall of Jerusalem. Instead she reverses it, using the rape metaphor to make explicit just who had the power to victimize.

3. Furthermore, the unfaithfulness to YHWH was continuing in Babylon, as the 'men of Israel' engaged in religious apostasy. Second Isaiah is enraged. The accusation of Jacob and Israel (although always in the context of redemption, such as at 43.1-5 or 44.21-22) is clear:

> Yet you did not call upon me, O Jacob;
> but you have been weary of me, O Israel! (43.22).

> Your first father sinned,
> and your mediators transgressed against me.
> Therefore I profaned the princes of the sanctuary,
> I delivered Jacob to utter destruction and Israel to reviling (43.27).

As has already been noted, ch. 48 begins with the clear charge of Jacob/Israel continuing sin of hypocritical faithlessness in exile:

> Hear this, O house of Jacob,
> who are called by the name of Israel,
> and who come forth from the loins of Judah:
> who swear by the name of the LORD,
> and who confess the God of Israel,
> *but not in truth or right* (48.1; italics mine).

This prophetic critique is brought against Jacob/Israel, who have sinned,

---

22. P. Bird, 'The Place of Women in the Israelite Cultus', in P. Miller Jr, P.D. Hanson and S.D. McBride (eds.), *Ancient Israelite Religion: Essays in Honor of Frank Moore Cross* (Philadelphia: Fortress Press, 1987), pp. 397-420.

continue to sin, and are nevertheless being redeemed. Jerusalem, by contrast, is pardoned of her iniquities at the very beginning of Second Isaiah because she has paid doubly for her participation in the transgression for which Israel was judged by YHWH:

> Speak tenderly to Jerusalem,
> and cry to her that her
> warfare is ended,
> that her iniquity is pardoned,
> that she has received from the LORD's hand
> double for all her sins (40.2).

From that moment of pardon, the rest of the text of Second Isaiah deals with Jacob/Israel's continuation of sin. 'Receiving double' is the prophet's reference to the women of Israel (Jerusalem/Zion) as both politically oppressed and sexually oppressed.

While her suffering has not effected redemption, Zion/Jerusalem is an agent of YHWH's redeeming of Jacob/Israel. Having stated Jerusalem's exoneration at the very beginning of the text, Second Isaiah quickly names Zion/Jerusalem as the bearer of good news:

> Get up to a high mountain,
> O Zion, herald of good tidings;
> lift up your voice with strength,
> O Jerusalem, herald of good tidings,
> lift it up, fear not;
> say to the cities of Judah,
> 'Behold your God!' (40.9).

The women of Israel-in-exile have saving knowledge to share. They have been emancipated, and it is their liberation that embodies (incarnates) the liberation of Jacob/Israel. The very shape of this literary composition replicates Second Isaiah's theology as summarized at 46.8-13, in which God declares 'the end from the beginning'. Just so, Second Isaiah presents the conclusions of her theological reflection in 40.1-2. Jerusalem has been exonerated and, now liberated, she is to be one of the agents of Jacob/Israel's redemption. This is reiterated at 46.13b: 'I will put salvation in *Zion* for Israel my glory' (italics mine).

When one hears a woman's voice within Second Isaiah, the Servant Songs are transposed into a slightly different key. If a woman has prophesied out of double oppression of gender and exile, does that reality not suggest the way in which she might have understood a marginalized individual within a marginalized community to have salvific power? This male servant, unattractive, unloved, nonviolent and perhaps silenced (53.7), becomes a paradigm of power that surely subverts the patriarchal paradigm of power.

There is no reason to deny the masculine gender of the servant; in both the third person pronouns and in imagery ('I gave my cheeks to those who pulled out the beard', 50.6) a man is described. But what a man this is—the reversal of Cyrus, the powerful military victor, who is also identified by Second Isaiah as an agent of divine will (44.28).

Is it a problem for the thesis of this paper that the two subjective songs, the two internal reflections by the servant (49.1-6; 50.4-9) reflect a male? To the contrary, the continuing debate as to whether the servant is one or many, individual or community, suggests that the boundaries here have been deliberately effaced for the sake of maintaining simultaneous levels of meaning.[23] To illustrate, in 53.10-11, in the song of community response to the servant presented in the first person plural voice, there are back-to-back images of promise, (1) that the servant will see his seed זֶרַע (RSV translates 'offspring'), and (2) that the servant will bear fruit from the travail עָמָל (or childbirth) of the soul. In this context of boundary confusion, sex becomes a trope, a rhetorical construct, not an attribute.

The Songs of this Servant, if they may be taken out of context and sung consecutively, have a chiastic structure of voice. They move from an external voice of God describing the servant ('Behold my servant', 42.1) to two internal, subjective reflections by the servant in first person (49.1-6; 50.4-9), returning to the external voice echoing the opening line ('Behold my servant', 52.13). At some editorial moment all of the text of Second Isaiah, in which this four-stanza song is embedded, became the community's responsorial song of affirmation of its relationship to this once despised servant. The songs can thus be heard as one song with a coherent structure of four stanzas, which have been interwoven throughout the text.

Consider now ch. 47 and the prophetic address to the 'virgin daughter of Babylon'. Could this figure stand for all the women of Babylon, just as 'the captive daughter Zion' stands for all the women of the exilic community? Here an empathetic (if not sympathetic) woman's voice

---

23. P. Wilcox and D. Paton-Williams, 'The Servant Songs in Deutero-Isaiah', *JSOT* 42 (1988), pp. 79-102.

speaks to a soon-to-be victimized sister, caught in the reversal of Babylon's political fortunes at the hand of Cyrus. The combination of scathing insight and empathetic understanding could most easily be understood as coming from a woman of exile.

Here is the prophetic critical tradition brought to bear by a woman on behalf of all women in both oppressor and oppressed cultures against the men, whose political control of the religious practices of the cultures has determined the women's futures. After inviting the Babylonian woman to join her in the conditions of oppression 'on the ground' (47.1), Second Isaiah tells her that these consequences are inevitable, but includes her in direct address under the care of Israel's God:

> I will take vengeance, and I will spare no man.
> *Our Redeemer*—the LORD of hosts is his name—
> is the Holy One of Israel (47.4; italics mine).

Chapter 47 details a political reversal soon to occur that will bring social and personal reversals in its wake. Second Isaiah has experienced such a reversal herself, and, reflecting upon that experience, she interprets political reversals as accomplishing God's purposes. Second Isaiah constantly affirms reversals of conditions to be theological: the exiled will become the new Jerusalem; the rough places will be made plain; the desert will bloom; and the pagan Persian conqueror Cyrus will be God's anointed, God's 'messiah'. A woman prophesies that exonerated, emancipated women are to comfort Israel-in-exile, and a mute male suffers. Such reversals are shocking, especially since their intent is redemptive.

Does it now seem a surprise that Second Isaiah—the only book of the Hebrew Bible outside of Genesis to do so—remembers Sarah, our matriarch? At Isa. 51.2 we have:

> Look to Abraham your father
> And to Sarah who bore you.[24]

Here in Second Isaiah is extensive imagery drawn from the experience of nurturing a child, often expressing tender solicitousness. Such nurturing is, of course, possible for either parent:

---

24. See M. Callaway, *Sing, O Barren One: A Study in Comparative Midrash* (Atlanta: Scholars Press, 1986).

40.11	he will gather the lambs in his arms, he will carry them in his bosom, and gently lead those that are with young.
41.13	For I the LORD your God hold your right hand; it is I who say to you, 'Fear not. I will help you.'
42.6	I have taken you by the hand and kept you.
43.4	Because you are precious in my eyes, and honored, and I love you...
49.25	for I will contend with those who contend with you, and I will save your children.

While it is possible for a male to base images on the experience of parenting, it would be remarkable for a man to accompany such images of nurturing with imagery from women's exclusive (biologically maternal) experience, as one finds in Second Isaiah. Imagery has been drawn from the explicitly female experiences of breast-feeding and birth:

49.15	Can a woman forget her sucking child?
49.23	Kings shall be your foster fathers, and their queens your nursing mothers.
42.14	...and now I will cry out like a woman in travail, I will gasp and pant.
45.10b	Woe to him who says...to a woman, 'With what are you in travail?'

There are several references to being formed in the womb (44.24; 49.5; 49.15), and P. Trible has done ground-breaking, critical work on the imagery of compassion as 'womb-love' in Second Isaiah.[25]

Many images have been drawn from women's socio-sexual roles, including the virgin daughter, the bride, the wife, the barren woman, the divorced woman and the widow:

47.1-4	The virgin daughter is the figure addressed in the extended metaphor.
49.18	The bride: 'you shall put them all on as an ornament, you shall bind them on as a bride does'.
54.6	The wife: 'For the LORD has called you like a wife forsaken and grieved in Spirit, like a wife of youth when she is cast off, says your God'.
49.21	The barren woman:[26] 'I was bereaved and barren'.
54.1a	'Sing, O barren one, who did not bear...you who have not been in travail'.

25. Trible, *God and the Rhetoric of Sexuality*, p. 520.

26. See the treatment of the barren woman tradition in Callaway, *Sing, O Barren One*.

50.1   The divorced woman: 'Thus says the LORD, "Where is your mother's
            bill of divorce with which I put her away?"'
47.8   The widow: 'I shall not sit as a widow or know the loss of children'.
49.20   '...the children born in the time of your bereavement'.

B.B. Kaiser has suggested that some of the sexually conditioned experience that informs the imagery and voices in the Hebrew Bible, including Second Isaiah, is a constructed *persona*, a mask behind which a male poet could express the fullest intensity of emotion.[27] In the case of Second Isaiah, such an analysis abstracts figures of speech (particularly Daughter Zion) from the text and obscures the fact that sexually conditioned experience becomes a hermeneutic within the text. Rape, an extreme example of power assymetry, epitomizes betrayal. Once the paradigm of betrayal was understood by those who had experienced it, the betrayal of women by men pointed beyond itself to the betrayal of YHWH by the men of Israel.

The question then arises, since most women's religious lives were expressed in the private realm through socio-sexual roles,[28] how could a sixth-century BCE woman have emerged as a poet of such stature? Feminist scholarship is uncovering a corpus of women's literature within the Old Testament. J.A. Hackett has suggested that Judges 5–11 is such an example.[29] Those chapters describe heroines—Deborah, Jael, Jephthah's daughter—and there are no negative comments about the women. Chapter 5, Deborah's song, which is a holy war battle cry, is suggested to have been written by a woman.[30] Work on such texts sheds light on women as historical agents within Israel. Moreover, Hackett suggests that women are most likely to have public power, to have visible central roles, in times of political and social chaos, such as the time described in Judges.[31] So too the Babylonian exile was a time of social chaos when traditional roles might have broken down, when ad hoc leaders might have emerged. There is, of course, scriptural evidence for women charismatics or women prophets (e.g. Huldah, Miriam).

27. B.B. Kaiser, 'Poet as Female Impersonator: The Image of Daughter Zion as Speaker in Biblical Poems of Suffering', *JR* 67 (1987), pp. 164-82.

28. Bird, 'The Place of Women', p. 401.

29. J.A. Hackett, 'In the Days of Jael: Reclaiming the History of Women', in C.W. Atkinson, C.H. Buchanan and M.R. Miles (eds.), *Immaculate and Powerful* (Boston: Beacon Press, 1985).

30. Hackett, 'In the Days of Jael', p. 32.

31. Hackett, 'In the Days of Jael', p. 19.

P. Bird suggests that 'the role of prophet...was the one religious office
with broad power that was not mediated or controlled by the cultic or
civil hierarchy and the one religious office open to women'.[32] Second
Isaiah, as prophet, was a historical agent; she was also a victim of exile,
and she reflected on and prophesied out of her victimization as a woman.

There is current scholarly consensus on the anonymity of Second
Isaiah,[33] yet the pronoun used to refer to this writer is almost always
'he'. To my knowledge, only K. Pfisterer Darr has published a reference
to Second Isaiah's anonymous author as 'he or she'.[34] There is no
prima facie evidence to indicate that this writer was male, nor any
reason why the weight of presumption needs to fall on male authorship.
Indeed, if we are enabled to hear a woman's voice speaking to us from
the text of Isaiah 40–55, should not the pronoun used to refer to the
voice of Second Isaiah more properly be 'she'?

Second Isaiah's method of knowing was to reflect theologically on
her experience of oppression in exile as double victimization—one
sexual and one political. Through that reflection the prophet placed the
responsibility for Israel's downfall as cult and nation with the male
leadership and that leadership's continuing arrogant, idolatrous betrayal of
YHWH by the making of idols in violation of their traditional monotheistic values. Second Isaiah brought the full force of prophetic tradition
against patriarchy. Nevertheless, it was always in the context of Israel's
ultimate redemption that the prophet cried, and it was always to accomplish YHWH's own purpose. Second Isaiah is the critical prophetic
tradition explicitly applied to the sin of patriarchy within the history of
Israel and within the canon.

---

32. Bird, 'The Place of Women', p. 407.

33. P.D. Hanson, *The Dawn of Apocalyptic* (Philadelphia: Fortress Press, 1975),
p. 41.

34. K. Pfisterer Darr, 'Like Warrior, Like Woman: Destruction and Deliverance
in Isaiah 42.10-17', *CBQ* 49 (1987), pp. 560-71.

JSOT 44 (1989), pp. 89-107

DAUGHTER OF ZION AND SERVANT OF THE LORD
IN ISAIAH: A COMPARISON

John F.A. Sawyer

This note[1] is a response to three recent developments in Isaiah research. The first is epitomized in the title of Tryggve Mettinger's monograph, *A Farewell to the Servant Songs: A Critical Examination of an Exegetical Axiom*.[2] The four passages about the Servant of the Lord which Bernhard Duhm isolated as 'Servant Songs',[3] can now be restored to their context in Isaiah, and this has made us think again, not only about what the Servant of the Lord imagery means, but also about its relationship to other images in the same context, in particular, the 'daughter of Zion'.

Secondly, there is the recent scholarly interest in feminine imagery in the Bible, and in particular in the second half of the book of Isaiah. Is it possible that the same male, Christian bias that had for a century preoccupied readers and commentators with the identity and role of the man in the 'Servant Songs', had prevented us from taking seriously the woman in the 'Zion songs'? Of course, in Christian tradition, from New Testament times, the Servant of the Lord has been identified with Jesus, and that provided a particular stimulus, not always admitted or recognized, to Christian scholars. But whatever the reason, feminine imagery in Isaiah and elsewhere in the Bible has, apart from typological references to the Virgin Mary, rarely received much scholarly attention until the last decade or two. Now Christian feminist interpreters, concerned to find scriptural authority for a less patriarchal Christianity,

1. Delivered at the winter meeting of the Society for Old Testament Study in London, January 1989.
2. Lund: Gleerup, 1983.
3. B. Duhm, *Das Buch Jesaia* (Göttingen: Vandenhoeck & Ruprecht, 1892).

have given new emphasis to a few striking passages, several of them in Isaiah, in which God is thought of as a mother (Deut. 32.18; cf. 32.11; Isa. 42.14; 45.10; 46.3; 49.15). In such contexts the feminine associations of the term רחמים 'love, warmth, compassion' (e.g. 49.13, 14), etymologically related to רחם 'womb', are acknowledged too.[4] When the numerous 'Zion' passages in these chapters are taken into account as well, the concentration of feminine language and imagery is quite exceptional and demands special critical attention.

The third new factor in the situation concerns method. Biblical scholars are increasingly going beyond traditional 'atomistic' approaches to scripture to study larger stretches of text, even whole books, whatever the original date and authorship of their separate components.[5] This often goes with a new interest in the history of interpretation, that is to say, in how the text has been understood and used by those religious communities, Jewish and Christian, for whom it is scripture.[6] Without entering into the debate on the relative merits of various approaches to biblical interpretation, it must be said that much has changed in the last twenty years or so, and perhaps the burden of proof is now on the 'atomizers' to justify their methods of handling scripture. For present purposes, at any rate, there are clearly themes and images which recur and develop through the text and to understand them fully they must be viewed together, as parts of a whole.[7]

---

4. Cf. P. Trible, *God and the Rhetoric of Sexuality* (Philadelphia: Fortress Press, 1978), pp. 50-56, 60-71; S. McFague, *Metaphorical Theology: Models of God in Religious Language* (London: SCM Press, 1982), pp. 145-92.

5. Cf. R.M. Polzin and E. Rothman (eds.), *The Biblical Mosaic: Changing Perspectives* (Philadephia: Fortress Press, 1982); R. Alter and F. Kermode, *The Literary Guide to the Bible* (Cambridge, MA: Harvard University Press, 1987).

6. Cf. J.F.A. Sawyer, 'Changing Emphasis in the Study of the Prophets', in R.J. Coggins *et al.* (eds.), *Israel's Prophetic Thadition* (Cambridge: Cambridge University Press, 1984), pp. 233-49; E. Schüssler Fiorenza, 'The Ethics of Biblical Interpretation: Decentering Biblical Scholarship', *JBL* 107.1 (1988), pp. 3-17; R. Morgan and J. Barton, *Biblical Interpretation* (Oxford: Clarendon Press, 1988), pp. 285-96.

7. Cf. L. Alonso Schökel, 'Isaiah', in Alter and Kermode, *Literary Guide*, pp. 165-83.

I

We begin with a brief survey of the relevant passages in Isaiah. The 'servant' passages are so familiar that I do not propose to say much about them at this stage, except to emphasize that, as well as those outside the 'Servant Songs' (e.g. 41.8ff.; 44.1ff., 21-22), I shall also include passages in which a man is described or addressed in similar language to that used of the servant, even although the term 'servant' does not occur (e.g. 40.27ff.; 43.1ff.).

Less familiar and more in need of some introductory remarks are the 'daughter of Zion' passages. Again I propose to include passages in addition to those in which the term 'daughter of Zion' actually occurs. There are in fact only seven of these in Isaiah (1.8; 3.16; 10.32; 16.1; 37.22; 52.2; 62.11).[8] 'Daughter of Zion' in my title is in effect shorthand for a female character who figures just as prominently in Isaiah 40–66 as the servant of the Lord. Like him, she is sometimes named, as in 49.14 ('But Zion said, The Lord has forsaken me...'), sometimes she is anonymous as in ch. 54 ('Sing, O barren one, who did not bear...fear not').

There are several passages in Isaiah where Jerusalem is compared to a woman. The lament beginning 'How the faithful city has become a harlot!' in ch. 1 is one of the best-known (vv. 21-26). There is another in ch. 37 where Jerusalem, standing firm against the Assyrians, is compared to a proud and courageous young woman tossing her head defiantly as she repels an unwelcome suitor (v. 22 NEB, JB). Jerusalem is not the only city to which such graphic feminine imagery is applied. Tyre is compared to a shameless and ageing prostitute, plying her trade 'with all the kingdoms of the world' (23.15-18), and Sidon to a childless, rejected old woman (23.4-12). The fall of Babylon is described in language as vivid and detailed as any of the passages we shall be considering (ch. 47). A powerful, elegant queen, who has been brought up to believe she is god, she is pulled off her throne, stripped of her fine clothes, raped and given menial tasks to do such as laundry work and grinding flour; her counsellors and astrologers are found wanting, her children and her husband dead. Now even though she is named in v. 1 as the 'daughter of Babylon', it is important to notice that there is not one detail in this chapter that refers explicitly to a city: nothing about

8. The term is more common in Jeremiah (13×) and Lamentations (17×), and also appears a few times in Micah, Zephaniah and Zechariah.

walls or gates or sieges. It tells the story of the overpowering and
humiliation of a woman. Feminine singular forms are used throughout:
'get down from your throne...sit in the dust...go into...there is no-one
to save you...' The personification is complete, the story autonomous
and consistent.

Most of the best known passages about the daughter of Zion are, like
the servant passages, in chs. 40ff. Following on the command to 'speak
tenderly to Jerusalem' (v. 1), Zion is addressed directly: 'Get you up to
a high mountain, צִיּוֹן מְבַשֶּׂרֶת herald of good tidings to Zion' (or 'Zion,
herald of good tidings'). whatever it means, the important fact is that the
person in question, the herald (מְבַשֶּׂרֶת) is female, addressed in feminine
singular forms. But I shall return to this famous passage later.

The main concentration of 'daughter of Zion' passages is in chs. 49–
66. Through these chapters, in a series of dramatic poems, runs the story
of a woman's life from bereavement and barrenness in ch. 49 to the
birth of a son in ch. 66. Sometimes but not always she is named as Zion
or Jerusalem. Sometimes but not always she is identified as the city of
Jerusalem by explicit references to her gates or her walls or builders.
Sometimes her identity, like that of the servant, is ambiguous. But the
feminine imagery is so vividly described as to create in almost every
case a story or picture, every bit as consistent and convincing as that of
the Servant of the Lord.

Her first words are a sceptical response to triumphant expressions of
faith in Yahweh's power and love: 'But Zion said, Yahweh has forsaken
me, the Lord has forgotten me'. This is precisely parallel to the servant's
doubts earlier in the chapter: 'But I said, I have laboured in vain...' (v.
4). In spite of Yahweh's assurances of his eternal love for her and the
promise of children—even if her sons and daughters were actually
brought back and placed in front of her—she still would not believe it: 'I
was bereaved and barren, exiled and put away... I was left alone: so
where could they have come from?' Her third question sums up her
feeling of powerlessness: 'Can the prey be taken from the mighty, or the
captives of a righteous man be rescued?' Against the physical strength
of a man, whether he is a 'lawful' (צַדִּיק) captor as the masoretic text
has it (cf. AV), or a 'tyrant' (עָרִיץ) as Isaiah Scroll A, the Peshitta, the
Vulgate and most modern commentators[9] take it, a woman is powerless.

---

9. E.g. Duhm, *Jesaia*; C.R. North, *The Second Isaiah* (Oxford: Clarendon
Press, 1964); C. Westermann, *Isaiah 40–66* (London: SCM Press, 1969);
P.-E. Bonnard, *Le Second Isaïe* (Paris: Lecoffre, 1972); cf. RSV, NEB.

In chs. 51 and 52, her plight is described in more detail: she is, as it were, drunk with the strong wine of her suffering, staggering helplessly, not one of her children there to take her by the hand and lead her to safety, a dirty, humiliated slave. In double imperatives so typical of these chapters, she is summoned to rouse herself: 'Awake, awake, put on your strength, O Zion, put on your beautiful garments...shake yourself from the dust...arise...loose the bonds from your neck, O captive daughter of Zion!' Part of 51.12 is also addressed to Zion: 'Who are you that are afraid of man who dies...?'[10]

Chapter 54 continues the imperatives ('Shout for joy, barren... enlarge your tent-space...do not be afraid...'), and depicts Yahweh swearing he will never again be angry with her or rebuke her. Chapter 50, beginning with the words 'Arise shine for your light is come', envisages the nations of the world bringing her, among other things, gifts of gold and frankincense. Chapter 52 celebrates her wedding, or at any rate the day on which the names Azubah and Shemamah (Abandoned and Desolate) are changed to Hephzibah and Beulah (My-delight-is-in-her and Married), and Yahweh rejoices over her 'as a bridegroom rejoices over his bride'. As the climax to the series, there is the remarkable poem in ch. 66 describing the birth of her children and the subsequent scene of her feeding them and carrying them on her hip and dandling them on her knee.

There is one discordant passage in all this, in which she has become a whore, involved in nameless orgies, oblivious to the enormity of her crimes: 'deserting me, you stripped and lay down on your wide bed and made bargains with men for the pleasure of sleeping together...' (cf. NEB) (57.6-13). We shall look at its parallel among the servant passages later (43.22-28).

But before comparing the two motifs, I propose to look in detail at two of the Zion passages (54.1-10; 66.7-14) in which the image is developed and elaborated to the point where one is tempted to take them out of their context, and consider them like the 'Servant Songs' on their own. This is merely to highlight the vividness and effectiveness of the story, and the resemblance between the two motifs, the one studied almost to the point of idolatry by Christian exegetes, the other almost totally ignored. I shall then put them back in their context in Isaiah, alongside all the other Zion passages, and examine them together.

---

10. The gender is ignored by most commentators (e.g. North): BHS emends to masculine singular מִי אַתְּ וַתִּירְאִי. Duhm keeps the feminine.

1.   *54.1-10*

1.   Shout for joy, barren woman, you who never had a child!
Break into cries of joy, you who have never been in labour!
A woman who was abandoned will have more children than one that was
        married, said Yahweh.
2.   Enlarge your tent-space; spread out the hangings in your
        home;
lengthen your guy-ropes; strengthen your tent-pegs.
3.   You will burst out to the right and the left;
your offspring will take over nations, and populate deserted
        cities.
4.   Do not be afraid; you will not be put to shame.
Do not be dismayed; you will not be disgraced.
You will forget the shame of your youth;
and remember no more the reproach of your widowhood.
5.   The one who made you, whose name is 'Yahweh Sabaoth' is to
        be your husband;
The Holy One of Israel, who is called 'God of all the earth', is to be
        your redeemer.
6.   Like a forsaken wife, distressed in spirit, Yahweh has called
        you,
the wife of his youth, though once rejected, said your God.
7.   I did forsake you for a brief moment,
but my love for you is deep and I will bring you home again.
8.   In a momentary outburst of anger[11] I turned away from you,
but I love you with a love that never fails,
said Yahweh, your redeemer.
9.   This is like the days of[12] Noah to me,
when I swore that the waters of Noah would never flood the world
        again.
So now I swear never again to be angry with you or to rebuke
        you.
10.   Though the mountains depart and the hills are shaken,
my love will never leave you,
and my promise of peace will never be shaken,
said the one who loves you, Yahweh.

This is a passage about reconciliation: a husband promises never again
to lose his temper, never again to walk out on his wife, leaving her
childless and humiliated. She was partly to blame, but the single

---

11. בשצף קצף...רגע: following the traditional view that שצף is a variant of שטף
'flood' (cf. Prov. 27.4).

12. Reading כִּימֵי for MT כִּי־מֵי cf. RSV, NEB, JB.

reference to 'the shame of her youth' (בשת עלומיך) in v. 4 is insigni-
ficant beside the repeated references to her suffering and his love. He
takes prime responsibility for the tragedy and swears he will never again
be angry with her or rebuke her. The new relationship will be characterized on his part by 'love that never fails' (חסד עולם) and 'deep tender
love' (רחמים) and enshrined in a 'promise of reconciliation' (ברית שלומי)
more lasting than the hills. Like the story of the suffering servant in the
previous chapter, the story of the suffering woman in ch. 54 begins at
the end: she will soon be singing again; her shame and loneliness are as
good as over; she will have a home and a family; she will see her
children and grandchildren growing up and prospering.

The story is as vivid, the language and imagery every bit as colourful
and dramatic as in the Servant Songs. It is not a story about Jerusalem,
any more than the servant songs are about Israel or Jesus or the
prophet. It is about a woman, and to neglect this is to miss the dynamic
of the passage. In the first place, there is not a single word in it that
refers exclusively to a city. שוממה 'abandoned', for example, in v. 1 is
used in some contexts of ruined city-walls and gates (e.g. 49.8, 19; 61.4;
Lam. 1.4), but here surely its usage in the story of Tamar, raped,
humiliated and abandoned by her brother (2 Sam. 13.20), is more
relevant—although few commentaries note this. There it is applied, as
Phyllis Trible puts it, to 'a woman of sorrows and acquainted with...cut
off from the land of the living, stricken for the sins of her brother;
yet she herself had done no violence and there was no deceit in her
mouth'.[13]

Allusions back to the stories of the patriarchs similarly shift the point
of reference away from rebuilding the ruined city of Jerusalem. Instead,
we have a scene of tent-erecting reminiscent of the story of Isaac in
Gerar, where freedom to expand and live in peace is celebrated in the
place-name Rehoboth: 'For now the Lord has made room for us (כי
עתה הרחיב יהוה לנו) and we shall be fruitful in the land' (Gen. 26). The
woman in this story is also the recipient of a promise very like those
given to Abraham (Gen. 12; 15), Isaac (Gen. 26) and Jacob (Gen. 28):
'your offspring (literally 'your seed, the seed in your womb') will take
over the nations and populate deserted cities' (v. 3). Here too the eternal
promise to Noah (Gen. 9) is cited as the model for reconciliation: 'when

13. P. Trible, *Texts of Terror: Literary-Feminist Readings of Biblical Narratives*
(Philadelphia: Fortress Press, 1984), p. 32.

I swore that the waters of Noah would never flood the world again...'
(v. 9).

Verse 7 contains another proof that the poem is not primarily or only
about a city: אֲקַבְּצֵךְ 'I will bring you home again'. The word קָבֵץ refers
here and in many other contexts to the ingathering of the exiles and, like
the word 'Israel' in the second Servant Song, points to a collective interpretation of the passage. We shall return to this later. For the present,
there is more to be said about the story itself

Unlike the woman in the poem—and the servant in the 'Servant
Songs'—the man is identified. He is of course Yahweh, and, if we take
the imagery of the story seriously,[14] this provides one of the most
strikng features of the poem. Yahweh, 'the Holy One of Israel... God of
all the earth' (v. 5) is represented as behaving like a remorseful husband,
pleading with his wife to trust him and take him back. The last four
verses of the poem are apologetic in tone: 'it was just for a moment—I
lost my temper (בשצף קצף) I won't do it again... I promise... I love
you'. She is physically weaker than he is and socially dependent on him.
He has the power to give her happiness and dignity and freedom; she
knows he also has the power to punish, humiliate and abuse her. So he
has to convince her that he really loves her and that she can trust him.
To do this he sets aside all hardness and pomposity, the frightening
manifestations of his power and his status as 'God of all the earth', and
comes to her, on bended knee as it were, to plead with her to let
bygones be bygones and start again.

If you find it hard to believe that such an image of Yahweh can really
appear in scripture, then you need only look elsewhere in these remarkable chapters to find evidence that it can. In ch. 42 God is described as
'crying out and panting like a woman in labour'. In ch. 63 he appears at
the gates of the city, unrecognized, a weary, bloodstained warrior,[15]
commanding our respect and sympathy rather than our fear, and in ch.
66, to which we shall return later, Yahweh is Zion's midwife when she is
in labour. The prophet was called to 'comfort his people... and speak
tenderly to Jerusalem'. Surely this is one of the most effective ways in
which he does this.

---

14. On the importance of 'taking seriously' metaphors or models in religious
language, see McFague, *Models of God*, pp. 31-66.
   15. Cf. NEB.

2. 66.7-14

7.   Before she was in labour she had a child.

Before her labour pains began, she gave birth to a son.

8.   Who ever heard of such a thing? Who ever saw anything like
        this?

Is a country born in one day? Is a nation brought forth in one
        moment?

No sooner was Zion in labour than she brought forth her
        children.

9.   Would I assist at the labour and then not deliver the baby? said
        Yahweh.

Would I who allow children to be born, close her womb?

said your God.

10.   Rejoice, Jerusalem, be glad for her, all you who love her.

Rejoice, rejoice for her, all you who mourn for her.

11.   Then feeding at her breast, you will be comforted and sated,

and savour with delight the abundance of her milk.

12.   This is what Yahweh said:

I will send peace flowing over her like a river

and the wealth of nations like a flooded valley.

You shall feed at her breast; you shall be carried on her hip and
        dandled on her knees.

13.   Like one comforted by his mother, so I will comfort you.

You will find comfort in Jerusalem.

14.   At this sight your heart will be filled with joy.

And your limbs will be as fresh as grass in spring.

The hand of Yahweh will be revealed to his servants,

but anger to his enemies.

The passage comes at the very end of the book. It describes two scenes in considerable detail. Both are about Zion. In the first, she gives birth to a son. In the second, she is already the proud mother of a large family and attention switches to the contentment of her children, feeding at her breast or being dandled on her knee. There are phrases in this poem which apply it to Jerusalem ('is a country born in one day?...the wealth of nations'). But, once more, if we are to appreciate the force of this passage, we should first take the language and imagery at face value.

Coming as it does at the very end of the book of Isaiah, it picks up themes familiar to us from earlier passages. Of these the most significant is 54.1-10, which we have just discussed, There the woman was promised a husband and lots of children: here the birth of her first child is described. Chapter 54 is written in the future tense, full of promises and assurances; this passage is in the past tense with an account of how she gave birth to a son. The birth of a son is of course celebrated elsewhere in Isaiah as a saving event in the royal, masculine language of chs. 9 and 11: 'for to us a child is born...there shall come forth a shoot from the stem of Jesse...' But here, as in ch. 54, the emphasis is on the birth itself, as an act of new creation, on the mother rather than on the child. In fact who is born here is not clear: one child as in v. 7, or more than one as in the second half of verse 8, or a whole nation as in the first half of v. 8. The conspicuous absence of the word בֵן 'son' from the first half of v. 7, as a parallel to זָכָר 'male child' in the second, has been noted: BHS inserts it; Duhm preferred the rather unidiomatic יַלְדָּה 'her child'. But that is to miss the point: this is not about the birth of a son as in 9 and 11, but about birth as opposed to death, fecundity as opposed to barrenness. Like rebuilding a city or bringing back exiles, having a child provides a marvellous image of restoration or revival.

In the first place, there is the sheer number of technical or semi-technical obstetric terms in these few verses: two different words for 'labour-pains' (the verb חִיל 3× and the noun חֶבֶל), two words for 'deliver' (הִמְלִיט and יָלַד),[16] and the word הִשְׁבִּיר 'to assist delivery' (by helping the baby through the מַשְׁבֵּר 'the neck of the womb'). There are some tragic stories of childbirth in the Bible, Rachel dying as she gave birth to Benjamin, for example (Gen. 35.16-20), and more often than not this language is applied figuratively to painful or catastrophic situations. The pain and distress of a birth that has gone wrong is used twice in such contexts earlier in the book (26.17-18; 37.3). But in ch. 65 among the characteristics of the new heaven and the new earth, where newborn babies will never die and the wolf and the lamb shall feed together, there is the idea that childbirth will never go wrong (65.23). So the ultimate occurrence of this image in ch. 66 completes the return to paradise before the curse of Eve: 'before her labour pains began, she gave birth to a son...no sooner was she in labour than she brought forth her children'. The unprecedented nature of this birth is described in language not unlike that used in the fourth Servant Song: 'who ever heard of such a thing? who ever saw anything like this?' Following on from ch. 54, we are perhaps to understand that Zion, like Sarah, was past child-bearing age. But there was another miracle as well: 'before she was in labour, she had a child'. This was childbirth without labour pains.

Before we leave this climax of the feminine imagery in Isaiah, there is

---

16. הִמְלִיט occurs only here in this sense in biblical Hebrew; it later became the regular word for 'to lamb, calve, etc'. מלט Pi. is 'to lay eggs' (Isa. 34.15).

one more detail to comment on. In ch. 54 we noted that Yahweh was somewhat daringly represented as a remorseful husband, pleading with his wife to trust him. Here again he has a humble role to play, this time as a woman's midwife: 'Would I assist at the labour and then not deliver the baby? Would I who allow children to be born, close her womb?' There are plenty of parallels to the second half of this verse, where Yahweh determines whether a birth takes place or not: for example, he 'closed all the wombs of the house of Abimelech' (Gen. 20.18; cf. Gen. 15.3). But this is the only passage in which he is the subject of the verb השביר the technical term for the midwife's task up to the point where the baby is delivered. One is tempted to suggest that the parallel term, הוליד *Hiph.* 'cause to bring forth', used elsewhere figuratively of Yahweh (55.10), is a scribal error for the technical term יֵלֵּד *Piel* 'to deliver a child' (hence מְיַלֶּדֶת 'midwife': Gen. 35.17; Exod. 1.15). Dittography הוליד occurs in the second half of the verse) and the radical anthropomorphism would explain the error. But even without that change, the anthropomorphism is there: Yahweh once more humbles himself to assist his beloved Zion.

II

Having looked at these two 'Daughter of Zion' songs in isolation, let us now put them back in their context and consider them as elements in a single story, parallel to the story of the Servant of the Lord. In the first place, there is the sheer extent of the elaboration of these two themes in Isaiah 40–66. In the dozen or so passages about Zion there is a clear progression, from abandonment, loneliness and fear to fulfilment and joy: and the same goes for the servant whose fortunes are traced from a time when he is weak and afraid and feels like a worm (41.14) to heroic suffering and triumph in ch. 53. Neither story is told as a continuous narrative, but the plot and the characters in both cases are referred to sufficiently often and regularly for the progression and continuity to be maintained. whether these graphic forms of expression, stories we might call them, constitute some kind of basic framework around which the rest of the material in Isaiah 40–66 has been woven, or whether the creative process was the other way round, is impossible to say.

There is still much work to be done on the way chs. 40–66 pick up themes introduced in earlier chapters: for example, the suffering of the servant in ch. 53 appears to echo the diseased body of Israel in ch. 1; the humiliation of the haughty daughters of Zion in all their finery in ch. 3 prepares the way for the story of her redemption in 40–66; and perhaps the defiant toss of her head in ch. 37 is a transition, heralding the moment when she shakes off her bonds in ch. 52.[17] But for reasons of time I shall restrict myself to chs. 40–66. Both characters are introduced afresh in ch. 40. But the story of the one is completed in 40–55, while the other is developed mainly in 49–66. So there is an overlap in 49–55. There above all the two stories intersect. Points of comparison have been noted by some of the commentators. The first half of ch. 49 describes the servant's sense of loneliness and failure: 'But I said, "I have laboured in vain, I have spent my strength for nothing and vanity"'. The second half begins: 'But Zion said: "Yahweh has forsaken me, the Lord has forgotten me"', and goes on later 'Behold I was left alone.' The servant in the first half is 'one deeply despised, abhorred by the nations'; Zion in the second half is 'bereaved and barren, exiled and put away'. The servant remembers that Yahweh 'called him from the womb... formed him from the womb to be his servant'; Yahweh tells Zion he loves her as a mother loves her own child. He tells the servant that kings and princes will prostrate themselves; he tells Zion that kings and queens shall bow down to her and lick the dust of her feet.

Continuity and verbal parallels have also been noted between ch. 53, the last of the so-called Servant Songs, and ch. 54, the first of the two Zion passages I discussed above.[18] Both are humiliated or afflicted, both are finally vindicated. Both the servant and Zion will live to see their offspring growing up. In both stories the nations of the world will be affected by what happens (52.15; 54.3). Perhaps most significant is the use of the word שלום in both passages: 'the chastisement that made us whole' (מוסר שלומנו) in 53.5, and Yahweh's 'promise of peace or reconciliation' ברית שלומי in 54.10. The differences in language and imagery are just as striking between the two stories, as we shall see, and of course the one reaches its climax in ch. 53, while the other is still just beginning in ch. 54. But there are clearly enough correspondences

17. On the literary unity of Isaiah, see D.R. Jones, 'The Traditio of the Oracles of Isaiah of Jerusalem', ZAW 67 (1955), pp. 226-46; P.R. Ackroyd, 'Isaiah 1–12: The Presentation of a Prophet', VTSup, 29 (1978), pp. 16-48; J.F.A. Sawyer, Isaiah, I (The Daily Study Bible; Edinburgh: St Andrew Press, 1984), esp. pp. 1-11; II (1986), esp. pp. 43-45.

18. Cf P.-E. Bonnard, Le Second Isaïe (Paris, 1972), pp. 488ff.

between them to justify, if not to demand, that these and all the other Zion and servant passages be studied together.

First of all, are there any ways in which Zion's story can help us understand the servant's story better? One example comes from a comparison of the two climaxes in chs. 53 and 66 respectively. As we saw, one of the elements in the Zion passage is the miraculous nature of the birth: 'Who ever heard of such a thing? Who ever saw anything like this?' Does the supernatural ending to the Zion story confirm that the servant's story also ends with a miracle, namely, his resurrection from the dead?

Both stories are interrupted by sarcastic rebukes: the one is reminded how he had burdened Yahweh with his sins (43.22-24; cf. 42.19-20); the other how she had indulged in all manner of licentious behaviour (57.6-13). As we saw, her past demeanours are only fleetingly alluded to elsewhere ('the shame of your youth' בשת עלומיך in ch. 54).[19] The discordant note sounded by this extended rebuke of the servant, amid all the salvation oracles, hymns of praise and other words of comfort that make up the bulk of Isaiah 40–55, has frequently been commented on. In the present context we may simply add that it is an element in the Zion story too and an explanation for the one must apply to the other.

A third implication of this comparison would be that Duhm's crude distinction between the servant in the songs and the servant elsewhere must go. It adds another argument to those of Tryggve Mettinger. If the story of the Daughter of Zion runs through continuously, in short one- or two-verse passages as well as much longer and more elaborate poems, then surely that is most likely to be the case with the Servant of the Lord passages as well. 'Why do you say... O Israel...my right (משפטי) is ignored (JB) by my God?' in ch. 40 must belong to the same story as 'But I said, surely my right (משפט) is with Yahweh' in ch. 49 (the second 'Servant Song'). And 44.1-5 is as much a 'Servant Song' as any of the others: 'But now hear, O Jacob my servant, Israel whom I have chosen...who formed you from the womb... I will pour my spirit upon your descendants, and my blessing on your offspring...' Almost every phrase in that quotation appears in the four so-called Servant Songs. The natural way to treat this image of the 'Servant of the Lord', like that of the 'Daughter of Zion', is surely to begin by assuming it is all one story, and then to tackle difficulties with that interpretation as they arise. This

---

19. If this term is taken as referring to the 'shame' of being unmarried, then no reference at all is made to any guilt in her past.

brings us now to the question of the identity of the two characters. What light, if any, does the comparison throw on this problem?

One of Duhm's main questions was: Who is the servant in the four songs? And it led to a quite extraordinary variety of answers.[20] Let us ask the same question about Zion: Who is the woman in these passages intended to represent? As in the case of the servant, it is not always made explicit. Some contain clear references to the city of Jerusalem. The familiar poem beginning 'Arise, shine, for thy light is come', for example, is a case in point (60.1-14). Although there are references in it to her sons and daughters, it is throughout a poem about a city, not a woman. 'Foreigners shall build up your walls...your gates shall be open continually...they shall call you the city of the Lord, the Zion of the Holy One of Israel...you shall call your walls Salvation and your gates Praise'. Some passages, on the other hand, tell the story of a woman, at first forsaken, humiliated, afraid, later married and having children. These need not refer to the city of Jerusalem. Indeed some passages certainly do not refer to a city, but to the people in exile. Like the servant, Zion is an image that is capable of various interpretations, both collective and individual. A collective interpretation is made explicit in 51.16, where she is identified with the exiled people of God: 'I am the Lord your God...stretching out the heavens and laying the foundations of the earth, and saying to Zion, 'You (masculine singular!) are my people'.

Sometimes the consistency of the story is sacrificed to one interpretation or another. As we saw above, ch. 54 ('Shout for joy, barren woman...') contains a detail that is inconsistent with an individual interpretation, whether a personified city or a woman: 'I did forsake you for a brief moment, but my love for you is deep and I will bring you home again'. The verb קָבַץ 'gather, collect' cannot easily be used with a singular object. The LXX has ἐλεήσω σε 'I will have mercy on you'. Duhm and others suggest אֲחַבְּקֵךְ 'I will embrace you', which would be most appropriate. What has happened is that the application of this language to the exiles has momentarily disturbed the consistency of the imagery. Then the addition of vv. 11-17 turns the image round again and makes it refer to the city: 'O afflicted one, storm-tossed and not comforted, I will set your stones in antimony, and lay your foundations

---

20. See H.H. Rowley, 'The Servant of the Lord in the Light of Three Decades of Criticism', in *The Servant of the Lord and other Essays* (London: Lutterworth, 1952), pp. 1-57.

with sapphires. I will make your pinnacles of agate, your gates of carbuncles and all your wall of precious stones'. Paul applies the first verse of the passage ('Rejoice O barren one, who does not bear...') to the New Jerusalem (Gal. 4.27).

The possibility of individual interpretations of the same motif, corresponding to Christian interpretations of the servant, is illustrated by Rev. 12.16 where the woman in Isaiah 66 is identified with the Virgin Mary, and by Christian interpretations of Zeph. 3.16-17 ('Do not fear, O Zion...the Lord your God is within you...he will renew you [LXX] by his love') where she is also identified with the Virgin Mary (cf. Zech. 2.14-15 (Eng. 2.10-11); Lk. 1.26-38).[21]

But obviously a collective interpretation of the feminine image is dominant, whether as applied to a people or a city. The first verse of ch. 40 makes it clear that the story of Zion's fortunes, from desolate loneliness and rejection to happiness, marriage and the birth of her children, is a story intended to comfort and inspire its listeners and readers: 'Comfort, comfort my people, says your God, speak tenderly to Jerusalem, and cry to her that her time of service is ended...' This verse introduces the other image as well, the masculine one, called here 'my people', and the same collective interpretation must surely be dominant in the story of 'Israel, my servant, Jacob whom I have chosen' throughout these chapters.[22]

I hope I have drawn enough parallels between the two stories to make this a convincing conclusion. But I would like to add two more, both of them often considered obstacles to the collective interpretation of some of the servant passages. The first is the innocence of the servant in ch. 53, in apparent contradiction to what is said elsewhere of the servant's sins and iniquities (e.g. 43.22-24). It seems to me that in both stories the guilt of the past is played down, with the exception of those colourlul passages I mentioned. The guilt of Zion, the reason why she suffered, is only fleetingly referred to in ch. 54, and nowhere else in the main story. The point is made there and in the opening verses of ch. 40, that her suffering is out of all proportion to her guilt ('she has received double for all her sins'). Other images are operating in ch. 53 as well, notably

---

21. Cf. M. Thurian, *Marie: Mère du Seigneur, Figure de l'Eglise* (Taizé, 1962), pp. 19-27.

22. P. Wilcox and D. Paton-Williams argue that the people are addressed as Jacob/Israel in chs. 40–48 and as Zion/Jerusalem in chs. 49–55 ('The Servant-Songs in Deutero-Isaiah', *JSOT* 42 [1988], pp. 79-102).

that of a sin offering (v. 10), but the notion that his suffering was out of all proportion to anything he could have deserved is definitely part of the story there too.

The other familiar problem about a collective interpretation of the servant is that, in some passages, he apparently has a mission to Israel: he was formed 'from the womb' to bring Jacob back to God and that 'Israel might be gathered to him' (49.5). How can Israel have a mission to himself? If we take the story of Zion as parallel to the story of the servant, we find that the same appears to be true of her as well. In 40.9 she is told, in language we have become familiar with from other parts of Zion story: 'get you up to a high mountain...lift up your voice with strength...fear not...say to the cities of Judah, Behold your God'. She is called מבשרת ירושלם...מבשרת ציון 'O herald of good tidings to Zion... Jerusalem', which indicates that Zion/Jerusalem is included among the cities of Judah that are to hear her message.[23] So the female figure who is elsewhere called Zion, is sent as a herald of good tidings to Zion/Jerusalem and the cities of Judah, just as the male figure, who is called Israel elsewhere, is sent to 'raise up the tribes of Jacob and bring back the survivors of Israel'. In 52.7 another herald (masculine מבשר) goes up on to a mountain to bring good tidings to Zion: 'How beautiful upon the mountains are the feet of a herald of good tidings who says to Zion, Your god reigns'. In a third passage (61.1-4) there is no indication as to which of the two it is: 'I have been anointed to bring good tidings (לבשר) to the poor...and to those who mourn in Zion', the female figure from ch. 40 or the male one from ch. 52. Naturally tradition, especially Christian tradition, starting with Luke 4, assumes it must have been the latter and identifies the herald in ch. 61 with Jesus. But even without this final example, it seems it is possible for the leading character in the one story, known sometimes as Zion, to be described as having a mission to Zion and Jerusalem, and for the leading character in the other, known sometimes as Israel and Jacob, to be described as having a mission to Israel.

Clearly there is in both stories some vacillation between the various possibilities, although by far the most frequent and consistent is the collective interpretation. Both stories tell of a sequence of events leading from suffering and humiliation to new beginnings, and in most contexts,

---

23. It is grammatically possible to understand מבשרת ציון as 'O Zion, herald of good tidings' (RSV; cf. NEB, JB). But the two parallels discussed here (52.7 and 61.14) are good evidence for the traditional view that the mission was *to* Zion.

both within the book of Isaiah itself and in the history of its interpretation, both Jewish and Christian, these events are reflected in the hopes and experiences of the people of God. Just as, some years ago, it became fashionable to drop the question of who the servant is, in favour or what his office or role is, or what figures have influenced the imagery (Moses, David, Jehoiachin, Cyrus, Jeremiah, etc.),[24] so now we should perhaps give a low priority to who the daughter of Zion is, and focus instead on her role in the story. To conclude, then, here are a few brief comments on the literary and theological significance of this powerful image.

III

In the first place, there is the sheer appropriateness and effectiveness of this feminine imagery in its present context, over against the masculine imagery of the servant. It goes beyond the language and imagery of the servant in a number of respects. In descriptions of the plight of a people in exile, an oppressed people, a people without a homeland, the physical weakness of a woman, her vulnerability and her dependence on another person give the Zion poems a special poignancy. To illustrate this one need only apply the imagery to the experience of real people. For instance, the servant passages can be very powerfully applied to the history of the Jews, and have been, but there is added poignancy in the Zion passages. They tell how she has been abused, humiliated, carried off, powerless in the hands of powerful men. The fate of Babylon (ch. 47) and the daughters of Zion (3.18-26) are telling Isaianic illustrations of the vulnerability of women in situations of violence.

Then there is the language addressed to her—as a woman. The servant is told not to be afraid. With God's help he will have the strength to overcome adversity by brute force: 'Behold I will make of you a threshing sledge, new sharp and having teeth; you shall thresh the mountains and crush them' (41.15); and in the end he shall share the spoils of war (53.12). Zion is also told not to be afraid, but beyond that the imagery is quite different. She is to wake up, loose the bonds from her neck, shake off the dust, put on beautiful garments and so on. These

24. Cf G. von Rad, *Old Testament Theology*, II (Edinburgh: Oliver & Boyd, 1965), pp. 257ff. (= *The Message of the Prophets* [London: SCM Press, 1968], pp. 224ff.); P.R. Ackroyd, *Exile and Restoration* (London: SCM Press, 1968), pp. 126ff.

images come closer to where the people actually find themselves. The idea that they could ever have the power to conquer their almighty oppressors is beyond their wildest imaginings; but that they would one day recover their freedom and self-respect—that is not so hard to imagine.

On the other hand, the repeated imperatives in chs. 51–52 ('rouse yourself...stand up...awake...put on your strength...shake off the dust...') do give a revolutionary dimension to the story. It is perhaps interesting to note in passing that the Arabic world *intafaḍa*, from which *intifāḍa* 'uprising' is derived, has the sense of shaking off the dust after a long period of inactivity. Like the servant, the Daughter of Zion is always dependent on her lord and master. Her role is primarily a domestic one. But like the young woman in 7.14 who shows up Ahaz's lack of faith by calling her son 'Immanuel, God-is-with-us', and the one who tosses her head defiantly at the taunts of another king in ch. 37, Zion is depicted in 52.1-2 as proudly laying claim to her rightful dignity and freedom.

The way Yahweh approaches Zion is also significant, and again highlights differences between the two stories. In the one he is like a judge or a king eager to demonstrate his power; in the other, he empties himself of that exalted status, and, almost on bended knee, expresses his love, as of a man for a woman, a bridegroom for his bride, promising to be faithful to her till the mountains depart and the hills be removed (54.10). There is love in Yahweh's words to his servant too: for example, 'you are precious in my eyes and honoured and I love you...' (43.4); but the almost kenotic love of Yahweh described in the Zion passages goes far beyond it.

Finally, in contrast to the very masculine imagery at the end of the heroic servant story, the sharing out of the spoils of war, the ending of the Zion story is a unique description of childbirth and the joy and contentment of a mother with her children. This appears shortly after an account of the creation of a new heaven and a new earth—and a new Jerusalem in ch. 65, and, as we saw, seems to pick up some of the details from there concerning children and childbearing. The connection between creation and childbirth is obvious, and, as elsewhere in these chapters of Isaiah (e.g. 43.15; 51.9-10), the result is in both cases the creation of a new Israel.[25] But here, the predominantly male imagery of

25. In avoiding the anthropomorphism, Targum Jonathan substitutes ברא cosmology for the childbirth image, and applies it to the return of the exiles:

traditional creation mythology—Yahweh, like a mighty warrior slaying the monsters of chaos (51.9-10) or a powerful king, imposing his authority on the world (43.15)—is offset by the feminine imagery of childbearing. ברא Cosmology (cf. Gen. 1.1, 27) is balanced by ילד cosmology (cf. Deut. 32.18; Job 38.8ff, 28ff; Prov. 8.24ff). God's role in both is stressed ('Behold, I create [בורא] a new heaven and a new...I create Jerusalem a rejoicing...' 65.17-18), but in the Zion passage, it is, as we saw, that of a midwife assisting at the birth. The first passage stresses the absence of injustice and violence in the new Jerusalem (ten negatives in nine verses); the second develops the positive images of maternal warmth, contentment and fecundity to a degree unparalleled in biblical tradition—a quite remarkable climax, both theologically and emotionally, to the story of the 'Daughter of Zion'.

J.F. Stenning (ed.), *The Targum of Isaiah* (Oxford: Clarendon Press, 1949), p. 221.

JSOT 70 (1996), pp. 63-86

PORNOPROPHETICS REVISITED: SOME ADDITIONAL REFLECTIONS

Athalya Brenner

Some seductive passages in the books attributed to the 'prophets' contain specifically allocated images of gender relations and gendered sexuality. These images are inflexible in that they invariably reflect female sexuality as negative and male sexuality as neutral or positive. Therefore such passages as Hosea 1–3, Jeremiah 2–5, Ezekiel 16; 23 and Deutero-Isaiah 47 have been branded 'pornography' by some readers, notably feminist readers. They are variations on the image of the faithful husband and his promiscuous wife. The husband is God; the wife variously represents Samaria, Jerusalem, Judah, the Israelites, the Judahites— in short, the addressed religio-political community.[1] The textual speaker sides with the divine 'husband' to the point of identification. For example, 'Hosea' is reportedly involved with a אשת זנונים, 'wife of harlotry' (chs. 1 and 2), and the same or possibly another woman depicted as promiscuous (ch. 3). Grammatically, the textual voice is a first-person singular masculine voice. Interpreters are divided on the question: Did Hosea's mission shape his marital life or did his unfortunate marital life shape his prophetic destiny? Be the answer to that interesting question as it may, and theological considerations do of course determine the interpretative position taken, the affinities of male mainstream commentators with 'Hosea' is more than pronounced.[2] This textual voice, then, can be con-

---

1.   Related passages which contain images of 'harlots' as other cities conquered by God and similarly punished are Nah. 3.4-7 (on Nineveh) and Isa. 47.1-12 (on Babylon).

2.   Cf. for instance C.R. Fontaine, 'Hosea' and 'A Response to Hosea', and Y. Sherwood, 'Boxing Gomer: Controlling the Deviant Woman in Hosea 1–3', in A. Brenner (ed.), *A Feminist Companion to the Latter Prophets* (FCB, 8; Sheffield:

structed as a male voice, and is in fact gendered by the reader as such. At any rate, the text is neither perceived as nor, perhaps, intended to be gender-neutral. The dual image of husband/wife and, implicitly, male/ female sexuality is consequently unbalanced. The 'husband' is divine, correct, faithful, positive, voiced. The 'wife' is human, morally corrupt, faithless, negative, silent or silenced: her voice, if heard at all, is embedded within the male discourse of the text. The message, although indirect, is clear. 'Wifely' loyalty is to be learnt through re-education and punishment, including exposure and public shaming. A metaphor for a wayward people who deserve their fate, a 'true-life' situation utilized for religious instruction: that was the critical consensus before feminist Bible criticism started to problematize the husband/wife image.

D. Setel has written about such passages in Hosea and other texts.[3] F. van Dijk-Hemmes has discussed Hosea 1–3[4] and Ezekiel 23.[5] I wrote a comparison of chs. 2–5 in Jeremiah with a modern pornographic novel, the *Story of O*.[6] But other readers have viewed and continue to view these same passages as merely 'erotic imagery' utilized for a theological purpose. Indeed, the latter approach has been standard in Bible interpretation from antiquity until quite recently. Objections to viewing the husband/wife image as pornography have been and still are numerous; and even when the pornographic contents are not denied, its anti-woman bias is disputed. In addition, ostensibly politically-correct attitudes towards pornography are invoked for the sake of personal freedom and personal choice[7] and, so, the social thrust of the image is ostensibly minimized.

Sheffield Academic Press, 1995), pp. 40-69 and 101-125 respectively, for comments on commentaries to Hosea and for alternative analyses.

3. D.T. Setel, 'Prophets and Pornography: Female Sexual Imagery in Hosea', in L.T. Russell (ed.), *Feminist Interpretations of the Bible* (Philadelphia: Westminster Press, 1985), pp. 86-95.

4. F. van Dijk-Hemmes, 'The Imagination of Power and the Power of Imagination: An Intertextual Analysis of Two Biblical Love Songs—The Song of Songs and Hosea 2', *JSOT* 44 (1989), pp. 75-88; reprinted in A. Brenner (ed.), *A Feminist Companion to the Song of Songs* (FCB, 1; Sheffield: Sheffield Academic Press, 1993), pp. 156-70.

5. F. van Dijk-Hemmes, 'The Metaphorization of Woman in Prophetic Speech: An Analysis of Ezekiel 23', in A. Brenner and F. van Dijk-Hemmes, *On Gendering Texts: Female and Male Voices in the Hebrew Bible* (Leiden: Brill, 1993), pp. 167-76.

6. A. Brenner, 'On "Jeremiah" and the Poetics of (Prophetic?) Pornography', in Brenner and van Dijk-Hemmes, *On Gendering Texts*, pp. 177-93.

7. For a refutation of such and similar arguments, in the American legal setting,

For instance, in a recent response to van Dijk-Hemmes's and my own work, R. Carroll severely chastises us both for our partisan attitudes in rejecting pornography in general, and hence for making too much of the biblical passages discussed.[8]

There is hardly disagreement about the function of such passages: they are widely recognized to be religio-political propaganda. So much of the authorial intent is considered obvious, whoever the author(s). I feel, however, that the allegedly propagandistic constituents should be articulated in the light of modern definitions of propaganda. Further, the debate about these loaded texts centres on the dual problem of the texts' definition as either eroticism or pornography, either realistic (objective?) metaphor or image rooted in anti-female disposition, on the one hand; and the issue of modern readings of 'historical' (that is, culturally different) texts of the past on the other hand. Somehow, interpreters who are seduced by the image tend to 'understand' its function and validity as 'erotic'. Resistant and more suspicious readers, those who refuse to be co-opted by the texts into adopting their inherent focalization, tend to disapprove of their pornographic thrust and anti-female bias. Both factions are motivated by their own worldviews and specific ideologies.

My personal position is a feminist variant, one of a few existing feminist approaches. I would like to add some reflections to the ongoing debate from that standpoint. The following remarks are based on previous work I have done on this issue and are much indebted to recent work by others.[9] The strategy I adopt is to move between the present and the past and vice versa, since I find that a rigid linearity of treating this loaded subject is impossible for me to attain. A consideration of propaganda in general will precede a change of direction, to the definition/examination of pornography vis-à-vis eroticism. That will be

---

see the short essays under the heading 'Pornography and the First Amendment' by various contributors in L. Lederer (ed.), *Take Back the Night: Women on Pornography* (New York: Morrow, 1980), pp. 239-58. Although written in the late 1970s, the refutation still rings fresh and true—and valid.

8.   R.P. Carroll, 'Desire under the Terebinths: On Pornographic Representations in the Prophets—A Response', in Brenner (ed.), *A Feminist Companion to the Latter Prophets*, pp. 275-307.

9.   My own work has been published in Brenner and van Dijk-Hemmes, *On Gendering Texts*, pp. 177-93, and a revised version in Brenner (ed.), *A Feminist Companion to the Latter Prophets*, pp. 256-74. Other works have been cited above and will be cited below.

followed by some brief notes on the propagandistic nature of 'prophetic' literature, and a discussion of the similarities between propaganda and pornographic representations, within modern contexts and also within the biblical materials. Then, some more aspects of biblical literature in general and the 'prophetic' husband/wife metaphor in particular will be referred to, again in order to answer the questions: Are these texts propaganda? Are they porno-religious propaganda? And what are the hallmarks of Hebrew Bible social order and pornography, of which the husband/wife metaphor is the most blatant example? In essence, then, the strategy I adopt here is akin to that of my previous work on what I and others view as biblical pornoprophetic literature. And, once again, I find it helpful to draw a comparison between modern representations and biblical ones.

What is Propaganda?

I proceed from a minimalist postulate: propaganda is a transaction of verbal (rhetorical) communication designed by its initiator(s) to persuade the recipients of communication to accept its message(s), then formulate new opinions, then act on the newly acquired position. The techniques employed for achieving persuasion may include the following techniques or devices.[10]

a. *Use of stereotyping.* Generalizations and catchphrases are a great aid to persuasion: details are perceived as hindrance. Hence, the use of a progressively more limited stock of stereotypes becomes more and more noticeable as the propaganda becomes more virulent. Suffice it at this point to mention just a few stereotypes that have featured largely in Western history: 'black', 'foreigner', 'mad', 'Jew', 'feminist'.

b. *Naming and name substitution* follows the principle of uncomplicated economy in much the same way stereotyping does.

---

10. The following list of devices and their use in pornography (see below) is largely derived from B. LaBelle, 'The Propaganda of Misogyny', in Lederer (ed.), *Take Back the Night*, pp. 174-78, 324; which is, in turn, based on J.A. Brown, *Techniques of Persuasion* (New York: Penguin, 1963).

c. *Selection.* In order to convince, only certain facts pertaining to a case are presented instead of as full a picture as possible. Consequently, the addressee's vision becomes limited.

d. *Exaggeration and lying.* Even the partial presentation of a situation constitutes a lie by omission; the manipulation of opinion by direct lying may be used as well, with the reasoning that the end may justify the means. Paradoxically, of course, propaganda always claims a truth, if not the truth.

e. *Repetition* is an integral part and parcel of propaganda, be it political or commercial. A cursory look at any contemporary large advertising campaign for consumer goods will verify this beyond any doubt. It may be monotonous or else varied repetition. At any rate, sheer repetition makes the verbally repeated entity acquire a non-verbal existence of its own: persuasion follows remembrance. Repetition also desensitizes the target audience as to the nature/origin of the claims made.

f. *Promotion.* The selected idea(s) is (are) promoted as positive, beneficial and possessing a liberating potential.

g. *Promises and threats.* By way of supporting the promotion, promises and threats are closely linked to the acceptance or non-acceptance of the idea propagated. An equation is made between acceptance and a liberation of sorts on the one hand, non-acceptance and oppression or lack on the other hand. Shaming of opponents falls under this heading as well as under others (like, for instance, lying and targeting a scapegoat; see below).

h. *Particular examples* are utilized to make general points, as a complementary technique to stereotyping. Heroes and anti-heroes feature largely in such examples.

i. *Anti-heroes* fill the important role of enemy. The pinpointing of an enemy or a scapegoat diverts attention, creates solidarity between propagandist and audience, and effectively bonds them through hatred and/or aversion. So the boundaries of the hoped for community of opinion and action are doubly defined by positive ('for') as well as negative ('against') markers.

j. *Authority*. So as to substantiate its claim for truth, propaganda always appeals to authority in order to legitimate itself and acquire respectability and authority. Appeals may be made to history and the wisdom of the past; to contemporaneous history and accepted wisdom; to 'common sense'; to the law, institutions, celebrities, culture, expertise, science; to religion and its institutions; and, ultimately, to God.

These techniques are hardly unique to propaganda. Some or most are routinely used as rhetorical devices in many kinds of communication. However, in propaganda—which is about the domination of the target's mind prior to its activation—they are present as a cluster. If propaganda's end justifies the means, all available means can be and are enlisted.

Before we can ask the question, Are the same or similar techniques deployed for (modern and ancient) propaganda and (modern and ancient) pornography?, some reflections on pornography *per se* are in order at this point, together with an evaluation of the differences between pornography and eroticism.

What is Pornography? What is Eroticism?

By general consensus, and as reflected in and by dictionary entries, pornography is the representation of sexual acts that arouses sexual excitement. Some definitions add that the pornographic representation is *designed* to arouse sexual desire; so, authorial intent and motive are implied. Even without going further, it can be noted at the outset that the prophetic husband/wife and related images fall well within the definitions on this count. Assuming for the moment that they do constitute propaganda, which virtually all commentators confirm (but which I shall come back to examine later), they must have had an appeal for their target audience.[11] The use of sex as an appeal for selling everything and anything is not a modern invention of the advertising world. In that sense, although religious ideas rather than sex or male control (see below) *per se* are being sold by the 'prophets', sexual arousal is used as a tool for securing attention and influence.

One of pornography's basic constituents is its appeal to, and/or attempt to create, sexual fantasy. The appeal to the seemingly imaginary and extra-ordinary may lead to one of the differences between erotic representations (of what is within personal experience) and pornographic

---

11. Brenner and van Dijk-Hemmes, *On Gendering Texts*, pp. 178-79.

representations (of what is conjured up as 'possible'). It so happens that usually, in mainstream definitions of sexual fantasy, no distinction is made between genders. It is widely assumed that female and male sexual fantasies are identical or similar; alternatively, when a need to admit gendered variables in fantasy is recognized, gendered fantasy is viewed as at least complementary, like in the sado-masochistic twin image. The fact that, culturally, male sexual fantasies have been and still are presented as universally and trans-genderwise valid is usually ignored or not commented upon. The assumed male dominance and female compliance in this representation of sexual fantasy is seldom contested. It is accepted unquestioningly. This is highly unsurprising. Why should representations of sexuality, be their definition what it may, differ from other gendered socio-cultural phenomena? And how does this fixed-role convention contribute to the definition of a representation as pornographic? In other words, once more, wherein lies the difference between 'erotics' or even so-called 'soft porn' on the one hand, and 'pornography' or 'hard porn' on the other hand? I shall by-pass the joke about pornography and geography, but not without a moment's pause. Conventions, variations in taste and norms, spatial and temporal and individual determinants do indeed motivate the making of distinctions between eroticism and pornography. Readerly location is certainly crucial here.

From my gendered perspective, the lack of gender differentiation in attributing or creating a sexual fantasy may mutate that fantasy into a pornographic fantasy through lack of knowledge about the other's desire. Other determinants may be the objectification of female sexuality and the representation of fixed sexual roles, with the female serving the male. The same goes for the repeated humiliation of woman or a woman's image through sexual violence, and 'her' bodily exposure (in language or vision) to public view within a shaming framework (and more on that later). The same applies to the all-too-frequent depictions of females as lesser than human males: as slaves, as servants, as minors, as animals. Admittedly, then, multiple criteria are necessary for distinguishing between pornographic and erotic representations, over and apart from the recognition of cultural and individual variations.

Some common ground can nevertheless be demarcated even though exact definitions are elusive or inefficient. To illustrate from the Bible, the Song of Songs is explicitly sexual and allows us to gaze at naked or partially naked women at our leisure; and yet, most readers—and I include myself among those—experience this gaze as erotic rather than pornographic. Although the Song of Songs contains the elements of female nakedness[12] and explicit references to sexuality, and so may activate sexual fantasy if the reader of either gender is that way inclined, there are neither gender debasement nor fixed gender roles in it. We do view female and male figurations in the Song of Songs, but the fantasies described are differentiated as well as mutually inclusive. It goes without saying, then, that pornography, according to the guidelines I adopt, does not concern just *what* is being seen and said (neither simply the bluntness nor the explicitness of the image conjured up and gazed at, be it male or female), but also the *how* used in the representation. Wherever I detect an underlying worldview of gender asymmetry and female otherness, there I tend to respond by screaming, 'Pornography'. And so far, the multiple criteria of exposure, shaming, asymmetry and objectification certainly feature in the 'prophetic' passages that we shall come back to later.

Furthermore and logically, pornography is not simply the representation of sexual fantasy but that of *violent* sexual fantasy. Even if we reject essentialism, the obvious fact that women (as a group) are physically weaker than men and that their bodies are physically penetrated in male–female sex should be given due consideration: potentially and literally, women's bodies are more deeply affected by sexual acts than men's. Women are also, again as a group, inferior social agents. Hence, sexual violence can and is exercised upon them in order to control their bodies and minds. How should sexual violence practised by the strong (male?, older person?, social superior of either gender?) on the weak (females?, children[13] of both genders?, socially inferior persons?) be assessed, then: as erotic or pornographic?

12. And, although to a lesser extent, male nakedness.

13. In Ezek. 16 a first-person voice speaking for YHWH narrates the story of a male who finds a female baby, raises and then weds her; the metaphorical female baby is Jerusalem (vv. 1-14). This fantasy of turning a 'daughter' into a 'bride' goes sour, according to the indignant speaker. Since the daughter figure is silent throughout the process, we may assume that she consents. We may also view the story, however, as reflexive of incest practices about which daughters had no say. The speaker certainly expects us to side with him against the disobedient daughter. Suffice it here to note that child molestation is well represented in modern pornography; cf. F. Rush, 'Child Pornography', in Lederer (ed.), *Take Back the Night*, pp. 71-81, esp. on Playboy and other soft-porn magazines. The link between the pornographization of women and children is well explained there. The depiction of the female object as doubly inferior—by gender and age—obtains also in Ezek. 23.3.

In my view violence does not have much to do with *eros*. Violence is
a distortion of *eros*, a corruption or sublimation. Although violence may
express *eros*, its ultimate motivation is physical and social control. It can
and should be admitted that when violence occurs in sexual relations
women are much more vulnerable than men. Is sexual violence motivated by desire? Perhaps by frustrated desire. In our culture, the license
to gratify desire, immediately and even violently, is the privilege of the
socially dominant. In our culture, this is the prerogative of males (as a
group). And when violence enters the sexual fantasy, it mutates that
fantasy into pornography. I shall not refer here to the platitude of the
eros/thanatos duality; suffice it to note that merely to equate violence
with *thanatos* is to miss the mark widely. I am also less essentialistic–
deterministic about gendered sexual mechanisms than other feminist
critics. Here I obviously part company from feminist writers like Andrea
Dworkin[14] or Camille Paglia.[15] I do not define heterosexual sexual
activity a priori as violence against women, nor necessarily view sex as a
war game. However, certain sex and gender differentials, although banal,
cannot be ruled out of the discussion.

In assessing the differences between erotics and pornography I take
my cue from Susan Griffin,[16] whose views in *Pornography and Silence*
I shall summarize briefly and comment upon. According to Griffin
pornography is a cultural phenomenon which, paradoxically, is accepted
as a positive antidote to (negative, threatening) nature. Culture triumphs
over nature through the agency of human knowledge. Knowledge is
control; to control is to know. The pornographic mind seeks to achieve
control over its own carnal (natural) self and the other's self by enslaving
the other's carnal body. The ensuing violence evidences the futility of
the project. No lasting epistemology of the self or the other can be
gained or sustained by it. The fatal split suffered by the pornographic
mind cannot be healed, and *eros* is destroyed by the fantasy rather than

14. A. Dworkin's work is well known and much objected to, sometimes with
violent criticism (cf. for instance Carroll, 'Desire', p. 281). For the sake of conve-
nience I will refer here to two items: her *Pornography: Men Possessing Women*
(New York: Perigee, 1981); and two short pieces in Lederer (ed.), *Take Back the
Night*: 'Why So-Called Radical Men Love and Need Pornography' (pp. 148-54), and
'For Men, Freedom of Speech; for Women, Silence Please' (pp. 256-58).

15. For instance in C. Paglia, *Sexual Personae: Art and Decadence from Nefertiti
to Emily Dickinson* (New York: Vintage Books, 1991).

16. S. Griffin, *Pornography and Silence: Culture's Revenge against Nature* (New
York: Harper & Row, 1980).

nourished by it. Since males are more likely to participate in or practise pornography voluntarily, women (and social inferiors, and minors of both genders) are its more common objects. The inferiors are educated to cooperate silently with their own demotion out of the cultural social order. So males may retain their superficial autonomy at the price of losing *eros*.[17]

Viewed like this, pornography permeates all facets of Western culture, including monotheistic religions and the cultures of their practitioners. In these cultures the pornographic fantasy simply waits to be enacted. It is likely to become an event, a series of events, a norm unproblematically built into the social system. Hence lies the danger of pornography: fantasy is not dangerous if it remains that; its violent enactment is much more of a threat, especially since the dialectics of cooperation dictate that weaker social groups actively participate in the enactment of their masters' fantasies.

At this point I could refer to other feminist critics, like Jessica Benjamin in her book *The Bonds of Love*;[18] or to works by male psychologists and sociologists and anthropologists who imply that females, by defini-tion, hover outside the symbolic, hence social, order. Such views are a faithful description of Western culture, but whether they constitute a justification of gender relations in that culture is another matter entirely. Instead, I shall return to the 'prophetic' divine husband/human wife image in order to problematize it further. Love, *eros*, is indeed being declared by the metaphoric husband. He claims he loves his wife. Is this *eros* or pornography? Lo and behold, in a moment we shall be called to witness a violent scene. If he has his way, she will be publicly shamed. She is called whore, deviant, uncivilized; she is animalistic. She is threat-ened with divorce, loss of status, loss of possessions and children, torture and deportation—before she is taken back. An attempt is made to silence her into submission. 'Her' implied behaviour is graphically described in Jeremiah and, even more so, in Ezekiel. Is this fantasy of female punish-ment by a (divine) male force a female fantasy?

'She'. The idea of metaphorizing woman into a rejected country, town, nation, land to be punished—an idea that receives readerly consent—is common throughout the Prophets, as has been pointed out

17. I would like to add, in passing, that the relatively modern phenomenon of female-authored pornography, when it involves hierarchic relations and S/M relation-ships, is in my view no more acceptable than any other type of pornography.

18. J. Benjamin, *The Bonds of Love* (New York: Pantheon, 1988).

by many commentators. Nevertheless, this common place usage should give us food for reflection,[19] especially so since the metaphoric 'woman' is to have her body exposed as part of punishment and re-education. The distance between metaphoric 'prophetic' speech and social potentialities is easily bridged here. The transition from one territory or community/'wife' into two territories or communities/'wives'—like Judah and Samaria, Oholah and Oholibah (Ezek. 23)—is quickly introduced; for example, in Jeremiah 3; 5 and Ezekiel 16; 23. 'They' are imaged as kin, sisters. From here to a stereotypic generalization, all women potentially are like this, there is but a short distance. And this brings us back to the question: Is the pornoprophetic literature discussed propaganda?

Is Prophetic Literature Propaganda?

There is hardly any doubt that many passages in the so-called prophetic books are propaganda. The form of address bears this out. The literary style is that of an attempt to persuade, to sway public opinion by the techniques delineated above, separately or mixed together. Stereotyping, name-calling, exaggeration and half-truths, repetitions, promotion of its own goals as the truth, promises alternating with threats, examples, generalizations, pinpointing enemies and appeals to divine as well as lesser-respected authorities all serve the ideology of YHWH as a single god of his people and their history. Be the attempts to influence public and private opinion successful or otherwise, be our own sensibilities in empathy with the message conveyed or otherwise, the utilization of propaganda techniques in such texts make them into just that: propaganda, an advertising of wares. The fact that the merchandise is spiritual does not invalidate the definition of the means. Neither are the means automatically justified by the underlying ideology. Therefore, the propagandistic features of the husband/wife metaphor should be examined for themselves, and for the additional light they might shed on the significance of this metaphor—not only for its religious ideology but also for its by-product, gender relations.

---

19. Brenner and van Dijk-Hemmes, *On Gendering Texts*, pp. 182-83; P. Gordon and H.C. Washington, 'Rape as a Military Metaphor in the Hebrew Bible', in Brenner (ed.), *A Feminist Companion to the Latter Prophets*, pp. 308-25.

Pornography and Propaganda, Modern and Biblical:
Similarities of Technique

Pornography advertises its wares in much the same ways used for propaganda in general. In order to show the similar techniques deployed, I shall review the ten propagandistic devices listed above and apply them to the pornographic media. Since it is easier to accept claims concerning modern pornography than claims concerning biblical pornography, I shall begin with the former then move to the latter.

a. *Stereotyping* is part and parcel of pornographic representations, be they 'soft' (non-violent) or 'hard' (violent), although the stereotyping becomes more rigid the more violent the representation. Women and femininity are mostly objectified into types: carnal, submissive, promiscuous, whores to be conquered, inexperienced-but-waiting-to-be-taught are some of the recurrent types. They hardly have a mind or undergo character development. They are breasts and genitalia. This stereotyping reaches a climax, so to speak, in the S/M fantasy of rigid gender roles: passive masochistic (the object and loving it) female and active sadistic (strong) male.

b. *Name-giving or name-taking is common.* Women are 'whores'. They are dehumanized into minors or playthings or animals, with the accompanying change of address (the Playboy Bunny is an appropriate example). They may even be stripped of a name completely, signifying a total departure from the social order (as for prison inmates, if not to invoke more painful analogies). So, in the *Story of O*, the female protagonist is the only person in the book to remain nameless. Whether the 'O' referring to her stands for 'zero', 'orifice' or some other explanation, or all put together, is less significant than the stripping act itself.

c. *Selection.* In pornography, a dual process of selection occurs. Basically one vision of female sexuality is presented: a woman that is turned on by violence. This selected vision excludes other visions of female sexuality almost altogether. Further selection is evidenced by the claim that pornography liberates desire and prevents repression, to the exclusion of its possible harmful effects.

d. *Stereotyped fantasy*. In line with the stereotyping, the fantasy of woman is not gender-neutral: it has little to do with actual women's fantasy. A good example is the myth of women's masochism, exploded only recently by woman writers.

e. *The story lines are few and repetitious*. Every woman is a whore, given a chance. They love violence, even if they protest the contrary. They enjoy being disciplined. They love oral sex. They love and obey strong, assertive males and so on.

f. *Promotion*. Pornography is promoted as erotics, the 'natural' expression of desire that is liberating, even necessary (see c, above). Its supporters present it as value-neutral or positive, free, uninhibited. Claims for its dissemination under the principles of freedom of speech, civil liberties, adult consent and so on are often made.

g. *Promises and rewards*. In pornography, women are threatened by violence, and rewarded by pleasure if they comply with their role. Potential consumers (all of us, regardless of gender) are threatened by being labeled 'spoilsports', 'reactionaries' or 'radical feminists' if they object to pornography, promised the reward of being considered 'politically correct' or 'liberal' if they consent to fulfilling their role as demanded. Pornography, like propaganda, tends to shame its target audience into submission while alleging rationality.

h. *Heroes and anti-heroes*. Men are the heroes of heterosexual pornography; they are the active ones. Women are the objects, the anti-heroes. As throughout my description, I am aware that exceptions to this formula exist as such—they are exceptional. The majority of pornographic representations follow the rules.

i. *The anti-hero is the scapegoat or enemy*. Woman, especially assertive woman, is the enemy to be conquered (tamed, educated) in the pornographic representation. The sight of this conquered enemy is a source of bonding for the males within and without it.

j. *Authority*. Appeals to authority are made in order to make pornography respectable and legitimate. The example of Playboy magazine again—its interviews with prominent public figures—springs immediately to the mind. The industry's appeal to science, ancient literatures and so on is a case in point.

Working back from the generalization of pornographic representation to its underlying ideology, the question asked earlier can be repeated: Is pornography simply about sexual desire? The specifics of its use of propaganda techniques exclude such a naive assumption. It is seen to propagate male supremacy. The propagation is indirect although not necessarily either innocent or else conscious. According to this ideology women exist as the object of male sexual gratification. Like in other areas of psycho-social relations, women are thereby dehumanized and de-socialized. Although pornography claims to entertain and to represent non-gendered desire, in fact it advertises an ideology of female bondage and upholds the gender split typical to our society.[20]

How are the same criteria applicable to the husband/wife metaphor in the 'prophetic' passages (Hos. 1–3; Jer. 2–5; Ezek. 16; 23; some Second Isaiah passages and Rev. 17–18, to name the most prominent examples)? The frequent depiction of turning away from the one true monotheistic god is in terms of female 'whoring'.[21] This is stereotyping as well as name-calling. Another instance of name-calling is in Ezekiel, where the names of Samaria and Jerusalem are changed into Oholah and Oholibah (ch. 23), presumably to indicate some property of their relationship with the divine. In Jer. 2.20-24 the nation/addressee gets to be called whore, animal and more. The shaming mechanism is much in evidence. Only one possible way of female sexual behaviour is selected for presentation, then generalized by enthusiastic repetition (cf. Ezek. 16 and 23) into a unshaken axiom. Exaggeration by repetition and exclusion amounts to a half-truth: the accused party, 'woman', is allowed no independent voice. The idea of violent sexual punishment is promoted as a justified solution, the only one possible.[22] Threats of violence and promises if submission is embraced are the essence. The woman–people–city is pinpointed as the enemy: of themselves, of YHWH's love. The bonding between the speaker and his target audience, essential to propaganda, is presumably to be achieved by the reference to the social enemy, woman. Finally, the

20. Griffin, *Pornography and Silence*.
21. P. Bird, '"To Play the Harlot": An Inquiry into an Old Testament Metaphor', in P.L. Day (ed.), *Gender and Difference in Ancient Israel* (Minneapolis: Fortress Press, 1989), pp. 75-94.
22. As also in the case of Jezebel (2 Kgs 9).

appeal to authority is absolute. The legitimizing authority is YHWH himself, and in most of the passages referred to he is presented in the speaking mode, the 'I' persona.

There is no doubt that, unlike modern pornography, the porno-prophetic passages are *not* intended as depictions of male desire *per se*. I would even venture the thought that they are not consciously misogynistic. That, however, is small consolation. The ideology of male supremacy is indispensable to the husband/wife metaphor: without this ideology the metaphor will not be understood, even less be acted upon. The fact remains that only one type of woman is presented, be she daughter (Ezek. 16) or wife and mother (Hos. 1–2). She is objectified and dehumanized by various means, including expulsion. She is the enemy of positive godly and male values. The authority appealed to is, ultimately, male authority as symbolized by and symbolizing divine authority. Throughout these pieces of religious propaganda, identification with the male god is sought at the expense of the humiliated, naked woman. In other words, a glimmer of liberation is offered by a model of female submission. Let us now look, then, at the biblical text's invitation.

Voyeurism and Pornography

In propaganda the addressees are required to assimilate a vision and make it their very own. They, we, are asked to comply with a message. Pornographic representations, be they verbal or visual, involve our senses directly. What about our complicity, our voyeurism of the figures it claims to represent, in general and in the biblical texts?

In our dominant Western culture—Judaeo-Christian, patriarchal and heterosexual—women are treated as collective or individual object(s) for gaze. This is borne out by many cultural facets of female socialization. Our clothes, behaviour, art, body image, self-image and so on are preparations for the gaze, although not only and simply the male gaze. By common consent, nowhere is this phenomenon more glaring than in American cinema, as succinctly analyzed by the film critic Laura Mulvey.[23]

In this world we recognize the possibility of eroticism wherever women are exhibited, or exhibit themselves, as naked or partly dressed. Female nudity functions as a social code. This is not to say that the male

23. L. Mulvey, 'Visual Pleasure and Narrative Cinema', *Screen* 16.3 (1975), pp. 6-18.

body always appears clothed in erotic representations, be they visual or verbal. However, the nude male body is treated with much more discretion; that is, coverage. The coverage extends particularly to male genitalia, as if by way of protection. Late at night one can watch films that conjure up such a world of 'erotics' on commercial television networks, which means that the films are socially acceptable as erotica or at least 'soft porn'. And erotics is 'healthy', is it not?, while pornography is more debatable and hardly tolerated by many social groups, prudery notwithstanding.

Clothing distinguishes culture from nature, as Susan Griffin asserts time and time again.[24] Images of females unwillingly undressed in/by film or other representations are stripped of their cultural identity; they become, literally and figuratively, more 'natural'. The same applies to male images, only that their stripping in art is much less frequent and follows different rules.

Is such a universe of habitual female exposure portrayed in the Bible and in related literature? Alice Bach has demonstrated how the male gaze, in the biblical text and of the reader, zeroes in on the biblical female object.[25] Jennifer Glancy[26] and Amy-Jill Levine[27] show how the male-gazing-and-female-gazed-at principle operates in Susanna. Mieke Bal discusses the gaze as knowledge in a new article on Judith and some of 'her' representations in visual arts.[28] Susan Durber writes about the difficulty for women to switch from being-looked-at-ness into looking;

24. Griffin, *Pornography and Silence*.

25. A. Bach, 'Mirror, Mirror in the Text: Reflections on Reading and Rereading', in A. Brenner (ed.), *A Feminist Companion to Esther, Judith and Susanna* (FCB, 7; Sheffield: Sheffield Academic Press, 1995), pp. 81-86.

26. J. Glancy, 'The Accused: Susanna and her Readers', *JSOT* 58 (1993), pp. 103-116; reprinted in Brenner (ed.), *A Feminist Companion to Esther, Judith and Susanna*, pp. 288-302.

27. A.-J. Levine, '"Hemmed in on Every Side": Jews and Women in the Book of Susanna', in F. Segovia and M.A. Tolbert (eds.), *Reading from This Place* (Philadelphia: Fortress Press, forthcoming); reprinted in Brenner (ed.), *A Feminist Companion to Esther, Judith and Susanna*, pp. 303-323.

28. M. Bal, 'Head Hunting: "Judith" on the Cutting Edge', *JSOT* 63 (1994), pp. 3-34; reprinted in Brenner (ed.), *A Feminist Companion to Esther, Judith and Susanna*, pp. 253-85.

that is, reading—in her case, into reading the New Testament parables of the lost.[29]

Indeed, clothing in the Bible does symbolize culture. Let us remember Genesis 2 and 3 to begin with. It is therefore worth noting that, in the Bible, female figurations are much more easily exposed—that is, presented as naked—than male figurations. Nakedness is a shameful state in culture. So representatives of culture should be especially careful about their clothing. This, presumably, is why (male) priests' clothing is prescribed with elaboration (Exod. 28 and 39); and they should wear linen pants while climbing the altar stairs to officiate so that their genitals, their 'nakedness' (ערוה) is not exposed (Exod. 28.42). How then should we evaluate the representations of females as naked, as being punished by being stripped naked, by having even their genitals exposed to the collective gaze of textual figures and readers of both genders—like in Isa. 3.17-24; Ezek. 16.37; 23.26; Hos. 2.5—all within a highly religious context?

There are exceptions, of course, like in Jer. 5.8 and Ezek. 23.20, where male genitals are on view through blatant language. In Jeremiah, the Jerusalemites—presumably a male community is so addressed—are compared to sexually-aroused horses; although the passage is corrupt, the physical reference is made clear by the accusation that the metaphorized 'horses' are keen on committing adultery. In Ezekiel human penises (of foreigners!) are vividly likened to horses' and asses' members. These descriptions are certainly explicit, albeit rare. In general, gazing at the carnal male body is hardly facilitated in and by biblical language. Let us, then, examine the semantic stock for signifying human sexual organs in the Hebrew Bible.

The Construction of the Male and Female Body in Biblical Language[30]
Biblical references to human erogenous zones, primary and secondary and of both sexes, are in general euphemistic. But over and above that (Jer. 5.8 and Ezek. 23.20 notwithstanding), the culture reflected in the

29. S. Durber, 'The Female Reader of the Parables of the Lost', in G.J. Brooke (ed.), *Women in the Biblical Tradition* (Studies in Women and Religion, 31; Lewiston, NY: Edwin Mellen, 1992), pp. 187-207.

30. Z. Zevit delivered a somewhat similar linguistic analysis of biblical terms for body parts in the AAR/SBL meeting in Chicago (1994) too. Unfortunately, I have not been able to consult his work although, as I have been told, it is similar to mine. Each of our two analyses, needless to say, was conducted independently.

Bible protects the penis and its physical environs with vigour. This zealous protection is extended by the language or rather, I should say, by the lack of specific relevant terminology as well as by scanty usage. This is surprising, because the society that created biblical literature is a phallic, phallocentric society. This characterization is not an empty generalization; it does not imply mere reduction of a socio-psychological state. The society so referred to posits the human penis as the explicit, characteristic symbol of religious identity. The penis is the special link between its god and the members of the community. Circumcision, taken over from other cultures and re-interpreted, defines males as members of the community of the covenant.[31] So, Christianity did not separate itself from Judaism until the connection between the penis and the divine was severed. By this same token, women are excluded a priori from that symbolic order. The bonding with the (male) god is stamped on the (male) body; the anti-woman bias is built into the symbolic order. Seen in this light, Griffin's definition of Western culture as 'pornographic' in its exclusion of the female as other acquires a fresh meaning. The link between male sexuality and the divine is so established; no symmetrical view of female sexuality obtains. It is therefore easier to demonize the latter while upholding the former.

To return from ideology to the language that expresses it, the 'foreskin', ערלה, designating the part removed from the penis and dedicated to the divine, is a specific term mentioned 16 times in contexts of circumcision; its only other contexts are either agricultural or martial. Yet, the penis itself is simply and politely 'flesh', בשׂר,[32] which also has many other denotations. This evasion is highlighted by MH—another, later layer of classical Hebrew—which has specific terms like זין and אבר for 'penis'. While these MH phrases are euphemisms too, their referent is much more limited than BH בשׂר. The same applies also to ירך, 'thigh'.[33] Both terms, בשׂר and ירך, may indicate female sexual organs

31. For psychological and literary aspects of biblical circumcision, its connections with the perception of female sexuality as a threat to males and, particularly, its castration contents, see I.N. Rashkow, *The Phallacy of Genesis: A Feminist-Psychoanalytic Approach* (Louisville, KY: Westminster/John Knox, 1993), pp. 91-109. References to secondary literature can be found there and in the Notes, pp. 125-28.

32. Notably in Gen. 17, in the compound בשׂר ערלה, and in Ezek. 16.26 (quoted above).

33. Gen. 24.2, 9; 32.25, 32; 46.26; 47.29; Exod. 1.5; Judg. 8.30. Cf. N. Sarna,

too, albeit less frequently.[34] BH רגלים, 'legs', may serve as a similar euphemism in compounds referring to sexual activity and physical relief for both males and females although, once more, the statistical bias (for whatever it is worth) is in favour of male bodily representation.[35] 'Testicle' (אשך) is mentioned only once (Lev. 21.20).[36] Other euphemisms for male genitals are מבושיו (Deut. 25.11), 'shameful', hence private, parts; and מרגלות, from רגלים, as possibly in Ruth 3 (vv. 4, 7, 8, 14).[37]

When nakedness is concerned, female nakedness far outstrips male nakedness in BH. ערוה, 'Nakedness', unlike its twin term, עירם, refers in numerous instances to genitalia. It is a polite term. A simple survey of the term results in a straightforward picture. In most cases a woman's ערוה is thus implied for/by both textual and readerly spectators.[38] The technical term for incest with both blood kin and marriage kin is לגלות ערוה or לראות ערוה, decorously and literally translated as 'to see, uncover nakedness'. Let us remember that the object of biblical incest taboos is always a female categorized by blood and marriage affini ties, whereas the law itself is always addressed to males (Lev. 18; 20; Deut. 27 and elsewhere).[39] Therefore the object of the incest taboo, the objectified 'nakedness' which is put on view in order to be avoided, is female nakedness. Furthermore, the mother's 'nakedness' is conjured up by a curse (1 Sam. 20.30), preserved also in modern Hebrew (following colloquial Arabic) usage. 'Womb', an innard unlike the penis, defines 'woman' (Judg. 5.30), somewhat like 'foreskin' defines despised non-community members such as the Philistines whom David kills

Understanding Genesis (New York: Schocken Books, 1970), pp. 170-71; and Rashkow, *Phallacy of Genesis*, p. 125 n. 13.

34. A woman's בשר in the sense of 'genitalia' in Lev. 6.20; 15.19; female ירך in Num. 5.21, 22, 27; Song 7.2.

35. As in Deut. 28.57; Judg. 3.24; 1 Sam. 24.3; 2 Kgs 18.27 = Isa. 36.12; Isa. 7.20; Ezek. 16.25.

36. In this reference, a man with a ruptured (? NEB) testicle, like any other male of marked physical defect, cannot officiate as an Aaronide priest before God.

37. The sexual connotation, perhaps even denotation, of מרגלות was already recognized in Jewish midrash. Cf. *Ruth R.* and *Y. Shimeoni* on Ruth 3.

38. Notable exceptions are Gen. 9; Exod. 20.23, 28.42; Isa. 20.4.

39. Not surprisingly, the euphemism becomes even more opaque in David's case (2 Sam. 6): when he dances in front of the ark, he simply 'uncovers' (נגלה) *himself*, not his own nakedness (ערוה), although his indecent exposure is the axis the story hinges on; and cf. Michal's punishment, and the care taken in 1 Chron. 15.27-29 to dress David up.

(1 Sam. 18.25, 27), hardly a complimentary reference.[40] Female breasts (דדים, שׁדים) are much on view (that is, verbally), but I counted more occurrences of 'female breasts' as erogenous zones than as fertility symbols or life-sustaining apparatuses.

Language and Sexual Exposure

Where does this (admittedly cursory and incomplete) survey of semantic stock lead us? Let us have a look at the available objects. Where can we view, so to speak, female breasts in the Bible? In the Song of Songs, of course; there is a concentration there. However, in order to view, touch, feel and handle female breasts *with violence* we must turn to the so-called prophets; to Hosea (ch. 2) and Ezekiel (16; 21.8; 23). There female nakedness is highly visible and doubly vulnerable for being explicit as well as repeatedly threatened. Accusations of female whoring abound in those passages and others (notably also in Jeremiah and other chapters of Hosea), and modern scholarship complies with the accusations by writing copiously about Israelite 'sacred' prostitution.[41] There is a veritable mass of female breasts and total or near-total nudity introduced with violence and verbal abuse. The literary trope of the promiscuous naked woman appeals not only to our implied experience of the female species, but also to the image we presumably have of female corporeality. How can it work otherwise? In turn, the image educates our bi-gender perception of its source. I follow Mieke Bal here to conclude that desire and viewing and the attempt to gain knowledge blend in such images into a kind of epistemology (a ידיעה) of female bodies, of their nature, of their (im)proper treatment through silencing and abuse. In the Bible, the man is the subject of the verb ידע, 'know' in the sense of 'have sex',

---

40. Indeed, the reference to woman as 'womb' is attributed to a foreign (Canaanite) female speaker-in-the-text within a 'female' poem in Judg. 5.30. This attribution, however, does not necessarily imply a female voice underlying the usage. For grounds for and against the gendering of Deborah's song as a woman's poem see Brenner and van Dijk-Hemmes, *On Gendering Texts*, pp. 42-43, with additional literature cited; and in more detail in van Dijk-Hemmes's Dutch dissertation, 'Sporen van vrouwenteksten in de Hebreeuwse bijbel' (Utrecht: Faculteit der Godsgeleerdheid, 1992), pp. 191-244.

41. But cf. M. Gruber, 'The Hebrew *qedesah* and her Canaanite and Akkadian Cognates', in *idem*, *The Motherhood of God and Other Studies* (Atlanta: Scholars Press, 1992), pp. 17-47.

while the woman is always the verb's object.[42] I suggest that this too reflects a worldview. The possessor of knowledge, the one allowed to see and act on the sighting, is the male. Moreover, when a woman 'looks' or attempts to 'look' in the realm of sex, she can meet misfortune, as it is implied that Dinah's encounter with Shechem is her fault since she 'goes out to see' (Gen. 34.1-2)[43]—not to mention what is prescribed when a woman dares to touch a strange man's genitals in public, presumably where her action can be seen by others, for her hand shall be cut off for this serious breach of modesty without mercy (Deut. 25.11-12[44]). For a textual woman, looking is immoral and touching male genitalia in public even more so. But a male, be he symbolic or otherwise, is invited to look at female private parts continuously and to act, if he so chooses, on the naked body; women are invited to look at the female body too. Ezekiel 23.10 and 46–49 contain explicit addresses for women to look and to learn; not surprisingly, the elusive demarcation lines between metaphor and 'reality' break down and the two worlds, the divine/human and the social, blur into one gendered schism.

What we, all of us, ultimately see in the woman–community of the divine husband/human wife metaphor is not just a metaphorical woman but a *naked* woman—silent, accused of prostitution, framed for sustaining male violence. And the metaphor is backed up by two uncontested male claims: a claim of love and desire, and a claim for absolute truth.

This image shows too much and too little: too much female flesh; too little of the female herself and of the multi-layered motivation of her accusers. Viewed together, by us, against the backdrop of promised violence, the nude female figure and her clothed, self-appointed male mentors constitute an asymmetrical S/M pornographic icon. I feel acutely uncomfortable with that paradigmatic icon. It contains an inflexible model for gender relations. I sense it is damaging to my gender and take no comfort in other biblical models for gender relations. I wish not only to suspect this pornographic icon that allows women neither knowledge nor sight, and its consequences, but also to resist it. I do not want to join

42. As Francis Landy remarked in conversation, a possible exception is Hos. 2.22. Cf. also Judg. 11.39 and 21.12.

43. For a dissenter, cf. now L.M. Bechtel, 'What if Dinah is Not Raped? (Genesis 34)', *JSOT* 62 (1994), pp. 19-36.

44. Cf. C. Pressler, *The View of Women Found in the Deuteronomic Family Law* (BZAW, 216; Berlin: de Gruyter, 1993), pp. 74-77.

in the game of undressing that woman. I do not want to leer at her uncovered body. I am a heterosexual woman. I would rather view Israel, God's chosen son, being paraded naked in the marketplace. Alas, this is not possible. The son's private parts have been established as linked with the divine. Hence, these private parts are covered, and are not visually and linguistically accessible for the likes of me.

In Conclusion

For me, a pornographic representation qualifies as such, as a fantasy of sexual desire to be distinguished from erotic fantasy, when it contains abuse and/or violence. The boundary is very clear. It is less the amount of flesh shown that bothers me than the manner with which it is treated in the representation, since the image created depends on the *how* as well as the *what*. When one of the imaged partners is almost always clothed, retains control, heaps abuse, threatens physical punishment, and the other is naked or threatened with nakedness, on view, not allowed to speak and is closely monitored, that is pornographic fantasy, despite the declarations of 'love' uttered, as shown by van Dijk-Hemmes in her article on Hosea.[45] From this perspective, the husband/wife metaphor is a pornographic fantasy of male desire.

The metaphoric and speaking and listening males assume the right to undress the female and to drive knowledge into her gazed at being, while they remain safely protected by layers of clothing and ideology. This attitude is both reflected in biblical language and the gender and cultural ideologies motivating it, and perpetuated by that language. If we identify with their religious position, we also buy their gender position. The two, in their own culture as reflected by its own literature, are intertwined and inseparable. Religious propaganda is not divorced from social norms but rather builds on them and perpetuates them. There is more to understanding biblical pornography than at first meets the eye: not only a gender picture is at stake here, but our knowledge—preferably unidealized—of the socio-cultural fabric in general. Our modern sensibilities are all we have to guide us. Because women are excluded, because their non-existent penis does not bear the sign of the divine covenant, they cannot tell us about their situation and their views of such texts. Neither

---

45. Van Dijk-Hemmes, 'The Imagination of Power and the Power of Imagination'.

can we resort to material evidence or to comparative literatures in this case.

I can see no reason for complying with biblical pornography, even at the price of being considered politically incorrect. Far be it from me to censure erotics. But, together with other feminist critics, like for instance Gordon and Washington,[46] I want to expose, so in effect censure, any representation of violence against negatively depicted female images— even in the Bible—as propaganda and pornography. The insistence that a community is thus primarily censured is not sufficient to obliterate the image and its damaging effects.

Afterword: Is There Anything to Be Gained from Such Texts?

One way of dealing with pornoprophetic texts is to expose and then reject them. This has certainly been the way I have chosen for myself. Other readers, although willing to employ a hermeneutic of suspicion to the point of exposition, might not be so willing to reject the texts. Troubled as they might become, they might wish to find an exegetical solution that might be theologically acceptable while neutralizing the texts' harmful effects for gender relations.

Traditional (male) unproblematizing efforts are well known, and can be found in mainstream commentaries. Other efforts have taken new directions.[47]

1. To identify with the male-position-in/of-the-text does not necessarily imply acceptance; insights into the male psyche from an M (Male/Masculine) approach can be critical if understanding, and a complement to feminist approaches. This has been the approach chosen by John Goldingay regarding Hosea 2.[48] Finally, violence such as contained in the husband/wife metaphor is self-destructive and self-deconstructive. This is a

46. Gordon and Washington, 'Rape as a Military Metaphor'.

47. I delivered part of this article at a faculty seminar of the Faculty of Theology at the University of Amsterdam in April, 1995. The 'what to do, where to go from here' approach was discussed at the meeting with great interest. I thank the Faculty members present for their illuminating remarks.

48. J. Goldingay, 'Hosea 1–3, Genesis 1–4 and Masculist Interpretation', in Brenner (ed.), *A Feminist Companion to the Latter Prophets*, pp. 161-68.

lesson important to theology and to gender relations, as formulated by Francis Landy, again on Hosea 2.[49]

2. To regard such negative, one-sided texts as lacking and to fill in the gap, so, paradoxically, turning them into a source of liberation theology for the oppressed and their signifier (women). Such texts are about human desire. The filling in with female desire, and the fuller symbol of bi-gender epistemology (ידיעה) of God supplied, can serve to sublimate the message.

3. To stress that such texts are time-, place- and culture-bound: their message for gender-relations can and should be separated from their message about God, since, primarily, they are about a society and not women.

4. To view the metaphor as an economic metaphor about land, people and God, rather than about gender relations. This path was taken, for example, by Alice Keefe in a recent article.[50]

5. To defer judgment until more work is done on sexuality and desire in the Bible, so as to understand whether those texts should indeed be exegeted rather than eisegeted as pornography.

6. To insist, once again, that the husband/wife metaphor is primarily directed at a community of *men*, since men are the privileged group within the community constructed in/by the text and since women are only indirectly implicated. After all, the passages are about the politics of religion, not of gender relations.[51]

---

49. F. Landy, 'Fantasy and the Displacement of Pleasure: Hosea 2.4-17', in Brenner (ed.), *A Feminist Companion to the Latter Prophets*, pp. 146-60.

50. A. Keefe, 'The Female Body, the Body Politic and the Land: A Sociopolitical Reading of Hosea 1–2', in Brenner (ed.), *A Feminist Companion to the Latter Prophets*, pp. 70-100.

51. For the last two suggestions, cf. Carroll, 'Desire'.

READING PROPHECY

JSOT 44 (1989), pp. 75-88

THE IMAGINATION OF POWER AND THE POWER OF IMAGINATION
AN INTERTEXTUAL ANALYSIS OF TWO BIBLICAL LOVE SONGS:
THE SONG OF SONGS AND HOSEA 2

Fokkelien van Dijk-Hemmes†

In his article 'Hosea and Canticles' van Selms (1964–65) discusses some similarities between the Song of Songs and Hosea 2. He concludes that

> there is every reason to assume that the repertoire of Hosea's wife—who was something of an expert in erotic arts—did not much differ from some of the songs of canticles... So it seems that the prophet Hosea, describing Israel's apostasy with metaphors borrowed from his wife's misconduct, was influenced by the words of her songs. This insight makes our sympathy with the prophet's personal plight somewhat more poignant and reveals to us something of the way he relived his own tragedy in his indictment of Israel (88-89).

As van Selms does not consider the possibility that the sympathy and interpretative frame of a woman reader might move in a different direction, I would suggest that there is every reason to re-examine the similarities between the Song of Songs and Hosea 2. A woman reader might, for example, feel rather sympathetic to the plight of Hosea's wife. And beyond that, she might be interested in the damaging effects that Hosea's metaphorical language has had for women. Hosea is one of the prophets who uses 'objectified female sexuality as a symbol of evil' (Setel 1985: 86).

My re-examination of the similarities between the Song of Songs and Hosea 2 aims to focus on the latter text. The question I pose is: How does the Hosean text use motifs figuring in the Song of Songs in order to convey its own message? The attempt to deal with this question will lead me to re-evaluate the reasons why Hosea's call for justice is 'packaged' in a specific sexual metaphorical language. My analysis will be based on a gender-specific, narratological and intertextual approach to the texts. I define this approach as follows:

a. The term 'gender-specific' refers to a distinct approach to the relationship between reader, text and author. It assumes first of all, that the reader is aware of his or her own gender and of the dissymmetry in the relationship between the sexes in his or her culture. Secondly, it takes the line that, with respect to the construction of gender-relations, there exists a certain continuity between social reality and the world which is described in literature. Thirdly, it argues that, in order to be able to analyze the latter as precisely as possible, the reader or literary theorist takes on the position of a woman reader (Culler 1983: 43-64). In other words, she leaves behind the position of the so-called gender-free but in fact male reader-position in which she has been trained and which so has become self-evident. She rather focuses her attention in the first place on the female characters in the text, looking at the way in which the relationships between men and women in the text are constructed, then at the gender ideology as it is inscribed in the text and finally at the intended effect of the text upon the reader.

For analysis of the power relationships in the social world as well as in the world which is created in a text I adopt the criteria set out by the anthropologist Joke Schrijvers (1983: 58). She investigates the position of women in a certain culture by putting forth the following questions:

1. To what extent do women have something to say about their own sexuality and fertility? Are they (exclusively) held responsible for the care and nourishment of children and other members of the household?
2. To what extent are women economically self-supporting or dependent on men?
3. To what extent are women isolated from contact with other women, both physically and socially?
4. To what extent are women, according to the dominant ways of thinking and in their own estimation, inferior to men as regards their work, their bodies and their intellect?

I use these criteria as the starting point for an ideological critical analysis of a text. The next step is an investigation into the literary strategies deployed in the text and into its assumptions and goals (see e.g. Fuchs 1985). How far are these strategies, assumptions and goals in complicity with the preservation of male authority?

Finally, 'reading as a woman' implies that the gender of the author is taken into account. With regard to the Bible the question of the author's gender is relevant, precisely because the possibility that women might be the authors of parts of the Bible was, until recently, seldom considered. And of course it is incontestable that the Bible is a collection of writings predominantly by men. This in itself testifies to the dissymmetry in the relationships between men and women in ancient Israel. One can thus assume that this dissymmetry is depicted as well as legitimized in the biblical writings. Whenever this is the case the woman reader will assume the position of the 'resisting reader' (Fetterley 1978). However, the resistance is not an uncritical one. We should not exclude the possiblility that the text may contain self-critical and even liberating elements. To quote Patricinio Schweickart in a slightly modified form:[1] 'Biblical texts merit a dual hermeneutic: a negative hermeneutic that discloses their complicity with patriarchal ideology, and a positive hermeneutic that recuperates the utopian moment from which they draw a significant portion of their liberating power'.

The author's gender is not automatically decisive for the gender ideology inscribed in his or her text. The question of how the author's gender works in the text is nevertheless important, as the many results of feminist literary criticism have shown (see e.g. Showalter 1986; Lemaire 1987). As far as the Bible is concerned, our problem is that we can only guess but maybe never prove that some of its texts stem from women's traditions. Here the woman reader will have to trace how these texts distinguish themselves from, first of all, equivalent male texts. She has to explore how in the supposed women's texts such themes as love, nature, religious experience, violence and death are presented and what images the women speakers in these texts have about themselves and about the other sex. An example of this procedure can be found in 'The Canon of the Old Testament and Women's Cultural Traditions', where Jonneke Bekkenkamp and I (1987) compare the Song of Deborah with the prose story of Judges 4, and the Song of Songs with Proverbs 7.

---

1.   '...certain (not all) male texts merit a dual hermeneutic: a negative hermeneutic that discloses their complicity with patriarchal ideology, and a positive hermeneutic that recuperates the utopian moment—the authentic kernel—from which they draw a significant portion of their emotional power' (Schweickart 1986: 43-44).

b. The narratological method developed by Mieke Bal (1984 and 1985) is very fruitful for a gender-specific analysis of literary texts, including biblical ones. This method implies that a text is analyzed on three levels. The first level concerns the distribution of speech: Who speaks? Who tells the story and at what points do speakers alternate with the (anonymous) narrator? The second level concerns the domain of vision, of focalization: Who sees? Which image of (the imaginative) reality is presented to us? From whose point of view? Through whose eyes do we read the story? The third level concerns the distribution of actions: Who acts? What relationships are there between the characters in the narrative and the events in which they are involved? How do the characters relate to one another?

An important characteristic of the narratological method is that it allows us to establish connections between textual features and social meaning. The text is seen here not so much as a window through which we can get a glimpse of reality but rather as a figuration of and a response to the reality that brought it forth. For the Bible this means that the textual figurations, for example the grammatical or semantic possibilities of women as subjects or objects are relevant. These figurations give some insight in what was imagined as possibilities to women's lives, to women's contributions to society. That is to say: these possibilities were conceived of as desirable or frightening by those who produced the biblical texts (Bal 1988: 32-39). There is a relation between the text and reality, but that relation is not straightforwardly reflective.

c. The aim of this paper is the comparison between two texts, or more precisely, the exploration of the way in which one text is 'quoted' in another. Therefore it is useful to combine the gender-specific and narratological analysis with an intertextual approach. The term 'intertextual' is used here in a narrow sense. It refers to the studying of concrete relationships between texts as the reader perceives them. These relationships can be described as transformations, which can be classified as 'repetition', 'addition', 'deletion' and substitution'. The next step is then the attribution of a function, a meaning to the different transformations. This function can be interpreted as constructive/positive or destructive/negative or deconstructive (Claes 1987a and 1987b). After these methodological remarks let me add a few words about my view of the texts that I want to analyse. As may already have become clear, I do not conceive of Hosea 2, nor of its immediate context, chs. 1 and 3, as a direct reflection of the 'real' life of Hosea. In line with what was stated earlier, I see the narrative in these chapters as a figuration of, and response to, the reality outside the text. This view is all the more legitimate because Hosea 1–3 as we have it now is the result of a long process of transmission (see e.g. Ruppert 1982 and Renaud 1983). The world which is created within this composite narrative and the characters which play a part in it are literary constructions. The same holds in principle for the Song of Songs which is, as we have it now, a more or less unified composition of orally transmitted love-songs (see e.g. Pope 1977). As these and other love-songs must have circulated in the society of ancient Israel through the ages, it is quite possible that parts of it are 'quoted' in different biblical texts, for example in Hosea.

The first question we have to deal with now is: From which of these love-songs do we find quotations in the Hosea text? Let me give a few cases. The first is Song 3.1-4 (I use the RSV: The Oxford Annotated Bible):

(1)   Upon my bed by night
      I sought him whom my soul loves.
      I sought him but found him not.
(2)   Let me arise now and go round about the city
      in the streets and squares.
      I will seek him whom my soul loves.
      I sought him but found him not
(3)   The watchmen who go round about the city found me
      Have you seen him whom my soul loves?
(4)   Scarcely had I passed them.
      when I found him whom my soul loves.
      I grasped him and would not let him go
      until I had brought him into my mother's house.
      into the room of her who was pregnant of me.

In Hos. 2.7 we read:

For their mother has played the harlot.
She who was pregnant of them has acted shamefully,
for she said:
      I will go after my lovers...

The parallel expression 'mother//she who was pregnant' occurs only in the Song of Songs and in Hosea 2. So we have here a rather literal quotation: only the suffix has changed. This means at the same time a substitution. In the Song of Songs the mother whom is spoken about is the mother of the woman lover. In Hosea the mother is the woman lover herself. This quotation could indeed be taken from the love-song in Song 3.1-4 since in both cases the expression is used in a context where the woman lover pursues her beloved. In the Song of Songs it is *she* who is speaking. She expresses her longing for her beloved, whom she wants to bring into the house of her mother, of 'her who was pregnant of me'. The woman speaker in the Song of Songs is at the same time the one who does the focalization. This means that we read the story that she tells through her eyes. In Hos. 2.7 the situation is different. There it is the male first person who speaks. The woman is presented to the audience through *his* words and seen through *his* eyes. This means that, before we are informed about her view and her desire, the woman is accused of being a harlot who behaves in a shameless way. The expression of her desire functions as a 'quote' in his speech:

> For she said:
> > I will go after my lovers.

This saying might also refer to Song 1.4 where the woman first person says to her beloved: 'Draw me, after you we will run'. In this line the woman speaker includes her woman friends in expressing her desire to run after her lover, while in Hosea he says that she says: 'I will go after my lovers'. This plural is, of course, another example of her shameless behaviour.

In Song 3.1-2 the woman who goes after her beloved describes herself as 'seeking but not finding him'. In Hos. 2.8-9 the male first person describes himself as preventing his wife from going after her lovers:

> Therefore I will hedge up her way with thorns
> and I will build a wall against her
> so that she cannot find her paths.
> She shall pursue her lovers
> but not overtake them
> *and she shall seek them*
> *but shall not find them.*

As van Selms states it: 'Here the wording is nearly identical and the situation in both instances is the same: the woman seeks in the streets of the town her lover or lovers but she does not come upon them' (van Selms 1964–65: 86-87). Again it is important to note that, whereas the woman in the Song of Songs speaks about seeking and not finding her beloved, the male speaker in Hosea 2 prevents his wife from seeking and

finding her lovers. The violence which he expresses against her in this
and in other passages of his monologue is absent in the love-song in
Song 3.1-4. But there is another song in which the woman describes
herself as seeking but not finding her beloved: Song 5.2-7. In this song
the woman says that her beloved knocks on her door but that he has
gone when she opens to him:

> I sought him, but found him not:
> I called him, but he gave no answer.
> The watchmen found me
> as they went about the city:
> they beat me, they wounded me.
> They took away my mantle,
> those watchmen of the walls.

So here too, the woman is violently prevented from going after her
beloved. She is even beaten and stripped. In Hosea 2 the role of the
watchmen is taken over by the vengeful husband who not only 'hedges
up her way with thorns', but again and again threatens his wife with
stripping her naked. Hence it is more likely that Song 5.27 is the source.
But to notice that, the reader has to be interested in the violent
opposition of the men, and not only in the autonomous erotic behaviour
of the woman.

The last example of an intertextual relation between the Song of
Songs and Hosea 2 which van Selms points out is the enumeration of
gifts which the woman in Hosea 2 receives from her lovers:

> My bread and my water,
> my wool and my flax,
> my oil and my drink (Hos. 2.7).

This reminds us of the gifts which the beloved receives from his woman
friend in Song 5.1:

> My myrrh with my spice,
> my honeycomb with my honey,
> my wine with my milk.

> Probably in this text the gifts are mentioned as metaphorical indications of
> erotic pleasure, but even so it is evident that the imagery has been
> borrowed from the lover's custom of exchanging presents... It is
> remarkable that in both passages six gifts are enumerated: that in both
> instances the gifts are paired: that all the gifts carry the suffix of the first
> person singular. And that the background in reality is always the
> exchanging of gifts among lovers (van Selms 1964–65: 88).

I want to stress here that in Hos. 2.5 it is the woman who according to the male speaker receives gifts from her lovers. *These* gifts are not so much 'metaphorical indications of erotic pleasure' but necessary means of subsistence. In enumerating these gifts the male speaker makes the woman ironically ignore the female role in the provision of food and clothing. So in the Song of Songs it is the woman who gives; in Hosea it is the woman who, according to the male speaker in the text, receives, while expressing her dependence upon male support. The implication is that males nurture females, which is a reversal of (at least certain aspects of) social reality at the time (Setel 1985: 92) as well as of the source song.

These examples make clear that the Hosean text indeed contains words and motifs which must have been borrowed from love-songs which later on have been collected in the Song of Songs. In these love-songs the woman character is the first person. Her feelings of love and her desire, which are extensively described, are presented to us through her viewpoint. In Hosea the woman appears through the eyes (focalization) of the male first person. This means, as we have seen, that her view, her practices and her words appear in a negative light. Her words of love and longing for her beloved are almost 'deleted': negative qualifications of her behaviour are added. She is 'quoted' in a destructive way. The woman who expresses her desire for her lover becomes in the Hosean context a harlot who, in a shameless way, goes after her lovers.

This conclusion raises the question of the status of the subject who quotes/distorts the Song. What exactly is the textual context in which this transformation of female desire occurs? Who is the male first person of Hosea 2? The answer is to be found in the first chapter of Hosea. It is there that the first person of ch. 2 is constructed. In Hos. 1.2 we see that Hosea becomes a metaphor for YHWH. He has to take a 'wife of harlotry' and 'children of harlotry' because the land commits 'great harlotry' by 'whoring away' from YHWH. The implication of this metaphor is that YHWH acknowledges himself as the husband of the Land of Israel while Hosea is transformed into a metaphor for YHWH, and Gomer, his wife, into a metaphor for the Land of Israel. The children who are born afterwards are immediately transformed into metaphors for the different aspects of the *people* of Israel. As it is nowhere explicitly stated who is the father of this metaphorical family there is, at least implicitly, a problem: who is the father of these 'children of harlotry'—that is, the question of paternity is raised. This problem, which appears to be one of the features of the people's behaviour as it is described in 4.1–5.7 (see e.g. Hos. 5.7 'for they have borne alien children') will be solved at the end of Hosea 2, as we shall see.

Hosea 2 is an extensive monologue by the deceived husband: the complex character which has been constructed in chapter 1 and which we could name: YHWH/Hosea. The monologue starts with an invitation to the (metaphorical) children/the sons of Israel to 'plead with their mother'/to 'attack their mother'. In other words: they are called upon to detach themselves from their mother who behaves like a harlot. According to the speaker she has, by playing the harlot, broken her relationship with him/her husband and therefore bereft her children of fatherly compassion: 'Upon her children also I will have no pity because they are children of harlotry' (2.6). The woman is described as an alienated creature who appears not to know to whom she owes her life and the life of her children and who attributes these gifts to the wrong 'lords'.[2] Therefore her 'real Baal' takes the right to threaten her in an extremely violent way:

> Therefore I will take back my grain in its time,
> and my wine in its season:
> and I will take away my wool and my flax,
> Which were to cover her nakedness.
> Now I will uncover her lewdness in the sight of her lovers.
> And no man shall rescue her out of my hand (Hos. 2.11, 12).

This statement inspires the authors of the Anchor Bible commentary to the following comment:

> Why the husband should now deliberately share this privilege [that is: the seeing and enjoying of his wife's naked body] with his rivals is not clear, although in view of the context of the former's outrage and legitimate demand for retribution, it is to be seen as a form of punishment appropriate to the crime. Just as in the past the errant wife has sought out her lovers and eagerly disrobed in their presence for the purpose of sexual gratification, so now she will be forcibly exposed to the same situation and publicly humiliated. The *subtlety* of the talion here is essentially that what she did secretly and for pleasure will now be done to her openly and for her disgrace (249, italics mine).

---

2.   Baal means 'lord'/'husband'; 'going after her lovers' implies 'going after alien gods' i.e. Baals, see e.g. 2.15.

From a gender-specific point of view it is obvious that this commentary is not an example of reading as a woman.

After his threatening speech-acts, which expose so much sexual violence, the deceived husband starts to sing *his* love-song (2.16-25). In this love-song *she* no longer goes after her lover in order to bring him into 'her mother's house' (Song 3.4). It is he who takes the initiative. He allures her, whom he had just before transformed into a 'wilderness' (2.11-15), in order to bring her into the wilderness (2.16), where 'he speaks to her heart'. It is interesting to note that 'to speak to her heart' appears in two other biblical stories about sexual violence: in Genesis 34 where Shechem 'speaks to the heart' of Dinah after having raped her, and in Judges 19 where a Levite 'speaks to the heart' of his woman who has 'whored away from him' to her father.[3] On their way back to his house he exposes her to a gang-rape from which she dies. He cuts her body into twelve pieces and sends them around to the tribes of Israel. From these examples we can conclude that the translation in the RSV (The Oxford Annotated Bible) 'and I'll speak tenderly to her' seems to be slightly out of place, to say the least.

After this alluring seduction the first person of Hosea 2 gives his gifts to the woman victim. He removes the names of her former lovers from her mouth (2.19) and he betrothes her to himself forever. She then becomes the object of his 'sowing': 'and I will sow her' (2.25), and finally he acknowledges the children, whom he had already detached from their mother, as his children. The problem of paternity is then resolved. The children of the mother have been transformed into the children of the father. The 'father'[4] succeeds in this project by disowning the children from their mother and by bringing his wife's sexuality fully under his control. From an active subject-lover whose words are 'quoted' in a distorted way she becomes the passive object of his 'sowing'. All this is supposed to imply, according to the introduction of

---

3. The translation of *znh ʿl* in Judg. 19.2 is problematic. For an illuminating discussion of this passage, see Bal 1988: 80-93, who argues that the book of Judges and esp. Judges 19 can be seen as a figuration of the struggle between patrilocality and virilocality.

4. The word 'father' is strikingly absent in the text. This explains why this specific aspect of Hosea's metaphorical language has been left unnoticed by so many commentators. On the other hand, I would suggest that it is precisely this aspect: the (implicit) pleading for the establishment of fatherhood, that 'speaks to the heart' of most male readers.

the RSV (The Oxford Annotated Bible) to the book of Hosea, 'a Gospel of redeeming Love'.

So far my analysis of Hosea 2 has disclosed some important literary strategies deployed in the text. The reason why the Hosean call for justice—which might be named the 'utopian moment' in the text—has been 'packaged' in this particular male metaphorical language has, at least partly, become clear. Nevertheless there still remain some question marks. Why is Israel, first the land but then also the nation, represented in the image of a faithless wife, a harlot, and not in the image of, for example, a rapist? This would have been more justified when we look at Israel's misdeeds which YHWH/Hosea points out in the following 4.1–5.7, which, according to me, should be considered as the immediate context of the metaphorical introduction in chs. 1–3 (see also Balz Cochois 1982a: 38). And beyond that, it is the men who are held responsible for social and religious abuses: it is the priests who mislead the people (4.4-6) and the fathers who force their daughters to play the harlot (4.13-14).

An important *motivation* for Hosea's metaphorical language is as we have seen, the implicit pleading for the establishment of fatherhood and of the authority of the father. Its *justification* can be found in 4.12 and 5.4 where YHWH/Hosea speaks of a 'spirit of harlotry' which is, according to him, within the people. This expression becomes more meaningful when we consider it to be a specific figuration of the Goddess(es). Maybe we should think here of Asherah and Astarte. Helgard Balz Cochois (1982a and 1982b) has shown that according to popular religion (which has to be distinguished from official religion) it is Asherah who embodies the secret of the renewal of life. She is the giver of the fruits of the earth and of the children. Astarte is the Goddess of (erotic) love who embodies the ambiguous power of sexuality. These two Goddesses who represent the Mother and the Woman-Lover are possibly hidden behind the 'spirit of harlotry'. In other words, the woman who is attached in Hosea 2 is not only the woman of harlotry Gomer/Israel, but also the Spirit by whom she is inspired: the Spirit of harlotry/the Goddess(es). Addressed as the sons of this Mother, the sons of Israel are invited to detach themselves from her and to become the children of the Father-God. This must be the fundamental reason for Israel's representation as a woman. Therefore the Mother/Woman-Lover is effectively bereft of her power in H/his love-song. Quoted by H/him, she herself attributes this power in her 'own words' to her lovers/the Baals. After having been victimized by her 'husband' she becomes his totally passive bride whose only task is to respond to her husband's initiatives. Her marriage to this lover is not a *hieros gamos*, but it reflects and legitimizes the ideal patriarchal marriage. In this type of marriage the woman has to remain faithful in order to prevent the birth of 'alien children'. The power of the Mother/Woman-Lover has been taken over by Him. Her song of desire has been distorted and then deafened by His song.

So metaphorical language reveals more than its user might realize and intend. We can state that the way in which Hosea constructs his vision of justice is at the same time its undermining, its deconstruction. The stones with which he constructs his vision appear to be the wall within which the Woman-Mother-Lover is imprisoned. Nevertheless *her* Song of Desire has never been totally deafened as we can see from the Song of Songs. The intertextual relationship between the Song of Songs and Hosea 2 enabled me to develop a reading strategy which I could use against the very literary strategies deployed in the Hosean text. By re-placing the 'quotations' back into the love-songs from which they were borrowed, the vision of the woman in this text is restored. Her love-songs showed us a different figuration of the reality that brought them forth. The world which is created in these songs is evoked by women's voices: the first person and the daughters of Jerusalem. So why should not women be the creators of these songs? (See also Brenner 1985: 46-56.) Women who, in spite of watchmen who beat them, and in spite of a prophet who violates their language, kept dreaming of being able to go freely after their beloved. Maybe we should detach the Hosean call for justice from his love-song and 'repackage' it into her love-song. The Song of Songs, too, can be read as a representation of the relation between God and his people or maybe Goddess and her people. And beyond that: when S/she in this song speaks to H/his heart there is no question of her appropriation of power.

BIBLIOGRAPHY

Andersen, F.I. and D.N. Freedman
    1980   Hosea: A New Thandation with Introduction and Commentary (AB, 24; Garden City, NY Doubleday).
Bal, M.
    1984   *Narratologie* (Utrecht: HES).
    1985   *Narratology: An Introduction to the Theory of Narrative* (Toronto: University of Toronto Press).

1988   *Death & Dissymmetry: The Politics of Coherence in the Book of Judges* (Chicago: University of Chicago Press).

Balz Cochois, H.
1982a   *Gomer. Der Höhenkult Israels im Selbswerständnis der Volksfrömmigkeit* (Frankfurt am Main: Peter Lang).
1982b   'Gomer oder die Macht der Astarte', *EvT* 42.1: 31-65.

Bekkenkamp, J. and F. van Dijk-Hemmes
1987   'The Canon of the Old Testament and Women's Cultural Tradition', in M. Meijer and J. Schaap (eds.), *Historiography of Woman's Cultural Traditions* (Dordrecht, Holland: Foris): 91-108.

Brenner, A.
1985   *The Israelite Woman: Sexual Role and Literary Type in Biblical Narrative* (Sheffield: JSOT Press).

Claes, P.
1987a   'Wat is intertextualeit', *Schrift* 114: 207-11
1987b   'Semiotiek van het citaat', *Eigen en Vreemd: Identiteit en ontlening in taal, literatuur en beeldende kunst* (Handelingenvan het 39ste Nederlands Filologencongres; Amsterdam: Vrije Universiteit): 223-30.

Culler, J.
1983   *On Deconstruction, Theory and Criticism after Structuralism* (London: Routledge & Kegan Paul).

Fetterley, J.
1978   *The Resisting Reader: A Feminist Approach to American Fiction* (Bloomington: Indiana University Press)

Fuchs, E.
1985   'The Literary Characterization of Mothers and Sexual Politics in the Hebrew Bible', in A.Y. Collins (ed.), *Feminist Perspectives on Biblical Scholarship* (Chico, CA: Scholars Press).

Lemaire, R.
1987   *Passions et positions: Contributions à une sémiotique du sujet dans la poésie lyrique médiévale en langues romanes* (Amsterdam: Rodopi).

Pope, M.H.
1977   *Song of Songs: A New Translation with Introduction and Commentary* (AB, 7c; Garden City, NY: Doubleday).

Renaud, B.
1983   'Osée 1–3: Analyse diachronique et lecture sychronique: Problèmes de méthode', *Recherches des Sciences Religieuses* 57 (193): 249-60.

Ruppert, L.
1982   'Erwägungen zur Kompositions- and Redaktionsgeschichte von Hosea 1–3', *BZ* 2: 208-33.

Schrijvers, J.
1983   'Weerstand tegen geweld', *Tijdschrift voor Vrouwenstudies* 13: 55-82.

Schweickart, P.P.
1986   'Reading Ourselves: Toward a Feminist Theory of Reading', in E.A. Flynn and P.P. Schweickart (eds.), *Gender and Reading: Essays on Readers, Texts and Contexts* (Baltimore: Johns Hopkins University Press): 31-62.

Selms, A. van
    1964–65   'Hosea and Canticles', in *OTWSA* 7.8.
Setel, T.D.
    1985   'Prophets and Pornography: Female Sexual Imagery in Hosea', in
                  L. Russell (ed.), *Feminist Interpretation of the Bible* (Philadelphia:
                  Westminster Press): 86-95.
Showalter, E. (ed.)
    1986   *The New Feminist Criticism: Essays on Women, Literature and Theory*
                  (London, Virago).

JSOT 66 (1995), pp. 65-85

INSIDERS AND OUTSIDERS IN THE BOOK OF JEREMIAH:
SHIFTS IN SYMBOLIC ARRANGEMENTS

Louis Stulman

1. *Introduction*

This essay will examine the 'insider–outsider' *Weltanschauung* in the book of Jeremiah as a way to account for its primary literary symbols. Following a brief introduction, the paper will examine several code words for danger in Jeremiah in order to identify whom the text stigmatizes with labels of 'outsider' and privileges with labels of 'insider'. These categories are employed next as indices of major shifts and transformations in symbolic and social arrangements in the book. In the final analysis the essay will attempt to show that the literary milieu of Jeremiah[1] is witness to two disparate cosmological codes, each attempting to make sense of anomie and counter-coherence in its own network of meanings.

2. *Insider–Outsider Perspective*

In his article on the history of Inner Asia in the *Encyclopaedia Britannica*, D. Sinor writes,

---

1. By the expressions 'literary milieu of Jeremiah', 'the world of Jeremiah' and the 'social environment of Jeremiah', I mean the 'presentation' of Jeremiah which is the resultant work of the shapers of the book for subsequent audiences. I do not refer to an actual person, or the Jeremiah of the Deuteronomistic redactor. (Identifying the various levels of tradition, given our current state of knowledge, is at best tenuous.) Rather, I use these terms for the amalgam of voices, meanings and codes embedded within the text (generally the MT), without reference, except when indicated, to the external world. The text, thus, is treated in this study as text giving expression to its focal concerns and dominant attitudes.

> Because the hearts of men stake out frontiers more clearly than do mountains, streams, or deserts, the real boundaries of Inner Asia are determined at any given time in history by the relationship between the 'civilized' and the 'barbarian'... In essence, the history of Inner Asia is that of the Barbarian.[2]

Sinor suggests that the ethno-political concept of the barbarian enjoys an almost universal place in ancient sedentary civilizations. Societies would often assert their identities and define their distinct personalities by contrasting them with those of a common enemy, real or imagined. This largely fictitious opposition between 'civilized' insiders and alleged inferior outsiders would produce inner cohesion and group solidarity. However, the primary aim of insiders, Sinor suggests, was the prevention of incursions and the banishment of the barbarian far beyond the borders.[3]

P. Machinist has argued recently that much of the biblical literature speaks of 'Israel or one of its representative groups or individuals, including its God, as distinct from *outsiders* [itals. mine], whether humans or gods'.[4] Israel's perception of its own distinctiveness carries with it a comparison which often describes the 'specific feature that the one side possesses and the other does not'.[5] Machinist concludes that the biblical understanding of distinctiveness stands 'at some distance from the views which appear in two of the great high cultures of the ancient Near East, Egypt and Mesopotamia'.[6] This *Tendenz* may be attributed to 'Israel's newness' in its cultural milieu and the resultant concern to 'forge an identity for a people that began on the margins of history and

2. D. Sinor, 'Inner Asia, History of', *Encyclopaedia Britannica* (15th edn), IX, pp. 595-601.

3. D. Sinor, 'Introduction: The Concept of Inner Asia', in D. Sinor (ed.), *The Cambridge History of Early Inner Asia* (Cambridge: Cambridge University Press, 1990), pp. 1-18.

4. P. Machinist, 'The Question of Distinctiveness in Ancient Israel: An Essay', in M. Cogan and I. Eph'al (eds.), *Ah, Assyria... Studies in Assyrian History and Ancient Near Eastern Historiography Presented to Hayim Tadmor* (Jerusalem: Magnes Press, 1991), p. 203. Similarly, J.W. Rogerson notes that in ancient Israel 'it was necessary to be aware of boundaries separating between friend and foe, and of boundaries enclosing relatives of nearer or remoter kinship' ('The World-View of the Old Testament', in J.W. Rogerson [ed.], *Beginning Old Testament Study* [Philadelphia: Westminster Press, 1982], p. 57).

5. Machinist, 'Distinctiveness', p. 203.

6. Machinist, 'Distinctiveness', p. 209.

thereafter was faced constantly with a return to marginality…as against older societies like Egypt and Mesopotamia on its outside, and Canaanites and others within its midst'.[7]

This 'in-group–out-group' cosmology or world view with its distinct categories of differentiation is discernible in many symbol systems (e.g. in the priestly culinary and cultic mores) and literary traditions of the Hebrew Bible. The conviction that Yahweh had chosen Israel to be a special people with a unique destiny is one of Israel's 'self-evident' assumptions.[8] This claim to a special relationship with the deity,[9] however, is often juxtaposed with that of the barbarian, setting the two in

---

7.   Machinist, 'Distinctiveness', pp. 210-11. While Machinist is no doubt correct that this concern for distinctiveness from outsiders is reflected in much of the Hebrew Bible, it is by no means expressed evenly there. Rather, the biblical corpus is witness to a wide range of symbolic categories and social voices. Consequently, Israel's xenophobia and its 'insider–outsider' orientation are far more complex than is often assumed. For instance, a certain degree of equivocation or ambivalence exists as to the identity of foreigners or outsiders, or just how foreign is a foreigner. In Deuteronomy, for example, certain groups are unequivocally outsiders and are thus considered dangerous and unworthy of land (Deut. 7.1-6; 9.1-3). Other groups, however, are considered semi-foreigners or half-brothers (Deut. 2.1ff.). *gērîm*—resident aliens—are to be included in the community and treated as insiders in many respects (Deut. 10.18-19; 24.17; 27.19).

8.   I use the term 'self-evident' here without ontological reference; that is, 'self-evident' or *a priori* to Israel. See M. Douglas, *Implicit Meanings: Essays in Anthropology* (London: Routledge & Kegan Paul, 1975), pp. 276-318.

9.   Seock-Tae Sohn suggests that

> the divine election of Israel is one of the major themes of the Hebrew Bible. Yahweh chose Israel to be his people and dealt with it as his own throughout biblical history. Since this idea was of central importance to the biblical writers, it is not easy to grasp the message of the Bible without a proper understanding of this theme (*The Divine Election of Israel* [Grand Rapids: Eerdmans, 1991], p. 1).

J. Goldingay agrees that 'the notion of election is a key to understanding the notion of Israel. It is not even that God makes an already existent people his own; he brings a people into being' (*Theological Diversity and the Authority of the Old Testament* [Grand Rapids: Eerdmans, 1987]), p. 62. As is well known, G. Ernest Wright argued that 'the Old Testament doctrine of a chosen people, one selected by God "for his possession above all the people that are on the face of the earth" (Deut. 7.6), is the chief clue for the understanding of the meaning and significance of Israel' (*The Old Testament against its Environment* [Chicago: Henry Regnery, 1950], p. 47). Wright, however, drew the much criticized conclusion that this focal point was 'one of the central factors which distinguish it from all other religious literatures' (p. 47).

stark opposition.[10] Accordingly, while Israel claims to be chosen and accepted, it envisages a (residual) category of enemies that places the community's existence in grave danger. This category is perceived by insiders as 'unclean', 'wicked' or 'sinister', because it defines behavior not in conformance with community restraints and the restraints of cosmic power. Groups that exhibit such conduct are labeled as 'outsiders', 'barbarians' or 'foreigners', because *they live outside the social order and the accepted symbol system* (even if they actually live within the community). Their non-conformity and deviant activity threaten the integrity of the internal boundaries and systems of control.

In response to a fear of encroachment, sharp lines of demarcation are drawn, and a focal concern for well-defined boundaries appears frequently in the Hebrew Bible. Large blocks of material reflect an interest in establishing and maintaining precisely distinguished social categories and clearly assigned roles in the classification system.[11] Blurred and ambiguous internal boundaries, thus, often contribute to Israel's profound sense of danger and contingency. As a result, attempts to 'keep straight' the internal lines of distinction are embedded within much of the Hebrew Bible.[12]

---

10. Certain traditions or pieties in ancient Israel, however, apparently did not view outsiders with fear and suspicion; as a result there is no demonstrable concern for protecting insiders from foreigners. The Wisdom literature, for example, represents a distinct piety in Israel which is apparently open to understandings of reality existing outside national boundaries. It is far more tolerant of outsiders than, for example, the 'Priestly' or Dtr approach to life. Its boundaries are not closed, and contact with 'foreigners' or 'outsiders' is not viewed as dangerous or risky, but necessary and even desirable (see R.E Murphy, 'The Hebrew Sage and Openness to the World', in J. Papin [ed.], *Christian Action and Openness to the World* [Villanova University Symposium 2–3; Villanova, PA: Villanova University, 1970], pp. 219-44; see also J.G. Gammie, 'From Prudentialism to Apocalypticism', in J.G. Gammie and L.G. Perdue [eds.], *The Sage in Israel and the Ancient Near East* [Winona Lake, IN: Eisenbrauns, 1990], pp. 490-92.). Exogamy is not seen as a breach of loyalty but as advantageous and integral to life (see e.g. 1 Kgs 3, where Solomon, the paragon of the wisdom tradition, enters into a marriage alliance [חתן] with Egypt [3.1]; see also, however, the Dtr assessment of Solomon's exogamous relationships in 1 Kgs 11.1-13).

11. 'It is probable that ancient Israelites were much more conscious than we are about the importance of different roles in society, and that boundaries between roles were clearly marked' (Rogerson, 'The World-View of the Old Testament', p. 56).

12. L.M. Bechtel has shown recently that the process of shaming was also employed as a means of controlling undesirable or aggressive social behavior. See

3. *Insider–Outsider Perspective as Transmitted in the Book of Jeremiah by Specific Vocabulary*

Is this 'insider–outsider' *Weltanschauung* reflected in the literary milieu of Jeremiah? The world of Jeremiah has long been recognized as a hostile place, vulnerable to forces beyond its control.[13] This world is fragile, fraught with danger, and at risk of becoming a system at war with itself. This paper examines this 'social environment' of contingency and scarcity and seeks to understand the forces that contribute to its marked sense of uncertainty and powerlessness. Who are the enemies or barbarians rejecting social and cosmic restraints? Is the book witness to a focal concern for establishing and maintaining clear and well-defined internal boundaries that protect insiders from menacing outsiders? What kinds of symbolic voices and hierarchical arrangements are presented to its 'interpretative communities?' With these questions in mind, a brief examination of the words א‏יב (enemy), צפֿון (north) and בבל (Babylon) will serve as our point of departure. These three terms in particular function as code words for alarm and danger.

The word א‏(‎ו)‏יב and its derivative forms occur 19 times in Jeremiah. In the vast majority of occurrences it appears without identification, although on occasion א‏יב is closely associated with בבל (20.4, 5). The word is often used with Yahweh as subject (speaking in the first person), doing the acting, and Judah as the object of the activity. For example, Yahweh causes Judah to serve 'its enemies'; Yahweh delivers (נתן) Judah to the sword before 'its enemies' (15.9); Yahweh will cause them to fall by the sword of 'their enemies' (19.7); Yahweh threatens to deliver Judah 'into the hands of enemies' (34.20; 21.7); Judah will be scattered

---

L.M. Bechtel, 'Shame as a Sanction of Social Control in Biblical Israel: Judicial, Political and Social Shaming', *JSOT* 49 (1991), pp. 47-76. Law 'codes' also serve in part to preserve social control and coherence by stigmatizing 'bad' insiders with labels of outsiders (see L. Stulman, 'Encroachment in Deuteronomy: An Analysis of the Social World of the D Code', *JBL* 109 [1990], pp. 631-32). Another recent article that examines social control in biblical materials is L. Rowlett, 'Inclusion, Exclusion and Marginality in the Book of Joshua', *JSOT* 55 (1992), pp. 15-23.

13. For a recent review of the history of research, see R.P. Carroll, *Jeremiah: A Commentary* (Philadelphia: Westminster Press, 1986), pp. 38-55; W.L. Holladay, *Jeremiah. II. A Commentary on the Book of the Prophet Jeremiah, Chapters 26–52* (Minneapolis: Fortress Press, 1989), pp. 1-24; W. McKane, *A Critical and Exegetical Commentary on Jeremiah* (ICC; Edinburgh: T. & T. Clark, 1986), pp. xv-xcii.

'before the enemy' in the day of calamity (18.17). Although these adversaries are not identified, they appear to be dangerous outsiders who either invade sacred space or exact punishment from outside the boundaries. In either case the איבים serve as instruments of Yahweh to punish 'faithless' Judah and particularly the upper tiers of its social hierarchy that reject the structures of control.

The word צפון and derivative forms occur 25 times. The 'north' in Jeremiah is often associated with peril, alarm, as well as outside forces invading the space allotted to insiders.[14] The danger coming from the 'north' is never associated directly with the word איבים, but rather with לכל משפחות ממלכות (1.13; 4.6; 6.1), עם 6.22; 46.24; 50.41), (ה)רעה (1.15), קול שמועה (10.22), and, in the Oracles against the Foreign Nations, with עגלה (46.20), מים עלים (47.2), השודדים (51.48), גוי (50.3), and גוים גדלים (50.9; cf. 50.41). B. Childs has noted that the northern foe comes

> from a distant land (4.16, 5.15, 6.22). It is an 'ancient' and 'enduring' nation (5.15) speaking a foreign tongue (5.15). All of them are mighty men (5.16) and without mercy (6.23). The suddenness of the attack is emphasized (4.20, 6.26). The enemy rides upon swift horses (4.13, 4.29) with war chariots (4.13) and is armed with bow and spear (4.29, 6.23). He uses battle formations (6.23) and attacks a fortified city at noon (6.4, 5).[15]

While a rich variety of metaphors is employed to describe the threat from the north, most צפון passages draw heavily on war imagery (see 4.5-8; 6.1-8; 6.22-23; etc.). The 'northern foe' is engaged in a military campaign that will result in utter desolation (ושבר גדול [4.6; 6.1], מעון [10.22], and לשמה [50.3]).

The attack from outside, however, is no mere military-political activity

14. The reference to an invader from the north is generally taken to be the Neo-Babylonian armies and not, as was once popularly held, the Scythians. W. Brueggemann notes that any attempt to 'specify an historical referent...is to miss the point' (*Jeremiah 1–25: To Pluck Up, To Tear Down* [Grand Rapids: Eerdmans, 1988], p. 50). The invading threat from the north

> is an act of poetic imagination that does not depend on historical referent. Its purpose is, rather, to evoke in the listening community an awareness and a sense that this religious, political enterprise (Jerusalem) which has seemed so secure is in fact under massive assault, and that any complacency or "ease in Zion" (cf. Amos 6.1) is misplaced and ill-informed (p. 50).

See also B.S. Childs, 'The Enemy from the North and the Chaos Tradition', *JBL* 78 (1959), pp. 187-98.

15. Childs, 'Enemy from the North', p. 154.

since the ominous northern forces have been clearly aroused by Yahweh.

> The Lord said to me:
> From the north (מצפון) disaster shall come forth
> upon all the inhabitants of the land
> For now *I* am calling all the tribes of
> the kingdoms of the north (צפונה),
> oracle of the Lord; and they shall come
> and set themselves on thrones
> at the entrance of the gates of Jerusalem,
> against all its surrounding walls and against all the
> cities of Judah. And *I will pronounce my judgments against them*,
> for all their evil in forsaking me;
> in making offerings to other gods,
> and in worshipping the works of their own hands (Jer. 1.14-16).

In this passage, for example, the formidable enemy from the north invading sacred space, spoken of in the plural (v. 15), has been commissioned by Yahweh.[16] The alien horde sweeping down from the north over Jerusalem and 'all the cities of Judah' represents God's instrument of judgment against bad insiders. Whether this invading force is mythological or historical is incidental, for the real agent of impending disaster is Yahweh himself. 'That of course makes the danger massive, ominous, inescapable. Yahweh is now engaged in a dread military exercise against God's own beloved Jerusalem.'[17]

In turning to the term בבל a somewhat similar configuration of meanings emerges. בבל is attested over 100 times in Jeremiah. In most of these occurrences in chs. 20–43 the word is used as reference to Yahweh's instrument of assault against culpable Judah. It is also employed in this context to denote the faraway place where Yahweh has chosen for Judah's exile.

The position of Babylon is nearly inverted in the world of Jeremiah. Babylon the outsider or barbarian is afforded semiotically the favored status of insider. The literature views Babylonia, its king and invading armies as 'chosen' by Yahweh to perform punitive acts against Judah. Except for the Oracles against the Foreign Nations, the inner literary world of Jeremiah shows little hostility towards Babylon. Quite the

---

16. Cf., however, the reading suggested by W.L. Holladay, *Jeremiah. I. A Commentary on the Book of Jeremiah Chapters 1–25* (Hermeneia; Philadelphia: Fortress Press, 1986), pp. 22-23, 38-43.

17. Brueggemann, *Jeremiah 1–25*, p. 51.

contrary is true. The book in its final forms is replete with pro-Babylonian rhetoric.[18]

Accordingly, the book of Jeremiah (in the LXX and MT) is markedly *gōlâ* oriented. That is to say, it favors and represents the viewpoint of the departed Judaeans residing in *Babylon* over against those who remain in Judah, or those who migrate south to Egypt (e.g. 24.1-10; 27.1–29.32). Yahweh promises mercy and good fortune to the *gōlâ* in Babylon but announces his total rejection of Zedekiah and those residing with him in Jerusalem. C. Seitz has noted that the text reflects a conflict between

> a viewpoint which held out for the continued existence of a people of God, in the land, under the governorship of Gedaliah and the leadership of the prophet Jeremiah, and a viewpoint which has left its stamp on the final form of the book of Jeremiah and which saw life in the land as, if not disobedient to the will of Yahweh, then certainly as misguided and doomed to failure.[19]

While the MT accentuates this *gōlâ* orientation,[20] it is still present in a demonstrable way in the LXX.

Moreover, Judah and its near neighbors (i.e. other Syro-Palestinian states) are urged by Jeremiah to submit to Babylonian sovereignty as the will of Yahweh. Such rule, according to Jeremiah, will not be short but a long-term reality. This particular viewpoint is represented in chs. 27–29

18. See, however, Jer. 50–51, which reflects a radically different attitude towards Babylon.

> The sense of outrage directed against the depredations of Babylon which appears throughout 50–51 makes this set of OAN a very good foil to the attitude expressed towards Babylon in 27–29, and raises most interesting questions about the ambivalences shown towards Babylon in the book of Jeremiah' (R.P. Carroll, *Jeremiah* [OTG; Sheffield: JSOT Press, 1989], p. 54).

19. C.R. Seitz, 'The Crisis of Interpretation over the Meaning and Purpose of the Exile', *VT* 35 (1985), p. 79. K.F. Pohlmann's work *Studien zum Jeremiabuch* sets the date and provenance of this redactional activity during the post-exilic period, specifically during the fourth century in Judah, whereas Seitz argues for the period of the Exile (K.F. Pohlmann, *Studien zum Jeremiabuch: Ein Beitrag zur Frage nach der Entstehung des Jeremiabuches* [Göttingen: Vandenhoeck & Ruprecht, 1978]; see also E.W. Nicholson, *Preaching to the Exiles: A Study of the Prose Tradition in the Book of Jeremiah* [New York: Schocken Books, 1970], pp. 71-93).

20. See L. Stulman, 'Some Theological and Lexical Differences between the Old Greek and the MT of the Jeremiah Prose Discourses', *Hebrew Studies* 25 (1984), pp. 18-23.

in which Jeremiah is pitted against the prophetic voices of mendacity. These voices, including Hananiah ben Azzur's, insist that the return of the temple furnishings and the deportees to Jerusalem will be imminent; therefore, they incite rebellion against Babylonian rule. Jeremiah, the voice of veracity, encourages submission to Babylonian rule and the long-term settlement of Judaeans in the distant country of Babylon (see e.g. Jer. 29).

Hananiah and his support group represent the well-established salvific tradition founded in *election*—that is, they affirm the chosenness of Judah[21]—but they fail to recognize that their present καιρός stands under the 'wrath' and not the 'love of God'.[22] The intrinsic world of the Jeremiah text, however, is for the most part clear and unequivocal. It claims that the present moment stands under the *Zorn* of Yahweh, and Babylonian hegemony is not only a political reality but also a 'theo-political' reality. R.P. Carroll suggests in this regard that 'movements of support for the king in exile, opposition to the Babylonians and beliefs in Jerusalem as the centre of divine activity are all dismissed in favour of Babylonian hegemony and the permanence of life in Babylon for the exiles of 597'.[23] In other words, rebellion against Babylon is equivalent to rebellion against Yahweh, and submission to Babylon is viewed as compliance to Yahweh's will. Outsider Babylon has been afforded the role of 'servant' to exact punishment on wayward and rebellious Judah. Jeremiah announces 'not only that Babylon will triumph but, aston-ishingly, that Yahweh wills the triumph of Babylon. "Pax Babylonia" is the plan of Yahweh.'[24]

Nebuchadrezzar plays a somewhat ambivalent role in the book's treatment of Judah's fate as a nation. He is referred to as Yahweh's instrument of wrath (21.2, 4, 7; 25.9, 11, 12; 27.6, 8, 12; etc.) as well as his servant (25.9; 27.6; see also 43.10), although following the completion of his mission, he will then in turn be punished (25.11; 27.7).[25] As

21. T.W. Overholt, 'Jeremiah 27–29: The Question of False Prophecy', *JAAR* 35 (1967), p. 241. See also T.W. Overholt, *The Threat of Falsehood: A Study in the Theology of the Book of Jeremiah* (Naperville, IL: Allenson, 1970).

22. E. Osswald, *Falsche Prophetie im alten Testament* (Tübingen: J.C.B. Mohr, 1962), p. 22.

23. Carroll, *Jeremiah*, pp. 102-103.

24. W. Brueggemann, 'The Book of Jeremiah: Portrait of the Prophet', *Int* 37 (1983), p. 140.

25. These references to Nebuchadnezzar as Yahweh's servant are from the more

Yahweh's servant or vassal, Nebuchadrezzar cannot be opposed. Non-compliance to his decrees is denounced as false and viewed as direct insubordination to Yahweh. The implications of these theo-political developments are astonishing. 'The king in Judah is no longer Yahweh's servant, shepherd, anointed. The king has forfeited his role, and therefore the linkage of Yahweh and Judah is jeopardized if not broken.'[26]

Approaching 'barbarians' thus play an important role in the book. Nonetheless, while enemies invade sacred space from outside, *they rarely contribute to fear of encroachment, contingency and danger in Jeremiah. Enemies from the outside are employed in the fragile world of Jeremiah as servants of Yahweh, as subservient instruments of God's judgment upon lawbreaking and obdurate insiders who bring disaster upon themselves.* As such, they produce cohesion rather than counter-coherence.

4. *Characterization of the Boundaries as Inverted*

We do not find, in the intrinsic world of Jeremiah, the establishment of boundaries intended to prevent incursions; nor do we find a social environment which attempts to banish outsiders beyond the borders of the *oikoumenē*. Instead, enemies from beyond the borders *cement* group solidarity and give inner cohesion. This solidarity and cohesion is not envisaged by setting insiders and outsiders in opposition, and dehumanizing the latter. Instead, outside forces, whether Babylonian, the 'enemy from the north', or other agents from distant places, are employed in a morally exacting universe to punish undesirable and unacceptable social behavior of insiders. Nearly every reference to an assault by invading armies in the book is accompanied by and related integrally to the prophet's charge that the community has rejected the hierarchical arrangements headed by Yahweh. Judah, for example, is accused of 'not listening' (3.13, 25; 7.27; etc.), 'playing the harlot' (2.20-25, 33-37; 3.1-10; etc.), 'trusting in lies' (7.4, 8; 13.25; cf. 27.16; 28.15), 'forgetting' or 'forsaking' Yahweh (3.21; 5.7; 13.25), 'stubbornness'

---

developed and later MT. Nonetheless, the Babylonian monarch is seen as the instrument of Yahweh in the earlier common text tradition as well.

26. W. Brueggemann, 'The Book of Jeremiah: Portrait of the Prophet', p. 141. See also W.E. Lemke, 'Nebuchadrezzar My Servant', *CBQ* 28 (1966), pp. 45-50; T.W. Overholt, 'King Nebuchadrezzar in the Jeremiah Tradition', *CBQ* 30 (1968), pp. 3-48; see, however, Jer. 50-51, esp. 51.34 and n. 18 above.

(7.24; 9.14; 11.8; etc.), 'provoking Yahweh to anger' (7.18; 11.17; 32.29; etc.), 'burning incense to other gods' (7.9; 11.12, 13; 19.4; etc.), and 'not inclining the ear' (7.24, 26; 17.23; etc.). As a result, and only as a result of such culpability, there is massive destruction wrought by outsiders—total and inescapable devastation.

Accordingly, the book of Jeremiah views invasion and deportation as the direct consequences of the nation's waywardness and obduracy. Hostile forces are instrumental in punishing guilty Judah and are therefore an integral part of a symmetrical and congruent world in which the non-submissive—that is, persons or groups rejecting the structures of control established by prophetic authority—are silenced and subjugated. Outsiders, thus, do not intrude upon this exacting moral universe; they do not place this coherent and stable world in danger, nor do they threaten to undermine the integrity of the internal boundaries or blur the existing cultural and symbolic lines of distinction. Foreign armies and kings, foes from the north, and all other אֹיְבִים serve to uphold and reinforce the prophetic structures of control. As such, they are rendered powerless and now form an inverted category of 'elect' rather than one of dangerous deviants.[27]

This is an intriguing inversion in light of the contingencies and marked sense of encroachment in the *Sitz im Buch* as well as the external world of the text.[28] The physical and symbolic boundaries of the community have been penetrated by outsiders/barbarians resulting in the collapse of the conventional understandings and perceptions of reality. R.E. Clements observes in this regard that

---

27. Notwithstanding this inversion, the text's coherent system of symbols cannot tolerate barbarians to go unchecked and unpunished forever—as indicated by the oracles against the nations (chs. 46–51), wherein Yahweh's moral judgment is directed against the foreigner as well.

28. For an excellent discussion of the literary and referential character of prophetic texts, see the very lively and incisive discussions of A.G. Auld, R.P. Carroll and T.W. Overholt, in this volume. Contemporary studies of language have made us more aware that the transition from orality to writing involves symbolic shifts and transformations. 'Writing is not merely an exterior tool, but a practice that alters human consciousness to the degree to which it is…"interiorized"' (G. Baumann [ed.], *The Written Word: Literacy in Transition* [Oxford: Clarendon Press, 1986], p. 3). Epistemological questions regarding the literary and referential nature of texts will no doubt continue to be addressed in greater detail and depth in the coming years.

at one stroke the year 587 witnessed the removal of the two institutions—the temple and the Davidic kingship—which stood as symbolic assurances of God's election of Israel. Their loss was greater than a loss of national prestige and left the entire understanding of Israel's special relationship to Yahweh its God in question.[29]

The *Unheil* associated with 598/587, therefore, dealt a deathblow to the complex of 'self-evident' assumptions, values and social meanings shared by the community prior to the first quarter of the sixth century. W. Brueggemann can argue with force that 587 serves as a metaphor for the 'end of the known world and its relinquishment'.[30] Exile, however, marks not only the end but also the advent of a social and religious reorientation involving the dismantling of old paradigms and domain assumptions for new approaches to reality to be embraced by the *gōlâ* in Babylon.

Consequently, many of the root metaphors and sacred symbols employed to 'keep straight' the internal lines of Judah's social system, to reinforce social and cosmic restraints, and *to define clearly boundaries that differentiate insiders from outsiders* are blurred, transformed and/or inverted. These symbolic shifts include: Judah, once chosen, is now rejected, or redefined, whereas Babylon, once rejected, is now chosen as an instrument of divine judgment. The land (of Judah) is rejected as sacred space and is deemed unfit for habitation (see e.g. 24.1-10), whereas Babylon—once regarded as profane space—is now transformed into 'sacred space' chosen for habitation by the *gōlâ*. The Davidic dynasty is renounced (see, however, salvific promises for the Davidic dynasty in, for example, 23.5-6; 33.14-26) and threatened with extinction (see e.g. 21.1–24.10), while Nebuchadnezzar, king of Babylon, is chosen as Yahweh's עבד, the servant of the Lord.

Even the temple cultus, once the source of security and confidence for the state, is now rendered impotent and threatened with destruction (e.g. 7.1-15). The royal-temple ideology, W. Brueggemann suggests,

> articulated in the Jerusalem establishment, fostered by the king and articulated by temple priests, claimed that the God of Israel had made irrevocable promises to the temple and the monarchy, had taken up permanent residence in Jerusalem, and was for all time a patron and

29. R.E. Clements, *Jeremiah* (Interpretation: A Bible Commentary for Teaching and Preaching; Atlanta: John Knox, 1988), p. 6.

30. W. Brueggemann, *Hopeful Imagination: Prophetic Voices in Exile* (Philadelphia: Fortress Press, 1986), p. 4.

guarantor of the Jerusalem establishment. Jeremiah's work only makes sense as an antithetical response to that ideology.[31]

The disaster of 587 put an end to the conventional royal-temple assertions. As a result of this experience of dissonance, Judah's symbol systems are in the process of restructuring,[32] and long-standing distinctions between 'us' and 'them' are blurred and at times reconceptualized.

5. Bad Insiders and the Resultant Environment of Moral Dissonance

Blame for the experience of dissonance and for resultant shifts in hierarchical arrangements is thus never placed directly upon 'foreigners' or 'barbarians'. The presence of dissymmetry in the book of Jeremiah is most often associated with malevolent forces inside the community structures. *Bad insiders*—indigenous outsiders—pose a profound threat to those who adhere to social and cosmic restraints (see e.g. 11.18-23; 12.1-6; 15.15-21; 17.14-18; 18.19-23; 20.7-13).[33] Moreover, Jeremiah's survival is continuously threatened not only by bad insiders but particularly by groups located at the upper tiers of the social hierarchy, that is, by priests (e.g. 20.1-6; 29.24-32) and (*pseudo-*)prophets (e.g.

---

31. Brueggemann, *Jeremiah 1–25*, pp. 5-6.
32.

> A time of crisis and the responses it generates is the best time to observe how structures react, disintegrate and are reconstructed. The crisis brought on by the collapse of Jerusalem in 587 led to the eventual editing of prophetic traditions that had announced such a disaster (e.g. Jeremiah, Ezekiel), brought to an end the history of the kings of Israel and Judah (the deuteronomic history) and was lamented in a collection of poems about the fall of the city (Lamentations)

(R.P. Carroll, *When Prophecy Failed: Cognitive Dissonance in the Prophetic Traditions of the Old Testament* [New York: Seabury, 1979], pp. 157-58).

33. The greatest evidence of this intrusive force and of good insiders floundering and suffering unjustly as a result of these wanton individuals is found in the so-called 'Confessions of Jeremiah'. See W. Baumgartner, *Die Klagegedichte des Jeremia* (Giessen: Töpelmann, 1917 [ET *Jeremiah's Poems of Lament* (Sheffield: Almond Press, 1988)]); A.R.P. Diamond, *The Confessions of Jeremiah in Context: Scenes of Prophetic Drama* (Sheffield: JSOT Press, 1987); K.M. O'Connor, *The Confessions of Jeremiah: Their Interpretation and Role in Chapters 1–25* (Atlanta: Scholars Press, 1988); M.S. Smith, *The Laments of Jeremiah and their Contexts* (Atlanta: Scholars Press, 1990). For an excellent bibliography of the Jeremianic laments see Diamond, *The Confessions of Jeremiah in Context*, pp. 283-91.

23.9-40; 14.11-16; 27–28), as well as by kings and those who govern with them (e.g. 21; 22.1-9; 36.11-32; 37.11-15; 38.1-6).

In the internal world of Jeremiah, therefore, a category of dangerous enemies co-exists within the defined boundaries and is encountered by the righteous somewhat regularly. Furthermore, this category of wanton individuals wields enough power to harm good insiders and to skew the stability of the established hierarchical arrangements of the universe. As a result, the literary world of Jeremiah 'the prophet'—the servant of Yahweh and insider par excellence—is a place of extreme vulnerability.[34] It is a harsh and perilous setting because few social and symbolic channels exist to protect good insiders from deviant persons. With such little insulation from enemies, it is no wonder that the language of adversity and suffering enjoys a wide semantic and symbolic range in the book.[35]

Accordingly, not only do the wicked—insiders living outside the accepted symbol system—go unpunished, but the righteous—those who do Yahweh's bidding (i.e. Jeremiah)—suffer unjustly. Jeremiah the righteous suffers hardship from his enemies, is ridiculed, cries to Yahweh for help, seeks vengeance on his persecutors, and even curses the day of his birth (20.14-18). The opponents of the prophet threaten to kill him unless he abandons his prophetic mission (11.18-23); they conspire against him (18.18-23; cf. 11.9) and dig pits to trap him (18.22); those who pursue Jeremiah attempt to 'prevail' over him (20.7-13); they arrest and imprison him (20.1-6; 37.11-16) and bar him from the temple precincts (36.5). Jeremiah, however, never responds to this adversity penitentially. Rather, not unlike Job or the embattled psalmist of the laments, he incessantly declares his innocence, expresses hostility towards those who mistreat him (11.20; 12.3; 15.15; 17.18; 18.21-22; 20.12), and prays for the restoration of justice and moral coherence.

34. It is difficult to imagine that the persona of Jeremiah does not reflect a group ethos of some sort. To some degree, Jeremiah's marked sense of impotence and scarcity represents the anguish of a sector in the larger community that feels itself in grave danger. The world of Jeremiah thus represents a social network beyond the boundaries of any single figure in history. Wilson, Lang and others contend that the prophet reflects some social grouping, whether it be the prophet's own support group or a subsequent grouping which adapts the prophet's words to its own network of meanings.

35. J. Muilenburg, 'The Terminology of Adversity in Jeremiah', in H.T. Frank and W.L. Reed (eds.), *Translating and Understanding the Old Testament* (Nashville: Abingdon Press, 1970), p. 45.

Notwithstanding his declaration of innocence, Jeremiah is tormented by this environment of dissonance. He suffers 'incurable pain' but not as a consequence of wrongdoing. Jeremiah has maintained his personal and prophetic integrity. He has practiced uncompromising obedience and has even encountered the anticipated social disdain (15.15-18; see also 18.19-20). Consequently, his anguish and suffering appear gratuitous or at least rationally unmanageable. A causal connection between misfortune and moral wrongdoing is untenable. Caged in the inexplicable, Jeremiah indicts Yahweh for his unreliability and 'deception' (e.g. 12.1-4; 15.18; 20.7).

The hostile forces presenting a grave danger to well-defined social and symbolic boundaries include not only unnamed enemies (most often), kin-group members, persons located at the upper tiers of the social hierarchy, and close friends (אֱנוֹשׁ שְׁלֹמִי, 20.10), but also *Yahweh himself*. That is to say, the forces that threaten the world of Jeremiah and contribute to the undoing of order and symmetry are both human and divine. How could such moral discord exist without Yahweh being an active participant (see 4.10; 12.1-4; 15.18; 20.7-12; etc.)! Even though there is some hope for future vindication and a restoration of moral equilibrium (see e.g. the language of vengeance, 12.3; 17.18; 18.21-23; also note divine promises of assurance, 15.19-20; and expressions of confidence, 20.11-12), the 'adversarial' role of Yahweh heightens the profound sense of anxiety. There is little protection from the hostility, since God is perceived as sharing in it. So, the world of Jeremiah the prophet is precarious and beset with incongruities; it reflects internal anxiety and a marked sense of powerlessness. Jeremiah is under siege by forces—divine and human— beyond his control. Bad insiders and even Yahweh himself threaten to undermine the orderly arrangements of the universe; as a result, the survival of good insiders is at risk.

6. *Two Codes in Conflict*

This hostile and unpredictable environment stands in stark contrast to that in which dangerous outsiders are tamed and employed to uphold and reinforce a morally exacting universe. In the latter, boundaries are clear and well-defined. *Good* insiders are safe and insulated from the perils posed by enemies, that is, by those persons and groups that reject and live outside the social order. *Bad* insiders are punished for their wrongdoing, a punishment that is just and fully deserved. This world is predictable and morally unambiguous; conduct and condition are directly correlated. A culpable community is responsible for bringing the mass destruction upon itself. In one stroke, the presence of outsiders or barbarians is justified, and invasion and conquest are made rationally manageable.

This representation of symbolic coherence is perhaps most clearly evident in the so-called Deuteronomistic prose discourses.[36] In the punitive universe of 'C', misfortune is always explicable; it is the direct consequence of divine punishment for non-compliance to Yahweh's dictates. Consequently, outsiders or foreigners pose no 'real' threat to the internal boundaries; instead, they serve to keep straight these markers by sustaining and reinforcing symbolic congruence and stability.

This ideological system of congruence is also present in the book's oracular utterances. While the language of 'A' is far more imaginative than that of the prose sermons,[37] it too blames the whole nation, and especially its ruling class (see 2.1-37; 4.5-9; 5.1-31), for the mass destruction by invasion. Moral symmetry is maintained at all cost. Counter-coherence in the symbol system, such as innocent or inexplicable suffering, is alien and forcefully denied.

Although the 'B' material depicts the world of Jeremiah as hostile and incongruous, his rejection and suffering, as J. Rosenberg rightly observes, 'underscore the Deuteronomic theme of an embattled prophetic tradition and set the destruction of Jerusalem and Judah firmly into the framework of reciprocal justice that shaped the Deuteronomistic history as a whole...'[38]

Even the 'Confessions' of Jeremiah, with their raw expressions of rage, have been tamed by their placement within the Deuteronomistic framework of chs. 1–25.[39] In context the prophet's rejection and attack

---

36. L. Stulman, *The Prose Sermons of the Book of Jeremiah: A Redescription of the Correspondences with the Deuteronomistic Literature in the Light of Recent Text-Critical Research* (SBLDS, 83; Atlanta: Scholars Press, 1986); J.M. Ward, *Thus Says the Lord: The Message of the Prophets* (Nashville: Abingdon Press, 1991), pp. 150-70.

37. See S. Mowinckel's poignant comparison of the 'A stratum' and the 'C source' in *Zur Komposition des Buches Jeremia* (Kristiania: Jacob Dybwad, 1914), pp. 33-39.

38. J. Rosenberg, 'Jeremiah and Ezekiel', in R. Alter and F. Kermode (eds.), *The Literary Guide to the Bible* (Cambridge, MA: Harvard University Press, 1987), p. 190.

39. For the placement of the laments in context, see R.E. Clements, 'Jeremiah 1–25 and the Deuteronomistic History', in A.G. Auld (ed.), *Understanding Poets and Prophets: Essays in Honour of George Wishart Anderson* (Sheffield: JSOT Press,

by enemies—that is to say, the presence of counter-coherence—no longer speak with the same compelling force and clarity. Now the poems function to 'make sense of the nonsense of exile', and as such they tend to support and uphold a symbolic representation of social and cosmic cohesion. Examining the macrostructures of chs. 1–25, R.E. Clements contends that in the present Deuteronomistic environment Jeremiah is

> the paradigmatic illustration of the degree of total national rejection of the message of the prophets... Now the figure of Jeremiah, typified in his rejection, serves to make plain that Israel has not kept the covenant and must suffer the inevitable curse spelled out in Jer. 11.1-8.[40]

Anomie serves to reinforce symmetrical and orderly hierarchical arrangements.

The former *Weltanschauung*—embodied in the untamed persona of Jeremiah—is far different. Boundaries of this world are ambiguous and ill-defined. Here we encounter an arbitrary, or at least morally inexacting, universe in which wrongdoing goes unpunished and obedience and fidelity are not (immediately) rewarded. Innocent suffering is a *given* in life, and misfortune is not attributed to moral failings. Gratuitous suffering is accepted, without resorting to 'high-grid' explanations. There is no assurance, moreover, that justice will prevail since good insiders enjoy little protection from social evil-doers. Attempts to repress undesirable behavior and to preserve social cohesion are apparently unsuccessful. Members of the community who do not recognize cosmic restraints go unchecked. As a result, contact with such persons is unavoidable and potentially harmful. This lack of protection and moral symmetry results in anxiety and vulnerability.

To heighten the level of anxiety and risk, the dangers from within, as we have seen, derive at least in part from the upper tiers of the social hierarchy (i.e. from the king, military, royal court, priests, prophets, as well as the land owning nobility).[41] Bad kings, bad priests, bad prophets

---

1993), pp. 93-113; see also W. Thiel, *Die deuteronomistische Redaktion von Jeremia 1–25* (Neukirchen–Vluyn: Neukirchener Verlag, 1973); Diamond, *Jeremiah's Confessions in Context*; O'Connor, *The Confessions of Jeremiah*.

40. Clements, 'Jeremiah 1–25 and the Deuteronomistic History', p. 102.

41. B. Lang, *Monotheism and the Prophetic Minority* (Sheffield: Almond Press, 1983), pp. 64-70. Mark S. Smith suggests that

> the 'enemies' presented in the laments opposed the true work of Yahweh embodied in the prophet's message; moreover, their refusal to hear his word resulted in their following false prophets. The enemies largely left unnamed in the laments emerge

are the voices of mendacity; they are the enemies; they reject the divinely established boundaries of 'legitimate' prophetic authority and engage in activities that place the welfare of the 'righteous' in jeopardy. They do not submit to the established systems of control and are therefore stigmatized in the book with labels of outsider.

Moreover, Yahweh himself is perceived as a dangerous part of this environment. Yahweh is so dangerous because he shatters all systems of control. He is neither outsider or insider. *He is an 'untamed' participant who can not be controlled or manipulated.* As such, he supports but does not always protect; he is petitioned but is not always responsive. He does not bring internal order but seemingly contributes to its chaos. Yahweh does not destroy the wicked or defend the righteous (12.1-4; cf. however, Yahweh's threat against the people of Anathoth in 11.21-22). Rather, Yahweh stands against Jeremiah and demands greater loyalty (12.5-6; 15.19-20). On a surface semantic level, therefore, this world (i.e. the wild world of Jeremiah's laments in particular) is a perilous place fraught with uncertainty.

On another semantic level, however, this environment of enraged suffering most likely represents attempts of later (or perhaps earlier!) interpretative communities to explore and resolve the social and religious incongruities present in their own networks of meaning. R.P. Carroll argues cogently that the world of the Jeremianic laments represents a 'protest on behalf of the innocent and the righteous who seek divine vindication through prayers and lament'.[42] He sees the origins of this viewpoint 'in circles which, like the producers of the laments in the Psalms, recognized a polarity of righteous and wicked within the one community'.[43]

P. Welten contends that Jeremiah gradually became identified with the exemplary righteous sufferer of the post-exilic period in two ways. 'Diese Identifikation geschieht einerseits durch die Einfügung biographischer Element in der Konfessionen, anderseits durch die Einfügung

in the following narratives *as the nation's leaders—all the people (cf. 11.2; 13.13; 18.6, 11; 19.3), including priests, prophets and kings'* (itals. are mine) (Smith, *The Laments of Jeremiah and their Contexts*, p. 41).

42. Carroll, *Jeremiah*, p. 49.

43. Carroll, *Jeremiah*, p. 47; see, however, T.W. Overholt, 'Prophecy in History. The Social Reality of Interpretation', *JSOT* 48 (1990), pp. 3-29. 'Prophecy is at home in times of crisis, and at such times differences of opinion are bound to arise' (p. 15).

der Konfessionen in den erzählenden Text des zu jener Zeit weitgehend vollständigen Jeremiabuches.'[44] According to Welten, this persona of the prophet counters a retributive theology that could no longer adequately make sense of anomie—a milieu in which righteous segments of the community would suffer for no apparent reason. The innocent suffering of good insiders found its justification in the suffering of Jeremiah. Misfortune would no longer be viewed as 'shameful, resulting from wrongdoing...but rather as a typical part of life'.[45] 'Diese sichtbar gemachte Leiden ist vielmehr ein Aufruf zur Bewältigung.'[46]

Consequently, the text privileges Jeremiah, the servant of Yahweh, as the insider par excellence, and as the *Imago der Armenfrömmigkeit*; he faces failure, abuse and rejection on account of his mission; the 'powerless' and scorned prophet is exiled to a faraway country. If Jeremiah encounters such hostility, should not the exiles in Babylon or the repatriates who return to Judaea expect the same? In a sense, these exiles in Babylonia or Judaean repatriates (as producers or recipients of

44. P. Welten, 'Leiden und Leidenserfahrung im Buch Jeremia', *ZTK* 74 (1977), p. 149.

45. Welten, 'Leiden', p. 149.

46. Welten, 'Leiden', p. 149; see also A.H.J. Gunneweg, 'Konfession oder Interpretation im Jeremiabuch', *ZTK* 67 (1970), pp. 395-416, who posits that Jeremiah's suffering in his 'Confessions' was employed by the community to depict the exemplary sufferer, that is, one who suffers as a result of obedience and fidelity to a vocation. Cf. O.H. Steck, *Israel und das gewaltsame Geschick der Propheten: Untersuchungen zur Überlieferung des deuteronomistischen Geschichtsbildes im alten Testament, Spätjudentum und Urchristentum* (WMANT, 23; Neukirchen–Vluyn: Neukirchener Verlag, 1967). Reading the 'Confessions' as self-referring statements of Jeremiah, von Rad concludes that in these poems

> the ultimate hopelessness of genuine prophetic service is recognized; but it is not merely recognized—it has burst into Jeremiah's life as suffering and is now something the prophet endures. Isaiah and Micah were solely proclaimers of God's word; in the case of Jeremiah something new in God's working through prophets presents itself. This man serves God not only with the bold proclamation of his mouth (his person), but his very life is unexpectedly involved in God's cause on earth. Thus the prophet... now becomes a witness to God not only by virtue of his charisma, but in his humanity—yet not as the person who is triumphant over human sin, not as the person who is gaining the victory, but as the messenger of God going down to destruction in the midst of humanity. Therefore even the bios of Jeremiah now takes on the authority of a witness. His suffering soul, his life bleeding to death in God's task—all this becomes a pointer towards God.

(G. von Rad, 'The Confessions of Jeremiah', trans. A.J. Ehlin, in J.L. Crenshaw [ed.], *Theodicy in the Old Testament* [Philadelphia: Fortress Press, 1983], p. 98).

the book) are the true insiders. Against overwhelming odds, they must face the challenge of creating a new life following devastation and disorientation. In either social location, the greatest opposition to the work of 'rebuilding' now derives from forces at work within the community instead of those operative outside its boundaries.

7. Conclusion

Two worlds co-exist in the intrinsic network of meanings that we have explored in the Jeremiah book; two disparate speech and cosmological codes find expression in the material we have examined.[47] One is orderly and congruent; its symbolic structures and social categories are clearly defined. This world is moral and stable, exacting punishment on wrongdoers and insulating good insiders from harm. The other, embodied in the wild persona of the prophet untamed by the Deuteronomists, is dangerous and unstable and marked by anxiety and vulnerability. Suffering and dissymmetry are primarily construed here as the product of forces inside the existing social structure.

Ironically, *outsiders* play a more integral part in the former world. They are employed to reinforce and 'keep straight' the internal boundaries; as a result, their place in the world is justified. Moreover, *unlike Jeremiah*, they are successful in their mission, which is not only to punish guilty Judah but also to establish a new military-political order in Babylon (cf. the role and function assigned to Cyrus in Isa. 40–55).

Taken together, both worlds of Jeremiah are witness to the dissolution and dismantling of life as it was once known. Both attempt to make sense of the nonsense of exile and post-exilic contingency and scarcity. Both dare to map out a new social and symbolic terrain during a period of great liminality. The 'givens' or 'a prioris' of a safe and congruent old order, with claims of chosenness and clear lines of distinction between insider and outsider, are no longer present. The old world is 'gone with the wind'. The voices of the text agree, however, that the losses are not the last word but themselves pave the way for new and profound understandings of reality. For only with the dissolution of the old is a future of hope made possible. The now world of the text is the topsy-

---

47. There are obviously many social environments and an amalgam of voices and codes embedded in the text. Taken together, the book of Jeremiah in its present form(s) is a polyphonic theodicy. It seems to me that the deuteronomistic voice is the dominant one under which others are to a certain extent subsumed.

turvy world of Jeremiah, for insiders have become outsiders and outsiders enjoy an ambivalent yet sanctioned place in this newly emergent
world. No longer can blame be placed on the barbarian. The amalgam of
voices, meanings and codes embedded in the text converge and speak
with clarity that the most perplexing problems facing the interpretative
communities lie with 'us' more than 'them'.

JSOT 57 (1993), pp. 99-119

PORTRAYING PROPHECY: OF DOUBLETS, VARIANTS
AND ANALOGIES IN THE NARRATIVE REPRESENTATION
OF JEREMIAH'S ORACLES—RECONSTRUCTING
THE HERMENEUTICS OF PROPHECY

A.R. Pete Diamond

1. *Introduction*

The modern critical interpreter of the so-called biographical narratives in
Jeremiah has been set a problem in reading. Faced with an account that
exists overall in dischronologized format, the critical interpreter attempts
to correlate the various temporally related episodes only to encounter
numerous inconsistencies.[1] Nowhere has this been felt more keenly than
in the prophetic oracles. The search for consistency of theme in
Jeremiah's message to the post-597 community in Jerusalem has seemed
almost impossible to discern.[2]

---

1.   These range from matters related to the historical and chronological setting of
the episode; to the personnel involved; to spatial location of the action; to diverse data
providing local color; to the orientation of the main characters toward the issues of
narrative concern and focus. For an accessible overview of the phenomena, see
R.P. Carroll, *Jeremiah: A Commentary* (OTL; London: SCM Press, 1986), pp.
669-750.

2.   I have in mind those oracles set within the reign of Zedekiah. The cases have
been much discussed. From the beginning of his reign, the prophet offers the
possibility of continued existence in submission to Babylonian hegemony (Jer. 27–
29) only to contravene these statements in 29.15-20 by predicting categorical
destruction: ונתתי אותם כתאנים הרשעים אשר לא תאכלנה מרע (29.17; cf. 24.1-10). By
and large the oracles during the final siege predict categorical destruction for the city,
king and people (32.1-5; 34.1-7; 37–38) but in 34.4-5 the prophet can still predict a
peaceful death for the king and in 38.17-23 offer the king an alternative that will
spare not only the king's life but also prevent the city from being burned. Along with

Current redaction critical study seeks to resolve this interpretative problem by analyzing the extant narrative into discreet self-consistent editorial layers.[3] The inconsistencies are interpreted as seams; the present narrative is declared unreadable; readability is effected by interpreting the text in its diachronic forms.[4]

The attractiveness of the redactional models is aided by the undeniable presence of these inconsistencies. Yet what renders such features 'problematic' to the critical reader should also be ascribed, in part, to a hermeneutics of prophecy underlying the modern reading of prophetic texts—that is, given a common historical occasion, inconsistent and contradictory oracles by one and the same prophet raise questions about the intelligibility, not to say the sanity, of the prophet, if the reader is seriously expected to correlate these oracles to the same setting. This, however, raises the question why the ancient editor(s) would have expected the narrative to be readable (an implicit contract between the author and reader) in its present form. For even if we are convinced of

these tensions in the narratives one should also note the prose sermons correlated within the same historical occasion (24.1-10; 21.1-10).

3. The major recent studies are: K.-F. Pohlmann, *Studien zum Jeremiabuch: Ein Beitrag zur Frage nach der Entstehung des Jeremiabuches* (FRLANT, 118; Göttingen: Vandenhoeck & Ruprecht, 1978); H. Migsch, *Gottes Wort über das Ende Jerusalems: Eine literar-, stil-, und gattungskritische Untersuchung des Berichtes Jeremia 34,1-7; 32, 2-5; 37,3-38, 28* (Österreichische Biblische Studien, 2; Klosterneuburg: Österreichisches Katholisches Bibelwerk, 1981); C.R. Seitz, 'The Crisis of Interpretation over the Meaning and Purpose of the Exile', *VT* 35 (1985), pp. 78-97; *idem, Theology in Conflict: Reactions to the Exile in the Book of Jeremiah* (BZAW, 176; Berlin: de Gruyter, 1989). Important older studies are: B. Duhm, *Das Buch Jeremia* (Kurzer Handkommentar zum Alten Testament, 11; Tübingen: Mohr [Paul Siebeck], 1901); H. Kremers, 'Leidensgemeinschaft mit Gott im Alten Testament', *EvT* 13 (1953), pp. 122-40; P.R. Ackroyd, 'Historians and Prophets', *SEÅ* 33 (1968), pp. 18-54; *idem, Exile and Restoration: A Study of Hebrew Thought of the Sixth Century* (OTL; London: SCM Press, 1968); E.W. Nicholson, *Preaching to the Exiles: A Study of the Prose Tradition in the Book of Jeremiah* (Oxford: Basil Blackwell, 1970); G. Wanke, *Untersuchungen zur sogenannten Baruchschrift* (BZAW, 122; Berlin: de Gruyter, 1971); W. Thiel, *Die deuteronomistische Redaktion von Jeremia 1–25* (WMANT, 41; Neukirchen: Neukirchener Verlag, 1973); *idem, Die deuteronomistische Redaktion von Jeremiah 26–45* (WMANT, 52; Neukirchen–Vluyn: Neukirchener Verlag, 1981).

4. For a broad theoretical discussion of the problems in reading posed by the Hebrew Bible for the critical reader see J. Barton, *Reading the Old Testament: Method in Biblical Study* (Philadelphia: Westminster Press, 1984).

the correctness of the redactional model, nevertheless the editor did not tell his account by telling different versions. On the foundation of many traditions, not all harmonious, this editor offers the reader only one.

This paper will investigate the narrative management of prophetic oracles in the tradition. The aim is to elucidate the way in which an editor's assumptions about the nature of prophecy shape his narrative portrayal. Recent developments in narrative poetics and the two edition model of the Jeremiah text tradition will provide methodological orientation.

2. Analysis

Research has long been convinced of the theological or ideological nature of the so-called biographical narratives. The contemporary study of biblical narrative reinforces this perception by showing the presence of a latent ideological dimension in the narrative representation of reality.[5] Attention to this latent ideological level with regard to the nature of prophecy/prophetic speech can go a long way in clarifying the editor's compositional strategy. The glaring tensions in the prophetic oracles addressed to Zedekiah will be the focus of this study. As a test probe, the weight of the analysis will be on the narratives of the final siege in chs. 37–38. I begin by examining the story as it is represented in the Hebrew *Vorlage* to the LXX (Jer.[1]).

2.1. *The Narrative Context of the Oracles in Jer.[1] (LXXV)[6]*
Plot Episode 1 (37.3-16). This episode is composed of two scenes. The first scene (vv. 3-10) is constructed to highlight a conflict over the nature of prophetic mission.

The royal mission makes a request for intercession (נא בעדנו התפלל).

---

5.   M. Sternberg, *The Poetics of Biblical Narrative: Ideological Literature and the Drama of Reading* (Indiana Literary Biblical Series; Bloomington, IN: Indiana Unversity Press, 1985); R. Alter, *The Art of Biblical Narrative* (New York: Basic Books, 1981).

6.   In a previous paper presented to the Israelite Prophetic Literature Section of the SBL, I have argued in greater detail that the MT and *Vorlage* to the LXX provide alternative versions of the narrative of the final siege. 'The textual variants represent a sophisticated, creative management of the whole system of meaning constructed by the two narratives'. A.R.P. Diamond, 'Genesis and Poesis in Jer. 37–38: The Story of the Final Siege of Jerusalem in MT and LXX' (unpublished paper, AAR/SBL, 1989).

Given the usage of this terminology,[7] the officials project an understanding of Jeremiah's function that includes efficacious intercessory
power to secure a beneficial oracle. They expect a positive bias. The fact
that Jeremiah's response is oracular indicates that he has understood
their request for intercession as a request for an oracle. But as the
disputational element in v. 9 indicates, although he is aware of the
hopeful interpretation that is desired (הלך ילכו מעלינו), he acts counter
to their expectations and crushes all hope[8] (...לא ילכו).[9] The prophet's
strategy is to offer a *prediction of disaster*[10] categorical in form. On one

---

7.   On התפלל בעד: in non-Jeremianic contexts the intercession is concerned in
most cases to avert divine judgment/wrath in a situation of communal or individual
sin. The intercessor is a 'prophetic' individual (Gen. 20.7; Num. 21.7; Deut. 9.20; 1
Sam. 7.5; 12.19, 23; 1 Kgs 13.6; Job 42.10). It need not, however, be a situation of
impending divine judgment. It can be a situation of distress in which deliverance by
YHWH is desired (1 Sam. 7.8) or more generally for wellbeing and blessing (Ps.
72.15). In Jeremiah (all prose texts), it occurs three times in the sense of intervention
to avert divine wrath and secure wellbeing (7.17; 11.14; 14.11). The other occurences
seem to involve a subtle development of meaning associated with an understanding
of the prophetic office. The root occurs without the idiom בעד in 29.12. There the
idiom התפלל אל is used, meaning 'pray to'. The people's prayers in general will be
answered in the time of the restoration. Notice that in the preceding context (v. 7) the
idiom התפלל בעד occurs in nuance parallel to the idea of general intercession for
well-being (cf. דרש שלום in the same verse). When it is the prophet who needs to אל
התפלל, the answer he receives is in the form of a prophetic oracle (32.16). These
associations must then account for semantic relationship to expressions refering to
oracular inquiry (cf. שאל/דרש הדבר). The expectation, however, of the intercession
idiom implies a positive connotation—to the benefit of the one for whom the request
is made (cf. 42.2, 20 with בעד parallel to v. 4 with התפלל אל).
8.   The prospect of help from the Egyptian force will come to naught; the
Babylonian forces will resume the siege and succeed; the only miracle that can be
expected would be to the favor of the enemy—that is, should the city's defenders
manage to defeat their attackers, then the Babylonian wounded would still be able to
destroy Jerusalem successfully. For later reference, the comprehensive specification
of the extent of the destruction should be noted: not only capture (לכדה), also burning
of the city (שרף באש).
9.   Notice that in v. 7 the prophet had studiously avoided any positive bias in his
rhetoric. To their התפלל בעד, he uses the bias-neutral לדרש.
10.   Except for one feature, the formal characteristics of the oracles as judgment
speech offer no surprises. The usual tropes identified by form critical research are
present, with the exception of an *accusation* or *diatribe* specifying the reason for
judgment. For form critical analysis and terminology see the standard surveys of
prophetic speech: C. Westermann, *Basic Forms of Prophetic Speech* (trans.

thing Jeremiah and the royal commission seem to agree: a prophet does provide inspired interpretation of events significant for the destiny of the community.

In the second scene (vv. 11-16), the plot shifts focus to the eccentric behavior of Jeremiah. In Jer.[1], the narrator manages the gaps surrounding the motivation and intent of the prophet's act in order to heighten ambiguity and suspiciousness. For the reader, the narrator appears to exonerate the prophet from the charge of treason at the outset (v. 12), but the other characters must infer the prophet's intentions in light of the timing of his actions (v. 11).[11] Should the reader side with

H.C. White; London: Lutterworth, 1967); K. Koch, *The Growth of the Biblical Tradition* (trans. S.M. Cupitt; London: A. & C. Black, 1969); J.H. Hayes (ed.), *Old Testament Form Criticism* (San Antonio, TX: Trinity University Press, 1974); G.M. Tucker, 'Prophetic Speech', *Int* 32 (1978), pp. 31-45. These features never occur. In other words the focus of the prophet's oracles is represented as *prediction* or *announcement of judgment*. This point must be modified somewhat; in episodes three (38.1-13) and four (38.14-28a) the oracles are in the form of positive and negative alternatives. This pattern in the third person narratives attracts attention to a distinctive form in the prose sermons which Thiel (*Jeremia 1–25*, pp. 290-95) identified as 'alternative preaching'. An implicit rationale for the *prediction of disaster* of the negative alternative becomes the failure to comply with the conditions of the positive alternative. Still this is quite different from what is usually expected of *accusation* in judgment speech. The contrast is heightened through comparison with the formal representation of judgment speech in Deuteronomistic narrative. To my knowledge, only 3 passages in Deuteronomistic judgment speech fail to include *accusation* (1 Kgs 13.2; 22.1-28; 2 Kgs 20.16-19). The narrative framework for the first and third example makes the basis for judgment clear. The second example takes place in the context of royal inquiry for war oracles. Westermann (*Basic Forms*, pp. 161-63) distinguishes between judgment speech and simple announcement of ill as a response to oracle inquiry. If this is correct, then the background to the formal patterns in Jer. 37–38 would become clear. In any case, the narrator of Jeremiah has produced a distinctive focus in the formal representation of Jeremiah's oracles. In a similar manner this exclusive focus on *prediction* sets these oracles in Jeremiah apart from the patterns in Chronicles. To my knowledge, no judgment oracle occurs in Chronicles without an explicit accusatory element. For general formal discussion of prophetic speech in Chronicles, see Westermann, *Basic Forms*, pp. 163-68; G. von Rad, 'The Levitical Sermon in 1 and 2 Chronicles', in *idem*, *The Problem of the Hexateuch and Other Essays* (trans. E.W. Trueman Dicken; London: Oliver & Boyd, 1965), pp. 267-80. This peculiarity of form is not haphazard on the narrator's part. As we shall see, it relates to the larger logic and theme of their narrative occasions.

11. The military situation remains unchanged (v. 11), thus linking this scene to

the princes' estimation of the prophet? Narrative privilege in v. 12 would suggest not. The identity of Jeremiah's accuser in v. 13, however, complicates the issue. In Jer.[1], the individual is a person with whom Jeremiah has been lodging (אִישׁ אֲשֶׁר יָלוֹן בּוֹ).[12] For the princes the privileged information of the prophet's close associate is enough to validate Saraya's accusation. The reader, however, is caught between the knowledge of the privileged narrator (v. 12) and the knowledge of Jeremiah's privileged associate. Does he betray Jeremiah with a false accusation or does he know hidden motives for Jeremiah's attempted departure that the reader does not see? The episode does not provide closure to this uncertainty for the reader.

Thematically the first episode sets Jeremiah's prophetic mission and word in the context of a quest for state security. From the point of view of the officials, the prophet's exercise of oracular power is eccentric. A second theme is introduced, ironically correlated with the first, and provides a second dimension to the narrative context for Jeremiah's oracles. A frustrated quest for national security now issues in a threat to the prophet's security.

Plot Episode 2 (37.17-21). The action is again initiated by a royal request for an oracle. The narrator, however, shifts plot tension to focus upon the threat that king and prophet represent for each other. For the king the agency of threat is not located merely in the military circumstances but more significantly in the prophet's oracles as *predictions of disaster*. From Jeremiah's perspective, the agency of threat is constituted by the legal mechanisms of state used to punish him for false prophecy. The narrator of Jer.[1] manages the episode in such a way as to enhance the sense of conflict and threat by having the prophet discern in the king's private face a scheming Machiavellian.

In the prophet's eyes, the king's request is motivated out of a quest for personal safety. The specifics of the oracle (v. 17) shift the central issue of the preceding context from the fate of the city in general to the topic of the king's personal destiny. Jeremiah's appeal (vv. 18-20)

---

the timing of the previous situation.

12. For MT בַּעַל פְּקֻדֹת, the LXX reads: ἄνθρωπος, παρ' ᾧ κατέλυε. ἄνθρωπος usually represents אִישׁ/אָדָם; it is not associated elsewhere with בַּעַל. καταλύειν primarily represents לוֹן (16× in OT); in Jer., 3× (שׁכן), 2× (*hiph.* שׁבת); it is never associated elsewhere with פְּקד.

abruptly refocuses the plot action to a judicial[13] proceeding designed to secure his own safety. In it the prophet reveals a sinister Zedekiah directly responsible for his imprisonment, the real threat behind the courtiers (v. 18 in LXX*V*: 2nd sing., כי נתת, 'you put me in prison'),[14] a king who intends to ignore Jeremiah's plea and return the prophet to the life-threatening imprisonment[15] (v. 20 in LXX*V*: ומה תשבני אל בית יהונתן הסופר ולא אמות שם, 'why do you intend to return me to the house of Jonathan the scribe; I will not die there').[16] Behind his illegal imprisonment, the prophet discerns a royal stratagem of intimidation designed to render him more cooperative and secure an oracle of more palatable character.[17] The prophet exposes the royal plot, and openly

13. For discussion of the legal background of terminology and forms employed here and throughout chs. 37–38, see: H.J. Boeker, *Redeformen des Rechtsleben im Alten Testament* (WMANT, 14; Neukirchen–Vluyn: Neukirchener Verlag, 1964); Migsch, *Gottes Wort*, pp. 215-18, 255-66.

14. LXX for v. 18: ὅτι σὺ δίδως με... Contrast MT (Jer.[2]) with 2p. pl.: כי נתתם אותי. The details of the retroversion vary without effect to the result—the king is the sole accused in LXX*V* (Jer.[1]). Alternative retroversions are possible: אתה נתן אותי (Wells, Migsch); נתתני אתה (Duhm); כי נתת אותי (Workman). For discussion see R. Wells, Jr, 'Preliminary Draft—Vorlage' (unpublished paper, 1989), p. 6 n. 31; Migsch, *Gottes Wort*, p. 22 n. 57.

15. If the conjectural emendation in v. 21 is not accepted, then in Jer.[1] the king returns the prophet to the very same place of incarceration (בית הכלא). This creates a significant tension with the formulaic phrase (וישב ירמיהו בהצר המטרה) at the end of the same verse. Cf. the textual variant in v. 21: codices Vaticanus, Sinaiticus and Alexandrinus read οἰκίαν τῆς φυλακῆς (cf. A. Rahlfs, *Septuaginta*). Ziegler emends to αὐλὴν τῆς φυλακῆς = MT. There is no mss. evidence for this conjecture. He bases it, with good reason, on the inner style of the formula בהצר המטרה throughout the episodes. On this view the inner Greek corruption occured by attraction to 37.4, 15, 18. For discussion, see J. Ziegler, *Beiträge zur Ieremias-Septuaginta* (Nachrichten der Akademie der Wissenschaften in Göttingen, 2; Göttingen: Vandenhoeck & Ruprecht, 1958), p. 35; Wells, 'Preliminary Draft', p. 7 n. 36.

16. For LXX (Jer.[1]): καὶ τί ἀποστρέφεις με...καὶ οὐ μὴ ἀποθάνω ἐκεῖ. Contrast MT (Jer.[2]): ואל תשבני...ולא אמות שם, 'Do not return me to the house of Jonathan the scribe lest I die there'. Alternative retroversion: ולמה (Wells). For discussion, see Wells, 'Preliminary Draft', p. 6 n. 34; Migsch, *Gottes Wort*, p. 23 n. 63.

17. Other features of the narrative also serve to support Jeremiah's perception of the king. It was the king who initiated the royal commission in the first place and who hoped for a good result (37.3). The king's delay before initiating this second consultation is suspicious (37.16, ימים רבים). That the king should be evaluated as weak, acting exclusively out of personal cowardice, is undermined by his presentation as the one fully in command (37.3, 17, 21). There is no hesitation on his part to alter

defies its effectiveness, a challenge Jeremiah has already made good by clinging to the rhetoric of disaster in his oracle.

In this episode, the narrator canvasses various perceptions of prophecy in the point of view of his characters. The scheming king's response to Jeremiah's oracular power implies a particular set of assumptions: predictions are not passive statements, rather they are effective shapers of events; the power of prediction is the prophet's to use and so it is politically negotiable. The prophet, on the other hand, does not appear willing at this stage to negotiate.[18] Nevertheless, he is quick to play off the assumption of the king about the effective power of prophetic oracles by issuing his oracle, rhetorically calculated to threaten the king at his point of chief concern—personal security. The king uses the mechanisms of state to threaten Jeremiah; the prophet in turn uses the mechanisms of prophecy as his personal weapon against the king. In v. 19, Jeremiah raises the issue of prophetic conflict and invokes the criterion of prediction/fullfilment to underline his claim to true prophecy. The fact that aspects of Jeremiah's earlier predictions concerning the military circumstances of the Babylonian campaign have received confirmation serves to intensify Jeremiah's claim to oracular power and hence, in the eyes of the king, the prophet's ability to undermine royal safety through his defiant prediction.

Both characters appear to agree about the destiny shaping quality of prophetic oracles. What is interesting is that the king does not tie connotations of fatalistic determinism to this prior assumption. This flies in the face of the categorical, emphatic, rhetorical form of Jeremiah's oracles. Jeremiah's understanding on this point remains opaque, unless the reader is to take the rhetorical form of the oracles at face value. The problem of the function of oracular speech in a context of threat to the person of the prophet emerges as a theme of the story.

publicly and boldly the arrangements of Jeremiah's imprisonment. Jeremiah recognizes the king's power and authority, and advances his legal appeal on the basis of it. The king, however, does not respond to the prophet's request for release. He only changes the circumstances of it. None of these details encourage an interpretation of the king as a weak belated supporter of the prophet.

18. It is uncertain what this indicates about Jeremiah's view of the negotiability of prophecy. The specifics of Jeremiah's oracle, however, are curiously reticent with regard to the mechanism and consequence of Zedekiah's capture and fate at the hand of the Babylonian monarch. Contrast the prior oracles in Episode 1.

Plot Episode 3 (38.1-13). The substantive issues of the third episode pit the security of the state against the security of the prophet. The catalyst for the episode is Jeremiah's continued oracular activity. In contrast to the preceding episodes, the alternative of desertion/surrender emerges coupled to the categorical prediction of disaster (vv. 2-3).[19] It is not clear why these changes have taken place (Does the prophet, in good faith, now provide for the amelioration of the impending defeat?). The princes, however, know how to read the prophet's intentions: Jeremiah engages in sedition. The character of their legal charges suggests assumptions about appropriate and inappropriate use of prophetic power. In their eyes, Jeremiah does the unthinkable by 'interceding' only to secure the state's destruction. For them, the use of oracular power should be dedicated to securing the state's well being (v. 4). They detect no fundamental change in the modulation of form and content of Jeremiah's oracles, but only a calculated attempt to sap the will to continued military resistance; in their eyes the prophet works as an active agent of their downfall.

The narrator's reticence concerning Jeremiah's motivation for modifying his oracle prompts the reader to fill this gap with ironic effect. On the one hand, there is agreement with the princes' assessment of the prophet's strategy, given Jeremiah's behavior in the prior episode. There the prophet employed his oracle as a weapon to defy the king and undermine his stratagem to win security. On the other hand, there is disagreement with the princes' view that such a use of prophetic power is criminal, given the subtle narrative pressure throughout chs. 37–38 to align the reader with Jeremiah as the true prophet (37.2). That pressure makes itself felt in the present episode in the voice of Ebed-Melek, Jeremiah's rescuer. According to Jer.[1], the wording of his appeal to the king is curious (v. 8, LXX*V*): האיש הזה הרעות את אשר עשית להמית מפני הרעב כי אין עודלחם בעיר, '"You have done wrong in that you have put this man to death because of the famine", for there was no longer food in the city'.[20] Not only does he hold the king personally (2nd sing.)

<hr>

19. Also, the prediction no longer speaks of both capture and destruction for the city—the notice of burning has been dropped (contrast 37.8, 10).

20. For LXX on v. 9: ἐπονηρεύσω ἃ ἐποίησας τοῦ ἀποκτεῖναι τὸν ἄνθρωπον τοῦτον ἀπὸ προσώπου τοῦ λιμοῦ, ὅτι οὐκ εἰσὶν ἔτι ἄρτοι ἐν τῇ πόλει. I have taken the ὅτι—clause as narrative comment, not as part of Ebed-Melek's address to the king. Contrast MT (Jer. v. 2): אדני המלך הרעו האנשים האלה את כל אשר עשו לירמיהו הנביא את אשר השליכו אל הבור וימת תחתיו מפני הרעב כי אין הלחם

responsible for injustice, but he also understands the basis for the death penalty not to lie in sedition per se but in the famine that the city currently suffers. One is reminded of the content of the negative alternative in v. 2, death by sword and famine. This discrepancy between Ebed-Melek's understanding of the charge and the charges brought by the princes in v. 4 suggests a ploy to redirect the king's attention to the fulfilment of Jeremiah's prediction.[21] It constitutes an implicit appeal to the prediction–fulfilment scheme and thus reminds king and reader that Jeremiah is a legitimated prophet.

The reader is led to fill the gap[22] regarding the prophet's motivation with an ironic fusion of the perspectives voiced by the princes and Ebed-Melek. To sustain this, the reader is required to see a double-edged moral test of the community, occasioned by the prophetic word. The prophet opens up the possibility of ameliorating the gravity of their defeat. Even the prophet does not view his prior predictions as immune to revision. Here the prophet apparently corroborates Zedekiah's earlier expectation (Episode 2: 37.17-21) that Jeremiah could modify his oracles if he so desired. But Jeremiah differs from the king as regards the criteria he employs in determining the appropriateness of oracular revision. Jeremiah's tack offers the community an opportunity for life on terms compatible with the fundamental direction of his judgment speech, at the same time continuing to undermine their current stratagems for security. When the leaders respond in opposition to Jeremiah, they reveal the extent of the state's religious decay and inability to prove responsive to the prophetic word. Consequently, Jeremiah's prophetic mission works the doom of the community in a manner that preserves the community's moral culpability for the reader. And the narrator persuades the reader to see prophetic speech functioning within a moral nexus that renders it contingent on audience response and posture.[23] Oracles constitute a

עוד בעיר, 'my lord king, these men have done wrong in what they have done to Jeremiah, the prophet, by casting him into the pit so that he may die, for there is no longer food in the city'. For further discussion of the retroversion see: Wells, 'Preliminary Draft', p. 11; Migsch, *Gottes Wort*, p. 27 n. 86.

21. See Pohlmann, *Studien*, p. 80, and Migsch, *Gottes Wort*, p. 57, on this discrepancy and other factors as indicators of a redactional seam.

22. For the concept of gaps in narrative, the strategies of narrators to enlist the reader in the process of filling these informational lacunae, and broad discussion of the phenomenon in biblical narrative, see Sternberg, *Poetics*, pp. 186-229.

23. I.L. Seeligmann ('Die Auffassung von der Prophetie in der deuteronomistischen und chronistischen Geschichtssschreibung', *Congress Volume, Göttingen*

moral test and crisis for the community, provoking the community to self-destruction should it prove recalcitrant or even hostile toward the prophetic mission. Ironically, the oracular power that endangered the prophet also becomes a flexible weapon in the hands of the prophet to defeat his enemies. For the narrator, the moral nexus in which prophecy is operative renders the latter invulnerable to community exploitation and manipulation.

Plot Episode 4 (38.14-28a). The sequencing of the episodes presents the reader with a conflict over conceptions of the prophetic office. The conflict is motivated by a polarity of interests—security versus threat to the safety of city and king, as over against security versus threat to the safety of Jeremiah. The fourth episode draws these plot tensions to an ironic resolution. A curious scene is developed in which the king and prophet bargain for security with oracular utterance as the currency of exchange.

For the narrator of Jer.[1], the war of nerves between prophet and king resolves to the prophet's benefit. Concerned for his safety, the prophet finally secures a guarantee of royal protection (v. 16). Jeremiah modifies his earlier oracle and provides a way of escape from the life-threatening situation for the king.[24] The contrast between the alternatives offered the

1977 [VTSup, 29; Leiden: Brill, 1978], pp. 254-84) notes this feature for 'source C' in Jeremiah and for the Chronicler over against the Deuteronomist. On repentance and the contingency of oracles elsewhere in Jer. prose, see T. Fretheim, 'The Repentance of God: A Study of Jeremiah 18.7-10', *HUCA* 11 (1987), pp. 81-92. I wonder, however, if Seeligmann has correctly detected the character of the Deuteronomist (contrast 2 Kgs 22.15-20 to his thesis) in light of recent work by D. van Winkle ('I Kings 20–22 and True and False Prophecy', in *IOSOT Congress, Louvain* [Beiträge zur Erforschung des AT und des Antiken Judentums, 20; Frankfurt am Main: Peter Lang, 1991], pp. 7-21). The latter has detected a similar feature in the narrative portrayal of prophecy in these chapters of the Deuteronomistic history. Also the Jeremiah narratives extend the contingency to human response to take in treatment of the prophet's person. Seeligmann does observe the latter for Jeremiah.

24. In effect, the prophet individualizes his seditious oracle of 38.2 to the king. Ironically, the king's oath succeeds where persecution and intimidation had failed. Tracing a process of character decay, the narrator depicts a king crumbling in the war of nerves, now ironically too weak to capitalize on the more favorable prophetic oracle (v. 19). Ironically, the episode closes with the safety of the prophet guaranteed by the latter's cooperation with, not defiance of, the royal stratagem for personal safety (v. 27). Also ironically, it is the failure of the prophet's opponents to 'hear' the oracle

king in this episode and the earlier categorical predictions of disaster is surprising. Why does not the narrator have Jeremiah offer the alternatives from the beginning? The prophet's bargaining with oracles in the context of personal threat with the clear motive of securing his own safety raises a troublesome possibility for the reader. The specter is raised of persecution subverting the integrity of oracular speech. Is the prophet trading away his authenticity, exploiting oracular power for reasons of personal security?

The framework of moral contingencies that the narrator erects, however, shields the prophet from such a conclusion. In the third episode, the modified oracle served as a double-edged weapon exposing the corruption of the leadership and testing the resolve of the community to prove responsive to the prophetic counsel. In Episode 4, when the king initially guarantees the safety of the prophet—a sign of his readiness to hear the word—the prophet's prior oracles become revisable. The broader historical and political circumstances have not changed, but the moral ones have! The moral nexus of oracular speech, that is, its contingency upon the audience's posture (repentance–obedience versus impenitence–disobedience), has been extended in the present narrative to include a guarantee of the prophet's personal safety. The prophet may open up a new alternative for the king. Failure to access it, however, reasserts the prophet's prior categorical predictions of disaster. The ironic outcome, in which the king is shattered by Jeremiah's prophetic cooperation, links back to the double-edged moral crisis and test occasioned by the oracular event; culpability is placed squarely on the moral failure of the king[25]/

which foils their scheme of silencing Jeremiah (v. 27, LXX: כי לא נשמע דבר יהוה, 'for they did not hear the word of YHWH'; contrast MT: כי לא נשמע הדבר, 'for they did not hear the conversation').

25. In Jer.[1], this moral failure is underlined all the more by having the king modify his earlier oath out of fear and narrow concern for personal security. He successfully coerces the prophet to conspire with him against his courtiers by personally threatening Jeremiah's life should he not maintain secrecy. I take the threat in v. 24 to have in view the king and not the courtiers as the source of danger. The king, in effect, counters the prophet's threat of v. 18 (ואתה לא תמלט) with a threat of his own, v. 24, ואתה לא תמות (contrast Jer.[2], ולא תמות, which has the king concerned to protect the prophet). The king is only interested in protecting himself from incriminating exposure (v. 25, מה דבר אליך המלך; contrast Jer.[2] which also has מה דברת אל המלך). The king will only honor his oath of protection if Jeremiah will agree to conspire against the princes for the king's safety. The details for this point have been argued in Diamond, 'Genesis and Poesis', pp. 12-13.

audience for the destruction of the community, rather than Jeremiah's failure as a prophet.

Summary. In the creation of this tableau between prophet, king and community, the narrator erects an ideological framework that overcomes the modulations, inconsistencies and shifts in Jeremiah's oracles during the final siege; an appropriate rationalization is provided for them by attention to the moral nexus in which oracular speech functions. My argument implies that the editor's sensitivities toward the Jeremiah tradition, and his interests in the use of it, are shaped by commitment to a particular ideological conception of prophecy. The elucidation of this factor is my next task.

2.2. *The Intertextual Context of the Oracles in Jer.[1] (Chapters 37–38).*
The narrator guides the reader to his underlying code for valuating the 'events' of his story through the construction of intertextual contacts. I refer to the strategy of creating narrative analogies and thematic associations with the Deuteronomistic history as well as intra-Jeremianic analogies created by the juxtaposition of chronologically disparate episodes.

Earlier studies have drawn attention to the stylization of Jeremiah 36 to link this episode in the reign of Jehoiakim to 2 Kings 22–23 and the reign of Josiah.[26] The link serves to contrast Jehoiakim's impiety with Josiah's piety.[27] Similarly, studies have detected in the stylization of Jer. 37.3-10 the creation of an analogy with 2 Kings 18–19.[28] The siege of Jerusalem during Hezekiah's reign provides a contrastive backdrop to the episodes of the final siege in Zedekiah's day.[29]

---

26. C.D. Isbell, 'II Kings 22.3–23.24 and Jeremiah 36: A Stylistic Comparison', *JSOT* 8 (1978), pp. 33-45.

27. Not only does the analogy create a framework for the valuation of the king, but it also enhances the valuation of Jeremiah's prophetic mission, for the authority of Jeremiah's prophecy is equated with that of Torah. Or to put it in Deuteronomistic terms, prophetic speech is subordinated to the Deuteronmic covenantal order and understood in terms of it.

28. S. de Jong, 'Hizkia en Zedekia', *Amsterdamse cahiers voor Exegese en Bijbelse Theologie* 5 (1984), pp. 135-46; Pohlmann, *Studien*, p. 55; Migsch, *Gottes Wort*, pp. 215-22. The latter has detected the analogy throughout Jer. 37–38.

29. This Hezekiah analogy comes to explicit expression in the doublet to Jer. 37.3-10 in 21.1-10 with Zedekiah's hope in v. 2: אולי יעשה יהוה אותנו ככל נפלאתיו ויעלה מעלינו, 'perhaps YHWH will act in accordance with all his wonders so that they break the siege'. So Duhm, *Jeremia*, p. 169; C.H. Cornill, *Das Buch Jeremia*

A second set of associations detected in the Jeremiah tradition also become important for our discussion—namely thematic interest in depicting Jeremiah as standing in the Mosaic succession of prophets.[30] This particular feature illustrates the narrator's preoccupation with the themes of prophetic intercession[31] and with the appeals to prediction–fulfilment criteria[32] in chs. 37–38.

(Leipzig: Chr. Herm. Tauchnitz, 1905), p. 241; W. Rudolph, *Jeremia* (HAT, 12; Tübingen: Mohr [Paul Siebeck], 3rd rev. edn., 1968), p. 135; A. Weiser, *Das Buch Jeremia: Kapitel 25, 15-52, 34* (ATD, 21; Göttingen: Vandenhoeck & Ruprecht, 1977), p. 178 (he sees the possibility of a more general reference to YHWH's saving deeds alongside this allusion); J. Bright, *Jeremiah: A New Translation with Introduction and Commentary* (AB, 21; Garden City, NY: Doubleday, 1965), p. 215; H. Weippert, *Die Prosareden des Jeremiabuches* (BZAW, 132; Berlin: de Gruyter, 1973), p. 71 n. 194; J.A. Thompson, *The Book of Jeremiah* (NICOT; Grand Rapids: Eerdmans, 1980), p. 467; W. McKane, *A Critical and Exegetical Commentary on Jeremiah. I. Introduction and Commentary on Jeremiah I–XXV* (ICC; Edinburgh: T. & T. Clark, 1986), p. 496; Contrast W.L. Holladay, *Jeremiah. I. A Commentary on the Book of the Prophet Jeremiah Chapters 1–25* (Hermeneia; Philadelphia: Fortress Press, 1986), p. 571. Interest in a Hezekiah analogy is present elsewhere in the prose tradition at 26.18-19, where elders defend Jeremiah by appeal to Hezekiah's regard for the sanctity of prophetic individuals. Verses 20-24 contrast Jehoiakim's violent posture to the same issue.

30. W.L. Holladay, 'The Background of Jeremiah's Self-Understanding', *JBL* 83 (1964), pp. 313-24; *idem*, 'Jeremiah and Moses', *JBL* 85 (1966), pp. 17-27; L. Alonso Schökel, 'Jeremias como anti-Moisés', in M. Carrez, *et al.* (eds.), *De la Tôrah au Messie, Mélanges Henri Cazelles* (Paris: Desclée, 1981), pp. 245-54; and C.R. Seitz, 'The Prophet Moses and the Canonical Shape of Jeremiah', *ZAW* 101 (1989), pp. 3-27. This theme surfaces explicitly at Jer. 15.1 in connection with the theme of intercession prohibited—a factor important for the conflicts over prophetic mission in Jer. 37–38.

31. See Seitz, 'The Prophet Moses', who has drawn attention to the intercession/Mosaic model connection.

32. Note Jeremiah's appeal in 37.19 and Ebed-Melek's appeal in 38.9 both discussed above. Also note Jeremiah's appeal in 38.22. The vision report, according to Jer.[1], also makes allusion to the prediction/fulfilment criterion in a context of prophetic conflict: הסיתוך ויכלו לך אנשי שלמך וילינו בחלקלקות רגלך נסגו מאהריך, 'They incited you and prevailed over you, your friends, made your feet rest on slipperiness, (then) they turned away from you'. Cf. LXX: ἠπάτησάν σε καὶ δυνήσονταί σοι ἄνδρες εἰρηνικοί σου καὶ καταλούσουσιν ἐν ὀλισθήμασι πόδας σου, ἀπέστρεψαν ἀπὸ σοῦ. Ziegler (see *Beiträge*, p. 35, for discussion) conjecturally emends καταλύω (Vaticanus, Sinaiticus and Alexandrinus—cf. Rahlfs, *Septuaginta*) to καταδύω based upon confusion of Λ/Δ. The emendation seems influenced primarily by MT. καταδύω occurs 4× in LXX; at Jer. 28(51).64 it

These intertextual and thematic connections permit Deuteronomistic conceptions of prophecy to function as the background code that the narrator enlists in the effort to further his apologetic ends, solve interpretative problems and overcome rhetorical obstacles for his readers. By creating a typological relationship with the Hezekiah narrative, the narrator places the piety of Zedekiah, the refusal of prophetic intercession and the fall of the city in an antipodal relationship to Hezekiah's piety, the successful intercession of Isaiah and the miraculous deliverance of Jerusalem. More important for the present discussion is the ironic effect of this typology on Jeremiah. Naturally one seeks to link Jeremiah with Isaiah, by virtue of prophetic office, only to encounter discontinuity—while Isaiah engages in prophetic intercession to secure the city's deliverance, Jeremiah does not. Jeremiah's function and the content of his oracles link him instead with the Rab-Shakeh and the latter's seditious speeches!

Important verbal and topical echoes exist between the statements of the Rab-Shakeh and Jeremiah's oracles or other plot elements in chs. 37–38. Both the Assyrian courtier and Jeremiah seek to crush hope in an Egyptian relief force (2 Kgs 18.21; cf. Jer. 37.7), and both seek to dissuade people from the deception of hope in a miraculous deliverance (2 Kgs 18.29; 19.10; note, אל ישיא לכם חזקיהו/אל ישאך אלהיך. Cf., Jer. 37.9: אל תשאו נפשתיכם). Both turn from the leadership to offer the inhabitants of the city the alternative of desertion and life (2 Kgs 18.31-32: צאו אלי ...Cf. Jer. 38.2: והיצא אל הכשדים יחיה; and, of course, Jeremiah extends this offer subsequently to the king: 38.17, 21: אם יצא חצא אל/אם מאן אתה לצאת). The desertion speech of the Assyrian is interesting as well, since he promises the deserters that they may 'eat, each one from his own vine and fig, and each one drink the water of his own well' (2 Kgs 18.31) prior to deportation. Attention is drawn to Jeremiah's suspicious attempt to leave the city in order to make a purchase among the people (Jer. 37.12, LXXV: לקנות משם בתוך העם[33]).

---

translates שקע. καταλύω primarily represents לון (14×; cf. 37.13) or שבת (7×). ὀλίσθημα is used elsewhere to represent חלקלקות (4×; cf. 23.12); דחי (2×); or חלקה (1×). See Wells, 'Preliminary Draft', p.16 n.78, for discussion.

33. LXX του ἀγοράσαι does not represent MT לחלק. ἀγοράζω occurs 23× in LXX. It never represents חלק. Statistically the best options are שבר (9×) or קנה (4×). Stylistically, the second of these is preferable for Jeremiah (13×; 9× in 32). שבר never occurs in Jeremiah. Note, however, that in Jeremiah 32 LXX uses κτάομαι to represent קנה. For discussion of the problem and a review of various emendations

The Rab-Shakeh reports in indirect speech a promise he views as false: ולא תנתן את העיר הזאת ביד מלך אשור, 'this city shall not be given into the hand of the king of Assyria' (2 Kgs 18.30; 19.10). Connection to the style and content of Jeremiah's predictions of disaster should be noted: Jer. 37.17, הנתן תנתן העיר הזאת ביד...; 38.3, ביד מלך בבל תנתן; 38.18, נתנה העיר הזאת ביד הכשדים... Also, 2 Kgs 18.3, כי יסית אתכם is echoed by Jer. 38.22, הסיתוך. Further, the link between Jeremiah and the Rab-Shakeh is strengthened through a contrast between Jeremiah and Isaiah. Jeremiah's taunt in Jer. 37.19 regarding the message of his prophetic opponents echoes the wording of Isaiah's oracle in 2 Kgs 19.32, 33, while at the same time undermining its relevance to Zedekiah: לא יבא לא יבא מלך...;ואל העיר הזאת cf. Jer. 37.19 (LXX*V*): לא יבא אל העיר הזאת... בבל על הארץ. Another oracle of Jeremiah ironically echoes Isaiah's oracle of deliverance, undermining its relevance to Jeremiah's situation. Compare 2 Kgs 19.7...הנני נתן בו רוח ושמע שמועה ושב לארצו/'I will put a spirit in him, he will hear a rumour, he will return to his land' to Jer. 37.7, 8: חיל פרעה...שבו לארץ מצרים. ושבו הכשדים...על העיר הזאת, 'Pharaoh's army will return to the land of Egypt; and the Chaldeans will return... against this city' (note also Jer. 37.5: וישמעו הכשדים את שמעם).

With this analogy, the narrator of Jer.[1] risks undermining Jeremiah's authority, for on the surface it enables the reader to view Jeremiah as an agent of the enemy king and a blasphemer (cf. 2 Kgs 19.4). This is where the intra-Jeremianic strategy of achronically related episodes[34] comes to the narrator's rescue. By prefacing Jeremiah 36 to the story of the siege, the narrator can effect a link between Zedekiah and Jehoiakim.[35] The association of Zedekiah with the impiety of Jehoiakim

that have been proposed, see Wells, 'Preliminary Draft', p. 4 n. 20; Migsch, *Gottes Wort*, p. 18-20; W. Holladay, *Jeremiah*. II. *A Commentary on the Book of the Prophet Jeremiah Chapters 26–52* (Hermeneia; Minneapolis: Fortress Press, 1989), p. 265.

34. By utilizing other episodes or doublets (21; 32; 34) of the siege narratives in other contexts, the editor also clears the way for the construction of the Jeremiah 36 and 37–38 narrative analogy.

35. Cf. Jer. 52.2, ככל אשר עשה יהויקים. This has been noted in earlier studies, e.g. Thiel, *Jeremiah 26–45*, p. 52; and esp. E. Martens, 'Narrative Parallelism and Message in Jeremiah 34–38', in C. Evans and W.F. Stinespring (eds.), *Early Jewish and Christian Exegesis: Studies in Memory of William Hugh Brownlee* (Atlanta: Scholars Press, 1987), pp. 33-49. Contrast Migsch, *Gottes Wort*, pp. 195-97, 211-14, who detects a broadly based attempt to contrast Zedekiah and Jehoiakim within the original kernal of the narratives of siege as he reconstructs this. A significant

(who has already been constituted as anti-Josiah by analogy with 2 Kings 22–23) firmly underlines the contrast with the circumstances of Hezekiah's reign. Jeremiah's role in Zedekiah's day is justified and the prophet is defended from the charge of dereliction of prophetic duty—in failing to intercede as Isaiah had done for the community's protection. The network of intertextual associations both sets the criteria of evaluation and guides the reader to make the appropriate judgment of the events of the story. Jeremiah is successfully assimilated to the Deuteronomistic model of prophecy at the same time that the Deuteronomistic ideology is adjusted in light of the realities of Jeremiah's prophetic mission.

2.3. *Jer.² as a Reader of Jer.¹*

This examination of narrative strategy has limited itself to the edition of Jeremiah reflected in the Hebrew *Vorlage* of the LXX (Jer.¹). I would like to enlist the expanded edition of Jeremiah reflected in the MT (Jer.²), viewed as a reader of Jer.¹, to test the sensitivities of one ancient Israelite reader[36] to the subtleties of this narrative strategy. Space permits only a summary discussion.

Through expansions and content variants, Jer.² manages the narrative system reflected in Jer.¹ to effect significant shifts in the characterization of king and prophet. Jer.² works to enhance and make explicit the apologetic interest of the prior edition in the legitimation and defense of Jeremiah's mission. So he works to enlarge the stature of Jeremiah as a prophet: at almost every opportunity, the title 'the prophet' is interpolated into the text;[37] more importantly, the character of the king is

problem of method attaches to Migsch's thesis, since he employs a composite text of readings drawn from LXX and MT.

36. Another reader of Jeremiah is provided in the person of the Chronicler. Interestingly enough, in 2 Chron. 36.12, the judgment of Zedekiah is understood as a result of failure to humble himself before Jeremiah's guidance. By implication, the prophet's preaching is understood as warning to evoke repentance. This is in line with the morally contingent understanding of prophecy/judgment speech developed in the Jeremiah narratives.

37. Jer.² adds the title at 37.2, 3, 6, 13; 38.9, 10, 14. This has frequently been observed—see e.g. Carroll, *Jeremiah*, p. 61; E. Tov, 'The Literary History of the Book of Jeremiah', in J.H. Tigay (ed.), *Empirical Models for Biblical Criticism* (Philadelphia: University of Pennsylvania Press, 1985), p. 228; Wells, 'Preliminary Draft', p. 1 n. 5.

reconfigured. As opposed to the shrewd Machiavellian who shatters on his own intrigues, Jer.[2] presents a weak figure caught in the options provided by those around him.[38] The invincibility of the prophet is highlighted in relation to royal weakness and the ineffectual intrigues of the royal courtiers. By such alterations Jer.[2] realizes an additional advantage: the contrast between Zedekiah and Hezekiah is increased. That Jer.[2] is aware of the 2 Kings analogy is suggested by the content variant at 37.10—the oracular reference to the dead or wounded on the battlefield (במקומו) now becomes a reference to the dead/wounded in their tents (באהלו). Allusion to the miraculous slaughter of the Assyrians in their camp becomes more explicit.[39]

Jer.[2] also exhibits increased interest in the persecution of the prophet. He works to enlarge his portrayal as an innocent victim as well as the gravity of the threat to Jeremiah's life and the comprehensive scope[40] of community opposition. In Episode 1, the ambiguity and suspiciousness of the prophet's motives are resolved so as to firmly exonerate Jeremiah. An explicit link to 32.6-44 is created at 37.12 to clarify Jeremiah's intentions for leaving the city. Instead of the vague לקנות משם בתוך העם, 'to make a purchase among the people', Jer.[2] has the prophet intending a patrimonial redemption, that is, ...לחלק, 'to receive a portion'.[41]

---

38. He vacillates in his support and recognition of Jeremiah's legitimacy, being too paralyzed by personal cowardice to rule effectively or follow the prophet's instruction. See my earlier paper (Diamond, 'Genesis and Poesis') for details. More briefly, it is to be noted for Jer.[2] that in Episode 2 (v. 18) the threat to the prophet is shifted from the king to the whole community (2nd sing. shifted to 2nd pl.). At v. 20 the prophet no longer discerns sinister intentions for the king (Jer.[1]—ומה תשבני, Jer.[2]—ואל תשבני). The king has become a belated, although weak, secret supporter of Jeremiah. Unable to back him publicly, he does seek, secretly, to protect the prophet. In Episode 3 (v. 5) third person narrative comment is altered so that the king is the one directly protesting his weakness on a broad scale (Jer.[1]—אתהם אין יוכל המלך, Jer.[2]—אתכם דבר...). Again, in v. 9, direct blame for the threat to Jeremiah is shifted from the king to the courtiers (הרעו האנשים האלה). Finally, in Episode 4, the king does not undermine his oath of protection in v. 24 (see above, n. 25, for details). As secret supporter and would-be protector, the king lacks the courage to take action on prophetic advice.

39. Further strengthening of the analogy is indicated perhaps by stylistic adjustment of v. 7 (Jer.[1]), שבו לארץ מצרים, to (Jer.[2]) שב לארצו מצרים. Cf. 2 Kings 19.9, וישב לארצו. If this is correct, the anti-Isaiah typology is made more explicit.

40. See above, n. 38, for details.

41. Or if the unusual MT is emended to לקחת חלק חלק, 'to take possession of his patrimony'. So Holladay, *Jeremiah*, II, p. 265.

Further, access to a contradictory, although privileged, interpretation of the prophet's motives from the fellow lodger is removed when the latter's status shifts to that of a military officer (בעל פקדת). For the reader, the new status immediately undermines the reliability of this character's charge. In Episode 3, the gravity of the threat to the prophet's life is increased through mention of his sinking in the mud (v. 6)[42] and of Ebed-Melek's fear that the prophet would starve (v. 9).[43] With these changes Jer.[2] achieves two things: first, in light of the narrative analogy with 2 Kings, intensifying the prophet's innocence reduces the risk entered upon by Jer.[1], namely, that a reader might be tempted to misappropriate the Rab-Shakeh typology for Jeremiah; secondly, by focusing attention on the prophet as an innocent victim of persecution, he increases recognition of the morally reprehensible environment of Jeremiah's mission, justifying the final outcome indicated by the oracles of disaster.

3. *Conclusion*

That interpreters have found in these narratives a theodicy of the exile seems correct; that the narratives also reflect party conflicts of the late exilic and early postexilic communities is attractive. On both views, the figure of Jeremiah has taken on symbolic significance for apologetic interests. But the appeal to Jeremiah carried rhetorical risks, especially given the matrix of Deuteronomistic assumptions about the nature of prophecy. Jeremiah's eccentricities vis-à-vis the Deuteronomistic model raise for the reader the problem of whether Jeremiah failed to live up to the prophetic calling, understood as Mosaic succession—or worse, that he exploited oracular power for his own personal well being.

---

42. In this connection, it should also be noted that Jer.[2] draws a connection between the threat to Jeremiah and the threat to Zedekiah. In a note of poetic justice, the prophet's vision (v. 22) forsees the king sinking in the mud of his courtiers' intrigues just as they had sunk the prophet in the mud at the bottom of the cistern. Jer. 38.22 (Jer.[1]) reads, אנשי שלמך וילינו בחלקלקות רגלך. Contrast Jer.[2]: אנשי שלמך הטבעו בבץ רגלך.

43. Jer. 38.6 (Jer.[1]): ויהי בטיט. Contrast Jer.[2]: ויטבע ירמיהו בטיט. For 38.9 (Jer.[1]): את אשר. Contrast Jer.[2]: להמית האיש הזה מפני הרעב כי אין עוד לחם בעיר השליכו אל הבור וימת תחתיו מפני הרעב כי אין הלחם עוד בעיר.

Set a rhetorical obstacle for the success of his apologetic interests by the tradition, the editor of Jer.[1] employs a strategy that permits multiple points of view and expectations regarding prophetic mission—all of which in some fashion derive from the Deuteronomistic model—to intermingle. In the determination of prophetic legitimacy, Jeremiah's opponents serve as exclusive advocates of prophetic intercession, directed toward the averting of divine wrath. Jeremiah, Ebed-Melek and the narrator function as advocates of the prediction–fulfilment criterion modified by the moral nexus of prophecy. So he creates an illusion of fairness that in fact subtly realigns the reader to Jeremiah as the model of true prophet. Through his characters, the narrator pits two aspects of the Deuteronomistic model of prophecy[44] against each other: intercession versus prophecy of disaster. And he subordinates both to the moral environment in which oracular speech functions. By attention to the moral nexus of prophecy, the narrator renders the criterion of prediction–fulfilment more flexible, making it contingent on the moral realities of the oracular context; and the theme of the persecution of a prophet becomes part of that moral environment. The latter also serves to evoke reader sympathies and bias to aid the ideological persuasiveness of the narrator's apologetic task—a task dependent on the reader's acceptance of Jeremiah's prophetic legitimacy in spite of his prophetic heterodoxy (vis-à-vis the Mosaic model).

Jer.[2], sensitive to the rhetorical task of the first edition, attempts to strengthen that goal by pursuing a strategy of the explicit while at the same time working to protect the representation of prophecy from the risks Jer.[1] was willing to permit. Jer.[2] is concerned to inhibit the freedom of the reader with respect to the ambiguities of Jer.[1]

For both, the existence in the tradition of alternative oracular possibilities besides disaster is rationalized in a framework of moral contingencies. The latter enables the narration of a process of invalidation in order to preserve Jeremiah's prophetic authority and, at the same time, to preserve the moral responsibility of the community for their destruction. The moral contingency of prophecy has served as an effective

---

44. The influence runs in two directions: the Deuteronomistic model provides the framework that enables the narrator to assimilate the eccentric Jeremiah to the Mosaic model. At the same time, extension of the Mosaic model to Jeremiah forces an adjustment of the former permitting the narrator to overcome normal expectations about the intercessory role of a Mosaic prophet.

hermeneutical assumption to enable the editor to synthesize variant postures of the prophet into a coherent tableau, subordinated to his rhetorical ends.

JSOT 21 (1981), pp. 59-81

'DELIVERANCE BELONGS TO YAHWEH!':
SATIRE IN THE BOOK OF JONAH

John C. Holbert

An appropriate analysis of any work of art depends squarely upon the proper recognition of the content, shape and *Tendenz* of the work. Any analysis is bound to misfire if the analytical tools are put to work in the service of the wrong questions. If I ask after the historical foundation of the myth of Narcissus, I run a dual risk. First, I will be in danger of missing the significance of the myth as myth, failing to hear its tone *for me* of mockery and warning. Secondly, although it *may* be valid to ask such a question—it used to be much in vogue to do so—the results of such a search are of necessity speculative, chimerical, and lead to the making of more myths rather than to the deeper understanding of the one at hand. It must be agreed at least that the question of the historicity of the myth of Narcissus is not the best question which might be asked of it.

In like manner, to search for the historical rootage of the book of Jonah remains, like the search of Gilgamesh for immortality, distinctly frustrating and finally useless.[1] To ask the historical question of Jonah is to ask the wrong question. The vast majority of modern commentators agrees with that judgment, yet the genre analysis of this short work of

---

1. Let the reader not think, however, that the historical question is not still asked. G.C. Aalders in *The Problem of the Book of Jonah* (London: Tyndale Press, 1948), was still seeking to defend the history of nearly all particulars. E. Bickerman in his stimulating analysis of Jonah in *Four Strange Books of the Bible* (New York: Schocken Books, 1967) notes (p. 4) that in 1956 one Catholic encyclopedia had accepted this view and in 1962 a Protestant biblical dictionary had also. See even more recently in J.H. Stek, 'The Meaning of the Book of Jonah', *Calvin Theological Journal* 4 (1969), pp. 23-50.

art is much in dispute.[2] Some sort of scholarly consensus does seem finally to be evolving, based on the very general designation of 'short story.' 'Perhaps the best we can do is call it a satirical, didactic (or theological) short story' says T. Fretheim.[3] Many have agreed with relatively minor variations.[4]

But to say that Jonah is a 'short story' or 'novella' is really not to say very much at all. As Burrows remarks, 'On the whole, however, the classification as a Novella is a satisfactory description of the general literary form; yet it still ignores the most distinctive characteristic of the book of Jonah...'.[5] Burrows goes on to delineate that 'distinctive characteristic':

> The book of Jonah is a satire. In purpose and method it belongs to the same general type of literature as *Don Quixote* or *Gulliver's Travels*.[6]

I agree with Burrows's recognition of satiric elements in the book of Jonah, but Jonah is not a satire any more than *Don Quixote* is a satire.

---

2. See above all the concise summary of this problem by M. Burrows, 'The Literary Category of the Book of Jonah', in H.T. Frank and W.L. Reed (eds.), *Translation and Understanding the Old Testament* (Nashville: Abingdon Press, 1977), pp. 80-107. Add now the more recent summary of T.E. Fretheim, *The Message of Jonah* (Minneapolis: Augsburg 1977), pp. 61-72.

3. Fretheim, *The Message*, p. 72.

4. H.W. Wolff's designation of 'Novelle', in his *Studien zum Jonabuch* (Neukirchen–Vluyn: Neukirchener Verlag, 1965), and in his later commentary *Dodekapropheton 3, Obadja und Jona* (BKAT; Neukirchen–Vluyn: Neukirchener Verlag 1977), p. 34, is approved by Burrows, 'The Literary Category', p. 91. See also M.E. Andrews, 'Gattung and Intention of the Book of Jonah', *Orita* I (1967), pp. 78-81, who while approving Wolff's suggestion of the genre 'Novelle' disagrees with Wolff's particular formulation of that genre and with his application of it to the book of Jonah. G.M. Landes, 'Jonah: A *māšāl*?' in J.G. Gammie *et al.* (eds.), *Israelite Wisdom* (Missoula, MT: Scholars Press 1978), p. 146, asks the question of his title, picking up on an earlier suggestion in the 1963 Columbia dissertation of P. Trible, 'Studies in the Book of Jonah', wherein Jonah is called a 'midrashic legend' (p. 177). K. Budde, 'Vermutungen zum Midrasch des Buches der Könige', *ZAW* (1892), pp. 40ff., and O. Loretz, 'Herkunft und Sinn der JonaErzahlung', *BZ* NF V (1961), pp. 27-28, have called Jonah a midrash although they disagree concerning the precise text upon which the midrash is based. A. Feuillet, 'Le Livre de Jonas', *La Sainte Bible* (Paris, 1957), p. 18, claims that Jonah at least foreshadows the later midrashic literature. Against Jonah as midrash, see A.G. Wright, 'The Literary Genre Midrash', *CBQ* 28 (1966), p. 431.

5. Burrows, 'The Literary Category', p. 91.

6. Burrows, 'The Literary Category', p. 95.

Don Quixote is a picaresque novel which leans heavily on satiric techniques in its rhetorical construction. In the same manner, Jonah is a short
story characterized by the use of satire.

Many scholars have found satirical elements in Jonah.[7] Yet few of
them have spent much time explaining just what satire is. Burrows's
says it may be 'roughly defined as a caricature in words'.[8] Fretheim
defines 'irony' briefly, including in his definition many facets reserved
more traditionally for satire: 'ridicule, absurdity, burlesque, exaggeration,
humor, or other ways of intensifying incongruities'.[9] There appears to
be a need for further clarification of the term before it may be successfully employed as a critical tool. A more careful definition of satire may
prove helpful in assessing whether or not it serves as the principal
characteristic of the construction of the book of Jonah.

---

7.   T. Paine in his *Age of Reason* (1793) believed that Jonah was written to
satirize a prophet (see Bickermann, *Four Strange Books*, p. 19). A. Feuillet, 'Le Sens
du Livre de Jonas', *RB* 54, pp. 346-52, entitles a whole section 'Le caractère satirique
et parenetique, et l'actualité du livre de Jonas'. Wolff in each of his works on Jonah
uses the words *Satire, Satirikal* and *satirisch* quite often, although as far as I can see
he never defines precisely what he means by his usage. E.M. Good, in his analysis
of Jonah in *Irony in the Old Testament* (Philadelphia: Westminster Press, 1965
[repr.; Sheffield: Almond Press, 1981]), p. 41, calls Jonah satire. Fretheim uses the
word often in his *The Message*. G. von Rad, *Der Prophet Jona* (Nuremberg: Laetere
Verlag 1950), rejects the designation of 'satirischen Charakter', because, he says, the
'Schärfe und Bitterkeit' are missing. S.D.F. Goitein, 'Some Observations on Jonah',
JPOS 17 (1937), pp. 63-77, claims (p. 74) that the 'whole tenor of the story is much
too earnest for a satire'. However, not all satires are 'titter'. For example, the famous
'idol satire' of Isa. 44.9-20 is not characterized by 'bitterness' at all, but rather by
light-hearted burlesque. Von Rad himself nicely describes this burlesque in vol. II of
his *Old Testament Theology* (New York: Harper & Row 1965), p. 340. This satire is
obviously in 'earnest', attacking both pointedly and playfully the absurdity of idolatry;
so Goitein's objection on that basis is facile. J.A. Miles, in a delightful article,
'Laughing at the Bible: Jonah as Parody', *JQR* 65 (1974–1975), pp. 168-81, narrows
Jonah's literary genre to parody, claiming that Jonah is a specific and satiric attack on
'familiar texts or familiar styles' (p. 168). It is significant to note that Miles sees
satire as the vehicle for parody in Jonah (see especially his analysis of the psalm of
chapter 2 [p. 174]). See also the insightful observations of K.H. Miskotte, *When the
Gods are Silent* (New York: Harper & Row, 1967), especially pp. 422, 430, 436.
Another entertaining and insightful analysis is that of D.F. Rauber, 'Jonah—the
prophet as Shlemiel' *TBT* 49 (1970), pp. 29-37. Rauber includes satire as one of the
many techniques employed by the author of Jonah (p. 31).

8.   Burrows, 'The Literary Category', p. 96.

9.   Fretheim, *The Message*, pp. 51-52.

In his now classic *Anatomy of Criticism*, N. Frye observes: 'Satire is militant irony'. Furthering this distinction between satire and irony, he writes:

> Irony is consistent both with complete realism of content and with the suppression of attitude on the part of the author. Satire demands at least a token fantasy, a content which the reader recognizes as grotesque, and at least an implicit moral standard, the latter being essential in a militant attitude to experience.[10]

One can conclude from this distinction that irony is best characterized by ambiguity of intention on the part of the author. For example, in Genesis 37 Joseph is introduced to the reader as either a disgustingly arrogant tattle-tale (so, his brothers) or as the God-inspired dutiful, well-loved child of his father's old age. The author's attitude appears suppressed here and Joseph's later behavior towards his brothers in Egypt makes ambiguity in Genesis 37 all the more likely.[11] Satire is more overt, more direct in style and intention. So, Frye concludes that there are two essentials to satire. First, the wit and humor are founded on fantasy or on a sense of the grotesque and/or absurd. Secondly, there is an object of the attack.

Leonard Feinberg has written a readable introduction to the subject which can serve to sharpen our definition further.[12] He first defines satire succinctly as a 'playfully critical distortion of the familiar'.[13] Like Frye he emphasizes the hyperbolic quality of satire:

> The satirist, then, has to exaggerate because he is facing formidable opposition: an audience indifferent to expression of unpleasant truths, and a throng of teachers, officials, and writers who insist that these truths do not exist.[14]

It is made the more obvious then that the grotesque and absurd are constitutive of satire.

10. N. Frye, *Anatomy of Criticism* (Princeton: Princeton University Press, 1967), p. 224.

11. See G. von Rad's comments in *Genesis* (Philadelphia: Westminster Press, 1972), pp. 349-355, and a rather different and in my judgment more sensitive literary analysis by G.W. Coats, *From Canaan to Egypt* (CBQMS 4; Washington, DC: Catholic Biblical Association of America, 1976), pp. 8-19.

12. L. Feinberg, *Introduction to Satire* (Ames: Iowa State University Press, 1967).

13. Feinberg, *Satire*, p. 19.

14. Feinberg, *Satire*, p. 14.

Feinberg also comments helpfully on the object of satire's attack. 'The excesses (which are always found in satire) that we laugh at are usually inferior excesses; the fat man, not the strong man...'[15]

> Great villains have always been hard to ridicule. They may be horrible but they are not entertaining. When he [the object of satire] tries to seem noble, he invites satiric treatment. By pretending to be something he is not, he becomes a hypocrite; and hypocrisy is an inferiority that we can laugh at, feel contempt for, and enjoy.[16]

So, we can see that the object of satire must be reduced to laughable proportions (or sometimes 'increased' as in *Gulliver's Travels*) in order that the satire can perform at its best, engendering laughter from the reader who is thereby offered 'the pleasures of superiority and a safe release of aggression'.[17]

Two other observations by Feinberg will prove helpful to this study. Although the assault of satire is often overt and unambiguous, one of its chief techniques is indirection. In this regard, Feinberg quotes another master satirist, John Dryden:

> How easy it is to call rogue and villain, and that wittily! But how hard to make a man appear a fool, a blockhead, or a knave, without using any of these opprobrious terms.[18]

Satire is often subtle even though always pointed.

Another characteristic is that of externality. Satire tends to concentrate on 'the act itself rather than on the psychology of individuals who commit the act'.[19] Satiric style is broad, bold and active, not inclined toward the introspective. The object of satire acts and by his/her actions is found ludicrous and laughable and finally is caught in the glaring spotlight of truth.

This brief look at satire has led to the following conclusions:

15. Feinberg, *Satire*, p. 6.
16. Feinberg, *Satire*, p. 30. Feinberg quotes Mark Twain at this point for a beautiful illustration of satire against hypocrisy: 'I will say this much for the nobility: that tyrannical, murderous, rapacious and morally rotten as they were, they were deeply and enthusiastically religious' (from *A Connecticut Yankee in King Arthur's Court*).
17. Feinberg, *Satire*, p. 5.
18. Feinberg, *Satire*, p. 91.
19. Feinberg, *Satire*, p. 94.

1. Satire is humor based on the fantastic, the grotesque, the absurd.

2. Satire has a definite target which must be familiar enough to make the assault meaningful and memorable.

3. Satire is characterized by indirection of attack. The charge comes from the flanks rather than head-on.

4. Satire pillories inferior excesses; hypocrisy is one classic and familiar example.

5. Satire is usually external in viewpoint. The actions of the character or the overt effects of the satirized idea are emphasized rather than the interior realm of the individual or idea.

I

With that more careful analysis of satire in hand, we can now proceed to examine the satiric elements of Jonah with special reference to chs. 1 and 2. It is not my intent to provide a complete analysis of the satiric elements of the book of Jonah, but it appears essential to examine chs. 1 and 2 for these elements, for thereby we can see of a certainty that a satiric attack is underway, can identify the object of the attack, and can better observe how the psalm in particular aids the assault.

The satirist does not waste our time. The very first two verses of his book set the satiric tone and identify the object of the satire.

> (1) Once, the word of Yahweh came to Jonah, the son of Amittai, (2) 'Arise! Go to Nineveh, the great city, and cry against it, because their evil has come up in my presence!'

This is a prophetic call from Yahweh. It is identical in form to Joel 1.1 in that it is rather sparse in detail, explaining only the name and immediate lineage of the prophet. By comparison, other prophetic calls provide more precise settings by offering the names of reigning kings (e.g. Hos. 1.1; Mic. 1.1) or other chronological determinants (e.g. Amos's famous earthquake). Verse 1 makes it clear that our hero is Jonah, the son of Amittai. It is he, and no other character, who is to be the focus of our attention. It is also made clear here that he is the object of a typically prophetic call from Yahweh. Commentators are fond of saying that Jonah is never called a prophet in the story[20] and so prophecy in Israel has little to do with the tale. Still, when we remember that indirection is

20. So Wolff, *Obadja und Jona*; Fretheim, *The Message*, et al.

a hallmark of satire, we cannot dismiss out of hand the observed fact that Yahweh calls Jonah precisely as a prophet and anoints him for a mission on behalf of the divine Word.

Why is the name, 'Jonah, son of Amittai,' chosen for the book? This prophet appears in 2 Kings 14.23-29 as a figure who prophesied during the lengthy reign of Jeroboam II over Israel in the eighth century BCE Some commentators call him a 'nationalistic prophet' who presided prophetically over the great expansion of the Northern Kingdom during the reign of Jeroboam.[21] Wolff calls this eighth-century Jonah a 'typical prophet of salvation' who is used as such by the author of Jonah to criticize, at least indirectly, the prophets of salvation of his own day.[22] But, as Fretheim shows, Jonah, the prophet of Jeroboam, is hardly the focus of the 2 Kings passage.[23] The passage rather emphasizes God's willingness, despite the habitual wickedness of Jeroboam, 'to save Israel'. We are meant to see the great compassion of God who saw the 'bitter affliction' of Israel, how it stood alone in the world 'without helper' (2 Kgs 14.26), and resolved to save. The analogy to Jonah seems obvious, at least on the surface. Despite great wickedness (Jeroboam/Nineveh), God resolves to save. So, thematically, the choice of this prophet seems generally an apt one.[24]

But the eighth-century Jonah announces the glad tidings of Israel's expansion in the face of wickedness. Our Jonah announces evil tidings in the face of wickedness, engenders thereby repentance (Jeroboam never repents, according to the Judean redactor of Kings) and witnesses, much to his shock and anger, God's compassion on Nineveh. So, the themes of prophetic announcement and divine compassion are indeed in evidence, but the ways in which those themes are employed bear little direct relationship to one another. There may be irony afoot here, since the prophet of salvation has become the prophet of doom, but the possibility seems remote.[25]

21. For example, Wolff, *Studien*, pp. 14-16.

22. Wolff, *Studien*; Wolff, *Obadja und Jona*, p. 76.

23. Fretheim, *The Message*, 41-42.

24. When the book of Jonah was written is not significant for this particular study of it. In my judgment, however, there is no conclusive internal evidence with which one might confine the book to a post-exilic date. For a rejection of the typical view that the Hebrew of Jonah is laced with 'Aramaisms' and is hence late, see the persuasive article of O. Loretz, 'Herkunft und Sinn der Jona-Erzahlung', *BZ* 5 (1961), pp. 18-29.

25. Fretheim, *The Message*, p. 42, says that the reader would conclude from the

I think rather that 'Jonah, son of Amittai' is chosen precisely because of his name. He is 'Dove, the son of faithfulness or fidelity'.[26] By choosing this name, the author establishes the expectation in the mind of the reader that God has got the right man for the job. Like the dove of Noah (Gen. 8.8-12), this dove will perform his duty.[27] And because he is the 'son of faithfulness', we can expect nothing but obedience to the call of God.

But, astoundingly, that is just what we do not get. Without a single word, the prophet called to 'cry' the Word of Yahweh, arises (*qûm*, v. 2)—not to 'cry' (*qr'*) but to 'flee' (*brh*) God says 'Go east, young prophet,' but Jonah flees west, to Tarshish.[28] And he flees more precisely 'from the presence of Yahweh', the very place to which the evil of Nineveh had come so bringing about the call of Jonah in the first place. Note, too, that Jonah 'goes down' (*yrd*) to Joppa, and upon finding a west-bound ship, 'goes down' (*yrd*) into the ship's hold. This 'descent' is intended to describe a sharp contrast to God's call to 'arise'

author's use of Jonah that the emphasis of the tale falls on God's compassion over against his judgment: God goes beyond simple justice in his dealing with his people. While I agree that this theme is an important one for the book, it is one-sided to find this the only theme. Also, to say that this is the reason why the author chose 'Jonah, son of Amittai' for his hero is to assume that the obscure prophet of Gath-Hepher, and the tiny note about him in 2 Kings, were better known than that text itself would indicate. For the theme of Jonah, see, above all, J. Magonet, *Form and Meaning, Studies in Literary Techniques in the Book of Jonah* (BET, 2; Frankfurt am Main: Peter Lang, 1976), pp. 85-112. For Fretheim's defense of his view of the theme, see T.E. Fretheim, 'Jonah and Theodicy', *ZAW* 90 (1978), pp. 227-37. R.E. Clements, 'The Purpose of the Book of Jonah', VTSup, 28 (1975), p. 24, has a similar reading.

26. The commentators note this fact: Good, *Irony*, p. 42; Fretheim, *The Message*, p. 43. Burrows, 'The Literary Category', p. 90, has the surprising statement that '"Dove son of Fidelity" is hardly an appropriate appellation for the prophet Jonah'. Yet, if satire is the key element, as Burrows rightly notes, a better appellation could hardly be chosen. Wolff, *Obadja und Jona*, p. 76, says that the *Satiriker* and *Didaktiker* chose 'sein Held' precisely to indicate his 'Flattergeist' (flightiness) and notes Hos. 7.11 in this regard. See also the comments of Feuillet, 'Les Sources', p. 168.

27. Wolff's claim that 'Jonah' is chosen because of the 'flightiness' of the nature of the dove (see note 26) is very one-dimensional. Hos. 7.11 is the only clearly negative comment on the dove's behavior out of 15 non-sacrificial uses of the term in MT.

28. The exact location of Tarshish is unimportant. That it is far west of Israel is the key. See the speculations for the location in Wolff, *Obadja und Jona*, p. 78.

and go to Nineveh. The very structure of this brief section, 1.1-3, is designed to highlight the total disobedience of our prophet, Dove, son of Faithfulness, from whom we expected only obedience. It opens with the coming of Yahweh's word to Jonah (1.1) and closes with the prophet fleeing headlong 'from Yahweh's presence' (1.3). The precipitous character of the flight is beautifully exemplified in the text of 1.3 where four finite verbs ('he went down,' 'he found,' 'he paid,' 'he went down') are framed by two infinitive constructs formed with the preposition *lamed* and joined to the same object, 'to Tarshish from the presence of Yahweh.' The prophet's whole intent is thus flight away from Yahweh[29] and 'down' from his command to 'arise'.[30]

So, the *Tendenz* of the text is established in the first three verses. Expectations are dashed; the Word has come to the faithful dove and he has flown away. The Word of divine judgment is in danger of 'coming back empty'. The refusal of the divine call is hardly unprecedented (see Moses in Exod. 3–4, and Jer. 1), but the wordless flight of a prophet is indeed unique (Elijah flees, but it is *toward* the mount of God, not away from it). If this be satire, and the grotesque flight of the prophet points in that direction, the object of the satiric attack is Jonah, the prophet. One cannot at this stage of the analysis claim that Jonah is a representative of anything or anybody other than himself, nor can it be said that prophets in general, prophecy in general, or certain kinds of prophets or prophecies are under attack. Jonah, the prophet, no more, no less, is the target.

And now in the following section, 1.4-16, the grotesqueries, so characteristic of satire, begin to appear in profusion. First, God 'hurls (*he̱ṭil*) a great[31] wind at[32] the sea; so there was a *great* tempest on the sea'. The result of the tempest is that the ship, engulfed by this extraordinary divine storm, 'threatened to break up' (RSV). In actuality, the literal rendering of the phrase just given is 'the ship thought to be broken up.' The implication is that the ship *itself* feared to be broken up.

---

29. Contra, G.H. Cohn, *Das Buch Jona* (Assen: Van Gorcum & Co., 1969), p. 89, who says Jonah flees from God's word, not God himself.

30. Note the interesting analysis of 1.3 as a 'concentric structure' in N. Lohfink, 'Jona ging zur Stadt hinaus (Jona 4, 5)', *BZ* 5 (1961), p. 200.

31. See Fretheim's analysis of the use of *gādôl* in Jonah in *The Message*, pp. 43-44, but a more sensitive and complete review is given in Wolff, *Studien*, pp. 39-40.

32. The preposition *ʾl* provides the vivid picture here of God on the 'mound of heaven' throwing a mighty wind at the sea which results, upon impact, in a 'great tempest'.

Notwithstanding Wolff's claim that the *piel* of the verb *ḥšb* is nowhere else used of inanimate objects,[33] a 'thinking ship' is fully in tune with a story world of men-swallowing fish, huge one day plants, not to mention repentant Ninevites.

In response to God's 'hurling', the sailors 'hurl' (*yāṭilū*) the ship's cargo 'at (*ʾl*) the sea'. Yahweh's action leads to a similar action by the sailors. Yahweh calls to Jonah 'to cry' and 'to go,' to do the job of prophet. The sailors 'cry' and they do their jobs as sailors. We are to contrast Jonah with these unknown pagans who are fulfilling God's call, while Jonah lies sleeping, a fact revealed to us *immediately* after the description of the sailors' actions. The target of the satire is falling further and further in our esteem, a fact matched physically by his own desire 'to go down'.

Jonah has gone down to the very bottom of the ship, has lain down (as low physically as he can get), and has gone to sleep. The word used for sleep here (*rdm*) has important Old Testament usages. It is this sleep which falls on *ʾādām* before God takes the rib from him (Gen. 2.21). It is this sleep which falls on Abram (Gen. 15.12) before God comes to covenant with him. It is this sleep which comes to Sisera in the tent of Jael before she brutally murders him (Judg. 4.21). In short, it is the deepest of sleeps, during which often great divine actions are undertaken (see also the comic use of this sleep by the author of Job in connection with Eliphaz's rather pathetic vision—Job 4.13). So, at the end of v. 5 Jonah is as far from the place where he is supposed to be as can be imagined; he is lying prone in the bottom of a ship bound for the west, wrapped in a deep trance-like sleep. This picture is certainly an example of the grotesque incongruity of satire. Jonah has apparently, as far as he is able, succeeded in fleeing the presence of God.

The captain of the ship approaches the insensate figure in the hold of his foundering vessel and demands him to perform some actions already very familiar to the reader:

> How can you sleep? Arise! Cry to your god! Perhaps that god will concern himself with us so that we do not perish.

The captain first recognizes Jonah for the deep sleeper that he is by using a participle from the same verbal root (*rdm*). He then uses two of the verbal commands given by God to Jonah in 1.2, 'arise' (*qûm*) and

---

33. Wolff, *Obadja und Jona*, p. 83. See D.N. Freedman, 'Jonah 1.4b', *JBL* 77 (1958), p. 162, for the reading of the verb *ḥbh* instead of *ḥšb*.

'cry' (*qrʾ*). This repetition of words, such a common feature of the Jonah style,[34] accomplishes three important things at this point in the story. First, it reiterates the huge gulf between the active, praying pagan sailors and the sleeping, disobedient, so-called prophet of Yahweh. Secondly, it tells the reader immediately that Jonah has not escaped God; his call comes even through the mouth of a pagan sailor. Thirdly, the pagan is commanding Jonah to do his duty, to be true to his calling; even though he, the sailor, has no idea what that is as yet. But we, the omniscient readers, hear the sailor's request for what it is—a reiteration of the call of God to the sleeping prophet. We can be certain that the author wants us to hear this dual meaning of the captain's command to Jonah when we hear the rest of the sailors say in v. 7, 'Come on'. (*lᵉkû*), which constitutes the third command God had initially given to Jonah. All three commands (*qûm*, *lᵉk*, *qrʾ*) have now been given again by the sailors in the hearing of the disobedient one.[35]

Moving on into v. 7, word repetition is again important as the sailors decide 'to cast lots in order to discover on whose account this evil (*rᶜ*) has come to us'. The 'evil' (*rᶜ*) of Nineveh has triggered the entire episode so far (1.2). But instead of responding to the call of Yahweh to deal with evil, Jonah has rather engendered further evil upon wholly innocent pagan sailors. Jonah, by his flight and inaction, has tacitly announced doom on the pagans—but they are the wrong pagans. Jonah has not only not done his duty for Yahweh; Nineveh's evil has fallen on him, and upon his unwilling and undeserving companions, due to his pronounced willfulness. Could the satire be more pointed? Jonah, by refusing to announce judgment which might lead to repentance, has instead brought judgment upon the innocent. But there is a way out, as faithful religious persons know. Again it is appropriate that in a satiric piece it is the unexpected one who offers the expected solution. It is the pagan captain who suggests, 'perhaps that God (*hāʾᵉlōhîm*) will stir himself on our behalf in order that we do not perish.' Crying for help to the source of help may lead to help; that is good religion. The 'faithful' prophet of God never thought of it; or if he did, he surely did not act

34. See Magonet, *Form*, pp. 13-28; Wolff, *Studien*, pp. 36-40; Fretheim, *The Message*, pp. 39-50.

35. Magonet, *Form*, p. 17, says that after the repetition of the verbs 'rise up' and 'call' by the captain the reader is forced 'from then on' to read the book at two levels. I have tried to show how the two-level reading is forced from the first verse of the book.

upon it. It is again significant that another famous pagan in the book, the Ninevite king, has nearly an identical suggestion at 3.9: 'Who knows? That God (*hāᵉlōhîm*) might reverse himself, be gracious, and turn from his fierce anger in order that we do not perish.' Must the pagans teach the prophets proper religion? Apparently, *this* prophet needs teaching.

The sailors cast the lots, and the lot 'falls' (*npl*) on Jonah. The descending motif of this first chapter continues as the action of lot-casting involves both throwing and falling; the lot falls on Jonah as the sailors 'throw them down' (*wayyappilû*). Does this action not prefigure the sailors' later action of throwing Jonah down into the sea? The lots have already revealed the truth: Jonah is the guilty party. The questions of the sailors in v. 8 become highly significant in the light of their certain knowledge of Jonah's guilt. Why do they not simply throw him overboard? Once again the reader is asked to contrast God's prophet with the pagan sailors:

> So they said to him, 'Tell us, now! On whose account has this evil come upon us? What is your occupation? Where do you come from? What is your home country? From what people are you?'

Because the sailors already know the answer to their first question to Jonah, many commentators delete the phrase from v. 8, 'on whose account has this evil come upon us?'.[36] Yet, we may ask: why do persons ask a direct question of someone when the questioner already knows the answer? The question here does not seek information; it seeks confession. It is an exact analogy of God's question to Adam in the garden (Gen. 3.11), 'Have you eaten from the tree of which I commanded you not to eat?' God wants Adam to say, 'Yes. Forgive me'. His response is hardly that. So, in like manner, the sailors want Jonah to say, 'I did it'. Like Adam, he does not. The Genesis analogy does not end here, as we shall see.

Jonah's famous reply to this storm of questions is, 'I am a Hebrew, and I fear Yahweh, the God of the skies, who made the sea and the dry

36. So K. Elliger in *BHS*; T.H. Robinson, HAT, p. 120; Wolff, *Obadja und Jona*, p. 83; W. Rudolph, KAT, *ad loc.* R. Pesch, 'Zur konzentrischen Struktur von Jona I', *Bib* 47 (1966), pp. 577-581 (p. 579), argues structurally that the phrase must be retained. This 'concentric' analysis has been seconded with slight variation by Lohfink, 'Jona ging' (who actually is the earliest commentator to note this structure); C.A. Keller, 'Jonas: Le Portrait d'un prophète', *TZ* 21 (1965); G.M. Landes, 'The Kerygma of the Book of Jonah', *Int* 28 (1967); Trible, *Studies*; Cohn, *Das Buch Jona*; and Magonet, *Form*, p. 56.

land'. He answers, but he does not answer. He confesses, but he does
not confess. The phrase is a stock one, and the satiric content is obvious.
Jonah does two things by his credal statement. First, he identifies himself
as a Hebrew among non-Hebrews. Secondly, he claims to be a worship-
ful Yahweh believer, whose belief in Yahweh rests on God's creative
omnipotence. Could hypocrisy be stated any more clearly? Jonah is
'fleeing', from the Yahweh whom he has just 'confessed' as omnipotent
on the very sea he has just 'confessed' that Yahweh has made. The
creed is empty; in Jonah's mouth it is ashes.[37]

The effect of the creed on the sailors makes its hypocrisy all the
clearer. No longer are they called 'sailors'; now they are only 'men',
and they are 'greatly afraid'. So, again, as before, Jonah's behavior has
led to unexpected results. His disobedience to God's call to deal with evil
brought evil. Now, his pious sounding creed has brought terror.

The 'men' once again remind us of Genesis 3 with their anguished
cry, 'What is this you have done?' As God evidences his sorrow to Eve
in Gen. 3.13, so in an *identical* phrase the men, once-sailors, evidence
their terror to Jonah. It is clear that they now understand all, as the next
phrase says. Some critics assume that Jonah really did tell the men
directly that he was fleeing from God; the author simply does not report
all of the conversation.[38] But, did Jonah 'tell them' that he was fleeing
from Yahweh? Clearly, the men understood his 'partial confession'[39] of
1.9 better than he. He told them more than he intended. They knew he
was fleeing from Yahweh; his 'confession' of 1.9 did indeed tell them all
they wanted or needed to know.

And, once again, the author leads us to contrast the behavior of our
'hero' with that of the innocent 'victims' of his evil. The victims ask
their very tormentor what they should do with him (1.11). He responds,
'Pick me up and hurl me (*ha'îlunî*) at the sea in order that the sea calm
down for you' (1.12). In this 'partial confession' Jonah offers the men
an open invitation to divest themselves of their real problem. But, again,

37. Landes, 'The Kerygma', p. 19, claims Jonah's confession is not here
hypocritical, because Jonah is not fleeing God's actual and omnipotent power but
rather his 'cultic presence'. I have argued against that view above. See also the
remarkable analysis of Keller, 'Le Portrait', where Jonah becomes the 'suffering
servant' (p. 339) and is hardly then to be seen as a hypocrite. I find Keller's
arguments totally unconvincing.

38. So, for example, Fretheim, *The Message*, p. 85.

39. See Magonet, *Form*, pp. 24, 52, 119 n. 56, for a description of this literary
device.

Jonah's behavior leads to unexpected consequences, as it has done twice before in this chapter. They do not hurl him at the sea, but 'they rowed hard to reach the dry land' (the other half of Yahweh's creation, as confessed by Jonah). These sailors are nothing less than exemplary human beings; they never take the easy way; they do not shirk responsibility. The contrast with Jonah is again pointed and significant. Jonah's request to be thrown into the sea is hardly an offer of self-sacrifice. His escape from Yahweh is being foiled; death, the final descent, is the only option now. So, his request to the sailors is Jonah's final self-serving act, a grand finale to a life of disobedience. One can imagine Jonah's chagrin as the pagan sailors try to save his wretched life while he screams so mightily to give it up.

Then, in a great satiric thrust, the author has the sailors 'cry to Yahweh' in intense piety. 'That God' of the captain's command (1.6) is now known as Yahweh. Yahweh's demand 'to cry' (1.2) has been denied by his prophet, but picked up by the pagan sailors. They humbly make two requests. First, 'Do not let us perish on account of the life of this man'. The prophet of God has become a man of death, from whom the innocent sailors must pray to God to be saved. Secondly, they cry, 'Do not lay upon us innocent blood'. Jonah is obviously not seen as innocent by the sailors; they are fearful that his blood—shed innocently by them—will stain them. They pray this will not occur.[40]

After the sailors' two humble requests to Yahweh, they add the phrase we have expected from Jonah, but never got. 'Surely you, Yahweh, have done as you pleased!' Complete and total submission is intended by the phrase, not unlike the famous line of Jesus in the garden prayer (Lk. 22.42; Mk 14.36; Mt. 26.39). Has not the satire now come full circle? The total obedience of the sailors is now vividly etched against the total disobedience of the prophet Jonah.

> Then they picked Jonah up and hurled him (*y^eṭiluhû*) at the sea, and the sea ceased its raging. Then the men feared Yahweh tremendously, they sacrificed to Yahweh and made vows.

The sailors' fear of the storm (1.5) became the men's terror of the power of Yahweh and of the disobedience of his prophet (1.10). Now their 'tremendous fear' (1.10 and 1.6 are identical in their opening phrases) has become one of worship where sacrifices are offered and

---

40. See Magonet, *Form*, p. 73 for another literary device called by Magonet 'the dividing up of quotations'.

vows for the future relationship with Yahweh are made.[41] In short, the sailors have undergone a tremendous, ardent and lasting conversion to belief in Yahweh. They are his 'men' now; not again are they referred to as 'sailors' after 1.10.

So, there is an obvious pattern of counter-movement in ch. 1. While Jonah descends and flees from God, the sailors rise in our estimation and in their recognition of the real power of Yahweh. As the sailors sacrifice in a final testimony to their new-found faith, Jonah has continued his inexorable descent, now below his prone position in the ship's hold; he is dropping like a stone in the depths of the sea.

Chapter 1 of Jonah bears all of the distinguishing marks of satire. There is the fantastic (great storms and their instantaneous calming), the grotesque (pagans worshipping Yahweh while Yahweh's prophet seeks for ultimate escape from him), and the absurd (sleeping prophets and worthy pagans). The target is the Hebrew prophet, Jonah, who is shown to be self-centred, lazy, hypocritical and altogether inferior to the wonderful pagans who surround him. Jonah's words and actions are indeed indicators of the satiric assault, our expectations are continually dashed, the results of Jonah's behavior always other than we imagined and always other than he imagined. The attack on Jonah is indeed indirect in that we see him for what he is with the help of his interaction with characters with whom we find great sympathy. So, the five elements of satire delineated earlier are all here in ch. 1.

II

Within ch. 1 it has become clear that satire is the hallmark of the narrative art of the book. But is the satire extended into the controversial psalm of ch. 2? We now turn to an examination of the psalm to see whether or not this is the case.

A substantial majority of Jonah commentators have judged the psalm of ch. 2 to be a later, and quite inappropriate, addition to the original story. G. Landes, one of the first critical commentators to defend vigorously the originality of the psalm and the necessity of its inclusion in the

---

41. Magonet, *Form*, pp. 31-33, sees here another technique of the author of Jonah which he calls the 'growing phrase'. He notes in addition to this example of 1.5, 10, 16, the growing phrase of a storm, 1.4, 11, 13 (see also Cohn, *Das Buch Jona*, p. 54). Another example is the growing designation of Nineveh: 1.2; 3.2, 3; 4.11.

book, places the arguments against its originality into three broad categories:[42]

1. The psalm just does not fit the situation described in ch. 1. The prayer is obviously a psalm of thanksgiving where one would expect a lament of some kind.

2. The 'psychological picture' of Jonah in chs. 1, 3, 4 is markedly different than the picture of ch. 2. The 'pious' Jonah of the Psalm seems very remote from the disobedient one we have just seen.

3. It is very odd to find Jonah in prayer at all. Why now does he suddenly pray when he had to be coerced into any speech at all by the pagans in ch. 1?

Answers to these questions and others which may arise will be given in the course of the analysis of ch. 2.

It can readily be seen that ch. 2 continues the grotesque character of ch. 1; a 'great fish' (compare the 'great city' and the 'great fear' in ch. 1?) swallowing a man, having that man inside the alimentary system for three days and nights, and finally vomiting him up on the 'dry land,' remains, no matter how hard some would wish it otherwise, the stuff of legend. No particular fish is in mind; it is a special one, which God has 'appointed' (*way^{e}man*) for the occasion. It is very important to note that it is appointed not to destroy or to threaten Jonah, but precisely to save him. So, the unexpected quality of ch. 1 continues. Jonah seeks to die, and he has done his best to do so. But Yahweh now seeks to save him by means of the extraordinary beast of the sea. So, now from the very belly of the fish, Jonah prays. We might expect a blast from Jonah to God for saving his wretched life, but that is precisely what we do not get. We get a classic song of thanksgiving for deliverance from danger and death.

Before we are overwhelmed by this new, pious Jonah, as some analysts clearly are, let us look with care at the words of the prayer and

---

42. Landes, 'The Kerygma', pp. 10-25. Other commentators now argue for the psalm's inclusion. Cohn, *Das Buch Jona*; Magonet, *Form*; Fretheim, *The Message*; see also J.G. Williams, *Understanding the Old Testament* (New York: Barron, 1972), p. 246. S.D.F. Goitein, 'Some Observations', says the prayer is 'appropriate' (p. 69) but hardly says more. T. Warshaw, *Literary Interpretations of Biblical Narratives* (Nashville: Abingdon Press, 1974); Miles, 'Laughing at the Bible'; B.S. Childs *Introduction to the Old Testament as Scripture* (Philadelphia: Fortress Press, 1979) who in terms of the book's 'canonical shape' of course deals with the psalm.

at their functions within the prayer. A key word appears immediately, 'I cried' (*qārāʾtî*). Is God's command finally to be fulfilled? Is the prophet of Yahweh at last 'crying out' (1.2)? Yes, but note, only for himself. Verse 3 sharply emphasizes the first person singular nature of this prayer by ending each of the four stichs of the verse with the appropriate first person singular ending. The 'cry' has come, but it is not for God and not against Nineveh; it is because of Jonah's distress, brought about only by his desire to die.

In v. 4, however, Jonah blames God for his predicament. '*You* sent me to the depths, to the heart of the seas', he says. But that is not so. He requested to be thrown there and was so thrown. The second person verb stands in stark contrast at the very beginning of v. 4 to those multiple first person references of v. 3. 'All *your* breakers and *your* waves' of v. 4b heighten God's culpability for his plight in the eyes of Jonah. And to emphasize Jonah's own innocence in the entire experience, at v. 5 he employs the passive of the verb (*nigraštî*) and claims, 'I have been cast out from before your eyes...' But again the reader must demur. Jonah is only half right at most. He has indeed been 'hurled at the sea' by the sailors (1.15), but it of course was Jonah himself who so requested it (1.12), and it was Jonah himself who *fled* God's very presence in the first place. (Note that the verbs 'cast out' and 'hurl' are different verbs.) I see here another 'partial confession' on the part of our 'hero'. In the midst of a very traditional and pious sounding thanksgiving psalm, he has revealed more of himself, while saying less, than he wanted. Can the reader fail to see the hypocrisy here? Jonah has fled from God; he has fled so far as to demand to be drowned in the sea. But, instead, that same God has saved him and in return, Jonah the pious prays an unctuous thanksgiving prayer. In v. 5a, however, the real Jonah, our satiric target, has appeared. Indeed, in the first three verses of the prayer, Jonah accuses God of his plight, while thanking him for rescuing him from it. *O mea culpa* has become in Jonah's mouth *O sua culpa*! So, those who have found a 'different' Jonah in ch. 2 have not read the chapter with an eye to its satiric possibilities.

Jonah continues in v. 5b: 'However, I will again see your holy temple'. Why now is 'the temple' mentioned? Surely, the temple can be nothing other than the very symbol of God's presence; the parallelism of 'your holy temple' and 'from before your eyes' in v. 5 makes that a certainty for our poet. So, what has Jonah said? Even though God has cast him out from his presence, he longs again to see that very presence. But this is the man in flight headlong *from* that presence. His actions have shown that he neither wants to see or to hear God again.

In vv. 5 and 7abc the description of his descent into the mythological realms of the bottom of the cosmos continues. It should be noted that the psalm beautifully continues the falling/descending motif seen in ch. 1. Indeed, as Magonet shows, the psalm is so constructed as to portray a 'geographical consecutive descent'.[43] It moves from 'stream/flood' (v. 4b) to 'breakers and waves' (v. 4c) to 'great deep' (v. 6b) to 'the roots of the mountains' (v. 7a) and finally to 'earth's bars closed on me forever' (v. 7bc). This provides a strong literary connection between chs. 1 and 2. Jonah's descent from God is only completed at 2.7c; he is there at the very farthest point from God that he could be. And it is there, most significantly, that a catch word from ch. 1, *yrd*, is used (1.3 twice and 1.5). Add this to the apparently consistent psychological portrayal of the man Jonah in both chapters and it becomes less probable that the psalm is secondary.

The first ascent of Jonah is an act of God at v. 7d, 'Yet, you brought up my life from the pit, Yahweh, my God'. And so God has, by means of the great marine creature from whose very belly Jonah is now recounting his adventure to God and revealing to the reader his understanding of it (false for the most part as we have seen) and what he has learned from it. What sort of 'ascent' Jonah is experiencing is made clearer by v. 8:

> When my spirit fainted from me
> > I remembered Yahweh.
> My prayer came to you,
> > to your Holy Temple.

At best, we have 'fox-hole' religion here, or perhaps better 'fish-belly' religion. Jonah remembers Yahweh only when his spirit, his *nepeš*, has fainted from him. Still, we cannot chide him for the words alone; they are common in the Psalter (e.g. Ps. 18.7). The danger here is to make too much of the words.[44] Jonah makes a statement of facts, not a confession. Just because he prays at this juncture is no certain sign of piety. After all, he prays at 4.2 also, and in that prayer Jonah is clearly

---

43. Magonet, *Form*.

44. Magonet, *Form*, p. 43; he claims that Jonah here submits to God's will. Landes, 'The Kerygma', p. 26, sees here 'a sincere cry to Yahweh'.

shown to be a hypocrite.[45] His prayer had come to God, to his 'Holy Temple,' to God's very presence, as v. 5 told us. While Jonah flees from Yahweh's presence, his words at least return to Yahweh's presence. And what is the result of his prayer?

> Those who keep worthless idols
> abandon their true loyalty (*ḥesed*).
> But I, with a voice of thanksgiving,
> I will sacrifice to you.
> What I have vowed, I will fulfill.
> Deliverance belongs to Yahweh.' (vv. 9-10)

Verse 9 is a theological claim of some kind, directed to idolators. To whom can he be referring? In the context it can only be the sailors, those worshippers of 'other gods', and perhaps the heathen Ninevites still to come (ch. 3). But the irony then comes clear: it is precisely those groups who do not abandon true loyalty. The behavior of the sailors has been seen as altogether laudatory. The wicked Ninevites hear the word and repent wholeheartedly—even the cows—and become cleavers to true loyalty. And it is Jonah, the one who has abandoned loyalty to God so completely, who at 4.2 quotes the famous theological statement of Exod. 34.6 concerning God's own 'loyalty' (*ḥesed*). But his quote is uttered precisely to disparage that loyalty, to decry the fact that God, by his *ḥesed*, has spared Nineveh. All, save Jonah, have not abandoned their true loyalty. Who is it then who 'keeps worthless idols'? Again, the hypocrite is skewered on his own words.

And then Jonah, to complete the prayer, promises 'sacrifice' to God and vows to 'fulfill' his vows. The sailors have already physically sacrificed, and they have made vows (1.16). Jonah *says* he *will* do both. He never sacrifices in this book, nor does he make a vow. Jonah does not do what the sailors so willingly have done. So, ch. 2 deepens the gulf between the sailors and Jonah.[46]

Jonah ends his psalm by saying, 'Deliverance belongs to Yahweh.'

---

45. It is interesting to note the synonymous and assonantal verbs of 2.8 (*ʿṭp*) and 4.8 (*ʿlp*). Jonah 'faints' in both cases. If his remembrance of God at 2.8 had meant much, why is it that his 'fainting' of 4.8 leads to a request, not to God for aid, but to his own spirit (*nepeš*) to die?

46. Thus, Landes's claim, 'The Kerygma', p. 27, cannot be sustained that the content of chs. 1 and 2 conform to one another. If this is so, then his analysis of why the psalm is here must be called into question, for he says the conformity of content of 1 and 2 is there precisely to contrast the lack of conformity of 3 and 4.

Here at the same time is the book's hallmark claim *and* its sharpest satiric thrust. After reading Jonah, the fact the reader knows for certain is that Yahweh can indeed deliver, in the most unlikely ways and in the face of the most incredible recalcitrance. Jonah himself can certainly not deny the fact for himself; he has been delivered from the furthest depths of the nether world—and against his will. But what does the pious shout mean for Jonah's continuing mission? He goes to Nineveh, albeit reluctantly, enters the massive city part-way, and utters a five word sermon of doom.[47] Fantastically, the entire city is seized with a fever for immediate repentance, from the king to the cows (3.5-9). And God, seeing their honest repentance, delivers them from the threat of destruction. Indeed, 'Deliverance belongs to Yahweh!' But Jonah's response is the most fantastic event of all. He is enraged! He even sees the repentance of the city as a '*great* evil' (*rāʿāh gᵉdôlāh*). Whether one finds the source of Jonah's anger in the fact of God's change of heart,[48] or in the repentance of Nineveh itself, as I have suggested, is not a crucial matter. The use of the word 'evil' (*rʿh*) in 3.10 both with reference to the evil of Nineveh and to God's intended evil makes the immediate referent of Jonah's 'great evil' of 4.1 difficult of determination. The point is still clear. The deliverance of Yahweh, a fact shouted by Jonah in his psalm, has in reality enraged the petty prophet, enraged him to such a pitch that death, his apparent intial desire, seems to him the only course (4.3). It is no wonder that immediately after Jonah shouts, 'Deliverance belongs to Yahweh!' the big fish throws up![49]

If the psalm is viewed with an eye to its satiric tone, its important functions can be seen. As Magonet says, by it 'Jonah, to his own satisfaction, has reconciled himself to God'.[50] But in the context of ch. 1 and the remainder of the book it can only be seen as another inappropriate, hypocritical, pious sounding affirmation like 1.9 before it and 4.2 after it. By it, Jonah shows the reader more clearly his true colors. His phrases sound good and right, but in the event they turn out to be

47. Good, *Irony*, pp. 48-49, finds irony here in the possible double meaning of the verb *hpk*. It can mean 'to be changed' or 'to overthrow'. Jonah naturally wants the latter, but the former is the result.

48. Fretheim, *The Message* and in his 'Jonah and Theodicy'.

49. This wonderful joke is not my own. I heard it first orally in a sermon given by Dr W.J.A. Power in 1968 in the Perkins School of Theology Chapel. I have since read it in Williams, *Understanding*, p. 246 and Magonet, *Form*, p. 53.

50. Magonet, *Form*, p. 53.

empty. The negative character portrayal of Jonah in ch. 1 is sharpened in 2, as he is further and further separated from those around him by his appalling behavior. This separation is not complete until the book's end, where Jonah is in fact physically separated from everyone.

The descent motif of ch. 1 is not finished until 2.7, where the descent ends only by an act of God. Jonah recognizes it, proclaims it for himself, but cannot transfer his knowledge to anyone else, hence cutting himself off from them and God. What else could he seek but death (1.12; 4.3, 8)?

It is, of course, Jonah who is the object of the satiric attack of the book, but who is Jonah? What is being satirized? Only a few suggestions can be made. First, he is clearly a prophet. Secondly, he tries very hard to limit, to prevent, the prophetic word of God. Thirdly, when the word is grudgingly given, and the deliverance is effected, his claim that this is a 'great evil' and that he would rather die than live if such events can occur, direct our attention to those who would limit both the scope and intention of God's word. Fourthly, he is a Hebrew (1.9), the only one in the entire book. He is also the only figure in the book (including the cows) who is at the end unrepentant. Hence, Jonah is a Hebrew prophet disobedient and hypocritical, angered by God's will to save, yet claiming to affirm God's power to do so, having witnessed it in his own person. Jonah is thus an attack on Hebrew prophetic hypocrisy. Which group or groups the author has in mind cannot be identified specifically, but do not all religions bring forth 'hypocritical prophets' who claim great insight and unique callings, but who ultimately are found empty of substance, save their real anger at those who do not agree with them? Yea, their number is legion. For them, and their incessant fulminations, is Jonah written.

JSOT 40 (1938), pp. 83-97

LEVELS OF NATURALIZATION IN OBADIAH

Robert B. Robinson

I

Do not forget that a poem, even though it is composed in the language of information, is not used in the language game of giving information.

Ludwig Wittgenstein

Wittgenstein's warning is routinely forgotten in exegesis of the poetic texts of the Bible. Critical exegetes mobilize the full range of modern scholarly tools precisely to ferret out information concealed within or behind the poetic language of the text. The poem resists, gives information grudgingly, ambiguously, against its inclination. Yet with perseverance it can be brought to account. Biblical studies has its ways of making the text respond to its questions. The text must be made to yield up its information because the interpretative strategy of most critical exegetes demands linkage between the text and extra-textual circumstances existing at the time of its composition. Before such a connection is established, the text presents itself to its interpreter as a problem, an unknown whose correct meaning is yet to be fathomed. The text becomes intelligible by coming into conjunction with historically reconstructed realities construed loosely as causes of the literary phenomena in the text, as objective referents for its concrete language, and as perspicuous analogies to its themes and interests. Something like this model of interpretation is implicit in most critical exegesis, particularly that exegesis most insistent on the historicality of the biblical text.[1]

1. A concise statement of this model of interpretation is given by Rolf Knierim ('Criticism of Literary Features, Form, Tradition, and Redaction', in D.A. Knight and G.M. Tucker [eds.], *The Hebrew Bible and its Modern Interpreters* [Philadelphia: Fortress Press; Chico, CA: Scholars Press, 1985], pp. 123-28). Knierim is typical in

Veronica Forrest-Thomson has termed the type of interpretative strategy applied to biblical poetry 'naturalization'.[2] Naturalization represents, in Forrest-Thomson's words, 'an attempt to reduce the strangeness of poetic language and poetic organization by making it intelligible, by translating it into a statement about the non-verbal external world, by making the Artifice appear natural'.[3] Naturalization proceeds until the poem has been completely reduced to 'a thematic synthesis stated in terms of the outside world'.[4] Forrest-Thomson finds this rush to convert verbal structure to natural theme if not wholly wrongheaded, at least mostly so, because it leads the critic away from the proper goal of poetry reading, namely, aesthetic appreciation of the verbal artifice of the poem.[5] If you want information about the world, read the newspaper; if you want to appreciate the pleasures of verbal artifice, read a poem.

Forrest-Thomson opposes the rush to naturalization because it refuses the poem the opportunity to tell us anything new. The theme synthesized for the poem is always rooted in the world we already know. The poem

arguing that this type of interpretative program is required by the essential nature of the text, by its intrinsic historicality. Against Knierim see the anti-essentialist argument of E.D. Hirsch, Jr ('Some Aims of Criticism', in F. Brady, J. Palmer and M. Price [eds.], *Literary Theory and Practice: Essays in Honor of William K. Wimsatt* [New Haven: Yale University Press, 1973]). Hirsch argues that a text does not have an inherent, essential nature, but that construal of the text is a preliminary choice made by an interpreter, a choice to respond to some elements of the kaleidoscope of the text and not others. The historicality of the text is not an unmediated brute fact, nor is anything else.

2.   The term was coined in a 1972 article (V. Forrest-Thomson, 'Level in Poetic Convention', *Journal of European Studies* 2 [1972], p. 36) and developed fully in her book *Poetic Artifice: A Theory of Twentieth-Century Poetry* (New York: St. Martin's, 1978).

3.   Forrest-Thomson, *Poetic Artifice*, p. xi.

4.   Forrest-Thomson, *Poetic Artifice*, p. x.

5.   Forrest-Thomson's privileging of the aesthetic level of the text, one of the dogmas of Formalism and American New Criticism, is as susceptible to Hirsch's anti-essentialist critique as Knierim's privileging of the historical elements in the biblical text. To move 'artifice' or any of a myriad other categories which can fit a text to the center of an interpretation is a choice. Whether that choice is sensible or not depends on what the interpreter is doing, or, to use Wittgenstein's image, what game is being played. The nature of the material does not determine the choice in advance, although as the quote from Wittgenstein used as an epigraph stresses, some forms of literature are not used in some games.

reveals nothing. Interpretation through naturalization is uninformative, static, finally, and most damningly, dull. Contemplation of artifice, by contrast, is continually revelatory, although Forrest-Thomson limits the revelation to recognition of the potentialities of language. This restriction is certainly to be challenged for its own reductionism, but her criticism of interpretation which reduces a poem either simply to a reflex of the circumstances of its composition or to merely an artfully formulated proposition about the extra-textual world seems right to the point. A thematic synthesis of a poem must, except under unusual circumstances, take account of more than the referential function of language.[6]

Jonathan Culler further developed the notion of naturalization in his *Structuralist Poetics*.[7] Culler was interested in giving an account of understanding, that is, how readers make sense of a text, but, one must judge, was uneasy with the hermeneutic traditions (of Schleiermacher and Kant) which sought the conditions of the possibility of understanding in divinatory mental acts or in transcendental conditions. Culler sought a somewhat less theory-laden account of the process of making sense which linked publicly accessible attributes of the text with equally scrutable processes on the part of the reader. Naturalization provided such an account. Texts consist of structure and information (not related as a dualism) which require processing to make sense. The reader processes these structures and information by aligning them with a number of pre-existing 'texts' which the reader has learned through experience. By texts Culler does not here intend specific literary works but the complete set of what the reader knows about the world and about how to read literature, a set of competencies. Calling this knowledge 'text' stresses its structured orderliness and also its public nature. The process of naturalization consists of aligning the givens of the literary text with the pre-existing text in the reader. This process, by which the reader 'makes sense' quite literally of the initially strange literary text, is guided by a set of rules and conventions which, like the literary text and the text in the reader, resides in the public domain. No recourse need be taken to hidden mental activities of understanding; the whole process of naturalization takes place publicly according to commonly maintained

---

6. Using a poem as a source of information for a historical reconstruction might constitute such unusual circumstances. Such a usage does not, however, constitute an interpretation of the poem but is a different game entirely.

7. J. Culler, *Structuralist Poetics: Structuralism, Linguistics, and the Study of Literature* (Ithaca, NY: Cornell University Press, 1975), pp. 131-60.

conventions and rules, rules open to scrutiny and dispute, so that validation of a reading by conformity to prevailing conventions is possible.

Culler identified five texts or levels of naturalization with which the
structure and information in the literary text can be aligned. The first is
the text of the real. The real encompasses all our common expectations
about the way the natural world works. Night follows day. Unsupported
objects fall. Life ends. Inevitably. Details in the literary work which follow
normal realistic expectations align the textual world with our natural
world. Strangeness gives way to familiarity. The text makes sense.
Culler's second level, the cultural text, is closely related to the real. Every
culture shares a web of prejudices, stereotypes and what passes for
common sense which, although less firmly rooted in external reality,
nonetheless is taken for granted as more or less self-evident. Fiery-
tempered Latins and stiff-upper-lip British are projections of the cultural
code. Such generalizations about the world are not subject to proof, but
they are held with nearly the same subjective certainty as assumptions
about the physical world. The third level of naturalization requires
specifically literary competence to assign the text to an appropriate
genre of literature. Disappearing Cheshire cats and little boys that don't
grow up but do fly (very strange realities indeed) easily shed their
strangeness when they are placed in the genre of fantasy or fairy tale.
The highly stylized and concentrated use of language often found in
poetic works is easily naturalized by recognizing its particular generic
character and applying the appropriate convention learned through train-
ing in the institution of literature. Culler's fourth level, the conventionally
natural, plays no part in this discussion and can be left out of view.
Culler's final level of naturalization, then, is parody or irony, the literary
text taken as commentary on an existing text or situation known to the
reader. Here I believe Culler may be too narrow. The category might
better be called explicit intertextuality, one text commenting on another
specific text without limiting the relationship between the two to parody
or irony.

Forrest-Thomson's charge was that external naturalization is a reduction to the familiar. Culler answers by describing three levels of
naturalization which are strictly textual or intertextual. But he does not
agree to discard the levels of the text which align with the text of the
extra-textual world, and he insists on retaining the possible referential
function of the poem.[8] Naturalization becomes a name for the reader's

---

8.   But note that the 'reference' of the language of the poem is not to the actual

orderly process of making sense of a text, a process broad enough to take account of all significant factors.

Rules and conventions govern the process of naturalization. In *Semiotics of Poetry* Michael Riffaterre describes one of the most important, the convention for naturalizing the text at the appropriate level.[9] Logically, if not temporally, there are two stages to reading a text, Riffaterre argues. In a first reading the reader undertakes to naturalize every element of a poem at the 'mimetic' level. 'Mimetic' here is roughly equivalent to Culler's first two levels, the real and the cultural texts. This first reading, however, stumbles over elements of the text which defy naturalization as mimesis of extra-textual reality. These non-mimetic elements, 'ungrammaticalities' in Riffaterre's linguistic metaphor, are ungrammatical and disruptive within the grammar of the real or cultural texts in the way that misplaced modifiers and sentence fragments are ungrammatical within the grammar of standard English. They disrupt the production of sense at the mimetic level. The Cheshire cat grins. But unlike errors in standard English, ungrammaticalities in the mimetic reading do not call for correction. Instead they direct the reader to a higher level of naturalization, a level at which mimetic ungrammaticalities are grammatical and literally make or produce sense.

All the familiar tropes and embellishments of poetry—rhythm, rhyme, alliteration, orthographic peculiarities, violations of verisimilitude, unusual vocabulary, literary allusions—disrupt simple mimetic reading, forcing naturalization to a higher level. Having attained the higher level of reading, according to Rilfaterre's theory, the reader ceases to take account of the mimetic level of the text. The mimetic level functioned solely to place the ungrammaticalities, the true bearers of poetic sense, in the foreground. Once the ungrammaticalities have been identified by their power to disrupt the mimetic reading, the mimetic reading is dispensable. In a second stage, a second reading, the reader now organizes the non-mimetic elements of the text, and only the non-mimetic elements, into a properly poetic synthesis.

---

outside world, but to the texts of the real and cultural worlds which the reader produces. Culler would not accept an inherently referential relationship between language and external world, a relationship which the reader could not ignore because it was, so to speak, built into the language of the poem. Taking the poetic language as referential is an interpretative decision, not a necessity.

9. M. Riffaterre, *Semiotics of Poetry* (Bloomington: Indiana University Press, 1978), pp. 3-22.

Rilfaterre's theory defends against charges that literary readings are arbitrary and completely subjective. The ungrammaticalities in the text itself warrant more complex naturalizations than a simple realistic reading. The progression to higher levels of naturalization is orderly and responsive to elements of the text itself All the same Riffaterre recognizes the important role of the individual reader in producing the final sense of the text, so that his theory is useful in providing a systematic account of differences in interpretation. In one area, however, Riffaterre's theory is hardly satisfactory. He allots the mimetic elements of the text no part in the final thematic synthesis. This is a somewhat strange argument, since the mimetic elements of the text are no less a part of a poem than the non-mimetic.[10] The mimetic elements are equally open to interpretation and as a matter of descriptive fact most readers do take account of them in their interpretations. Riffaterre, then, is not so much describing the conventions of actual reading at this point as prescribing a new normative set of conventions—the two-stage reading—for ideological reasons, in this case a defense of pure aesthetics against contamination from the mundane world of the mimetic.[11] Whatever the justification for seeking to insulate a pure aesthetic or linguistic domain for literature, cutting the cord between the text and the world outside must itself trouble the biblical critic. Most of the uses which the biblical critic envisions both for the biblical text and for his or her

10. Riffaterre ('Interpretation and Descriptive Poetry: A Reading of Wordsworth's "Yew-Trees"', *New Literary History* 4.2 [1972], pp. 229-56) presents a tour de force example of non-mimetic naturalization in his interpretation of Wordsworth's 'Yew-Trees', a naturalistic poem. Riffaterre presents a brilliant synthesis which takes no account of the mimetic level of the poem. But the artificiality of Riffaterre's self-restriction was graphically demonstrated by Geoffrey Hartman ('The Use and Abuse of Structural Analysis: Riffaterre's Interpretation of Wordsworth's "Yew-Trees"', *New Literary History* 7.1 [1975] pp. 165-89) who, in effect, topped Riffaterre's interpretation without denying its brilliance by adding the mimetic elements back into the final poetic synthesis.

11. Riffaterre's (and Forrest-Thomson's) antipathy to the mimetic level has its roots in the efforts of the Russian Formalists to identify a formal characteristic which would distinguish literature (i.e. art) from more mundane uses of language. The characteristic they seized upon was precisely the deviant nature of literary language when compared to everyday usage (the mimetic functions of language). See V. Shklovsky, 'Art as Technique', in L.T. Lemon and M.J. Reis (eds.), *Russian Formalist Criticism: Four Essays* (Lincoln: University of Nebraska Press, 1965), pp. 3-24. The issue for Riffaterre and Forrest-Thomson is to preserve poetry's claim to be art.

interpretation of the text emphasize the connection between the text and the world. Riffaterre, and Forrest-Thomson with him, are right to protest against criticism which takes account exclusively of the mimetic level in its thematic synthesis, thereby grossly overdetermining that level. But they are wrong to exclude mimetic effects from interpretation in order to maintain a pristine concept of literature. In the exegesis that follows the goal will be a synthesis which naturalizes all the levels of the text. Indeed, in some ways the relationship between the mimetic and non-mimetic levels will be the key to the thematic synthesis of Obadiah's vision.

II

Obadiah begins with a superscription, which provides important preliminary information to guide the reader in naturalizing what follows. To begin, the key generic designation 'vision' is singular, a single vision. This reinforces the conventional disposition, already strong, to read the work as a unified whole and works against any inclination to dissolve productive tensions within the text by ascribing them to different sources or distinct visions. Inconsistencies, abrupt changes of voice, mood, vocabulary, to say nothing of more problematic variations in putative historical situations presupposed by the text, must be taken as 'ungrammaticalities' leading to higher level naturalization rather than being neutralized by source divisions.

A number of commentators have remarked that 'vision' is not particularly apt as a description of the content of the book, which begins with the reception of a word from the Lord and is dominated by words and formulas of hearing and speaking rather than seeing.[12] The discrepancy indicates that 'vision' here is not an anticipatory description of the content of the work but constitutes a genre designation (as also in Isaiah and Nahum) which institutes a set of conventional expectations controlling the naturalization of the whole. Disruptions of the mimetic level by such devices as temporal indeterminacy or referential ambiguity, for instance, will not be naturalized in a vision as failed mimesis but as typical and constitutive elements of the genre. Nor may the poetic devices in which Obadiah is so rich, anaphorae, chiasms, assonance,

---

12. A. Weiser, *Das Buch der zwölf kleinen Propheten* (ATD, 24.1; Göttingen: Vandenhoeck & Ruprecht, 1949), p. 182; W. Rudolph, *Joel-Amos-Obadja-Jona* (KAT, 13.2; Gütersloh: Gerd Mohn, 1971), p. 302.

parallelism, alliteration, be dismissed as mere stylistic niceties and orna-
mentation. In a vision they are constituent of the genre and so of the
meaning. Finally, seeing Obadiah as a vision will lead the reader to make
the final integration of the work significant theologically, as a communication of divine purpose.

The superscription so points unequivocally to a non-mimetic genre.
But throughout the work there is much that can be naturalized on the
mimetic level, signalling a thematically important complexity. The text
refers on numerous occasions to known places—Teman, the Shephelah,
the Negeb, Jerusalem, or Samaria. Even place names such as Zarephath
and Sepharad, which are less well known and so might seem to locate
the vision in an exotic realm, are still taken on the same realistic level as
the others because nothing marks them as distinctive from the run of
known places. The agents of the vision are also residents of the real
world—Edom, Judah, Philistines, Benjamin—although, as we shall see,
their names can take on symbolic and thematic importance beyond the
simply referential. Still, the major actors are at least partly naturalized at
the realistic level. Most pronounced and most realistic is the tone.
Outrage dominates Obadiah, an outrage completely natural to a people
laid waste by a neighbor nation. The cultural code makes sense of this
outrage, certainly without emptying the tone of thematic importance.
There is much in Obadiah that is mimetic to go along with much that is
not. The complexity and much of the interest of the work lie in the ways
the levels interact.

This complexity is already typified in the superscription by the figure
of Obadiah, to whom the vision appears. To all appearances Obadiah is a
concrete individual. Attempts to see Obadiah as a title, Servant of Yah,
which would support a non-mimetic or perhaps even allegorical reading
of the book, are very unlikely.[13] So Obadiah appears to be a real individual but unlike the prophetic figures mentioned in other superscriptions
using the term $ḥ^azôn$ or some form of the verb $ḥāzâ$ (Amos 1.1; Isa. 1.1;
Mic. 1.1; Nah. 1.1). Obadiah is not identified by ancestry nor placed in a
specific temporal or spatial frame by indicating the kings ruling during
his activity. Obadiah lacks personal or historical fixity, rootedness in a
historical context. Although taken as a concrete figure, Obadiah pointedly does nothing to fix his vision in a specific temporal or spatial frame
which demands to be taken as the necessary context for interpreting the

---

13. H.W. Wolff, *Dodekapropheton 3: Obadja und Jona* (BKAT, 14.3;
Neukirchen–Vluyn: Neukirchener Verlag, 1977), p. 26.

vision. Even the figure of Obadiah, the prophetic recipient of the vision, points to a complex mimetic and non-mimetic interpretation of the book.

The reference in the superscription to Edom is also concrete and serves to root the book at the mimetic level. But even Edom, which seems clearly referential, demands a complicated naturalization. Edom is certainly a historical reality in the extra-textual world.[14] Archeology provides independent information on this indubitable reality. But Edom also forms a state in the literary world of the Bible, a world which does not always precisely coincide with the historical world of the archeologist but, despite this, exhibits coherence and demands to have its integrity respected. The allusions are familiar. Edom refused passage to Israel wandering in the desert (Num. 20.14-21). Saul defeated Edom (1 Sam. 14.47) and David subjected it to Israel's hegemony (2 Sam. 8.13-14). Hostility between the states continued until the reign of Joram (1 Kgs 11.14-22), when Edom broke away from Judah's control (2 Kgs 8.20-22). These are all realistic, 'history-like' texts which describe political events and relations readily imaginable as actual events in the concourse between Israel and Edom. But each passage is also a literary text, an episode within the connected narrative which constitutes Obadiah's immediate literary context when the Bible is read as in some sense a literary unity. The reference to Edom in such a reading represents an intertextual allusion at least as much if not more than an extra-textual one. The reference to Edom takes one in the first instance to other texts, not to events known independently of the text. But these texts are themselves mimetic, so that naturalization becomes complex, hovering between two levels. By its allusions to realistic texts Obadiah assumes a mimetic or realistic aura, but the naturalization involved is actually intertextual, reality as mediated by another text.

Earlier it was noted that the superscription failed to provide a fixed temporal frame for Obadiah or his vision. The temporal indeterminacy runs throughout the book, disrupting at every turn the mimetic reading. In the opening section of the work, directed to Edom's pride, an extremely complex verbal sequence obscures the temporal reference. The sequence begins with a perfect, *nᵉtattîkā* (v. 2), normally translated as past tense. Indeed, a school of scholars following Wellhausen took this

---

14. For the extra-biblical evidence, see J.R. Bartlett, 'The Moabites and Edomites', in D.J. Wiseman (ed.), *Peoples of Old Testament Times* (Oxford: Oxford University Press, 1973), pp. 229-58.

section as a reference to a past judgment already visited on Edom.[15] But the perfect could also represent the so-called prophetic perfect.[16] Future events are so certain of accomplishment that they may be represented as already complete, so the theory runs. Read the verb as present, read the verb as past. The ambiguous verb is followed by a passive participle, essentially a stative, defining Edom's nature and having no independent temporal significance. The alternation of perfects and participles continues to the last line of the section, the judgment, *miššām ʾôrîdʿkā* (v. 4), 'Thence I will bring you down', which is an imperfect and unambiguously future. There is no simple syntactical explanation for this temporal indeterminacy.[17] But there is a clear enough effect. The judgment on Edom breaks free from a single concrete temporal reference point in either past or future. Mimetic naturalization is startlingly frustrated. Obadiah's vision is not of realities conclusively located at a single point on the familiar continuum of past to future.

A similiar phenomenon occurs in vv. 11-14, the list of Edom's depredations against Jerusalem and the most mimetic section in the poem. The vividness of these descriptions and their fully comprehensible tone, which I mentioned before, seem to demand that they refer to actual past actions of Edom, presumably Edom's participation in the Babylonian overthrow of Jerusalem. The incensed tone of this section is easily naturalized at the level of the cultural code, Israel's natural response to overwhelming provocation, but once again the tempus of the verbs interferes with and complicates the naturalization. Throughout this very regular section the verbs are imperfects negated by *ʾal* a construction which normally has either prohibitive or negated future force. Scholars have noted the difficulty the imperfects present for a naturalistic reading of the section as past justification for impending judgment, but they have tended to dispel the problem by reading the verbs modally, 'You should not have...' A modal reading is grammatically acceptable but somewhat ad hoc, deriving its plausibility from the

15. J. Wellhausen, *Die kleinen propheten: Übersetzt und erklärt* (Berlin: Georg Reimer, 3rd edn, 1898), p. 211.

16. Weiser, *Zwölf kleinen Propheten*, p. 183; Rudolph, *Joel-Amos-Obadja-Jona*, p. 296.

17. K. Matti (*Das Dodekapropheton* [Tübingen: J.C.B. Mohr, 1904], p. 231) took the mixture of perfects and imperfects as an attempt to represent the contemporaneity of the events described. This explanation is very ad hoc, an attempt to derive some firm temporal fixity from a sequence that dramatically resists temporal determination.

prior assumption that the passage describes actual historical events and therefore must be read mimetically. Leave aside that assumption and the future tense here deflects the straight fall of mimetic reading. The deflection in naturalization is not accomplished by undermining the vividness of description. Condemnation falls on specific acts of betrayal. But the temporal frame of these specific acts is uncertain, so that it is impossible to situate them temporally, as events in the real world are normally situated. Consequently, a completely realistic naturalization is blocked, and again in precisely the same manner as in the first section, by temporal indeterminacy.

To be sure, at several points in Obadiah there is determinate temporal language. So, for example, v. 8, 'Will I not on that day, says the Lord, destroy the wise men out of Edom?' The deictic 'that' appears to refer to a specific time. But what time? None is mentioned. Or at least not proximately. In v. 15a there is another reference to a day, 'For the day of the Lord is near upon all the nations'. This is the most pointed reference to a day within Obadiah, but the reference is not to an actual day in realistic time, but to the eschatological day, that envisioned and visionary day when God will judge all nations. If the reference to 'that day' in v. 8 is connected to the day of the Lord in v. 15, and there is no other candidate within the literary context of the book, then the judgment on Edom is not precisely historical but an eschatological event, an event within history, to be sure, and exhibiting the concreteness of historical events, but not bounded by history. The diatribe against Edom and the bill of particulars of its betrayal could not be fixed chronologically as either past or future because their true temporal frame is not historical time but eschatological time, a time which is, the reader is given to understand, both within history and outside it. Friction at the mimetic level, the grammatical uncertainty and resultant temporal indeterminacy, aptly expresses the nature of this particular eschatological event by necessarily breaching the conventions of mimetic description. Inability to resolve the grammatical inconsistencies presses the reader to a thematically productive naturalization at the level of genre, the genre of eschatological vision.

Other incongruities also disrupt a simple mimetic reading. According to the superscription the oracle is addressed to Edom.[18] Edom stands as

18. Or concerns Edom. The ambiguity of the preposition *l^e* in *le^{,e}dom* makes it initially uncertain whether God addresses a word to Edom or a word to Israel concerning Edom. At issue is whether this is a diatribe from within Israel directed

a mark of the concreteness of the text; it is naturalized at the mimetic level. But early in the vision an alternate designation appears which runs against a mimetic reading: 'How Esau has been pillaged, his treasures sought out'. According to Gen. 36.1, of course, Esau is simply equivalent to Edom. But the personal name 'Esau' has an entirely different valence in the poem from the political or national 'Edom'. 'Edom' led us to a whole series of history-like narratives of political relations which established Edom as a concrete national entity. But the personal name Esau takes us to a strikingly different world of familial relations and intrigues, recounted in a single complex of texts, the ancestral narratives of Genesis. Esau and Jacob are brothers, Esau the elder, the naturally favored. But Esau despises his birthright (Gen. 25.40; the same root is used in Obadiah 2: 'You are greatly despised') and Jacob takes the remaining and all-important blessing by deceit. Esau received in his own turn a 'blessing', but it is to serve his younger brother. Service to Jacob, who bears the promise originally given to Abraham, henceforth defines Esau's role in the divine economy. Images which depict the issue between Israel and Esau as betrayal of a brother by a brother reinforce the family associations introduced by the inter-textual reference to the ancestral stories: so v. 10, 'For the violence done to your brother Jacob, shame shall cover you'; v. 12, 'But you should not have gloated over the day of your brother, in the day of his misfortune'. A mimetic reading would have us see the issue as exclusively political; Edom has revealed itself an enemy. But it is only by denying the imagery its full weight, by doctrinaire reduction, that is, to strictly mimetic terms, that one can hear in these passages no more than political machinations. The political dimensions are doubtless present; Esau is Edom. But Esau and Jacob are brothers, relations between them personal and complex and inextricably bound to their life together in the tent of Isaac and Rebekah. Without totally sublimating the political level, the familial language forces the reader once again to a higher level naturalization, a level that can draw together thematically the distinctive nature of the familial imagery and the force of the intertextual allusions.

It is fortunate that a higher level naturalization is possible, because a strictly mimetic reading cannot avoid a question which threatens to trivialize the whole book. Why should Edom be condemned for getting

against Edom, in which case Obadiah is yet another sad instance of Jewish particularism, or whether it is an eschatological word from God encompassing Edom, in which case the horizon of the work is much broader than Jewish national interests.

even for centuries of subjugation to Judah or for looking to its own compelling national interest in supporting the triumphant Babylonians against a doomed neighbor? On the political level, there is no real answer, except to aver that the book is written from Judah's self-interested perspective. Obadiah appears as nothing more than Jewish particularism (understandable under the circumstances, if regrettable). But if Israel and Esau are brothers, indeed brothers whose destinies are linked by the promise to Abraham, then the condemnation of Esau for betrayal makes sense, in fact, very rich sense. Nothing justifies the betrayal of a brother, especially this brother, chosen to bear the promise.

The imagery of familial betrayal lifts the naturalization of Obadiah above the realistic level. But how does this complex level integrate with the eschatological level signalled by the indeterminacy of the time frame and the reference to the Day of the Lord? It seems to me that there are two different, but not incompatible, integrations. The first is called to our attention by the historical critics. Scholars have long been accustomed to divide the book into two sections, which are normally ascribed to different authors or historical periods.[19] The first section is roughly vv. 2-14 and 15b. This section concerns Edom and its actions against Israel. The second section consists of vv. 15a and either 16-18 or 16-21, depending on the critic consulted. This section contains the description of an eschatological judgment set to engulf Edom and indeed all nations, while Judah and, surprisingly, Israel will be restored with all under the lordship of God. The key verse is v. 15. Scholars noted that the *talio* formula in v. 15b, 'As you have done, it shall be done to you, your deeds shall return on your own head', makes a fit conclusion for the bill of particulars against Edom ending in v. 14. The betrayal of Judah will be avenged. And v. 15a makes a good beginning for the broader eschatological section: 'For the day of the Lord is near upon all nations'. Usual scholarly practice is therefore to reverse vv. 15a and 15b in order to produce two self-contained units which can be linked to two distinct historical situations. A mimetic reading would prefer 15b in front of 15a, but this is precisely what the text does not give. Placing the announcement of the eschatological Day of the Lord before the last word in the particular accusation against Esau draws the events described in the bill of particulars against Edom into the eschatological period, yet without

---

19. For an overview of the actual diversity of opinion on divisions within Obadiah, see G. Fohrer, 'Die Sprüche Obadjas', *Studia Biblica et Semitica Theodoro Christiano Vriezen Dedicata* (Wageningen: H. Veenan en Zonen, 1966), pp. 81-93.

destroying their concreteness. The effect is similar to that achieved by
the temporal indeterminacy: any clear line between historical time and
eschatological time is broken down. But the 'disorder' in v. 15 does
more. The temporal indeterminacy by itself could be seen as a local
effect, not to be ignored but not necessarily crucial to the thematic sense
of the whole. But the effect of v. 15 is not local; it draws what critics
would characterize as the two distinct sections of the vision together
and, as it does, it moves the theme of the relation of historical time to
eschatological time to the center of the poem.

The second line of integration of the poem must focus on the intertextual naturalization of the work. The designation of Edom as Esau,
even though it is not consistent in Obadiah, refers the reader to the
stories of Israel's ancestors and invites a thematic connection between
texts. The ancestral age represents an *Urzeit*, a time which is certainly
not separate from the continuing line of Israel's story, but which sets the
course of that line. In particular the promise to Abraham dominates the
ancestral stories, a promise which represents a divine plan not to bring
blessing on one clan, but to all nations (Gen. 12.3). The troubling stories
of relations between Jacob and Esau—Esau spurns his birthright, Jacob
cheats his brother of the promise, stories that often outrage our moral
sensibilities—somehow both follow the divine plan and establish its
concrete direction. A younger brother who has stolen it bears the
promise. Esau, the older brother, receives a blessing, to be sure, but it is
to serve the younger brother who carries the promise.

Subsequent stories, now far more history-like, work out the relationship set in the *Urzeit* by the two brothers and incorporated into the
developing line of the promise. Edom and Israel become nations, but
their relationship is still stamped by the events recounted in the ancestral
stories. Their relationship continually reflects the fact that Israel received
the promise while Esau's role was to serve the bearer of the promise.

If this dynamic of the promise is taken as the literary backdrop of
Obadiah, then the outrage at Esau's treachery and the judgment
announced on him fit together in the eschatological vision. Edom's
despoliation of Jerusalem is not simply an act of political treachery, nor
yet even the betrayal of a brother, but a stroke against the divine plan,
established in the *Urzeit*, to be realized now in the *Endzeit*. Because
Esau has not fulfilled his role to serve the bearer of the promise but has
in fact opposed the promise, attempting to eliminate its bearer, in the
final judgment, Esau is condemned.

In this fashion naturalizations at the level of the genre of eschatological vision and at the intertextual level can be integrated. But what of the mimetic level. Is there a unified synthesis which includes the mimetic or do the mimetic levels of the naturalization only serve to set off the higher levels? A synthesis is possible, I believe, indeed essential to understanding Obadiah, but it involves the recognition of tensions which are themselves thematically productive. In Obadiah the mimetic and non-mimetic levels of naturalization continually subvert one another. Familial imagery in the intertextual naturalization runs against and calls into question the national and political reality of the mimetic level. But the influence is reciprocal. Esau becomes national and political, a player on the stage of history, which becomes the stage on which the promise to Abraham is played out. Then again, the mimetic view of history and its underlying logic of linear time are confronted by eschatological time in a way that does not allow either to reduce the other to its terms. This continual undermining of each other by historical time and eschatological time, by familial, promise categories and political/national is a dialectic which simply will not come to rest in Obadiah. The final synthesis is not stable but kinetic. But then, what should we expect? Obadiah is not the news. It is a vision of the will of God.

INDEXES

INDEX OF REFERENCES

OLD TESTAMENT

INDEX OF AUTHORS

Miles, J.A. 336
Miles, M.R. 231, 349
Millard, A.R. 124
Miller, P. Jr 226
Miller, P.D. 116
Miscall, P.D. 90
Miskotte, K.H. 336
Momigliano, A. 117
Moore, C. 218
Moore, G.F. 192
Moore, S.D. 75, 164
Morgan, R. 234
Morgenstern, J. 196
Mowinckel, S. 207, 307
Muilenburg, J. 305
Mulvey, L. 266
Murphy, R.E. 295
Murtonen, A. 160

Narasimhan, R. 125
Nelson, R.D. 34, 36, 55
Neusner, J. 218
Nicholson, E.W. 299, 314
Nielsen, K. 150, 166
Nielson, E. 169
Nock, A.D. 191
Noort, E. 116
North, C.R. 129, 188, 193, 236, 237
Noth, M. 35, 44
Novak, M.E. 99

O'Connor, K.M. 304
Olsen, T. 223
Olson, D.R. 125
Ong, W. 92, 125
Osswald, E. 300
Oswald, H.C. 130
Overholt, T.W. 46, 69-71, 81, 88, 91,
    110, 212, 300-302, 309

Paglia, C. 260
Paine, T. 336
Palmer, J. 356
Papin, J. 295
Pardee, D. 210
Parpola, S. 114
Paton-Williams, D. 228, 247
Paul, S. 214
Pelikan, J. 130
Perdue, L.G. 295
Pesch, R. 345
Petersen, D.L. 44, 46, 51, 52, 178

Pfisterer Darr, K. 232
Phillips, A. 203
Pohlmann, K.-F. 101, 110, 299, 314,
    322, 326
Polzin, R.M. 35, 40, 90, 234
Pope, M.H. 282
Porter, S.E. 88
Poulet, G. 74
Powell, M.A. 164
Pressler, C. 272
Price, M. 356
Puech, E. 125

Qimron, E. 170

Rad, G. von 37, 145, 203, 215, 249, 310,
    317, 336, 337
Rahlfs, A. 320
Rashkow, I.N. 269
Rauber, D.F. 336
Reed, W.L. 305, 335
Reis, M.J. 360
Renaud, B. 282
Rendtorff, R. 147, 160, 163, 165, 171,
    172, 180, 213
Riffaterre, M. 359, 360
Ringgren, H. 110
Roberts, A. 88
Roberts, J.J.M. 112, 165
Robinson, H.W. 170
Robinson, T.H. 345
Rodd, C.S. 89
Rogerson, J.W. 93, 293, 295
Rosenberg, D. 219
Rosenberg, J. 307
Rothman, E. 234
Rowlett, L. 296
Rowley, H.H. 186, 196, 246
Rudolph, W. 209, 211, 326, 345, 361,
    364
Ruether, R.R. 221, 222
Ruppert, L. 282
Rush, F. 259
Russell, L.T. 253

Sarna, N. 269
Sawyer, J.F.A. 165, 166, 171, 234, 244
Schmidt, W.H. 48
Schmitt, A. 116
Schmitt, H.-C. 40, 101, 110
Schmitt, J.J. 224
Schökel, Alonso L. 234, 327

THE BIBLICAL SEMINAR

GOSHEN COLLEGE / GOOD LIBRARY

3 9310 01013564 6

DATE DUE

MAR 1 2 1999		
OCT 1 9 1999		
OCT 1 8 2000		
OCT 3 1 2000		
MAR 0 9 2001		
APR 2 9 2008		
JAN 0 5 2009		
GAYLORD		PRINTED IN U.S.A.